THE HIGH-PERFORMING SCHOOL

Benchmarking the 10 Indicators of Effectiveness

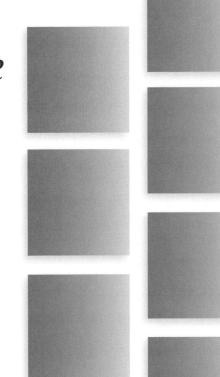

Solution Tree | Press

a division of

Solution Tree

Mardale Dunsworth and Dawn Billings

555 North Morton Street

Bloomington, IN 47404

800.733.6786 (toll free) / 812.336.7700

FAX: 812.336.7790

email: info@solution-tree.com

solution-tree.com

Visit **go.solution-tree.com/schoolimprovement** for additional information.

Printed in the United States of America

13 12 11 10 09   1 2 3 4 5

Library of Congress Cataloging-in-Publication Data

Dunsworth, Mardale.
  The high-performing school : benchmarking the 10 indicators of effectiveness / Mardale Dunsworth, Dawn Billings.
       p. cm.
  Includes bibliographical references.
  ISBN 978-1-934009-47-5 (perct bound) -- ISBN 978-1-935249-14-6 (lib. bdg.) 1. School improvement programs--United States. 2. Academic achievement--United States. 3. Educational indicators. I. Billings, Dawn L. II. Title.
  LB2822.82.D86 2009
  371.2'07--dc22
                              2009010695

_____

President: Douglas Rife

Publisher: Robert D. Clouse

Director of Production: Gretchen Knapp

Managing Editor of Production: Caroline Wise

Senior Production Editor: Risë Koben

Proofreader: Elisabeth Abrams

Text Designer: Amy Shock

Cover Designer: Pamela Rude

Acknowledgments

Solution Tree Press would like to thank the following reviewers:

Julie Anderson
English Language Arts Specialist
Oregon Department of Education
Beaverton, Oregon

Anita Archer
Education Consultant
Anita Archer Consulting
Portland, Oregon

Jon Bridges
Administrator for Accountability
Beaverton School District
Beaverton, Oregon

Glen Fielding
Director of Curriculum, Assessment, and
   Research
Willamette Education Service District
Salem, Oregon

Don Grotting
Superintendent
Nyssa School District #26
Nyssa, Oregon

Jeanne Harmon
Executive Director
Center for Strengthening the Teaching Profession
Tacoma, Washington

Shirley Hord
Scholar Laureate
National Staff Development Council
Austin, Texas

G. Sue Shannon
Senior Researcher
Office of the Superintendent of Public Instruction
Olympia, Washington

Marilyn Simpson
Former Director, Professional Development IN
   ACTION
Office of the Superintendent of Public Instruction
Olympia, Washington

Dannelle D. Stevens
Professor
Portland State University
Portland, Oregon

Visit **go.solution-tree.com/schoolimprovement** for additional information.

Table of Contents

PART 1
THE 10 EFFECTIVENESS INDICATORS: RESEARCH AND RUBRICS

Chapter 1

Chapter 2
Effectiveness Indicator 2: Instructional Program. . . 25

Chapter 3

Effectiveness Indicator 3: Student Assessment . . . 51

Chapter 4

Effectiveness Indicator 4: School Leadership 65

Chapter 5
Effectiveness Indicator 5: Strategic Planning 85

Chapter 9
Effectiveness Indicator 9: Family and Community Involvement 171

Chapter 10
Effectiveness Indicator 10: District Support 183

PART 2 THE PROCESS: CONDUCTING AN ON-SITE SCHOOL REVIEW

Chapter 11
Leading the Way

Chapter 12
Preparing for the On-Site Visit 211

Chapter 13
Examining Data and Other Documents 221

Chapter 16

Conclusion

About the Authors

Mardale Dunsworth is a founding partner of School Synergy, an educational consulting firm. She was formerly director of learning and teaching technology for Washington State. In that capacity, she led the design and development of an innovative web-based statewide professional development and certification system. Previously, as director of the Office of Curriculum, Instruction, and Professional Technical Education in the Oregon Department of Education, Mardale led the development of the research-based Comprehensive School Review process, supervised services to low-performing schools, coordinated regional technical assistance, and administered federal grant programs. She was a small-business owner prior to entering public service. Mardale holds a bachelor's degree in public policy and administration and a master's degree in curriculum and instruction.

Dawn Billings is also a founding partner of School Synergy. Before forming School Synergy, Dawn was assistant superintendent for professional development for Washington State. She led the statewide professional development initiative, including the creation of Washington's Professional Development Standards. Previously Dawn was director of curriculum and instruction in the Oregon Department of Education. She led the development of state content standards, directed Reading First and Title II, and supervised charter schools. She has held a variety of teaching and administrative positions in both public education and business and industry. Dawn holds bachelor's and master's degrees in education.

Mardale and Dawn have been involved in the design, development, and use of the on-site school review process since 2000.

Preface

We don't accomplish anything in this world alone . . . and whatever happens is the result of the whole tapestry of one's life and all the weavings of individual threads from one to another that creates something.

—Sandra Day O'Connor

In 2005, we formed School Synergy, an educational consulting group, to offer schools, districts, and states practical support in improving teaching and learning. Our core belief is that students and adults, when given good reasons and effective tools, can accomplish almost anything they set their minds to. We have seen this belief lead to extraordinarily positive results.

We have yet to encounter a school, district, or state that is not working to improve its effectiveness. What we have also seen is that there is a hunger for the knowledge and tools needed to improve student learning. This hunger isn't a consequence of federal or state regulations or external pressures—it is an intrinsic motivation—it's what has drawn us to the helping profession of education. This drive inspires all of us, whether we are teachers, administrators, or state-level leaders. It is a need to make a positive impact on children's lives.

Our purpose in writing this book is to lead schools into action—action that will result in increased student learning and achievement and that will be sustained over time. We want to provide a comprehensive resource that will enable schools and districts to embark on the same kind of improvement process that we facilitate in our consulting work.

Because it is essential that improvement efforts be based in research, we first offer readers a series of research briefings, grouped around 10 themes of school effectiveness. Then we explain step by step the On-Site School Review process we have developed to both illuminate current practice at a school and arrive at specific strategies for increasing student learning. We also share the set of tools we use to carry out the process.

This book is written for five audiences. The first is school or district administrators who are not satisfied with the current performance of their own schools or schools in their districts. Administrators will find well-laid-out and clearly defined rubrics that will enable them to measure school performance against that of the most effective schools nationwide—in other words, to conduct a sort of whole-school benchmarking process. The research chapters provide a description of research-based practices and what they look like both in the most effective schools and in schools in which student achievement is lagging.

The second audience is school staff members—teachers, specialists, and support (both paraprofessional and noninstructional) staff members who want to improve their practice or who work at a school considering a school review. For those asking, "Why and how should we change our practices to improve student learning?" familiarity with the research base will create confidence in the rubrics and in the recommendations resulting from their application.

The third audience is the leaders or potential leaders of school review teams. In addition to becoming familiar with the research, rubrics, and tools, a team leader will use the communication tools we provide to select the review team, lead the team in carrying out the review with the school staff members, and deliver the results and recommendations to the school and district administrators and school staff members.

The fourth audience is the members or potential members of school review teams. These are the people who use the tools to carry out a school review. This team needs to know how the rubrics reflect research-based practices and how to evaluate a school using the rubrics and applying the other tools with fidelity. The process chapters (chapters 11–16) and the tools (CD and appendix) are aimed particularly at the school review team. The review team is typically made up of educators external to the school. While a review team could perhaps include internal school staff members, it is more likely that a team whose members are from outside of the school community would be better positioned to provide objective feedback and would be regarded by the school staff as impartial.

A fifth and final audience is aspiring or developing school administrators. This book is a primer on effective schools research and best practice. It provides up-and-coming principals and other administrators with an overview of current research on the 10 most important dimensions of an effective school. An educational administration program could use this book to guide a project-based study in which prospective administrators would apply the rubrics in an actual school setting and then regroup to discuss their findings. The group would evaluate the state of current practice at the school and determine the best next steps to lead the school toward higher student achievement—again, all based on research.

We have conducted on-site reviews in schools of all grade levels and sizes; in urban, rural, and suburban locations; and with student populations that well reflect the diversity of the United States. We have seen firsthand the power of the research base, the focus on student learning resulting in increased student achievement, and the transformation of a school when, together, the staff is able to create a high-performing working environment. We hope that this book and its tools and processes will enable ever greater numbers of educators to experience the exhilarating transformation of their own schools into high-performing schools.

Knowing What to Do

The power to question is the basis of all human progress.

—Indira Gandhi

We frequently read and hear that we are making no headway in solving education's greatest dilemmas; that the reason student achievement is not where our society wants and needs it to be is because teachers and administrators refuse to accept new ideas, programs, practices, and strategies. We would propose an alternative explanation. We believe that the reason we in education continue to grapple with the same problems is not because we have done nothing, but rather because—as we are often not exactly sure what we should do—we have tried everything.

Consider the succession of trends just since the late 1990s. We have embraced building leaders as managers and administrators. We have embraced school administrators as instructional leaders. We have embraced homogeneous grouping. We have embraced heterogeneous grouping. We have embraced schools-within-schools, in which every student is known personally and well. We have embraced distance learning. We have embraced teacher-designed curriculum, eschewing textbooks. We have embraced direct instruction, in which teachers precisely follow scripted lessons. We have embraced schools that are open and welcoming to the public. We have embraced schools in which doors are locked at the morning bell and police patrol the hallways. We have embraced efforts to increase graduation rates by keeping more kids in school. We have embraced zero-tolerance policies that force kids out of school.

Still, we can see that these practices have not resulted in the overall gains in student achievement that we had hoped for. When we look at disaggregated student performance data, we can see, in black and brown and white, which of our children are not coming close to learning what they need to, what we want for them. So we conclude that strategy "A" is not working. We hear from a school nearby about a great new program that is working for them. We try it. It doesn't give us the results we had hoped for, or it works well only for the same, or perhaps a different, 70% of our students. So we look around for a new program or strategy or practice that might help us reach all of our students. We hear at a conference about a great new program that is working for schools that sound a lot like ours. We try it. It doesn't give us the results we had hoped for, or it works well only for the same, or perhaps a different, 70% of our students. This cycle is repeated all too often in schools across the country, leading teachers to intone the eight words administrators most dread when they propose new ideas: "We already tried that, and it didn't work."

Schools are becoming much better consumers of data, and, by and large, they know the academic areas in which they need to improve. What they don't know is what to *do* about it. Richard Elmore (2003, p. 9) calls this the "central problem of school improvement." He has found that while schools have clearly heard the message from policymakers and others that they must increase student achievement, no one is telling them what they need to know to act on that message. He explains:

> Holding schools accountable for their performance depends on having people in schools with the knowledge, skill, and judgment to make the improvements that will increase student performance. . . . These improvements are often not obvious even to people who are committed and knowledgeable themselves. . . . In the absence of careful analysis of the kind of practice that would lead to success, . . . they continue to do what they regarded as good teaching—and what many would tell them was good teaching—without recognizing that it was precisely that kind of teaching that was producing the disappointing performance. (pp. 9–10)

This book is about *knowing* and *doing*. In order to *know* what to do to improve achievement, educators must have a clear picture of the key characteristics of effective schools and be able to determine whether those characteristics are present in their schools. Then they need to know what to *do*, what next steps to take, to instill those characteristics in their schools.

Today, we have entered the greatest moment in educational history. We are beginning to see the fruits of high-quality research into what works in education and why. New insights are emerging from the marriage of educational research and medical research—helping us understand both what needs to be in place in order for all children to reach high learning goals and how the brain works to take in, store, and use information. These exciting developments prompted us to ask, As research converges, what does it tell us about practices, taken together, that work and those that don't? That was the genesis of this book.

That same convergence of research is helping us understand why practices work in some instances and with some children but don't in other instances or with other groups of children, and what to *do* to reach all children. This knowledge promises to relieve us of the wearying parade of new ideas, practices, programs, and strategies that are embraced, tried out, discarded as ineffective—or not as effective as we had hoped—and replaced with new ideas that are tried out, discarded as ineffective, and replaced with yet newer ideas.

Today we have a much clearer picture of what must be in place in order for students to attain high levels of learning while thriving and growing in a system that supports them. We also know what needs to be in place for the adults surrounding those students—teachers, staff members, school administrators, parents, and community members—to partner in that success. In short, we have the necessary knowledge to create high-performing schools.

The Essential Elements of Effective Schools

Ten themes have emerged from studies of schools in which all groups of students are performing at high levels. These themes can be used to create a detailed picture of what an effective school looks like.

Written Curriculum Aligned to Standards, Assessments, and Instructional Materials

Not surprisingly, the first theme is the central role of a written curriculum aligned to standards, assessments, and instructional materials. Because state standards provide continuity in education across each state, they provide an important and necessary baseline for curriculum alignment. In our mobile society, it is important to ensure that children transferring from one school or district to another encounter the same educational expectations and instructional progression. According to Census Bureau data on national mobility from 2000 to 2005, 42.4% of children between the ages of 5 and 19—nearly 26 million—moved *at least once* during that 5-year period. Of these mobile children, 14.5 million moved within the same county, 5.4 million moved outside of the county but within the same state, and 4.5 million moved to a different state (United States Census Bureau, 2008a). Had written curriculum aligned to state standards existed in every school district, it would have provided a degree of continuity for those *19.9 million* children who moved within their state. Had national standards existed, that continuity would have extended to an additional 4.5 million students.

While there is widespread agreement that the quality of state standards is improving (Achieve, Inc., 2009), in many states standards (1) are still too numerous and broad in scope, (2) do not focus on the most important areas, and (3) lack the necessary degree of coherence, specificity, and academic rigor.

In curriculum, instruction, and assessment, the big idea is coherence. In a coherent instructional program, all parts are aligned and working together toward the same goal: meeting the standards. The written curriculum lays out the specifics of the instructional program. It describes the assessments to be used and the program of intervention and enrichment opportunities that are keyed to the results of those assessments. This coherence ensures that every student is both challenged to do his or her best and supported in that effort should progress falter. Instructional materials support (but cannot replace) the written curriculum. Teachers rely on the written curriculum to help them know exactly what parts of books or other materials are to be used and in what context.

Instructional Practices That Challenge and Support All Students

In effective schools, a well-designed written curriculum is paired with a strong instructional program. To maintain coherence, leaders and peers work together to ensure that the written curriculum is the one that is taught in every classroom. Teacher teams develop pacing charts to guide instructional organization and delivery so that important concepts and content are not skipped. School administrators conduct frequent classroom observations to confirm that instruction is moving along as laid out in the pacing chart.

Effective schools acknowledge student learning as their highest priority. In such a context, teachers have high expectations of all of their students, and they have the instructional supports in place to ensure that all children have the real opportunity to meet those expectations. Students are simultaneously encouraged and supported to stretch their knowledge and skills in an instructional program that engages their interest.

Assessments That Improve Student Learning

To assess student progress through the instructional program and toward the standards, three types of assessments are necessary:

1. Formative assessments are used during the lesson or unit to guide and improve instruction and to group and regroup students within classes as skill levels increase.

2. Summative assessments are used to determine how well the student or group met the learning targets of a lesson or unit.

3. Diagnostic assessments are used to pinpoint individual students' specific needs for intervention or remediation and are keyed to specific instructional strategies to address identified areas of concern.

Research indicates that while summative assessments are overused, formative and diagnostic assessments are underused. Formative and diagnostic assessments are both powerful tools to improve classroom instruction and increase student achievement.

Leadership for Learning

Instructional programs need the support of strong leadership in order to thrive and to withstand challenges from competing school demands and priorities. This support is so important that researchers have found that "leadership is second only to classroom instruction among all school-related factors that contribute to what students learn at school" (Leithwood, Louis, Anderson, & Wahlstrom, 2004, p. 5). Effective leaders create a school climate in which academic achievement is the primary goal, and they ensure that policies, procedures, and resources support that goal. They maintain an unwavering focus on student learning. They work to put the supports in place so that teachers can focus on learning with minimal distractions and make sure that their instruction is aligned with the written curriculum and of high quality.

To allow school administrators to focus on student learning, others in the school or district must be empowered to carry out other important duties at the school that have traditionally been the work of the principal. This arrangement has a triple advantage in that it:

1. Distributes leadership responsibility and authority throughout the school

2. Adds health to the organization because all staff members are responsible for and committed to school improvement

3. Recognizes expertise rather than position as the factor that determines leadership within the school (Bennett, Wise, & Woods, 2003b; Morrison Institute for Public Policy, 2006)

As school administrators work to enhance the culture of the school or reform it from one that is organized to produce teaching to one that is set up to produce learning, healthy disagreement, even conflict, will arise from differing concepts of what is best for students. School administrators realize the positive power in conflict and encourage staff members to express concerns; they then work to identify and address the core issues. A positive by-product of this approach to conflict management is that when staff members see that school administrators are not threatened by disagreement, they feel empowered to suggest additional ideas and solutions that in the past they might have elected to keep to themselves.

Planning for Learning

Educators have sometimes been accused of random acts of improvement, and, as noted earlier, with some justification. Strategic planning ensures that actions are aligned with other initiatives at the school and work together toward a common goal. It begins when school administrators and others use data to identify and understand a problem that is interfering with student learning, propose a solution, work toward it, and use data again to evaluate progress toward the solution.

Strategic plans are not massive tomes, nor do they need to address only the broadest and most complex problems of the school. They can also be short, intervention-like plans focused on specific problems of student learning. In fact, shorter, more targeted strategic plans have distinct advantages in that they can result in small victories that "form the basis for a consistent pattern of winning that appeals to people's desire to belong to a successful venture" (DuFour, DuFour, Eaker, & Karhanek, 2004, p. 187).

Professional Development That Addresses Student Learning

An area that is commonly the target for strategic planning is teacher professional development. This makes sense because teacher expertise is the single most important school-related factor in student learning, accounting for 40% of the total impact (Darling-Hammond & Ball, 1997).

To be most effective, teachers need to have expertise in three domains: subject matter, understanding of how children learn (general pedagogy), and understanding of the instructional, assessment, and intervention practices associated with the specific subjects taught (content-specific pedagogy) (Elmore, 2002).

For teachers and other staff members who may need additional preparation in one or more of these three areas, professional development can provide that expertise. The "how" of professional development is as important as the "what." Professional development is most powerful when it focuses on student needs identified through data, builds on and is aligned with state standards and the instructional program of the school, is job-embedded, and provides opportunities for collaboration over time.

Job-embedded professional development gives teachers a way to apply what they are learning directly to their regular work with students. In collaborative professional development, teachers from the same school, department, or grade level work together in groups of two or more, observing lessons and learning from, as well as providing peer coaching for, one another; planning lessons or assessments; studying student work; scoring student work; or participating in more formalized coaching or mentoring (Abdal-Haqq, 1996; Resnick, 2005).

All Children Connected, Engaged, and Ready

A frequent focus of both strategic planning and professional development is the need to reduce the number of students who leave school prior to graduation. Helping children stay in and graduate from school has enormous benefits both for the student and for society as a whole. Children who drop out of school are more likely to be unemployed, in poor health, and impoverished; they are also more likely eventually to become the parents of children who themselves later drop out of school.

The decision to drop out of school is rarely made suddenly or precipitated by a single event. Instead, it is the culmination of a gradual process of disengagement that begins in elementary and middle school. In fact, the single most accurate predictor of leaving school before graduation is being held back a grade. In the Baltimore School District, for example, 71% of students who were held back a grade eventually dropped out of school (Ogle, 1997).

Most children who display symptoms of disengagement from school, including excessive absences, repeated suspensions, low reading skills, and low grades, have already experienced and failed in a traditional linear skills-progression model. To reengage these students, the curriculum must be both richer and deeper. Students at risk need to experience interesting and challenging learning that makes plentiful use of higher-order thinking skills in a strong and authentic curriculum, delivered by teachers with high expertise in both subject matter and pedagogy.

Whether children will be involved in an engaging, stimulating curriculum in which each child is challenged to excel while simultaneously supported in working toward high academic goals is to a large extent dependent on what the adults in the school prioritize and value. Effective schools differ measurably from less effective schools in this regard. One example of these differences comes from a large survey in which teachers from high- and low-achieving schools were asked to select what they valued most from a list of possible priorities. Teachers from high-performing schools selected "a hunger for improvement, raising capability, helping people learn, focusing on the value added, promoting excellence, and making sacrifices to put pupils first." Teachers from low-performing schools most valued "warmth, humor, repartee, feet on the ground, recognizing personal circumstances, making allowances, toleration, and creating a pleasant and collegial working environment" (Jerald, 2006, p. 4).

What is striking about these responses is that the priorities of the high-achieving schools demonstrated teachers' belief that they could make a difference in student achievement, as evidenced by selections such as "pushing the boundaries of achievement" and "helping people learn." In lower-performing schools, the priorities were excuses for low performance, such as "recognizing personal circumstances" and "making allowances."

A Safe and Supportive Learning Environment

In addition to emphasizing a strong and aligned instructional program and encouraging teachers and leaders to have high expectations of their students, effective schools protect instructional time from disruptions, including those resulting from negative student behaviors. Effective discipline systems have two major goals: to create and maintain an environment that is consistently conducive to learning, and to ensure the safety of students and staff. Behavior systems that support these goals and are supported by students, families, and school staff members are seen as fair, consistent, equitably applied, and having consequences commensurate with infractions.

Teachers in whose classrooms student behavior poses few or no problems hold and communicate high expectations for student learning and behavior. First, these teachers attend to instruction. They maintain a brisk pace of instruction, smoothly transitioning between activities. They pay attention to what is going on in their classrooms and acknowledge student behavior, both positive and negative. They establish and teach the classroom rules and procedures to be followed and then share with their students the responsibility for classroom management. They enforce classroom rules promptly, consistently, and equitably, using consequences that have been specified in advance (Cotton, 1990).

Effective schools avoid the overuse of suspension and expulsion. Because these punishments carry so many more negative consequences than all other options for addressing discipline issues, suspension and expulsion must be reserved for only the most serious offenses. Blomberg (2004) points out that suspension

tends to push away the very students who need the most support from school. . . . There is little evidence that students learn from their behavior and that students who are suspended avoid further misbehavior. Students most at risk for suspension often have difficult home lives and dangerous peer groups. The act of suspending these students and leaving them at home in a (typically) unsupervised setting can actually create more problems for them. (p. 4)

Building Positive Relationships With Families and the Community

Family and community members can be and are important partners in student success. High-functioning family involvement programs build trust and positive relationships between parents and the school. Because children learn from observing, they learn from positive encounters between school staff members and families, just as they learn from negative encounters. When children see their parents and school staff members interacting respectfully, they learn that school matters and that parents and teachers are working together toward their success.

Districts That Support Student Learning

While schools are most frequently the primary unit at which improvement efforts are aimed, rarely do they operate independently of a school district and board. Research into effective districts is not as plentiful as that into effective schools, but it is clear that in high-performing districts, the roles and responsibilities at each level (student, teacher, building administrator, district administrator, superintendent, and board) are clear, each level acts within its scope of authority, and each level is accountable to the others for its performance.

Effective districts maintain a relentless focus on student learning. They have clear expectations for adults, students, and the instructional program and "apply consistent pressure on schools for improved outcomes for students" (Shannon & Bylsma, 2004, p. 22).

Moving From Research to Improvement

So how does the research, taken together, add up? It paints a picture of what needs to be in place to ensure that every child achieves at a high level and graduates from high school prepared to enter the world of work or, even better, postsecondary education.

Replicating that picture starts with an absolute commitment on the part of teachers, administrators, the superintendent, and the board to prioritize student learning above all else. Decisions about whom to hire, what to pay for, and on what basis to evaluate staff—as well as every other decision that is made daily, monthly, or yearly—must all revolve around student learning. A second broad brushstroke is the alignment of all parts of the system so that they work together toward the common goal of student learning. A third is the development and enactment of an aligned K–12 curriculum, instruction, and assessment system. The fourth is data-based decision-making. If something matters, schools should find a way to measure it—and then use the results to improve what they measured. If it doesn't matter, they should stop doing it.

As schools lay claim to student learning as their core mission, they must transform from teaching organizations into learning organizations. School administrators and staff members must answer three key questions:

1. What has high-quality research identified as essential elements of effective schools?

2. How can we tell the extent to which those characteristics and traits are present in our school?

3. What are the next steps for our school to take to become more effective?

The on-site school review process can help schools find the answers to these questions. This book will describe in detail the specific tools and steps of this process. By committing to an on-site review, schools can move from *knowing* to *doing*. They will learn what they are doing now and where they fall on the continuum of effectiveness. Most important, they will be given direction for the next steps to take as they begin, refine, or complete their journey toward high achievement for all children.

The Building Blocks of an On-Site School Review

A principal or district superintendent is often the first person to recognize the potential of an objective external review of a school. The idea of such a review is that a team is invited into a school, gathers various types of data that allow it to identify a school's strengths and challenges, and then presents recommendations for specific steps the school can take to increase student learning and achievement.

An on-site school review derives its validity from research. The evaluation component of the review works by comparing the state of current practice at the school to what research tells us is in place in the most effective schools.

To identify and describe the benchmark characteristics of effective schools—those schools in which all students are learning to high levels, achievement gaps have narrowed, and both students and adults feel successful—we have reviewed thousands of publications, including research studies, literature reviews, data reports, trend reports, journal articles, and books. We conducted our initial research in 2000 and have since updated it twice: in 2005 and then again in early 2009 for this publication. In combing through the research, we looked first for empirical studies that had adequate sample sizes and, ideally, had been replicated. When the research did not meet these criteria, we looked for strong evidence of links between specific strategies, programs, and practices and student learning.

Next we condensed the research into the 10 broad themes of school effectiveness that we summarized in the introduction to this book. We then translated these themes into the benchmarks against which to compare a school under review. We call these benchmarks "Effectiveness Indicators," and they are the foundation of our school review process.

Effectiveness Indicators, Characteristics, and Traits

Each effectiveness indicator points to one dimension of a school's overall program that can be thoroughly evaluated through an on-site school review. The 10 effectiveness indicators are:

1. Written Curriculum

2. Instructional Program

3. Student Assessment

4. School Leadership

5. Strategic Planning

6. Professional Development

7. Student Connectedness, Engagement, and Readiness

8.   School Environment

9.   Family and Community Involvement

10.   District Support

Each effectiveness indicator is defined by between 5 and 12 "Characteristics." These are short statements describing elements that research has identified as being important to and in place in successful schools. For example, the first characteristic of Effectiveness Indicator 1: Written Curriculum is "The written curriculum is aligned to state standards or the standards of national disciplinary organizations."

The characteristics, in turn, are further broken down into between 1 and 5 "Traits." A trait is a measurable or observable component of a characteristic. It is at the level of the traits that a review team performs its evaluation. For example, to evaluate a school's written curriculum, the review team would first look at the extent of the written curriculum—that is, for which subjects and classes a written curriculum exists.

We have devised a shorthand system to identify the effectiveness indicators and their associated characteristics and traits. Each effectiveness indicator is assigned a number (for example, Effectiveness Indicator 1). The characteristics of that indicator are assigned the same number, followed by their own letters (for example, Characteristic 1A, 1B, and so on). The traits are assigned the number/letter combination of the characteristic they define, followed by their own numbers (for example, Trait 1A1, 1A2, and so on). These number/letter codes will be used consistently in the various tools that the review team employs in conducting its evaluation.

The Rubrics

The rubrics (scoring guides) are the basic tool of the school review process. They provide a systematic way to determine the extent to which each characteristic of each effectiveness indicator is, or is not, in place within a school. The rubrics enable the review team to conduct an objective evaluation of complex processes and activities. They also give the administrators and staff members at the school material for self-evaluation and reflection.

The rubrics for the effectiveness indicators break each characteristic down into its respective traits and describe what each trait looks like at three different points on a continuum of school effectiveness: low performing, effective, and high performing. For example, Table I.1 (page 10), the rubric for Characteristic 1A, shows the traits that are examined to determine the degree to which a school's "written curriculum is aligned to state standards or the standards of national disciplinary organizations" and describes what each will look like depending on the school's place on the effectiveness continuum.

Each of the 10 chapters in part 1 will be devoted to one effectiveness indicator. The chapters are divided into sections, one for each characteristic of the indicator. Each section begins with a summary of the research pertaining to that characteristic and ends with the rubric for that characteristic. The rubric is the guide that a review team will use to compare the school's practices with those of the nation's most effective schools.

Table I.1: Rubric for Characteristic 1A

Characteristic	Trait	Effectiveness Continuum		
		Low Performing	Effective	High Performing
1A. The written curriculum is aligned to state standards or the standards of national disciplinary organizations.	1A1. Extent of written curriculum	Some or all classes for which there are state standards lack written curriculum.	There is written curriculum for all subjects and classes for which there are state standards.	There is written curriculum for all subjects and classes.
	1A2. Alignment to content of standards	The written curriculum is not aligned to the content of state standards.	The written curriculum is aligned to the content of state standards.	The written curriculum is aligned to the content of state standards in those subjects for which there are state standards and the content of the standards of national disciplinary organizations for other subjects.
	1A3. Alignment to cognitive demands of standards	The written curriculum is not aligned to the cognitive demands of state standards.	The written curriculum is aligned to the cognitive demands of state standards.	The written curriculum is aligned to or exceeds the cognitive demands of state standards in those subjects for which there are state standards and the cognitive demands of the standards of national disciplinary organizations for other subjects.

The On-Site School Review Process

Part 2 of the book (chapters 11–16) will describe in detail the entire on-site school review process, from preparation through execution and follow-up. The chapters provide guidance for each step of the process so that the school staff will know exactly what to expect and plan for and the reviewers will know exactly how to conduct the review and make recommendations that will result in the greatest increases in student achievement.

During the school visit, the review team gathers information about the state of current practice at the school from many sources, including:

+ State and local assessments

+ Student work

+ Classroom observations

+ Curriculum documents

+ Surveys of teachers, classified staff members, parents, and students

+ Interviews and focus groups with teachers, administrators, staff members, and students

+ Parent and community meetings

+ Statements of school policies and procedures

+ School improvement plans

The power of the on-site review lies in the relationship between research, data collection, and the effectiveness indicators. Every trait of every effectiveness indicator is research-based and is tied to specific sources of evidence from the list above. For example, a focus group with teachers will yield information about particular traits, while classroom observations will yield information about others. At an even finer level, every survey, interview, and focus group question, as well as every item on the classroom observation checklist, is keyed to a specific trait. Finally, once the data related to a trait have been gathered and analyzed, the reviewers are ready to begin the scoring process by determining which column of the rubric best describes the school's performance on that trait. From the rubrics, the final evaluation takes shape.

The Tools

The CD accompanying the book provides the many tools that a review team uses to communicate about the visit and to collect and validate evidence. Thirteen of these tools also appear in the appendix to the book. The chapters describing the on-site school review process will refer readers to the specific tools that are needed to carry out each step—for example, surveys, templates for conducting interviews and focus groups, worksheets, and observation forms. Now, however, we want to alert readers to three comprehensive tools that will serve as handy references throughout the course of the book:

1. **Tool 5: Effectiveness Indicator Overview** (CD and appendix, page 262). This tool is a summary, in text form, of the 10 effectiveness indicators and their characteristics.

2. **Tool 46: Effectiveness Indicator Map** (CD and appendix, page 274). This tool is the one place in the book where readers will find the complete rubrics for all 10 effectiveness indicators.

3. **Tool 16: Master Matrix** (CD). This tool is a table that indicates which sources of evidence will be used to examine every trait of every effectiveness indicator.

The CD also includes PowerPoint presentations, agendas, letters, schedules, report samples, and other tools for planning and communication.

Using This Book

While this book is intended as a resource that will make it possible for educators to plan for, participate in, or conduct on-site school reviews, it can serve another function that also relates to school improvement. Schools that are considering being reviewed, or are unfamiliar with what a review entails, or are perhaps hesitant to commit to a review, will find rich material here for a book study. An administrator could introduce the book at a staff meeting and ask teachers to select the effectiveness indicators they are most interested in learning more about. Subsequent meetings could be devoted to discussions of the research and rubrics, which relate directly to what every teacher is doing on a daily basis. The reflection and conversation that the study engenders will surely have a positive effect on practice, whether or not the staff ultimately decides to move forward with a review.

PART 1

The 10 Effectiveness Indicators:
Research and Rubrics

Effectiveness Indicator 1
Written Curriculum

There are two ways of being creative. One can sing and dance. Or one can create an environment in which singers and dancers flourish.

—Warren G. Bennis

The written curriculum is the foundation of the school's instructional program. In effective schools, the written curriculum is aligned to standards, assessments, and instructional materials. From this principle, we derive Effectiveness Indicator 1. An on-site school review examines the written curriculum to gauge its alignment with state content standards; its horizontal and vertical alignment; its alignment with instructional materials; the supports available for it, such as assessments and interventions; and the degree to which it is implemented in classrooms every day.

Five characteristics define Effectiveness Indicator 1: Written Curriculum:

1A.   The written curriculum is aligned to state standards or the standards of national disciplinary organizations.

1B.   The written curriculum is vertically and horizontally aligned.

1C.   Textbooks and other instructional materials are aligned with the written curriculum.

1D.   Formative and summative assessments are identified in the written curriculum.

1E.   Intervention and enrichment materials are identified in the written curriculum.

Characteristic 1A: Alignment to Standards

Summary of Research

Research on increasing levels of student learning supports the importance and effectiveness of developing high-quality, rigorous curriculum aligned to standards. Joseph Murphy and his colleagues found that "in the array of factors that define high-performing schools, curriculum alignment enjoys a position of exceptional prominence" (Murphy, Elliott, Goldring, & Porter, 2006a, pp. 5–6).

Providing just the right instruction to equip every student with what is needed to learn to his or her highest potential is a complex process. It requires judgments about the knowledge and skills students need to meet state or national disciplinary standards as well as their own individual learning goals. It involves choices about instructional delivery, sequence and pacing, how instructional materials (such as textbooks and technology) will be used, and what assessments to use, when to use them, and for what purpose. It calls for determinations about the selection and use of strategic and intensive interventions when student learning begins to falter and of enrichment strategies for those students who are ready for them. And it requires all of these pieces to come together at just the right time. These decisions are simply too complex and interrelated to be made haphazardly.

A written curriculum document spells out how instruction and assessment will fit together into a seamless, or nearly seamless, whole. It formalizes agreements made by staff about the instructional program and how it will be enacted. It ensures that students receive the instruction that is judged by the staff to be the best progression for meeting individual learning goals and state and disciplinary standards. It provides continuity when new teachers are hired and is the starting place for evaluating and refining the instructional program. The process of putting all of these pieces together into a coherent whole is known as curriculum alignment.

Since the 1980s, "academic content standards have served as the foundation of state education systems. Standards provide the underpinning for decisions on curriculum, instruction and assessment, and they communicate core knowledge and skills to teachers, parents and students" (Achieve, Inc., 2009, p. 8). Since state and disciplinary standards (and their associated benchmarks) have been developed for most content areas to help define what it is students should know and be able to do, they are a logical starting point for curriculum development.

Written curriculum that provides the information teachers need to make sound instructional decisions should be aligned to these standards (and other learning goals selected by the school or district) in two ways. First, the curriculum should address the concepts described in the standards, such as supply and demand in economics or spatial and numeric patterns in mathematics. Second, the curriculum should take into account the cognitive demand of the standards.

Sometimes called depth of knowledge, *cognitive demand* refers to the kind or level of knowledge a student must demonstrate to show that he or she has met the standard. A standard's level of cognitive demand is keyed to descriptors that help in distinguishing between types of understanding. For example, some standards may require students to demonstrate an understanding of what they have learned by recalling or reciting facts, such as recognizing a definition of supply and demand. Other standards will require a deeper understanding of the topic, to be demonstrated by using knowledge to solve problems, applying what has been learned to make decisions about new situations, or predicting the results of certain courses of action, such as how a new law might affect supply and demand, and thus the pricing of related products. To be effective, written curricula are aligned both to the topic and to its associated cognitive demand.

Chapter 3, on student assessment, will go into more detail about cognitive demand and how students' attainment of it is measured.

The Rubric

A review team wanting to determine how a school's written curriculum measures up against the benchmark of Characteristic 1A would look at three traits of that characteristic. The rubric in Table 1.1 describes each trait as it manifests in low-performing, effective, and high-performing schools.

Table 1.1: Rubric for Characteristic 1A

Characteristic	Trait	Effectiveness Continuum		
		Low Performing	Effective	High Performing
1A. The written curriculum is aligned to state standards or the standards of national disciplinary organizations.	**1A1. Extent of written curriculum**	Some or all classes for which there are state standards lack written curriculum.	There is written curriculum for all subjects and classes for which there are state standards.	There is written curriculum for all subjects and classes.
	1A2. Alignment to content of standards	The written curriculum is not aligned to the content of state standards.	The written curriculum is aligned to the content of state standards.	The written curriculum is aligned to the content of state standards in those subjects for which there are state standards and the content of the standards of national disciplinary organizations for other subjects.
	1A3. Alignment to cognitive demands of standards	The written curriculum is not aligned to the cognitive demands of state standards.	The written curriculum is aligned to the cognitive demands of state standards.	The written curriculum is aligned to or exceeds the cognitive demands of state standards in those subjects for which there are state standards and the cognitive demands of the standards of national disciplinary organizations for other subjects.

Characteristic 1B: Vertical and Horizontal Alignment

Summary of Research

Curriculum needs to progress smoothly and logically, with each lesson and unit building knowledge and skills that can be used in the next lesson or unit and as students advance from one grade level to the next. A written curriculum that forms the basis for instruction and is coordinated within and between grade levels is a key feature of effective schools and one that is not typical of lower-performing schools (Fouts, 2003).

Alignment from one grade to another is called *vertical alignment*. This articulation has been shown to be effective in increasing student learning and achievement, even in schools with high levels of poverty and high populations of English language learners (Corallo & McDonald, 2002). When the curriculum is well-aligned vertically, teachers know in advance what has been taught to and learned by students at earlier grade levels and what is expected of students in the following grade levels. This knowledge can greatly reduce the amount of time spent reviewing and reteaching at the beginning of each school year. In addition, assessments from previous years provide useful information to teachers at the following grade levels because the assessments are tied to a curriculum that progresses logically from one grade or class to the next.

A second kind of alignment is *horizontal alignment*. Horizontal alignment occurs when the written curriculum forms the basis for instruction and assessment for all teachers working at the same grade level or teaching the same course. It provides answers to teachers in five areas:

1.   What do we teach?

2.   How do we teach it?

3.   When do we teach it?

4.   How do we assess it?

5.   How and when do we provide interventions and enrichment?

Horizontal alignment is characterized by *pacing charts*, which guide the time devoted to each standard, unit, or lesson. Porter (2004, p. 2) explains that "pacing decisions are important determinants of the content of the . . . curriculum because a slow pace covers less content. Teachers must negotiate between how much content they would like students to learn and how much content students can learn within the constraints of time, pedagogy, and effort."

Without pacing charts, teachers lack shared understandings about how much time should be spent on what. For example, in elementary school, should mathematics be taught every day or every other day? Should it be taught for 30 minutes or 90 minutes? Left without guidance, by midyear "one teacher may have spent as much time teaching mathematics as another will have spent by the end of the school year" (Porter, 2004, p. 2).

Effective pacing charts provide time frames for each standard in each unit. These "time frames help to govern time distribution among competing subject matter and topics. When curriculum appropriately governs time *and* content, academic learning time—time students are on task while learning challenging content not learned previously—increases, and so will student achievement" (Louisiana Department of

Education, 2005, p. iv). Pacing guidelines ensure that students receive similar instruction no matter to which teacher they are assigned.

The Rubric

A review team wanting to determine how a school's written curriculum measures up against the benchmark of Characteristic 1B would look at two traits of that characteristic. The rubric in Table 1.2 describes each trait as it manifests in low-performing, effective, and high-performing schools.

Table 1.2: Rubric for Characteristic 1B

Characteristic	Trait	Effectiveness Continuum		
		Low Performing	Effective	High Performing
1B. The written curriculum is vertically and horizontally aligned.	**1B1. Vertical alignment**	The curriculum is not aligned vertically between grade levels or sequential courses.	The curriculum is aligned vertically between grade levels and sequential courses.	The curriculum is aligned vertically between grade levels and sequential courses, and periodic analyses are conducted to review the appropriateness of grade-level curriculum loads.
	1B2. Horizontal alignment	The curriculum is not aligned horizontally within grade levels and courses.	The curriculum is aligned horizontally within each grade level and course.	The curriculum is aligned horizontally within each grade level and course, and periodic analyses are conducted to review the appropriateness of the pacing charts.

Characteristic 1C: Alignment of Textbooks and Other Instructional Materials

Summary of Research

In 2002, the National Education Association surveyed 1,000 teachers across the United States about their use of instructional materials. Among the findings were:

- Textbooks remained the most frequently used teaching tools, with nearly half (47%) of all teachers reporting that they used textbooks every day and another 14% reporting that they used textbooks three or more times per week.

+ Handouts were the second most frequently used instructional material, with 32% of teachers reporting that they used handouts daily and another 23% reporting that they used handouts three or four times per week.

+ Twenty-one percent of teachers reported that they used workbooks every day, and 10% more reported that they used them three or more times per week.

+ Eighteen percent of teachers reported that they used specialized instructional software, either computer-based or online, every day, and another 9% reported that they used it at least three times each week.

Because teachers rely on textbooks, handouts, workbooks, and software as important instructional tools, effective schools review these materials to determine their degree of alignment to the standards and written curriculum. A good way to do this is to conduct a match/gap analysis. In this activity, teacher teams analyze at which points the instructional materials match the written curriculum at the appropriate level of cognitive demand. This is the "match" part of the match/gap activity. The sections in which there is a match are then noted on the written curriculum.

There will be other areas in which instructional materials match the curriculum poorly or fail to match it. These areas are "gaps," which will need to be filled in with supplemental materials. The specific supplemental material to be used is noted along with the parts, sections, or pages of those materials.

The final step in the match/gap analysis is to identify extraneous content that does not need to be included in classroom instruction. Examples would be reviews of previously taught content or parts of the materials that the teacher team agrees will not help to meet the identified standards of a particular course or class. Sections determined to be unnecessary should be clearly identified, and permission given to teachers to skip these sections during instruction. These decisions then also become part of the written curriculum documents guiding instruction.

Many publishers provide some of this information as part of their sales or purchase package. This is a help in the match/gap analysis; still, schools should be sure to check that the publisher's analysis considers not only the topics of the written curriculum but also the cognitive demand of the standards at which the curriculum is aimed.

The Rubric

A review team wanting to determine how a school's written curriculum measures up against the benchmark of Characteristic 1C would look at two traits of that characteristic. The rubric in Table 1.3 describes each trait as it manifests in low-performing, effective, and high-performing schools.

Characteristic 1D: Identification of Formative and Summative Assessments

Summary of Research

Assessments are critical to the effectiveness of the written curriculum. Ideally, as part of the curriculum development process, teacher teams review the standards, determine what it is that all students should know and be able to do, and select or create assessments that measure student progress toward, or attainment of, the standards. These assessments then become part of the written curriculum, and the window within which they will be administered is included in the pacing chart.

Table 1.3: Rubric for Characteristic 1C

Characteristic	Trait	Effectiveness Continuum		
		Low Performing	Effective	High Performing
1C. Textbooks and other instructional materials are aligned with the written curriculum.	1C1. Identification of instructional materials	The written curriculum does not identify aligned instructional materials.	The written curriculum identifies aligned instructional materials.	The written curriculum identifies specific pages or units from instructional and supplemental materials that address each learning objective or standard.
	1C2. Availability of instructional materials	The instructional materials identified in the written curriculum are not available or are not being used in all classrooms.	The identified instructional materials are available in sufficient quantities and are being used in all classrooms.	The identified instructional materials are available in sufficient quantities, are being used in all classrooms, and are in excellent condition.

Formative assessments are used by students to improve their work or their understanding of a topic or concept and by teachers to improve or differentiate their instruction. Mathematics pretests are diagnostic assessments that help teachers better design instruction. Initial drafts of writing assignments, read by teachers or peer editors who suggest ways to improve the writer's work, are examples of formative assessments used by both students and teachers. Formative assessments are not graded, though they may be scored in order to provide information to the teacher about needed interventions or enrichments. Summative assessments, on the other hand, are typically given at the end of a unit, class, or course. They are nearly always scored or graded. Summative assessments are used to determine individual and group attainment of an educational objective, such as a grade-level standard or unit objective. State tests are examples of summative assessments, as are final exams and culminating course projects.

To ensure that students have the knowledge and skills they will need to demonstrate the proficiencies defined by the standards, classroom instruction and assessments must be aligned with the standards. Moreover, "research on the results of aligning curriculum and instruction with standards and assessments shows a strong positive relationship to student achievement" (Appalachia Education Laboratory at Edvantia, 2005a, p. 1).

The Rubric

A review team wanting to determine how a school's written curriculum measures up against the benchmark of Characteristic 1D would look at one trait of that characteristic. The rubric in Table 1.4 (page 22) describes that trait as it manifests in low-performing, effective, and high-performing schools.

Table 1.4: Rubric for Characteristic 1D

Characteristic	Trait	Effectiveness Continuum		
		Low Performing	Effective	High Performing
1D. Formative and summative assessments are identified in the written curriculum.	1D1. Identification of assessments	Formative and summative assessments are not identified in the written curriculum.	Formative and summative assessments are identified in the written curriculum.	Formative and summative assessments are identified in the written curriculum, and result ranges are keyed to interventions and enrichments.

Characteristic 1E: Identification of Intervention and Enrichment Materials

Summary of Research

Effective schools develop strategies or programs both to assist students who begin to fall behind learning targets and to challenge those who surge ahead of, or meet expectations well before, the rest of the class. The written curriculum should clearly describe the intervention and enrichment materials or strategies that have been selected by the school or district and should designate the events that would trigger their use, such as score ranges from specified formative assessments. These can take many forms, including teacher-made assessments, informal oral reading fluency measures, or skills checks included in software programs or classroom texts.

Well-designed assessments are the key to the early identification of learning difficulties, and targeted interventions based on the results of those assessments are the key to early remediation (National Joint Committee on Learning Disabilities, 2005). The curriculum needs to clearly spell out what interventions will be used, how they will be used, and by whom they will be delivered.

The Rubric

A review team wanting to determine how a school's written curriculum measures up against the benchmark of Characteristic 1E would look at two traits of that characteristic. The rubric in Table 1.5 describes each trait as it manifests in low-performing, effective, and high-performing schools.

Table 1.5: Rubric for Characteristic 1E

Characteristic	Trait	Effectiveness Continuum		
		Low Performing	Effective	High Performing
1E. Intervention and enrichment materials are identified in the written curriculum.	1E1. Identification of intervention and enrichment materials	The written curriculum does not identify intervention and enrichment materials.	The written curriculum identifies intervention and enrichment materials.	The written curriculum identifies intervention and enrichment materials keyed to specific learner needs.
	1E2. Availability of intervention and enrichment materials	Intervention and enrichment materials either are not available or are not available in sufficient quantities to meet identified student needs.	Intervention and enrichment materials are available in sufficient quantities to meet student needs.	Intervention and enrichment materials are available in sufficient quantities to meet student needs and are available in the major languages of the school.

Conclusion

As Baker (2004, p. 5) makes clear, the importance of alignment cannot be overstressed:

> Without alignment, nothing hangs together. Goals may or may not be exemplified in practice, children may or may not learn what is expected, and test scores could represent standards or miss their mark entirely. . . . Deficiencies in alignment result in ambiguity that may affect some or all parts of the system, like an incubating virus—dangerous but not that obvious.

Aligning the curriculum is the process of ensuring a match between the state standards and the lessons taught in classrooms every day (Corallo & McDonald, 2002). In effective schools, the written curriculum, instruction, and assessments create a coherent system in which gaps and repetitions have been eliminated, instructional materials support the curriculum, instruction is coordinated within and between levels and moves along at an appropriate and lively pace, and intervention and enrichment opportunities ensure that every student is both challenged to do his or her best and supported in that effort.

Effectiveness Indicator 2
Instructional Program

Live as if you were to die tomorrow. Learn as if you were to live forever.

— Mahatma Gandhi

The instructional program is the school's core mission. In effective schools, instructional practices challenge and support all students. From this principle, we derive Effectiveness Indicator 2. An on-site school review looks at the instructional program as a whole, focusing on its rigor (access, challenge, and support for all students), its flexibility (individualized tools, strategies, and assessments for all students), and the supports it provides for teachers (curriculum cohesion, professional collaboration, and instructional leadership). Teachers are key to the implementation of the instructional program. Their deep content knowledge, mastery of a broad range of instructional strategies, and commitment to student achievement are essential to the delivery system.

Ten characteristics define Effectiveness Indicator 2: Instructional Program:

2A.   Teachers integrate content standards into classroom instruction.

2B.   The instructional program is rigorous and provides access, challenge, and support for all students.

2C.   Teachers expect all students to make substantial learning gains each year, and students have high expectations of themselves.

2D.   Teachers organize instruction to support clearly articulated and communicated learning targets.

2E.   Teachers provide students with activities and assignments that are rigorous and engaging and that extend their learning.

2F.   Teachers have deep knowledge of their subject matter, possess expertise in a wide range of effective instructional strategies, and are committed to closing achievement gaps.

2G.   Teachers plan together to ensure that instruction and assessment meet the needs of all learners.

2H.   Instructional time is fully and effectively used.

2I.   School administrators support and promote effective instructional practices, program coordination, and resource allocation.

2J.   School administrators ensure that the taught curriculum reflects the written curriculum and aligns with the pacing charts.

Characteristic 2A: Integration of Content Standards

Summary of Research

A key premise of standards-based education is that curriculum, instruction, and assessment must be tightly aligned. This is the concept of coherent instruction, in which each part of the instructional system fits with, supports, and is supported by each of the other parts. In order to attain instructional coherency, the written curriculum, based on the standards, determines what is taught in the classroom. Classroom instruction is, in turn, supported by aligned instructional materials, assessments, and intervention and enrichment programs.

Increasing instructional coherency results in higher student achievement. In a study looking at the achievement of students in more than 200 schools in Washington State, Jeffrey Fouts (2003) concluded that schools that had aligned their curriculum and instruction to state standards improved student performance on state assessments. Conversely, schools in which curriculum and instruction were less well or poorly aligned registered lower student performance. Fouts' results replicate those of the Committee on the Foundations of Assessment, which found that improvement in student achievement depended on how well assessment, curriculum, and instruction were aligned with learning goals (Pellegrino, Chudowsky, & Glaser, 2001).

In a study of 257 California schools that shared similar demographics but differed substantially in student achievement, teachers in higher-performing schools were much more likely to report that their classroom instruction was guided by the state academic standards than were teachers from lower-performing schools. Teachers from higher-performing schools also reported that their school's curriculum materials and teachers' individual lesson plans were mapped to the standards (Williams et al., 2005).

The Rubric

A review team wanting to determine how a school's instructional program measures up against the benchmark of Characteristic 2A would look at one trait of that characteristic. The rubric in Table 2.1 describes that trait as it manifests in low-performing, effective, and high-performing schools.

Characteristic 2B: Rigor, Accessibility, and Challenge

Summary of Research

Students need access to a rich instructional program that prepares them for postsecondary opportunities. To accomplish this goal, schools must provide an ample array of rigorous courses; encourage students, particularly poor and minority students, to enroll in them; and support student success in these classes.

Table 2.1: Rubric for Characteristic 2A

Characteristic	Trait	Effectiveness Continuum		
		Low Performing	Effective	High Performing
2A. Teachers integrate content standards into classroom instruction.	2A1. Integration of standards	Instruction in those subjects for which state content standards exist does not reflect, or is only loosely coupled with, the content standards.	State content standards are explicitly integrated into instruction in those subjects for which state content standards exist.	State content standards or those of national disciplinary organizations are explicitly integrated into instruction in all classes.

Yet when researchers from WestEd studied the transcripts of 67,000 California high school students, they found that by the end of the ninth grade, a third of the students had not completed the freshman-level English class required for college entrance, and more than 40% had not completed the required full year of mathematics. More than 23% had failed to complete both freshman English and mathematics requirements (Finkelstein & Fong, 2008). Thus at this early point in their high school careers, not only had these students already slipped far behind in meeting the requirements necessary for college entry, but many classes were closed to them because freshman English and mathematics were prerequisites for these higher-level courses.

The Ohio Department of Education (ODE) looked at both course-taking patterns and rigor in relation to an initiative aiming to prepare students for careers in science, technology, engineering, and mathematics (2008). Researchers concluded that in Ohio and across the nation, too few students of color took the necessary coursework or were prepared to take postsecondary steps toward careers in science, technology, engineering, or mathematics. For evidence, the researchers drew from the data showing which students in Ohio took Advanced Placement exams and which groups of students were, and were not, taking rigorous science and mathematics classes. They found that only 6% (1,961) of the students taking the AP exam were African American, fewer than 2% (537) were Hispanic, and fewer than 5% were from low-income families.

ODE also reported that when the College Board studied course-taking patterns "in 2007, only 12 percent of blacks and 11 percent of Hispanics took physics, pre-calculus or calculus courses" (p. 1). The department concluded that poor and minority students "either don't have access to challenging courses or don't choose to take them, even when they're headed to college" (p. 1).

While challenging courses are essential, it is what happens during instructional time that largely governs how much or how little a student extends his or her learning. Teachers must constantly perform a delicate balancing act. Instruction either too far or not far enough above a student's current level of knowledge and skills is not effective. In the early 1900s, psychologist Lev Vygotsky first explored what this means. His education theory, known as the zone of proximal development, held that the greatest learning strides are made when instruction both engages a child and is aimed at a point that is just beyond his or her ability to function alone but where he or she can succeed with scaffolding or support from a teacher, mentor, or peer. Vygotsky asserted that it is the "teacher's job to push the child into his or her zone of proximal development, coach for success with a task slightly more complex than the child can manage alone, and, thus, push forward until the student reaches the area of independence" (Tomlinson et al., 2003, pp. 5–6).

Instructionally rigorous content challenges every student to do his or her best thinking and work. In a rigorous instructional program, teachers call upon their students to combine newly acquired knowledge and skills with their existing knowledge base and then use those assets to create or explore new ideas rather than simply to reproduce information. Students demonstrate conceptual understanding of important content through the use of higher-order thinking skills, such as organizing, interpreting, evaluating, or synthesizing information, and then clearly communicate those new ideas. They continue to revise their work (based on feedback from teachers, experts in the field, or their peers) until it represents their best effort (Mitchell et al., 2005).

The teacher's task is to encourage each child in every lesson to stretch into his or her zone of proximal development, to engage in deep thinking, and to produce his or her best work. Aiming instruction at this range produces the greatest learning gains (Torgeson, Granger Meadows, & Howard, n.d.). Urging the child forward into new learning that challenges his or her understanding but is not beyond his or her ability to be successful, the teacher provides scaffolding and coaching until the student reaches the level at which the scaffolding can be removed and the skill or knowledge can be applied independently (Simpson, 2005). Tomlinson et al. (2003) explain, "It is through repetition of such cycles [engagement, support, independence] that learners grasp new ideas, master new skills, and become increasingly independent thinkers and problem solvers" (pp. 5–6). Research also shows that "when students encounter tasks at moderate levels of difficulty, they are . . . more likely to sustain efforts to learn, even in the face of difficulty, than when tasks are either too difficult or under-challenging" (Tomlinson et al., p. 6).

But what of the children for whom grade-level expectations are beyond their zone of proximal development? Some of these children may need short-term interventions to help them gain specific knowledge, others may need skills remediation to give them additional background that will enable them to take the next large step, and others may need intensive intervention and support provided by special educators or others. From a systems perspective, these differing needs mean that, in addition to an effective core curriculum, a school must have in place systematic "procedures to identify students who need additional intervention." These procedures must be sensitive enough to determine specifically what knowledge and skills need to be taught. Schools must also have established "a mechanism to deliver additional intervention (time, personnel, curriculum, space) and procedures to escalate the amount of instructional support if needed to achieve benchmark goals" (Good et al., 2002, p. 8). And it is here that something exciting is taking place, bringing the worlds of special education and general education a little closer.

In 2002, in preparation for the reauthorization of the Individuals with Disabilities Education Act (IDEA), the legislation governing special education, the President's Commission on Excellence in Special Education issued a report detailing specific changes to strengthen the act. Many of the commission's recommendations were included in the final language of IDEA 2004. One of these was an endorsement of the assessment and intervention strategy known as response to intervention (RTI).

RTI contributes to more effective instruction by encouraging earlier intervention for students experiencing difficulty. While RTI has a history of use in both general education and special education, under IDEA 2004 it can be used to meld the diagnostic-assessment, intervention, and remediation systems of general and special education into a continuum of services. An important foundation of this continuum is the premise that if a student responds to intervention, it is unlikely that he or she has a learning disability.

RTI uses frequent individual assessment and monitoring to determine a student's need for specific instructional interventions and then to identify next steps, which may include interventions of more or less intensity or cessation altogether. To summarize,

> the function of assessment in RTI is to identify at-risk students as early as possible, to gather relevant data to support educational decision-making and to impact what the teacher is doing to improve achievement. The framework of assessment tools must be increasingly sensitive to detect subtle changes in achievement in student performance as assessments move from screening to diagnostics to progress monitoring. (National Association of State Directors of Special Education & Council of Administrators of Special Education, 2006, p. 4)

The Rubric

A review team wanting to determine how a school's instructional program measures up against the benchmark of Characteristic 2B would look at two traits of that characteristic. The rubric in Table 2.2 describes each trait as it manifests in low-performing, effective, and high-performing schools.

Table 2.2: Rubric for Characteristic 2B

Characteristic	Trait	Effectiveness Continuum		
		Low Performing	Effective	High Performing
2B. The instructional program is rigorous and provides access, challenge, and support for all students.	2B1. Access to rigorous program	Students do not have access to an instructional program that is rigorous and provides challenging opportunities to extend their learning.	Students have access to an instructional program that is rigorous and provides challenging opportunities to extend their learning.	Students have access to an instructional program that is rigorous and provides challenging opportunities to extend their learning. Enrollment patterns in advanced and honors classes reflect the demographics of the student population.
	2B2. Availability of intervention, support, and enrichment programs	Students are not systematically matched with intervention, support, and enrichment programs based on individual student needs.	Teachers have access to a variety of intervention, support, and enrichment programs to address individual student needs.	Teachers have access to a variety of research-based intervention, support, and enrichment programs to address individual student needs.

Characteristic 2C: High Expectations for Learning

Summary of Research

Students whose teachers believe they are capable of meeting high standards tend to do so. Conversely, teachers who believe their students will not master complex knowledge and skills may unintentionally communicate that belief to their students, who may then internalize it, creating a self-fulfilling prophecy. Simply stated, student achievement tends to rise or fall to the level of teacher expectations (Bamburg, 1994).

In an examination of 22 studies and evaluations and 23 research reviews and meta-analyses on the effect of teacher expectations on student achievement, Kathleen Cotton (1989, p. 5) concludes, "The most important finding from this research is that teacher expectations can and do affect students' achievement and attitudes. Among the research materials supporting this paper, all that address this topic found relationships between expectations and student outcomes."

Cotton also reported other major findings. Among these were the following (p. 9):

- High expectations are a critical component of effective schools.

- Teacher expectations and accompanying behaviors have a very real—although limited—effect on student performance, accounting for five to ten percent of student achievement outcomes.

- Communicating low expectations has more power to limit student achievement than communicating high expectations has to raise student performance.

- A minority of teachers see student ability as static, and thus do not perceive and respond to changes in students' performance in such a way as to foster their growth.

- When teachers engage in differential treatment of high- and low-expectation students, students are aware of those differences.

- Younger children are more susceptible to expectancy effects than are older students.

Cotton's analysis also identified the following effective strategies that teachers can use both to improve the way they form expectations and to avoid communicating low expectations to their students:

- Confront and overcome stereotypes.

- Avoid basing judgments on the biases of others.

- Reinforce that you believe your students can achieve.

- Use heterogeneous grouping and cooperative learning activities to capitalize on students' strengths, not their weaknesses.

- Demonstrate that all students are good at different things by creating opportunities for students to see one another's products and performances.

- Monitor student progress closely to test your perceptions.

- Increase wait time to improve the quality of responses, increase participation, and give students time to think about and formulate responses.

- ❖ Give students feedback.

- ❖ Focus on giving information that students can use to improve their work, not just grades.

- ❖ Break down the tasks required and reteach in a different way when students struggle with understanding.

- ❖ Challenge students to continuously increase their skills and knowledge.

- ❖ Concentrate on extending warmth, friendliness, and encouragement to all students.

Other studies have identified many student characteristics, or perceived student characteristics, that are directly associated with teachers' expectations. These include students' race, socioeconomic status, country of origin, English-speaking skills, special education status, appearance, and choice of friends (Kuykendall, 1989; LoGerfo, 2006).

As important as it is for teachers to have high expectations of their students, students must hold high expectations of themselves. For children who may be underestimated by their teachers, it becomes even more important to have high self-expectations, in a sense fortifying themselves against the low expectations of those around them.

In a 4-year study, Janine Bempechat (1999) and her colleagues surveyed more than 1,000 fifth- and sixth-graders who were considered at risk because of poverty or minority status or because their first language was not English, they lived in single-parent homes, or their mothers did not complete high school. Bempechat found that the higher-achieving students "believed that success was due to high ability and, perhaps more important, they did not believe that failure was due to lack of ability. In contrast, regardless of ethnicity, the lower achievers believed that success was due to external factors [such as good luck] and that failure was due to lack of ability" (pp. 9–11). For the low-achieving children who have come to believe that they do not have the ability to succeed in school, trying harder, persisting through initial failure, or taking on challenging coursework simply does not make sense.

In order to be successful in school, students must believe in their own abilities to master complex and sometimes difficult concepts and processes (National Literacy Trust, 2005). This concept of self-efficacy allows students to persist when they are trying to learn new skills that are difficult for them to master, to take on assignments that are beyond their current knowledge and skill level, and to persevere in the face of academic challenges.

The Rubric

A review team wanting to determine how a school's instructional program measures up against the benchmark of Characteristic 2C would look at two traits of that characteristic. The rubric in Table 2.3 (page 32) describes each trait as it manifests in low-performing, effective, and high-performing schools.

Characteristic 2D: Support of Learning Targets

Summary of Research

It is important that *students* understand what they will be learning, why they should learn it, and how they will be asked to demonstrate that they have learned it. For *teachers*, thinking about these questions before creating and teaching a lesson enables them to provide well-designed, high-quality instruction.

Table 2.3: Rubric for Characteristic 2C

Characteristic	Trait	Effectiveness Continuum		
		Low Performing	Effective	High Performing
2C. Teachers expect all students to make substantial learning gains each year, and students have high expectations of themselves.	2C1. Teacher expectations	Some teachers convey low or modest academic expectations of students or high expectations of some, but not all, students.	Teachers express confidence in the ability of their students to make substantial learning gains.	Instructional goals and activities, teacher talk, and the classroom environment all convey high expectations of all students.
	2C2. Student expectations	Some students express low or modest academic expectations of themselves.	Students express confidence in their ability to make substantial learning gains.	Students express confidence in their ability to make substantial learning gains, and student academic achievement supports that confidence.

Knowing the what, why, and how of a lesson or unit gives students a much-needed framework to organize information, which allows for higher levels of both recall and knowledge transfer from one context to another. Ellis and Worthington (1994) call these frameworks "advance organizers," and their research has confirmed that using them results in increased student learning. They propose that the most effective advance organizers include information about:

+ The topics to be covered in the lesson

+ The physical acts that the learner must perform to accomplish the task

+ How to bring background knowledge to the new material to be learned

+ The sequence in which the new material will be presented

+ The new vocabulary that will be introduced

+ The expected outcomes

+ Why this knowledge will be important to the students

Advance organizers contribute to personalized learning. Personalized learning is based on the premise that students will do mental work on information they perceive as useful. Simpson (2005) notes that "how usable the information is perceived to be has everything to do with the learner's willingness to do mental work on the new information as well as how this information is stored in the brain" (p. 2). When teachers explain how their instruction is organized, "students see how each learning target fits into the larger content discipline to which it belongs. They see learning as a continuum of interrelated experiences where one learning experience builds on another. They are aware of their placement and progress along that continuum" (p. 14). In other words, students know where they are, can articulate the progress they have made toward the target, and know what they have left to do.

As part of this process, students are taught to increase their levels of self-direction—for example, to look to the teacher as only one of many sources of help or additional information should they need it (Simpson, 2005).

The Rubric

A review team wanting to determine how a school's instructional program measures up against the benchmark of Characteristic 2D would look at three traits of that characteristic. The rubric in Table 2.4 describes each trait as it manifests in low-performing, effective, and high-performing schools.

Table 2.4: Rubric for Characteristic 2D

Characteristic	Trait	Effectiveness Continuum		
		Low Performing	Effective	High Performing
2D. Teachers have organized instruction to support clearly articulated and communicated learning targets.	2D1. Student understanding of importance of content	Some students cannot explain why what they are learning is important.	Students know why what they are learning is important.	Students know why what they are learning is important and can explain how it might be used outside of school.
	2D2. Student awareness of progress	Some students do not know where they are in the progression of steps to meet their learning targets.	Students know where they are in the progression of steps to meet their learning targets.	All students know where they are in the progression of steps to meet their learning targets and what evidence will be required to demonstrate mastery of the next step.
	2D3. Student access to additional help	Some students do not know where to access additional help when they need it.	Students know how and where to access additional help when they need it.	Procedures are in place to ensure that all students who need extra help have access to and are using that assistance.

Characteristic 2E: Rigorous and Engaging Activities and Assignments

Summary of Research

Even the best-planned instruction will not be effective if the students in the class are concentrating on things other than the lesson at hand. Managing students means getting their attention and keeping it on their work. Engaging students means motivating them to get involved in their work and maintaining that level of involvement. Phillip Schlechty (2001) characterizes student engagement as that which:

> requires the student to be attentive as well as in attendance, requires the student
> to be committed to the task and find some inherent value in what he or she is being
> asked to do. The engaged student not only does the task assigned but also does
> the task with enthusiasm and diligence. Moreover, the student performs the task
> because he or she perceives the task to be associated with a near-term end that he
> or she values. (p. 64)

The more engaged students are, the more they will profit from the lesson. The National Research Council and Institute of Medicine (2003) commissioned a study on student engagement in urban high schools. The study committee concluded that learning and succeeding in school require active engagement and that this finding is applicable to all schools. The committee further found that the "likelihood that students will be motivated and engaged is increased [when] family and friends effectively support their purposeful involvement in learning and in school. Engaging schools promote a sense of belonging by personalizing instruction, showing an interest in students' lives, and creating a supportive, caring social environment" (p. 3).

In 2000, Cori Brewster and Jennifer Fager, researchers from the Northwest Regional Educational Laboratory, examined the research on student engagement and motivation. Consolidating the findings from many studies, they identified five strategies that lead to high levels of student engagement:

1. Provide course materials that relate to students' lives, and make explicit connections to how the learning could be used in life outside of school. Students want to know that the work they are doing is significant and has value.

2. Provide students with choices among assignments and different ways of demonstrating their learning. Even small choices, such as working either with a partner or independently, give students a greater sense of self-direction. Giving students the opportunity to self-evaluate their progress toward the learning targets and giving groups more autonomy also lead to increased student engagement.

3. Assign challenging but achievable tasks for all students, and be sure to include special education students and students at risk in these challenging assignments. Assignments that seem completely out of reach as well as assignments that are without challenge do not result in high levels of learning gains.

4. Involve students in real problems or questions that require investigation or research.

5. Find ways for students to share what they have learned.

Over 10 years, Strong, Silver, and Robinson (1995) asked students about the kind of work they found engaging and the kind of work they disliked. The responses remained surprisingly alike over time:

> Students who are engaged in their work are energized by four goals—success, curi-
> osity, originality, and satisfying relationships. Engaging work, respondents said, was
> work that stimulated their curiosity, permitted them to express their creativity, and
> fostered positive relationships with others. It was also work at which they were good.
> As for activities they hated . . . students cited work that was repetitive, that required
> little or no thought, and that was forced on them by others. (pp. 1–3)

Engaging assignments alone are, of course, not enough. Those assignments need to build upon and extend classroom learning and be of sufficient rigor to move students into their zones of proximal development. In a study comparing high-achieving and low-achieving rural schools, Bottoms, Presson, and Han (2005) found that "leaders and teachers at high-achieving rural schools hold students to higher standards" (p. 25). Students in those schools felt they had to work hard to meet the standards. For example, they were often asked to revise and rewrite their work. Teachers worked together to encourage students to do their best, giving them frequent writing assignments, urging them to take science and mathematics at every grade level, and ensuring that they were both challenged and supported to meet the standards.

An approach known as authentic instruction has earned high marks for its power both to engage students and to increase achievement, particularly in low-income, high-minority schools (Lewis & Paik, 2001). In authentic instruction, students are asked to complete work similar to that which adults perform in the workplace. They go far beyond the mere memorization and reproduction of knowledge, such as using formulas to "solve routine mathematics problems," identifying the different parts of speech, or matching "authors with titles, or explorers with their feats" (Newmann & Wehlage, 1995, pp. 8–9).

The first step of the authentic work strategy is asking students to construct knowledge using higher-order thinking skills, such as synthesizing, interpreting, explaining, or evaluating information. To do this well, students must build on prior knowledge and what others studying the subject have learned. Using this knowledge,

> they should hone their skills through guided practice in producing original conversation and writing, building physical objects, or through artistic and musical performances. . . . The mere reproduction of prior knowledge does not constitute authentic academic achievement because it does not involve the thoughtful use or application of knowledge found in authentic adult accomplishment. (pp. 8–9)

In the second step, students engage in disciplined inquiry, working to solve real-world problems. They might address pressing issues (for example, the loss of native habitats or how to increase crop yields), create products (for example, working models, videos, or sculptures), or take part in performances for audiences (for example, concerts, dance performances, or plays).

Students use what they have learned to "elaborate on their findings both orally and in writing" (Newmann & Wehlage, 1995, p. 9). They "engage in extended conversations with the teacher or their peers about the subject matter in a way that builds an improved and shared understanding of ideas or topics" (Lewis & Paik, 2001, p. 27). These activities differ markedly from what is commonly asked for in school—multiple-choice answers, brief responses, short sentences, choosing true or false, and matching cause with effect.

In addition to being more rigorous than the usual classroom work, authentic work must have value beyond school. This means that the tasks asked of students must have meaning beyond demonstrating achievement of a standard. To be authentic, projects must have "value to the persons constructing them and to others in society" (Newmann & Wehlage, 1995, p. 8).

We recently saw an example of authentic instruction in two schools in Hawaii. Over the course of their high school career, students in these schools were required to demonstrate that they had met each of the Hawaii state content standards. They did not attend classes focused on memorizing what others had already learned. In these project-based schools, students, with the help of one or more advisors, designed projects that centered on real-world questions or problems, crossed a number of subject areas, and resulted in a tangible service to the community. They studied the effects of invasive species on the last of Hawaii's native forests, figured out how to increase vegetable harvests in poor and volcanic soils, and re-created traditional sustainable taro farming.

At various points in the projects, students presented their work and emerging data to knowledgeable adults, including teachers, scientists, artists, and community elders. These adults asked hard questions and required alterations in a project if they were not convinced it was progressing as it should. Talking with the students (in one of the schools, more than 30% were identified for special education and more than 90% were children of poverty) made it readily apparent that the standards set by the school were challenging, the students were deeply involved in their learning, and they took great pride in their accomplishments. These authentic projects brought learning to life for the students.

Teacher feedback to students plays an important role in student engagement, motivation, and persistence. There are two general categories of teacher feedback: summative and formative. Summative feedback is evaluative ("You missed 4 out of 10 questions," "I think you could have done a better job on this," or "You missed the point"). The research on summative feedback shows that it has little or no positive effect—and, in fact, some negative effect—on levels of learning or motivation to succeed (Chappuis & Stiggins, 2002).

Formative feedback, on the other hand, has been shown to be effective in increasing student learning and motivation. This feedback differs from summative feedback in that it provides specific advice about what a student can do to improve his or her work:

> Instead of simply labeling student errors or omissions, effective feedback guides students to better performance throughout the learning process. . . . Teacher feedback for learning draws an even bigger picture by telling students where they are now relative to the defined learning targets—where teachers ultimately want them to be. (Chappuis & Stiggins, 2002, section 3)

Finally, a word about a practice that does not appear in the rubrics for Effectiveness Indicator 2: the assigning of homework. The value of homework in increasing student achievement has been and remains a controversial topic in education circles, with arguments about its effectiveness, fairness, and over- or underuse the topic of many articles. A look at the research can be as confusing as it is helpful. First, many of the research studies on homework have used small groups or unrepresentative samples, such as only high-achieving or college-bound students, or have drawn conclusions exclusively from questionnaires or perception data. Second, even in studies using larger and more representative samples, many of the conclusions are based on very small effect sizes. Finally, there is nothing standard about homework. It can be of high quality or low quality, challenge students to use higher- or lower-order thinking skills, build upon and enhance what was introduced in the classroom, or be rote memorization or drill work (Center for Public Education, 2007; Hallam, 2004; Sharp et al., 2001).

Even high-quality homework is probably not equally valuable at all grade levels. It appears to result in greater achievement gains for high school students in grades 10–12. The effectiveness declines with each earlier grade level, so that there are only weak correlations at grades 6–9 and nearly a zero correlation for grades 3–5 (Sharp et al., 2001).

What we do know for sure about homework is that it should share the characteristics of other high-quality work assigned to students (Brewster & Fager, 2000):

   ✦   It should be engaging.

   ✦   It should have a clear purpose that is understood by the student.

   ✦   It should be connected to the lives of students in the world outside of school.

   ✦   It should be challenging but within reach.

The Rubric

A review team wanting to determine how a school's instructional program measures up against the benchmark of Characteristic 2E would look at two traits of that characteristic. The rubric in Table 2.5 describes each trait as it manifests in low-performing, effective, and high-performing schools.

Table 2.5: Rubric for Characteristic 2E

Characteristic	Trait	Effectiveness Continuum		
		Low Performing	Effective	High Performing
2E. Teachers provide students with activities and assignments that are rigorous and engaging and that extend their learning.	2E1. Student engagement	Some students are not attentive during instruction, not on task, or not engaged in classroom activities.	Students are actively engaged in classroom activities.	Students are attentive during instruction and engaged in classroom activities. Activities are varied for the range of student skill levels, and enrichment activities are readily available.
	2E2. Rigor of activities and assignments	Activities and assignments lack rigor or do not extend student learning.	Activities and assignments are rigorous and contribute to student understanding or extend concepts addressed in the lesson.	Activities and assignments are rigorous and extend concepts addressed in the lesson. Assistance and supports are readily available to enable all students to complete assignments.

Characteristic 2F: Teacher Knowledge and Expertise

Summary of Research

Having a teacher in every classroom who has content knowledge and pedagogical skills is critical to student achievement. This factor is so important that Linda Darling-Hammond (2005, p. 2) sums up her findings by stating, "It's now clear that the single most important determinant of what students learn is what their teachers know. [Teachers'] qualifications, [their] knowledge and skills, make more difference for student learning than any other single factor." Teachers must master both the content knowledge of their subjects and the pedagogical skills to transmit that particular knowledge to students, who often have widely diverse knowledge and skills, learning styles, and experiences. Teachers who are strong in only one or the other lack some of the essential tools to meet this challenge.

Weiss and Miller (2006) found that teachers with shallower content knowledge tend to spend more time telling students about the subject. Teachers with deeper knowledge "pose more questions, and are more likely to have students consider alternative explanations, propose more investigations, and pursue unanticipated inquiries" (p. 10).

It seems astounding that arguments still swirl around the importance of teacher content knowledge in instruction. Teachers' abilities "to pose questions, select tasks, evaluate their pupils' understanding, and to make curriculum decisions all depend on how they themselves understand the subject matter" (McDiarmid, Ball, & Anderson, 1989, p. 13). Ball and McDiarmid (1990) point out that

> what teachers need to know about the subject matter they teach extends beyond the specific topics of their curriculum. Teachers must not only be capable of defining for students the accepted truths in a subject but they must also be able to explain why a particular proposition is deemed warranted, why it is worth knowing, and how it relates to other propositions. For example, while English teachers need to know about particular authors and their works, about literary genres and styles, they also need to know about interpretation and criticism. A history teacher needs detailed knowledge about events and people of the past but must also understand what history is: the nature of historical knowledge and what it means to find out or know something about the past. (p. 3)

Those teachers whose students are most successful have a deep understanding of appropriate instructional methods (National Staff Development Council, 2001a). Research-validated strategies in the area of pedagogy include:

- Us[ing] techniques such as advance organizers, study questions, prediction, concept mapping and computer simulations to prepare students for learning activities

- Provid[ing] clear and focused instruction

- Routinely provid[ing] students feedback and reinforcement regarding their learning progress

- Review[ing] and reteach[ing] as necessary to help all students master learning material

- Develop[ing] students' critical and creative thinking skills

- Us[ing] effective questioning techniques to build basic and higher-level skills

- Foster[ing] the development of self-directed learning skills (Northwest Regional Educational Laboratory, 2005, section 3.1)

Effective teachers are skillful in engaging students in their learning. Teachers who actively engage students "use hands-on lessons that require students to use multiple learning skills and higher-order thinking to construct meaning and knowledge" (Appalachia Educational Laboratory at Edvantia, 2005b, p. 2).

As every teacher can attest, designing and delivering instruction to a classroom full of students, all of whom are at different places in their learning and who learn best using a variety of strategies, is a challenge. In working to meet the diverse needs of students, effective teachers differentiate their instruction so that it meets "learners where they are and offers multiple avenues through which they can access, understand and apply learning" (Corley, 2005, p. 3).

Carol Ann Tomlinson has worked for more than 20 years in the area of differentiated instruction. She describes three essential elements of differentiated classroom instruction (Tomlinson, n.d.):

1. Assessment is continuous, and results are used to plan and improve instruction. Teachers gather information in a variety of ways to better assess current levels of students' knowledge, skills, interests, and readiness for next steps.

2. All students are engaged in instruction that is "equally interesting, equally appealing, and equally focused on essential understandings and skills." All students are "working with tasks that students and teachers perceive to be worthwhile and valuable."

3. Teachers use flexible grouping, in which all students work with a variety of other students over a short period of time. Sometimes the teacher assigns the students into groups, and sometimes they self-select into groups, which the teacher forms and re-forms frequently. Students are sometimes homogeneously grouped by current skill level, sometimes heterogeneously grouped, sometimes grouped with students who have like interests, sometimes grouped with those who have different interests, and frequently placed in a large group.

To meet learners' diverse needs and learning styles, Tomlinson advocates varying four components of classroom instruction, based on what is most effective for each child. She labels these components content, process, products, and the learning environment.

Content refers to both "what the student needs to learn" and "how the student will get access to the information." Examples of differentiating content include giving reading assignments at higher and lower readability levels, presenting ideas both orally and through the written word, and meeting with small groups, either to "re-teach an idea or a skill to struggling learners or to extend the thinking or skills of advanced learners" (p. 4).

Processes are the "activities in which the student engages in order to make sense of or master the content." Examples of differentiating processes include engaging students in "tiered activities through which all learners work with the same important understandings and skills but proceed with different levels of support, challenge, or complexity" (p. 5) and varying the time allotted to tasks in order to provide additional supports for struggling students or to give those who have mastered the learning an opportunity to engage in a topic more deeply.

Products are the work that students complete in order to demonstrate that they are able to "apply and extend" what they have learned in the unit (p. 6). Teachers can differentiate this component by giving students options such as completing exhibitions individually or in small groups or finding their own ways to show that they have learned the material.

The *learning environment* is the way the classroom works and feels. Examples of differentiation in the learning environment include providing differentiated areas for group and individual work and "developing routines that allow students to get help when teachers are busy with other students and cannot help them immediately" (p. 7).

In schools in which all students are learning to high levels, there is a commitment not only to raising achievement but also to closing any gaps between groups of students. Achievement gaps may exist between students of racial or ethnic minorities and those of the majority population; between students of poverty and those whose families are earning living wages; between students identified for special services (such as special education) and students in general education; between students who are native speakers of English and those who are just learning English; and between boys and girls. Achievement gaps that are persistent "can tell us a lot about which students are given the preparation they need to succeed in college and work, and which ones continue to be left out" (Education Trust, 2003, p. 1).

The 2007 National Assessment of Educational Progress (NAEP) measured some of these gaps. In eighth-grade reading, only 12% of African American students, 14% of Latino students, and 19% of Native American students reached the proficient level. This was contrasted to 38% of white students and 40% of Asian students. Even more troubling, 46% of African American, 43% of Latino, and 42% of Native American fourth-graders did not even reach the basic level, contrasted to 17% of white students and 21% of Asian students (Education Trust, 2007, slide 9).

In mathematics, the 2007 NAEP results show a similar pattern. At the eighth grade, only 11% of African American students, 15% of Latino students, and 17% of Native American students reached the proficient level, contrasted with 41% of white students and 49% of Asian students. Fifty-three percent of African American, 46% of Latino, and 44% of Native American eighth-graders did not even reach the basic level, contrasted to 19% of white and 18% of Asian students (slide 12).

U.S. graduation rates too are alarmingly low. *Education Week* reported in its 2008 *Diplomas Count* analysis that 1.23 million students would fail to graduate in 2008. Nationally, "about 71% of 9th graders make it to graduation four years later . . . and that figure drops to 58% for Hispanics, 55% for African Americans, and 51% for Native Americans" (p. 2).

Researchers in 2004 reported that for boys, state-reported graduation rates were yet lower, with African American males at 43%, Native American males at 47%, and Latino males at 48% (Orfield, Losen, Wald, & Swanson).

If these figures were not disturbing enough, another study found that by grade 12, those African Americans and Latinos who are still attending school have achievement levels in reading and mathematics that are equal to those of white eighth-graders (American Educational Research Association, 2004).

While these numbers represent the very real and sobering problem that exists today, they do not have to represent our future. Research exists to point the way toward programs that lead to very different results. In fact, we can already begin to see those results in the small but significant closure of achievement gaps since the late 1990s. In 2002, the National Research Council and Institute of Medicine conducted a meta-analysis examining school- and community-based programs (such as Boys and Girls Clubs, Big Brothers Big Sisters) that were experiencing success in reengaging children from widely diverse backgrounds with school. The researchers concluded that the most powerful strategy for schools was to combine the elements of authentic instruction (discussed under Characteristic 2E), with "practices that support positive motivation," such as stressing "mastery and improvement rather than current levels of knowledge" (pp. 108–109).

The Rubric

A review team wanting to determine how a school's instructional program measures up against the benchmark of Characteristic 2F would look at three traits of that characteristic. The rubric in Table 2.6 describes each trait as it manifests in low-performing, effective, and high-performing schools.

Table 2.6: Rubric for Characteristic 2F

Characteristic	Trait	Effectiveness Continuum		
		Low Performing	Effective	High Performing
2F. Teachers have deep knowledge of their subject matter, possess expertise in a wide range of effective instructional strategies, and are committed to closing achievement gaps.	2F1. Teacher content knowledge	Some teachers make or fail to correct content errors.	Teachers demonstrate strong content knowledge in the subjects taught.	Teachers demonstrate strong content knowledge in the subjects taught and are adept at diagnosing student gaps in understanding and knowledge.
	2F2. Repertoire of instructional strategies	Teachers demonstrate a limited number of instructional strategies or use strategies that are not well-matched to the needs of their students.	Teachers use a variety of instructional strategies matched to the needs of their students.	Teachers differentiate instruction to meet the diverse needs of students by varying content, processes, products, or the learning environment.
	2F3. Teacher commitment to closing achievement gaps	Teachers do not convey a commitment to raising achievement or closing achievement gaps between groups of students.	Teachers are committed to raising achievement and closing achievement gaps between groups of students.	Teachers' commitment to raising achievement has narrowed or closed achievement gaps between groups of students.

Characteristic 2G: Collaborative Planning

Summary of Research

Mike Schmoker (2006) believes that isolation is the "enemy of improvement" (p. 23). His assertion is supported by 30 years of research showing that "teacher isolation has adverse consequences for students, for teachers, and for any effort to improve schools" (DuFour, DuFour, & Eaker, 2008, pp. 171–172). DuFour, DuFour, and Eaker state that this isolation works against improving teaching because it shields teachers from accountability for

> what takes place in their classrooms. Educator evaluations are almost invariably perfunctory, and teachers are rarely called upon to provide concrete evidence of what they are teaching, how they are assessing, the criteria they use in determining the quality of student work, the instructional strategies and materials they utilize in the classroom, the factors they consider in determining a student's grade, and most importantly, the degree to which their students are acquiring the intended knowledge, skills, and dispositions. (p. 171)

The opposite of the situation just described is meaningful collaboration, which occurs when school staff members work "together interdependently in systematic processes to analyze and impact professional practice to improve individual and collective results" (p. 183). DuFour and his colleagues "argue that effective collaborative teams will engage in collective inquiry into the four critical questions of learning" (pp. 183–184):

1. What is it we want our students to learn? What knowledge, skills, and dispositions do we expect them to acquire as a result of this course, grade level, or unit of instruction?

2. How will we know if each student is learning each of the essential skills, concepts, and dispositions we have deemed most essential?

3. How will we respond when some of our students do not learn? What process will we put in place to ensure students receive additional time and support for learning in a timely, directive, and systematic way?

4. How will we enrich and extend the learning for students who are already proficient?

This approach is supported by findings from studies that grew out of the 1997 Third International Mathematics and Science Study (TIMSS). A common theme of high-performing nations was teacher collaboration on instruction and instructional planning.

One of the many groups to study TIMSS was the National Institute on Educational Governance, Finance, Policymaking, and Management (1998). This group looked closely at the instructional practices of those nations whose students substantially outperformed students in the United States. Japan was one of those nations. Researchers found that Japanese teachers worked to "develop and refine their lessons through a structured, collaborative group process characterized by 'lesson study groups'—small teams of teachers who met weekly to design, critique, revise, and try out lessons" (p. 21). In this process, teachers both tried new approaches and revisited previously used lessons. Teacher groups then critiqued the lessons with a focus on student learning. Questions included: "What did this student say, and, how much did that student understand?" The study found that as a result of planning, working, and refining their work together, "teachers not only produced better lessons, but they also learned more about pedagogy and effective practice, and engaged in rich intellectual conversations" (p. 21). The resulting lessons were, in fact, so good that it was common practice for them to be shared across the nation.

In a study of small high schools in Chicago, Stevens and Kahne (2006) found that an important first step in the collaborative process was to formally create common meeting times to discuss instruction. However, creating the time and even soliciting and receiving the buy-in of teachers did not always result in the hoped-for results. Stevens and Kahne found that it was equally important to set up procedures that protected teachers from the competing demands and pressures that could either distract them or cause them to regard other activities as more important than the time set aside for instructional discussions.

This finding too was supported by the aforementioned TIMSS study, which found that in order to encourage (and in some cases require) teachers to work together on important instructional issues, the high-performing schools and nations provided both time and a structure for them to do so (National Institute on Educational Governance, Finance, Policymaking, and Management, 1998).

The Rubric

A review team wanting to determine how a school's instructional program measures up against the benchmark of Characteristic 2G would look at two traits of that characteristic. The rubric in Table 2.7 describes each trait as it manifests in low-performing, effective, and high-performing schools.

Table 2.7: Rubric for Characteristic 2G

Characteristic	Trait	Effectiveness Continuum		
		Low Performing	Effective	High Performing
2G. Teachers plan together to ensure that instruction and assessment meet the needs of all learners.	2G1. Extent of collaborative planning	Most teachers do not meet or infrequently meet together to plan common lessons or assessments.	Teams of grade-level or content-area teachers frequently meet together to review student work and plan common lessons and assessments.	A formalized process exists and sufficient time is allocated for teams of grade-level or content-area teachers to plan common lessons and assessments. Planning time is used effectively, and teams document strategies and results.
	2G2. Scheduled collaboration	The daily schedule does not support instructional collaboration.	The school schedule provides time for joint planning or collaboration within grade levels and content areas.	The school schedule fosters collaboration and planning within and across grade levels, content areas, and programs (for example, ELL, special education).

Characteristic 2H: Effective Use of Instructional Time

Summary of Research

Effective use of instructional time is another key element cited in the research on high-performing schools. And here we stress the term *effective*. There are many, and at first blush conflicting, reports and studies on the relationship between the time spent on instruction and the level of student learning. First brought to the forefront in *Prisoners of Time*, the 1994 report of the National Education Commission on Time and Learning, and in David Berliner's 1990 report, *What's All the Fuss About Instructional Time?* the role of instructional time has occupied an important place in school improvement research. Both studies found that time spent on instruction is strongly related to levels of learning. Yet more recent studies have found that instructional time does not appear to increase or decrease student performance overall unless the time spent is either much more or much less than is generally provided in schools worldwide (Baker & LeTendre, 2005).

The reason for this apparent conflict in research is that *merely* increasing time dedicated to instruction may not result in increased student learning. This lack of impact is related to the concepts described in the literature as first- and second-order change. First-order change is doing more or less of something in the same way that it has been done up to that point. It does not cause or result in lasting change. First-order change does not require new learning, it is accomplished within the existing structure, and it is easily reversible. Second-order change, on the other hand, is doing something significantly different from what has been done before. It generally requires new learning to be carried out successfully, and it typically affects the entire organization rather than just one or a few individuals (Cuban, 1988).

In a common example of first-order change, a school increases minutes of instructional time in a subject. The problem here is that lots of poor instruction will not yield the hoped-for increases in student learning. In second-order change, when a school increases instructional time, it also provides high-quality professional development to help teachers more effectively use the additional class time. Looked at in isolation, instructional time (first-order change) can only provide a piece of the puzzle. However, when it is coupled with effectiveness (second-order change), it is a key strategy resulting in increased student learning.

An important consideration in looking at effective use of instructional time is to determine how much time in the school day is actually spent on academic activities and how much is lost to nonacademic pursuits. In a 2005 review of research, Richard Allington found two studies that closely looked at instructional time in classrooms. In the first, Jodie Roth and a team of researchers looked at more than 500 elementary classrooms across the nation. They found that "an average of 2 hours and 10 minutes each day was spent on nonacademic activities" (Allington, 2005, p. 1). These numbers seem almost impossible to believe, but Allington found they were supported in the second study, this one by Claire E. Cameron, published in the *Journal of School Psychology* in 2005. Looking at first-grade classrooms, Cameron found that "anywhere from 15 minutes to over 2 hours a day" were devoted to such noninstructional activities as "lining up, waiting for lessons to start, distributing materials, taking attendance, cleaning up, eating a snack, and managing disruptions" (p. 1). Cameron further noted that schools with the shortest school days were most often those with the highest levels of poverty and highest percentages of minority students (Allington, 2005).

Researchers have also found that "in many schools, considerable instructional time is lost to excessive loudspeaker announcements and other administrative intrusions, too-frequent assemblies, and other all-school gatherings . . . over which the principal has total or partial control" (Cotton, 2003, p. 37). In these schools, the reduction in the total instructional time may result in lower student performance. Principals of effective schools, on the other hand, not only are careful to protect instructional time but also arrange for additional instructional time outside the regular school day as needed (Cotton, 2003).

The Rubric

A review team wanting to determine how a school's instructional program measures up against the benchmark of Characteristic 2H would look at two traits of that characteristic. The rubric in Table 2.8 describes each trait as it manifests in low-performing, effective, and high-performing schools.

Table 2.8: Rubric for Characteristic 2H

Characteristic	Trait	Effectiveness Continuum		
		Low Performing	Effective	High Performing
2H. Instructional time is fully and effectively used.	2H1. Use of instructional time	Some teachers do not use instructional time effectively, losing time to behavior problems, classroom management, attendance, and noninstructional activities.	Teachers use instructional time effectively and lose little time to behavior problems, classroom management, attendance, and noninstructional activities.	Teachers use instructional time effectively with minimal time lost to behavior problems, classroom management, attendance, and noninstructional activities. Schoolwide interruptions such as announcements and assemblies during class time are rare.
	2H2. Clarity of instruction and procedures	Instruction and procedures in some classes are not clear to students, and instructional time is lost as clarifications are made.	Instruction and directions are clear to students, and little time is spent on clarifying directions, reteaching, or repeating previously described procedures.	In all classes, the teachers' directions and procedures are clear to students. Teachers anticipate areas of possible student misunderstanding and proactively address those areas in their instruction.

Characteristic 2I: Administrator Support

Summary of Research

Scores of studies show that student achievement is strongly affected by the leadership of school principals. Principals who serve as instructional leaders, in particular, are much more likely to have high-achieving students than are principals who do not (Cotton, 2003; Mendez-Morse, 1992).

In their meta-analysis on leadership, Marzano, Waters, and McNulty (2005, pp. 54–55) identified three specific traits that are associated with principals in effective schools:

1. Being directly involved in helping teachers address instructional issues

2. Possessing extensive knowledge about effective instructional practices

3. Providing conceptual guidance regarding effective classroom practices

Principals and other school administrators can demonstrate these three traits in many ways. For example, principals could initiate instructional walk-throughs and follow-up coaching, remain current with emerging educational research on effective instruction, share new learning with staff members, participate in reviews of student work, or join in collaborative scoring sessions.

We have frequently been called upon to work with schools that are already well along with plans and efforts to improve their performance in a number of areas. Often they have so many schoolwide initiatives under way (from grant programs to curriculum mapping, from discipline and behavior programs to schoolwide literacy projects, from adopting new instructional materials to implementing differentiated instruction) that they are unable to give any of the initiatives the time and attention they need to be successful. This is a case where more is not necessarily better. While each initiative may be research-based and, in and of itself, have the real potential to increase student learning, in many schools there are simply way too many things going on.

As teachers and administrators try to put each of the new schoolwide initiatives into place, more and more time and energy are required. Faced finally with simply too much to do well, teachers wind up trying to decide for themselves in which "schoolwide" efforts they will participate. Predictably, these schools do not realize the desired increases in student achievement.

Effective school administrators not only provide vision in selecting and undertaking new initiatives. These instructional leaders also help school staff members let go of initiatives. They ensure that the work of the school, including decisions regarding abandoning or deemphasizing existing initiatives and adopting new initiatives, is coordinated—ideally, through the school strategic plan.

In effective schools, leaders make sure that sufficient time, resources, and energy are available and will continue to be available to carry out planned new initiatives as they were designed, before the staff moves forward to implement even newer ideas. These school administrators create explicit processes that ensure sustained and systematic attention to a limited number of schoolwide instructional undertakings and protect teachers from the interruptions and distractions caused by the introduction of unexpected new initiatives.

The Rubric

A review team wanting to determine how a school's instructional program measures up against the benchmark of Characteristic 2I would look at three traits of that characteristic. The rubric in Table 2.9 describes each trait as it manifests in low-performing, effective, and high-performing schools.

Table 2.9: Rubric for Characteristic 2I

Characteristic	Trait	Effectiveness Continuum		
		Low Performing	Effective	High Performing
2I. School administrators support and promote effective instructional practices, program coordination, and resource allocation.	2I1. Administrator support of effective instructional practices	School administrators provide little instructional guidance.	School administrators support and promote effective instructional practices.	School administrators provide instructional leadership, support effective instructional practices, and actively seek out and acknowledge high-quality instructional strategies.
	2I2. Administrator efforts to coordinate instructional program	School administrators do not, or do not always, ensure coordination of the instructional program.	School administrators ensure coordination of the instructional program.	School administrators ensure coordination of the instructional program and ensure that new initiatives are coordinated with existing instructional efforts.
	2I3. Administrator provision of time and resources	School administrators do not, or do not always, ensure that sufficient time and resources are available to support the instructional program.	School administrators ensure that sufficient time and resources are available to support the instructional program.	School administrators ensure that sufficient time and resources are available to support the instructional program and ensure that new initiatives are fully resourced prior to implementation.

Characteristic 2J: Match Between Taught Curriculum, Written Curriculum, and Pacing Charts

Summary of Research

It is difficult to overstate the importance of classroom instruction to student learning. Coherency in the instructional program, as in so many other areas, is key to sustainable, schoolwide gains in achievement. School administrators have an important role in ensuring not only that the written curriculum provides coordination within and between grade levels but also that every teacher teaches that curriculum and follows the pacing charts (Fouts, 2003). Lashway (2003) points out that effective instructional leaders create and maintain a coherent instructional vision, attending to those issues that threaten the alignment of the written, taught, and tested curriculum. These leaders have a clear vision as to what rigorous standards and high-quality instruction should look like in the classroom and work to make that vision a reality. Without the alignment Lashway refers to, no matter how tightly the written curriculum is aligned to instructional goals or how well-conceived it is, student performance will still lag (Corallo & McDonald, 2002).

The curriculum that is transmitted in school classrooms is sometimes referred to as the *enacted curriculum*. When the enacted curriculum reflects rigorous standards delivered within a system of instructional supports, students have the foundation they need to achieve. Porter (2004, p. 1) has found that "the content of the enacted curriculum is a powerful predictor of variance in student achievement gains, and helps explain a portion of the achievement gap between White, Black, and Hispanic students."

Effective school administrators serve two important functions in the development and delivery of curriculum. First, by being directly involved in developing the curriculum of the school, they ensure that it is both rigorous and of high quality, and they signal the value they place on this work (Murphy et al., 2006a).

Second, effective administrators are attentive to the enacted curriculum, using pacing charts in their observations to ensure that the instruction occurring in every classroom is tightly coupled with the written curriculum. They make sure that standards-based instruction, curriculum materials, and assessments are all carefully orchestrated so that "there is a high degree of coordination (a) across subjects within grades, (b) across grade levels and phases of schooling (e.g., from the elementary to the middle school), and (c) among teachers within and across departments and grade levels" (Murphy et al., 2006b, p. 14).

The Rubric

A review team wanting to determine how a school's instructional program measures up against the benchmark of Characteristic 2J would look at one trait of that characteristic. The rubric in Table 2.10 describes that trait as it manifests in low-performing, effective, and high-performing schools.

Table 2.10: Rubric for Characteristic 2J

Characteristic	Trait	Effectiveness Continuum		
		Low Performing	Effective	High Performing
2J. School administrators ensure that the taught curriculum reflects the written curriculum and aligns with the pacing charts.	2J1. Match between taught and written curriculum and pacing charts	School administrators do not observe, or infrequently observe, classroom instruction to ensure that the taught curriculum matches the written curriculum and pacing charts.	School administrators ensure that the taught curriculum matches the written curriculum and pacing charts.	School administrators and all instructional staff members hold one another accountable to ensure that the taught curriculum matches the written curriculum and pacing charts.

Conclusion

For students to achieve at high levels, it is crucial that their teachers possess both deep content knowledge and strong pedagogical skills. As the range of student skills becomes more varied in every classroom, the ability to match instructional methods to student needs becomes increasingly important. To differentiate instruction for general education students, special education students, English language learners, gifted students, and others who in the past were served through pull-out programs, teachers must have tremendous instructional versatility. At the core of an effective school is a high-quality instructional program focused on rigor, flexibility, and supporting teaching in order to meet the needs of all students.

Effectiveness Indicator 3
Student Assessment

It's easy to make a buck. It's a lot tougher to make a difference.

—Tom Brokaw

Effective schools use assessment to improve student learning. From this principle, we derive Effectiveness Indicator 3. Student assessment can be used to determine individual students' levels of specific knowledge and skills; to improve classroom instruction; to adapt instruction or prescribe interventions for individuals or groups of students; to evaluate and improve larger instructional programs; and to measure and compare schools, districts, and states for broad public accountability. An on-site school review examines the range and quality of a school's assessment system.

Six characteristics define Effectiveness Indicator 3: Student Assessment:

3A. Local assessments are aligned to the cognitive demand of the standards and to the written curriculum.

3B. Teachers employ a variety of formative and summative assessment strategies.

3C. Diagnostic assessments are used to identify student skill levels and to determine appropriate interventions or remediations.

3D. Data from diagnostic assessments are used to place, group, and regroup students.

3E. Aggregated and disaggregated data from state assessments are used to improve the school's curriculum and instructional program.

3F. State and local student assessment data are collected, disseminated, and readily available.

Characteristic 3A: Alignment With Standards and Curriculum

Summary of Research

In a standards-based education system, one purpose for student assessment is to measure students' progress toward meeting state standards. In order for these measurements to be accurate, they must be part of a system, aligned to content standards, performance standards, curriculum, and instruction.

Content standards are statements of overarching goals. They provide a broad description of what students are expected to know and be able to do at certain points in time. Standing alone, they do not provide enough information to design assessments that will reliably measure students' progress toward the standards. To meet this need, performance standards are developed.

Performance standards provide additional details to flesh out the broad definitions contained in the content standards. They define how good is good enough by more specifically describing the knowledge and skills that students will be expected to acquire and demonstrate. Performance standards also describe various levels of performance. These levels usually carry very short descriptors, such as emerging, basic, proficient, or advanced. Ideally, examples of student work at each level illustrate even further what is expected.

Performance standards also address the level of cognitive demand entailed in meeting a standard. Cognitive demand, sometimes referred to as depth of knowledge, is the level of thinking required in order to complete a given task. For an assessment to yield accurate information about the progress of a student or group of students toward the standard, the cognitive demand of the assessment must match the cognitive demand of the content standard.

The concept of cognitive demand as it relates to higher- and lower-order thinking skills is familiar to many of us from taxonomies such as that developed by Benjamin Bloom. Bloom's Taxonomy is divided into six levels, three encompassing lower-order thinking skills and three, higher-order thinking skills. Since Bloom's original work, different authors and researchers have made many modifications to his taxonomy, but his concept of lower- and higher-order thinking as well as his progression of skills within those orders remains the taxonomy in widest use.

Bloom's Taxonomy is as follows (Bloom & Krathwohl, 1956):

Lower-order thinking skills

1. Knowledge. Recalling or remembering information without necessarily understanding it. Students may be asked to arrange, define, duplicate, label, list, memorize, name, order, recall, recognize, relate, repeat, or reproduce.

2. Comprehension. Understanding learned material. Students may be asked to classify, describe, discuss, explain, express, identify, indicate, locate, recognize, report, restate, review, select, or translate.

3. Application. The ability to put ideas and concepts to work in solving problems. Students may be asked to apply, choose, demonstrate, dramatize, employ, illustrate, interpret, operate, practice, schedule, sketch, solve, use, or write.

Higher-order thinking skills

4. Analysis. Breaking down information into its component parts to see relationships and ideas. Students may be asked to analyze, appraise, calculate, categorize, compare, contrast, criticize, differentiate, discriminate, distinguish, examine, experiment, question, or test.

5. Synthesis. The ability to put parts together to form something original. This skill involves using creativity to compose or design something new. Students may be asked to arrange,

assemble, collect, compose, construct, create, design, develop, formulate, manage, organize, plan, prepare, or propose.

6.   Evaluation. Judging the value of evidence based on definite criteria. Students may be asked to argue, assess, conclude, criticize, defend, estimate, evaluate, judge, predict, prioritize, rate, select, support, or value.

To illustrate how assessments measure standards' different levels of cognitive demand, we have drawn three questions from released items on the 2006 Ohio State Citizenship Ninth-Grade Proficiency Test (Ohio Department of Education, 2006). In the first question (p. 13), students are asked to demonstrate recall, a lower-order thinking skill, by selecting the response that best describes how a United States representative is most commonly selected:

44.   A congressional representative of the United States usually acquires office by which of the following methods?

A.   appointment by the President

B.   appointment by the Senate

C.   election by members of the presidential cabinet

D.   election by voters

A higher level of cognitive demand is illustrated by the next question (p. 14), which asks students to demonstrate the thinking skill of application—using recalled knowledge to make a decision:

49.   Which of the following actions performed by Kenji is the best example of active community service?

A.   serving on the recreation board

B.   joining a community softball league

C.   attending a Labor Day parade

D.   subscribing to a local news magazine

Still higher on the scale of cognitive demand are questions that require students to demonstrate the thinking skills of synthesizing or evaluating. In this example (p. 11), students are asked to predict how the specific actions of one group of people—nonvoting citizens—might affect the future of another group—candidates for office:

37.   A survey of the citizens of Lawnacre revealed that many of them did NOT vote because they believed that their candidate would be elected by other voters. If this trend continues in upcoming elections in Lawnacre, what will be the most likely result?

A.   Candidates will run for reelection less frequently.

B.   Candidates preferred by a majority of the citizens will continue to be elected into office.

C.   Candidates will call for more frequent recounts of votes.

D.   Candidates preferred by a majority of the citizens will not always win elections.

Local assessments are those which are created or administered by teachers, schools, or districts to measure student progress toward meeting state standards or meeting local curriculum goals. Local assessments allow students to demonstrate what they know in more ways than are possible in large-scale state assessments, including hands-on demonstrations, oral presentations, and work created over time. Additionally, these assessments can better reflect the local school context. For example, several years ago we worked with one state that included on its state assessment a question on using a bus schedule and route map to get from one area of town to another. While this question may have worked well in cities, many children in rural areas have never used mass transit, much less used a schedule or route map. Local assessments, on the other hand, can be tailored to match more closely the experiences of children within a school or district. However, there are also some challenges to developing local assessments. For example, they typically do not have the technical accuracy of large-scale assessments and may result in higher levels of subjectivity.

The Rubric

A review team wanting to determine how a school's assessments measure up against the benchmark of Characteristic 3A would look at one trait of that characteristic. The rubric in Table 3.1 describes that trait as it manifests in low-performing, effective, and high-performing schools.

Table 3.1: Rubric for Characteristic 3A

Characteristic	Trait	Effectiveness Continuum		
		Low Performing	Effective	High Performing
3A. Local assessments are aligned to the cognitive demand of the standards and to the written curriculum.	3A1. Alignment to cognitive demand and to written curriculum	Local assessments are not aligned to the cognitive demand of the standards and to the written curriculum.	Local assessments are aligned to the cognitive demand of the standards and to the written curriculum.	Local assessments, aligned to the cognitive demand of the standards and to the written curriculum, are sufficient to measure attainment of all standards.

Characteristic 3B: Formative and Summative Assessment

Summary of Research

Assessment plays a key role in instruction. In effective classrooms, assessments aren't just what teachers do at the end of a lesson or unit; instead, they are integral to instructional design, defining what it is a teacher, school, or district wants students to know as a result of the instruction. High-quality assessments take many forms, from traditional paper-and-pencil tests to oral reports, writing assignments, performances, scientific experiments, and mathematical problem-solving. The choice of what type of assessment is the most appropriate depends on the purpose for which the results will be used. In many instances, multiple forms of assessment may be necessary to measure full attainment of the educational goal (LaMarca, Redfield, Winter, Bailey, & Handsche-Despriet, 2000).

Assessments can be categorized into two main groups: norm-referenced and criterion-referenced. In norm-referenced assessments, the achievement of an individual or group is compared to that of a larger group or representative sample of a larger group. Student achievement is evaluated based on how much higher or lower individual student scores are than the mean or norm of the larger group. Scores are usually reported on a percentile basis. Examples of norm-referenced tests include tests graded on the curve, the Iowa Tests of Basic Skills, and traditional IQ tests.

In criterion-referenced assessments, the achievement of an individual or group is compared to a criterion or standard that does not change, regardless of group performance. Success in this kind of assessment depends not on surpassing the performance of others but on demonstrating attainment of knowledge and skills at a level that remains stable regardless of how many or how few reach that level. Examples of criterion-referenced tests are state standards-based assessments and state driver's license examinations.

Within each of these broad categories of tests, there are a variety of different assessment types. Some of these include:

- Portfolio assessments, in which a collection of student work completed over time is evaluated

- Performance assessments, in which specific, usually complex, demonstrations of knowledge and skills are evaluated

- Authentic assessments, in which the tasks assigned are closely related to the kinds of projects students might encounter in the world of work

Assessments can also be divided into the broad categories of formative and summative. Summative assessment is sometimes referred to as assessment *of* learning, while formative assessment is referred to as assessment *for* learning.

Formative assessments are those that are administered prior to the culmination of the lesson or unit. Ideally, formative assessments are not graded. Instead they are used to obtain information for the student and the teacher about the student's progress toward the goal of the lesson or unit. These assessments are given while there is still time for the student, and often the teacher, to make improvements. Formative assessment achieves its maximum power when it is used to identify students who can move faster, those for whom additional or supplemental instruction would be beneficial, and the areas in which particular students are struggling.

High-quality formative assessments are powerful tools for improving instruction. They give teachers the information they need to adjust and readjust instruction, even in the midst of a lesson or unit. Moreover, they help teachers "provide feedback that explicitly helps students see how to improve" (Darling-Hammond & Bransford, 2005, p. 275).

The positive impact of formative assessments in increasing student achievement has a strong research base. In a review of more than 40 empirical studies, Black and Wiliam (1998, p. 2) found that increasing the number and quality of formative assessments produced "significant and often substantial learning gains . . . from five-year-olds to university graduates, across several school subjects and over several countries," and that this positive effect was even greater for lower achievers than for other students.

In reviewing Black and Wiliam's research, Darling-Hammond and Bransford (2005, p. 277) con-cluded that

> focused efforts to improve formative assessment produced learning gains equiva-lent to raising the score of an average student from the 50th percentile to the 85th percentile. In other words, formative assessment, effectively implemented, can do as much or more to improve student achievement than any of the most powerful instructional interventions, intensive reading instruction, one-on-one tutoring and the like.

Formative assessments are most effective when there are no grades attached. When grades are assigned to formative assessment, "they often seem to predominate in students' thinking, and to be seen as the real purpose of the assessment" (Crooks, 2001, p. 3). Black and Wiliam (1998, p. 2) put it more strongly. They argue that grades are overemphasized, "while the giving of useful advice and the learning function are underemphasized."

The National Forum on Assessment, a coalition of more than 200 education and civil rights orga-nizations, has developed a set of principles and indicators for the design of student assessment systems, particularly classroom assessments that provide an equal opportunity for all students to demonstrate their knowledge and skills. Among these is the principle that the primary purpose of assessment is to improve student learning. To meet this purpose, assessments must:

- Grow out of and be interwoven with curriculum (state standards) and instruction

- Provide students with multiple ways to demonstrate their learning

- Be connected to clear statements of what is important for students to learn (standards)

- Provide students with ways to apply their learning through projects, performances, experi-ments, interviews, and observations as well as tests

- Promote student choice, self-evaluation, and individual and group work

- Limit the reliance on multiple-choice and short-answer tests (Neill, 1996)

We would add that, in using assessments to improve student learning, schools must:

- Provide frequent formative assessment opportunities

- Ensure that results from the formative assessments are used to provide short-term and timely interventions when needed

Summative assessments differ from formative assessments in that they occur at the end of a lesson or unit and are typically those from which grades derive. Summative assessments are also aligned with previously administered formative assessments. The highest-quality summative assessments are those that challenge students by requiring them to use higher-order thinking skills in a culminating performance—to "exhibit mastery and to use their knowledge in ways that generalize and extend what has come before" (Darling-Hammond & Bransford, 2005, p. 297).

In 1992, researchers studied 8,800 test questions drawn from K–12 classes, finding that nearly 80% of them required students to operate at the lowest level of Bloom's Taxonomy: the knowledge level. Ten years later, in a second review, researchers examined both textbook-designed and teacher-designed summative assessments in elementary and high school mathematics classes. They found that more than 95% of questions and problems called for responses at the knowledge level (Darling-Hammond & Bransford, 2005, p. 302).

Summative tests must avoid the pitfall of drawing heavily from lower-order thinking skills. Instead, they should have a high degree of cognitive demand, requiring deep analysis. They should ask students to perform conceptually rich, real-world, meaningful instructional tasks (Darling-Hammond & Bransford, 2005). Such tasks both provide better data for teachers to use in assigning grades and result in positive cognitive and motivational benefits for students. To realize these benefits, summative assessments should involve students in "an active search for meaning, underlying principles, and structures that link different concepts" (p. 302).

The Rubric

A review team wanting to determine how a school's assessment program measures up against the benchmark of Characteristic 3B would look at one trait of that characteristic. The rubric in Table 3.2 describes that trait as it manifests in low-performing, effective, and high-performing schools.

Table 3.2: Rubric for Characteristic 3B

Characteristic	Trait	Effectiveness Continuum		
		Low Performing	Effective	High Performing
3B. Teachers employ a variety of formative and summative assessment strategies.	3B1. Repertoire of assessment strategies	Teachers do not employ a variety of formative and summative assessment strategies.	Teachers employ a variety of formative and summative assessment strategies.	Teachers employ a common set of formative and summative assessments and use the results to improve instruction within grade levels or courses.

Characteristic 3C: Diagnostic Assessments

Summary of Research

Diagnostic assessments are pre-assessments that differ from formative assessments in that they are used prior to instruction, primarily to provide information to the teacher, rather than the student, about the current knowledge and skill level of each child. These assessments break learning into fundamental skills and then measure student attainment of those skills so that patterns of error or miscues can be identified. From these patterns a diagnosis is suggested. Instructional strategies are keyed to the diagnosis and create the prescription for treatment.

This means that for students whose achievement is lagging, diagnostic assessments can pinpoint which skills need to be built before launching into new learning (Swearingen, 2002) and can help the teacher zero in on specific areas for intervention or remediation. Some diagnostic assessments come with aligned professional development should a teacher not be familiar with the instructional techniques suggested to address the areas of concern.

Diagnostic assessments can also provide more general information about the knowledge and misconceptions students bring to a new learning activity, which gives the teacher information to help him or her design and deliver instruction more precisely where it is needed to move students toward the learning goal.

The Rubric

A review team wanting to determine how a school's assessment program measures up against the benchmark of Characteristic 3C would look at two traits of that characteristic. The rubric in Table 3.3 describes each trait as it manifests in low-performing, effective, and high-performing schools.

Table 3.3: Rubric for Characteristic 3C

Characteristic	Trait	Effectiveness Continuum		
		Low Performing	Effective	High Performing
3C. Diagnostic assessments are used to identify student skill levels and to determine appropriate interventions or remediations.	3C1. Assessment of knowledge and skill levels	Diagnostic assessments are not used to identify student knowledge and skill levels.	All students participate in diagnostic assessments to identify current knowledge and skill levels in reading and mathematics.	All students participate in diagnostic assessments to identify current knowledge and skill levels in reading, mathematics, science, and social studies.
	3C2. Assessment for interventions or remediations	Diagnostic assessments are not used to determine needed interventions or remediations.	Diagnostic assessments are used in reading and mathematics to determine needed interventions or remediations.	Diagnostic assessments are administered in reading, mathematics, science, and social studies throughout the year to determine needed interventions or remediations.

Characteristic 3D: Grouping and Regrouping

Summary of Research

Diagnostic assessments provide teachers with the data they need to differentiate instruction for groups of students within similar skill levels or for those who are experiencing difficulties. Using the data to place students into small and flexible work groups—each having the same instructional goal but with differences in the time allotted, the materials being used, the amount of individual work demanded, or the time devoted to a particular task—is the philosophy behind differentiated instruction.

Research in mathematics and reading achievement supports the effectiveness of short-term, homogeneous grouping based on current skill levels when that strategy is used appropriately (Marzano, Pickering,

& Pollock, 2001). Used appropriately means, among other things, that children are placed in homogeneous groups for only short periods of time while they work on specific skills—not throughout the whole class, school day, or even semester. Groups should be structured so that as children gain skills, they can move nearly seamlessly from one group to another.

In his 1986 review of research on the effectiveness of various student grouping practices at the elementary level, Robert Slavin looked at five different ability or achievement groupings. He found that:

1. Traditional ability-grouped (or tracked) class assignments, in which students were placed in a single self-contained class based on ability or achievement, did not enhance student achievement at the elementary level.

2. Regrouping, in which students spend most of their day in heterogeneous homerooms but spend one or two periods a day in achievement-grouped mathematics or reading classes, can improve student achievement in reading and mathematics when the level and pace of instruction are adapted to the achievement level.

3. In the Joplin Plan, students are heterogeneously grouped for most of the day, but for reading, they are regrouped across grade levels based on their current skill levels. For example, a reading class at the level of the first 6 weeks of the third grade might include high-achieving second-graders, average-achieving third-graders, and low-achieving fourth-graders. There is strong evidence that this plan results in increased reading achievement.

4. In nongraded plans, grade-level designations are not used, and students are placed in flexible groups based on performance rather than age. Students move from group to group based on their current skill levels in different subjects, for example, mathematics and reading. There is some evidence to support the use of the nongraded model.

5. In within-class ability grouping, teachers assign students within their classroom to one of several groups based on current skill levels. Each group works on different materials and at different rates appropriate to the needs and skill levels of its members. Research existing in 1987 clearly supported this practice for mathematics but had not been carried out for reading. (Hollifield, 1987)

Since Slavin's review, that research on reading has been completed and has shown that "students in small groups in the classroom learned significantly more than students who were not instructed in small groups" (Vaughn, Hughes, Moody, & Elbaum, 2001, p. 16).

Over time, some have expressed concern that even flexible grouping could be emotionally detrimental to children. In its position statement on this issue, the National Association of School Psychologists (2005, p. 10) noted:

> Homogeneous grouping by skill level has been demonstrated to be effective for instruction in the areas of mathematics and reading (Marzano, Pickering, & Pollock, 2001). Three keys to flexible grouping are using it sparingly, monitoring student progress closely, and allowing for the continual remixing of assigned groups. This allows students to move between smaller homogeneous skill-based groups and then back to larger heterogeneous groups for creative and problem solving activities. Flexible grouping surrounding student skills and across age grouping allows

students performing at various levels to share their combined areas of knowledge and strength (Marzano, Pickering, & Pollock, 2001). If utilized effectively and in a sensitive manner, the method of flexible grouping does not have to carry a negative stigma for the learner (Tieso, 2003).

The Rubric

A review team wanting to determine how a school's assessment program measures up against the benchmark of Characteristic 3D would look at one trait of that characteristic. The rubric in Table 3.4 describes that trait as it manifests in low-performing, effective, and high-performing schools.

Table 3.4: Rubric for Characteristic 3D

| Characteristic | Trait | Effectiveness Continuum | | |
		Low Performing	Effective	High Performing
3D. Data from diagnostic assessments are used to place, group, and regroup students.	**3D1. Assessment for grouping**	Data from diagnostic assessments are not used to place, group, and regroup students.	Data from diagnostic assessments are used to place, group, and regroup students across grade levels based on knowledge and skills.	Data from diagnostic assessments are used to group and regroup students, student progress is monitored closely, and a continual remixing of assigned groups occurs throughout the year.

Characteristic 3E: Aggregated and Disaggregated Data

Summary of Research

The federal No Child Left Behind (NCLB) Act required states for the first time to report assessment data both by overall results (aggregated data) and by subgroups for race/ethnicity, gender, socioeconomic status, English-language proficiency, and disability status (disaggregated data). Since the law was implemented in 2002, the examination of such data has become a more routine part of every school's analysis of its performance.

Statewide assessment data provide valuable information for schools and districts, allowing them to compare their own performance with that of schools or districts with similar characteristics. These data can then be used to begin the work of school improvement overall. When a school teases apart, or disaggregates, its own assessment data, it can understand more about how specific segments of the school population or specific programs are doing and thus can target its improvement efforts to the areas that would most benefit from them.

We have seen firsthand how looking at schoolwide test results without disaggregating data can provide an incomplete picture, with serious consequences for some students. We worked with a school that had selected, as its school improvement goal, the improvement of mathematics scores at the eighth grade.

The school was meeting its NCLB adequate yearly progress (AYP) goal, but its students were achieving at a rate 12 percentage points below the state average. In disaggregating the school assessment data, we saw that not a single one of its Hispanic eighth-graders (none of whom were English language learners) had met the mathematics standard. In fact, in looking even more closely at scores, we saw that the scores of Hispanic students were not even close to the bar. Because there were just 15 Hispanic students at the eighth-grade level (in this state, a subgroup had to have a minimum of 30 students to be included in the AYP disaggregation), those scores were not reported for AYP compliance, and the lagging performance of the Hispanic children was overshadowed by the higher performance of students overall. The faculty had looked at the overall results, but had no idea that the performance of these students was masked until they disaggregated the data student by student.

In another school with which we were working, the improvement goal was to increase the freshman graduation rate, which stood at 72%. When the staff members drilled down in the data to look at the various ethnic groups represented at the school, they were dismayed to find that the freshman graduation rate for the school's Native American population was only 30%. Looking even closer, they found that the graduation rate for Native American boys was only18%.

Disaggregated student assessment data can also provide essential information about the effectiveness of the overall and grade-level curricula and of particular school programs with respect to groups of students. Examples of such programs include the special education program, mathematics and reading interventions, and after-school and extended-learning opportunities.

The Education Commission of the States (2002) conducted a study to learn how the most successful school districts used data. They found that all of these districts collected and used more data than was mandated by federal law. They collected three kinds of data: demographic data, such as gender, ethnicity, attendance, and number of years in the school district; achievement data, including results from state, district, and teacher-created tests; and instructional data, such as information about the effectiveness of interventions and to which teachers students had been assigned. Then they *used* the data to make instructional decisions regarding placement, intervention, and enrichment and to identify needs for teacher professional development.

The Rubric

A review team wanting to determine how a school's assessment program measures up against the benchmark of Characteristic 3E would look at two traits of that characteristic. The rubric in Table 3.5 (page 62) describes each trait as it manifests in low-performing, effective, and high-performing schools.

Characteristic 3F: Data Collection and Dissemination

Summary of Research

Because state assessment data are such a powerful indication of the health of the instructional program, they are too important to be held close to the vest. NCLB has required states and districts to share state assessment data with parents, but teachers, paraprofessionals, students, and business and community members are also very interested in this information and are becoming more vocal in their demands to be included when data are released, as well as to have ongoing access to them.

Table 3.5: Rubric for Characteristic 3E

Characteristic	Trait	Effectiveness Continuum		
		Low Performing	Effective	High Performing
3E. Aggregated and disaggregated data from state assessments are used to improve the school's curriculum and instructional program.	3E1. Analysis of data	Aggregated and disaggregated data from state assessments are not analyzed by school staff.	Aggregated and disaggregated data from state assessments are analyzed by school staff.	Aggregated and disaggregated data, including state assessment, local assessment, and student demographic data, are analyzed at least annually by school staff.
	3E2. Use of data for school improvement	The school's curriculum and instructional program are not reviewed and refined based on disaggregated data from state assessments.	Disaggregated data from state assessments are used as a basis to review and refine the school's curriculum and instructional program.	Teachers meet as a faculty and in grade-level or content-area teams at least annually to discuss possible modifications to the curriculum and instructional program based on disaggregated results from state assessments.

Access alone however, is not sufficient. Effective districts present the data in a way that is concise and understandable to all audiences and that helps them see the significance of the numbers. The reports to stakeholders should identify important trends as well as questions that the school or district is considering as a result of its review of the data. The public should be given information about how groups and individuals may participate in the discussions surrounding the questions posed. How seriously stakeholders take student assessment data is reflected in a 2005 position paper of the League of Women Voters of California: "There should be a state level student assessment system that is timely, accessible, and understandable to teachers, administrators, and the public" (p. 13).

The Rubric

A review team wanting to determine how a school's assessment program measures up against the benchmark of Characteristic 3F would look at two traits of that characteristic. The rubric in Table 3.6 describes each trait as it manifests in low-performing, effective, and high-performing schools.

Table 3.6: Rubric for Characteristic 3F

Characteristic	Trait	Effectiveness Continuum		
		Low Performing	Effective	High Performing
3F. State and local student assessment data are collected, disseminated, and readily available.	3F1. Availability of assessment data	Student-level state assessment data are not readily available to teachers and staff members.	State and local student assessment data are collected, disseminated, and readily available to teachers and staff members.	State and local student assessment data are collected, disseminated, and readily available to teachers, staff members, families, and students.
	3F2. Reporting of assessment data	State assessment data are not communicated in a way that is understandable.	State assessment data are communicated in a way that is understandable to staff, members, students, families, and the public.	State assessment data are communicated in a clear and concise manner to all stakeholders. Trends over time are included in the communication.

Conclusion

Student assessment is a powerful tool for understanding student knowledge and skills, for designing targeted instruction to help students meet learning goals, and for evaluating the effectiveness of programs. It allows us to see which students the system is serving well and who is being shortchanged. It can also serve to spur parents, community members, and other stakeholders to action if they are included as partners in raising student achievement in their schools.

Effectiveness Indicator 4

School Leadership

Time is neutral and does not change things. With courage and initiative, leaders change things.

—Jesse Jackson

School leadership exerts a powerful influence on student learning. For a school to be effective, its leaders must maintain an unwavering focus on learning. From this principle, we derive Effectiveness Indicator 4. An on-site school review examines the role of school administrators in developing, implementing, and maintaining improvement efforts that are focused on student learning.

Recognizing student learning as the foremost priority of the school and its teachers, effective school administrators ensure that a culture of high expectations nurtures student and teacher efficacy. These administrators maximize their influence by increasing leadership capacity schoolwide and widely distributing leadership responsibilities. Effective leaders model the characteristics they expect of staff members and students, including optimism, fairness, respect, collaboration, and an openness to constructive feedback. They are learners themselves who recognize and acknowledge staff expertise. They provide the foundation on which school improvement is built, including adequate resources.

Twelve characteristics define Effectiveness Indicator 4: School Leadership:

4A.	School administrators provide leadership in strategic planning.

4B.	School administrators create a culture of high expectations for student and adult success and support those beliefs schoolwide.

4C.	School administrators see student learning as the foremost priority for the school.

4D.	School administrators ensure that adequate resources are allocated to achieve school improvement goals.

4E.	School leadership is distributed schoolwide.

4F.	School administrators recognize staff members' accomplishments, expertise, and leadership potential.

4G.　School administrators encourage and promote collaborative relationships.

4H.　School administrators address existing and potential conflicts.

4I.　School administrators are accessible and model optimism, integrity, fairness, and respect.

4J.　School administrators are adaptable and encourage innovation.

4K.　School administrators ensure that teachers receive constructive feedback through periodic observation, coaching, and lesson study.

4L.　School administrators provide formal staff evaluations.

Characteristic 4A: Strategic Planning

Summary of Research

The concept of strategic planning is fairly new to the field of education, coming from the business arena. Of course, today, federal and state laws impel schools with problems of lagging performance to create strategic plans, but in a culture of continuous improvement, all schools strive to improve. The gist of strategic planning is that in order for an organization to remain healthy, it needs to be in the business of continual reflection on current performance, coupled with intense effort to move beyond current performance to something even better—a quest to identify "what is vital and what is not" (Collins, 2001, p. 205).

Companies and schools that are continuously working toward improvement have been described as "learning organizations." In *The Fifth Discipline*, Peter Senge (1990), who originated this concept, characterizes the leader's new work as building learning organizations. He states, "In learning organizations, leaders are designers, stewards, and teachers. They are responsible for building organizations where people continually expand their capabilities to understand complexity, clarify vision, and improve shared mental models, that is, they are responsible for learning" (p. 340).

In 2008, the Interstate School Leaders Licensure Consortium (ISLLC) updated its standards for school leaders based on research into effective leadership. The first standard defines an education leader as one who "promotes the success of every student by facilitating the development, articulation, implementation, and stewardship of a vision of learning that is shared and supported by all stakeholders" (p. 1).

Leaders in successful schools strongly believe that the purpose of schools is to meet the academic needs of students (Mendez-Morse, 1992). They then take responsibility for and lead a focused school improvement effort by creating a coherent and strategic plan that describes how the school will "transmit [its] vision to others so that they become motivated to work toward the realization of the vision" (p. 7).

More information on strategic planning can be found in Chapter 5, "Effectiveness Indicator 5: Strategic Planning."

The Rubric

A review team wanting to determine how a school's leadership measures up against the benchmark of Characteristic 4A would look at four traits of that characteristic. The rubric in Table 4.1 describes each trait as it manifests in low-performing, effective, and high-performing schools.

Table 4.1: Rubric for Characteristic 4A

Characteristic	Trait	Effectiveness Continuum		
		Low Performing	Effective	High Performing
4A. School administrators provide leadership in strategic planning.	4A1. Development of strategic plan	The school lacks a current strategic plan, or the plan was developed without significant staff input.	The school has a current strategic plan that was developed with significant staff participation.	The school has a current strategic plan that was developed by school leadership and staff members and approved by district leadership or the school board.
	4A2. Focus of strategic plan	The school lacks a strategic plan, or the plan is not focused on student learning.	The school strategic plan is focused on student learning.	The school strategic plan is focused on student learning and includes disaggregated student achievement data and analysis supporting the goals and action plans.
	4A3. Relationship of strategic plan to decision-making	School decisions are made without regard to the strategic plan.	The strategic plan guides school decision-making.	The strategic plan is the pivotal factor in school decision-making.
	4A4. Responsibility for strategic plan	School administrators do not take responsibility for implementing the strategic plan.	School administrators take personal responsibility for the strategic plan.	School administrators take personal responsibility for the strategic plan and lead its implementation.

Characteristic 4B: High Expectations

Summary of Research

Leaders in effective schools hold high expectations for students, staff members, and themselves. They are able to infuse this belief into the school culture. In a study of principals, Cotton (2003, p. 11) noted that these high expectations form the basis for "the vision that guides high-achieving schools and is a critical component in its own right." The faith in the ability of all segments of the school population to succeed, even in the face of sometimes daunting challenges, is what inspires school administrators to persist through difficulties, setbacks, and failures. As Cotton observed, "in spite of challenges and frustrations, school administrators did not stop trying to improve their schools" (p. 13).

In their review of research into effective organizational leadership, Murphy, Elliott, Goldring, and Porter (2006b, p. 21) found that "learning-centered leaders in high-performing schools work ceaselessly to create an environment of high performance expectations for self, staff, and students." How important are those expectations? In *10 Strategies for Improving High School Graduation Rates and Student Achievement*, Gene Bottoms (2006) calls for "fostering a school culture of high expectations and relevance" (p. 9) and asserts that "two-thirds of high school dropouts report they would have worked harder if more was demanded of them" (p. 6).

Translated into action, this leadership characteristic can be thought of as leading for learning. That phrase acknowledges the role of leadership in bringing about lasting improvements in the way students learn, teachers teach, and the system responds. It "means creating powerful, equitable learning opportunities for students, professionals, and the system, and motivating or compelling participants to take advantage of these opportunities" (Knapp, Copland, & Talbert, 2003, p. 12).

The Rubric

A review team wanting to determine how a school's leadership measures up against the benchmark of Characteristic 4B would look at two traits of that characteristic. The rubric in Table 4.2 describes each trait as it manifests in low-performing, effective, and high-performing schools.

Table 4.2: Rubric for Characteristic 4B

Characteristic	Trait	Effectiveness Continuum		
		Low Performing	Effective	High Performing
4B. School administrators create a culture of high expectations for student and adult success and support those beliefs schoolwide.	**4B1. Expectations for students**	School administrators do not have high expectations for the success of all students.	School administrators have high expectations for the success of all students.	School administrators have high expectations for student success and consistently reinforce that belief in interactions with students, staff members, and parents.
	4B2. Expectations for staff members	School administrators do not have high expectations for the success of all staff members.	School administrators have high expectations for the success of all staff members.	School administrators have high expectations for the success of all staff members and consistently reinforce that message in interactions with staff members, students, parents, and the community.

Characteristic 4C: Student Learning

Summary of Research

Research over the last 30 years has consistently demonstrated that schools that make student learning their top priority see higher levels of student achievement than other schools (Cotton, 2003). The role of the school leader in setting and maintaining this priority is pivotal. Cotton found that "effective principals create a school climate where academic achievement is the primary goal, and policies and procedures are instituted to achieve that goal" (pp. 14–15).

School administrators who are also instructional leaders regard the oversight of the school's instructional program as a key leadership responsibility (Murphy et al., 2006b). They have a strong focus on student learning and are knowledgeable about and deeply involved in the school's instructional program (Marzano, Waters, & McNulty, 2005). They work to ensure that all students have access to a rigorous curriculum, one that prepares them for a world in which a lack of a high school diploma equals a lack of opportunity (Murphy et al., 2006b).

In 2000, the Institute for Educational Leadership, a nonprofit, nonpartisan organization funded by the United States Department of Education, the Ford Foundation, the Metropolitan Life Foundation, the UPS Foundation, and the Carnegie Corporation of New York, joined in an initiative to examine the needs for school leadership in the 21st century. The group's report designated "facilitating student learning" as the single most important role of school administrators, stating, "Everything principals do—establishing a vision, setting goals, managing staff, rallying the community, creating effective learning environments, building support systems for students, guiding instruction and so on—must be in service of student learning" (Task Force on the Principalship, 2000, p. 4).

This finding has important implications for all of the other areas about which school administrators must be concerned. Learning-centered leaders know that if learning is the foremost priority, other duties "that have historically occupied center stage in school administration—management, politics, organization, finance—are no longer ends in themselves, but rather assume importance to the extent that they strengthen the quality of the instructional and curricular program and enhance student learning" (Murphy et al., 2006b, p. 21).

The Rubric

A review team wanting to determine how a school's leadership measures up against the benchmark of Characteristic 4C would look at one trait of that characteristic. The rubric in Table 4.3 (page 70) describes that trait as it manifests in low-performing, effective, and high-performing schools.

Characteristic 4D: Adequate Resources

Summary of Research

In order for the improvement effort to succeed, sufficient resources must be allocated to and aligned with attaining and maintaining those improvement goals. Research in the areas of school improvement and instructional leadership consistently finds that leaders in high-performing schools are more successful

Table 4.3: Rubric for Characteristic 4C

Characteristic	Trait	Effectiveness Continuum		
		Low Performing	Effective	High Performing
4C. School administrators see student learning as the foremost priority for the school.	4C1. Priority assigned to student learning	School administrators do not see student learning as the highest priority in decision-making.	School administrators see student learning as the highest priority in all decision-making.	School administrators see student learning as the highest priority for the school and take direct responsibility for the quality of the school's instructional program.

than their peers in locating and securing additional resources for their schools (Murphy et al., 2006a). In addition, high-performing school administrators have a "gift for acquiring and using resources in support of every student reaching ambitious learning targets" and in ensuring that these resources are "thoughtfully linked to school goals and student needs" (p. 20). A review of research over the last 20 years shows that effective principals are "adept at finding and providing resources—financial, human, time, materials, and facilities—for all kinds of instructional needs" (Cotton, 2003, p. 36).

The Rubric

A review team wanting to determine how a school's leadership measures up against the benchmark of Characteristic 4D would look at one trait of that characteristic. The rubric in Table 4.4 describes that trait as it manifests in low-performing, effective, and high-performing schools.

Table 4.4: Rubric for Characteristic 4D

Characteristic	Trait	Effectiveness Continuum		
		Low Performing	Effective	High Performing
4D. School administrators ensure that adequate resources are allocated to achieve school improvement goals.	4D1. Sufficiency of resources for school improvement	School administrators have not ensured that sufficient resources have been allocated to support school improvement goals.	School administrators ensure that sufficient resources are allocated to support school improvement goals.	School administrators allocate sufficient resources to support implementation of the school improvement efforts and actively seek additional resources that support school goals.

Characteristic 4E: Shared Leadership

Summary of Research

The concept of shared or distributed leadership "entails the view that varieties of expertise are distributed across the many, not the few" (Bennett, Wise, & Woods, 2003a, p. 7). School leaders holding this view believe that "all teachers harbor leadership capabilities waiting to be unlocked and engaged for the good of the school" (Barth, 2001, p. 445). In fact, Roland Barth states that "ample evidence suggests that effective principals don't work harder than less effective principals; instead they 'encourage and enlist teachers' leadership' and use it to strengthen their leadership" (p. 444).

The rationale behind distributed leadership is that there are simply too many leadership responsibilities to be accomplished by one, two, or three school administrators and that, in fact, it adds to the health of an organization to distribute these responsibilities widely. It becomes expertise rather than formal position that determines the leadership within the school (Bennett, Wise, & Woods, 2003b, p. 6). Administrators in schools adopting this practice find that everyone has something to contribute toward leadership, and they create the "organization conditions, the climate and the support" for all staff members to be able to take on leadership roles in which they have expertise (Jackson, 2002).

Richard Elmore (2000) agrees that in order for all of the leadership tasks cited in effective schools research to be carried out successfully, leadership responsibilities must be widely distributed throughout the school. Those with particular knowledge and skills are identified and matched to the task at hand. Elmore illustrates how defining the core role of school leadership as improving instruction and learning can help leaders think about and focus on the most important leadership responsibilities. He stresses that "the skills and knowledge that matter in leadership, under this definition, are those that can be connected to, or lead directly to, the improvement of instruction and student performance" (p. 14).

Creating a schoolwide system of distributed leadership requires thoughtful planning, professional development, and time. Somewhat ironically, implementing the concept will initially add to the principal's responsibility: "By virtue of their strategic position, principals must not only carry out their own assigned duties, but must develop leadership capacity in teachers and others who are not necessarily accustomed to thinking and acting as leaders" (Lashway, 2003, p. 7).

The Rubric

A review team wanting to determine how a school's leadership measures up against the benchmark of Characteristic 4E would look at one trait of that characteristic. The rubric in Table 4.5 (page 72) describes that trait as it manifests in low-performing, effective, and high-performing schools.

Characteristic 4F: Recognition

Summary of Research

Principals of high-achieving schools "make a point of recognizing achievement and improvement. . . . Such recognition, when public and formalized, is one of the symbolic rituals that enhance affiliation with the school and help to fortify its identity" (Cotton, 2003, p. 40). Yet within school systems, many teachers tend to look with skepticism, even displeasure, at the singling out of coworkers for awards, distinction, or even overt praise. Mary Hatwood Futrell, dean of the Graduate School of Education and

Table 4.5: Rubric for Characteristic 4E

Characteristic	Trait	Effectiveness Continuum		
		Low Performing	Effective	High Performing
4E. School leadership is distributed schoolwide.	4E1. Sharing of leadership	School leadership is restricted to those in administrative positions.	School leadership is shared among staff members based on knowledge, skills, and interests.	School leadership is widely shared among staff members based on knowledge, skills, and interests. There is formalized acknowledgment of staff members' leadership roles.

Human Development at George Washington University, puts it bluntly: "Let's face it. When the teachers are identified as leaders, even their colleagues probably are going to mistrust them." She notes that teachers commonly make such comments as "Who do you think you are?" (Usdan & Hale, 2001).

Barth (2001, p. 446) sums up this undercurrent of resistance to teacher recognition: "There is something deep and powerful within school cultures that seems to work against teacher leadership. Ours is a cautious profession, top to bottom. To distinguish—or even appear to distinguish—oneself from the rest places the teacher at risk."

Yet research consistently identifies public recognition of school staff accomplishments as a factor in successful schools. DuFour and Eaker (1998, p. 112) argue:

> Regardless of the eloquence of the vision and values statements, those statements will not have an impact on people in a school unless progress toward the vision is apparent and unless the implementation of the values is recognized and celebrated on a consistent basis. When reaching a milestone in the journey toward the vision is noted and celebrated, and when examples of the commitment to values are publicly acknowledged and rewarded, everyone in the school is reminded that vision and values are important.

Another way leaders provide public recognition is by acknowledging expertise within the existing school staff. Teachers may have deep knowledge in any number of areas, including differentiated instruction, high-quality formative assessments, use of data, and powerful instructional techniques. Schools can also harness teacher expertise in the selection of textbooks and other instructional materials, curriculum development, behavior management, promotion and retention policies, school budgeting, design and delivery of professional development, evaluation of new teacher performance, and hiring decisions (Barth, 2001).

The late Sandra Feldman, who served as president of the American Federation of Teachers, recommended calling on teacher expertise in hiring, evaluation, and tenure. She pointed out that "teachers want competent colleagues.... No one is smarter and tougher about teachers than expert teachers ... [and] no one is more able to help struggling colleagues" (Education Trust, 2000, p. 13).

Schools and districts that support teachers' interest in developing leadership skills or other expertise that is then shared with their colleagues, both formally and informally, make a wise investment. This investment is

> primarily about enhancing the skills and knowledge of people in the organization, creating a common culture of expectations around the use of those skills and knowledge, holding the various pieces of the organization together in a productive relationship with each other, and holding individuals accountable for their contributions to the collective result. (Elmore, 2000, p. 15)

The Rubric

A review team wanting to determine how a school's leadership measures up against the benchmark of Characteristic 4F would look at three traits of that characteristic. The rubric in Table 4.6 describes each trait as it manifests in low-performing, effective, and high-performing schools.

Table 4.6: Rubric for Characteristic 4F

Characteristic	Trait	Effectiveness Continuum		
		Low Performing	Effective	High Performing
4F. School administrators recognize staff members' accomplishments, expertise, and leadership potential.	4F1. Recognition of staff accomplishments	Staff accomplishments receive little or no recognition.	School administrators informally recognize and acknowledge staff accomplishments.	School administrators formally and informally recognize staff members' individual and group accomplishments.
	4F2. Recognition and utilization of staff members' expertise	No processes exist to identify or utilize staff members' expertise.	School administrators identify and utilize internal staff members' expertise.	School administrators identify and utilize internal staff members' expertise and ensure that professional development is targeted to continue to build these internal resources.
	4F3. Professional development for staff leadership	Staff members with an interest in leadership roles pursue that interest without school or district assistance.	Staff members are encouraged to seek professional development to build their leadership capacities.	A formal professional development program exists to identify and prepare staff members for shared leadership opportunities and to provide them with ongoing support.

Characteristic 4G: Collaboration

Summary of Research

The effect of high-functioning collaborative teams extends well beyond an individual classroom. Darling-Hammond and her colleagues found that "collaborative approaches to professional learning can promote school change. . . . When all teachers in a school learn together, all students in a school benefit" (Darling-Hammond, Wei, Andree, Richardson, & Orphanos, 2009, p. 5).

DuFour, DuFour, and Eaker (2008) caution that

> there is nothing inherently "good" about collaboration. It represents a means to an end rather than the end itself. Collaboration can serve to perpetuate the status quo rather than improve it, to reinforce the negative aspects of the culture rather than resolve them, to reiterate faulty assumptions rather than subject them to collective inquiry. Collaboration can, and sometimes does, dissolve into grouping by griping, a forum for petty grievances, and a reaffirmation of resignation and helplessness. (p. 183)

Herein lies the role of the principal in developing collaborative teams working to improve teaching and learning.

In order to create and nurture high-functioning collaborative teams, effective principals provide the teams with a clear charge backed by the resources and support they need to accomplish their task. DuFour, DuFour, and Eaker (2008) stress that

> if teachers are being asked to collaborate, principals have an obligation to create structures that make collaboration meaningful rather than artificial, to guarantee time for collaboration during the contractual day [see the discussion of Characteristic 2G], to establish clear priorities and parameters so that teachers focus on the right topics, to help teams make informed decisions by making the essential knowledge base easily accessible to them, to provide meaningful and timely training based on the specific needs of each team, to offer templates and models to guide their work, and to specify clear expectations and standards to help teachers assess the quality of their work. (p. 312)

When inertia is overcome, momentum increases. Research shows that when a principal is successful in creating, nurturing, and valuing a collaborative environment, interest in this work grows throughout the organization, leading to increasing participation and support for school-based learning communities (Murphy et al., 2006b).

As in so many other areas, clear communication is a key. Successful school administrators encourage and promote collaboration and collaborative relationships through frequent and open communication (Marzano et al., 2005).

Leaders in schools in which collaborative work teams and disciplined collaboration are the norm ensure that teachers have specific and frequent opportunities to meet in grade-level, content-area, and other team meetings and that their meeting times are not layered on top of other responsibilities (or relegated to lunch or preparation times). In exchange, leaders clearly spell out the work to be accomplished, the group norms, and the expectations for deliverables. Fullan (2001a, p. 87) notes that "effective leaders understand the value and role of knowledge creation. They make it a priority and set about establishing and reinforcing habits of knowledge exchange among organizational members."

The Rubric

A review team wanting to determine how a school's leadership measures up against the benchmark of Characteristic 4G would look at two traits of that characteristic. The rubric in Table 4.7 describes each trait as it manifests in low-performing, effective, and high-performing schools.

Table 4.7: Rubric for Characteristic 4G

Characteristic	Trait	Effectiveness Continuum		
		Low Performing	Effective	High Performing
4G. School administrators encourage and promote collaborative relationships.	4G1. Provision of opportunities to collaborate	Opportunities for staff members to communicate, plan, and work with one another are limited, informal, and self-organized or primarily occur outside of the school day.	School administrators ensure that there are ample organized opportunities for staff members to communicate, plan, and work with one another.	The school calendar provides specific and frequent opportunities for grade-level, content-area, and other team meetings. Contract hours provide paraprofessionals with the opportunity and responsibility to participate as appropriate.
	4G2. Focus of collaborative efforts	Collaborative efforts are not focused on student learning.	School administrators ensure that collaborative efforts are focused on student learning.	School administrators ensure that collaborative efforts are focused on student learning, and instructional teams document and communicate strategies and results.

Characteristic 4H: Conflict Resolution

Summary of Research

Leaders are often called upon to help staff members work through conflict and to arrive at solutions that reflect shared decision-making. Leading effectively "means guiding people through differences and, indeed, enabling differences to surface" (Fullan, 2001a, p. 114).

Conflict can arise from differing views of what is best for students. These beliefs may surface when the school staff as a whole examines curricular issues and decides to move from individual or even departmental decision-making to whole-staff agreements—for example, when schools or districts begin the work of aligning curriculum and instruction to state standards. Agreeing to do this work is the first hurdle. The much higher bar is set when monitoring occurs to ensure that what happens in classrooms tightly reflects that alignment.

The argument that raged for years over the teaching of reading, sometimes called the "whole-language" debate, was a great source of conflict in schools that made schoolwide decisions to adopt one approach over another. (A similar debate has occurred in the area of mathematics instruction.) Teachers on each side of the debate believed deeply that one way of teaching reading would lead to higher skills and a better life for their students, while the teaching of the "other" way would limit children for a lifetime.

No matter what the source of the conflict, once all sides have been heard and a shared agreement reached, school administrators must take ultimate responsibility for ensuring that all staff members enact the agreement consistently and positively. "Principals who are unwilling to defend and protect the vision and values of their schools put improvement initiatives at risk. The school suffers when individuals are free to act in a manner that the staff as a whole has agreed is contrary to the school's best interest" (DuFour & Eaker, 1998, p. 113). The responsibility of reinforcing vision and values most often falls to the principal. However, it can, and should, extend to all who participate in school leadership in any of its many forms.

A second kind of conflict centers on adult issues. School administrators in effective schools make a concerted effort to be aware of situations that could undermine effectiveness or create dissatisfaction in the workplace. These leaders address such issues before they become problems by promoting healthy relationships among staff members and providing opportunities for frank and constructive discussions to relieve potential conflict. Examples of issues that may arise in this arena include dissatisfaction with classroom or teaching assignments, concern about the availability of opportunities for professional development, and lack of teacher-to-teacher or teacher-to-administrator trust.

When issues are likely to rise to the level of conflict, successful leaders bring them out into the open and then work with staff members to solve the underlying problems. If leaders ignore conflict, school improvement is in peril: "Whenever smart and well-intentioned people avoid confronting obstacles, they disempower employees and undermine change" (Kotter, 1996, pp. 30–31).

What are the processes that effective school administrators use to address conflict? Murphy et al. (2006b) observe that "these leaders model effective skills in the areas of (a) problem framing and problem-solving, (b) decision-making, (c) conflict resolution, (d) group processes and consensus building, and (e) communication. They also see to it that these important processes permeate the organization" (p. 19).

The Rubric

A review team wanting to determine how a school's leadership measures up against the benchmark of Characteristic 4H would look at two traits of that characteristic. The rubric in Table 4.8 describes each trait as it manifests in low-performing, effective, and high-performing schools.

Table 4.8: Rubric for Characteristic 4H

Characteristic	Trait	Effectiveness Continuum		
		Low Performing	Effective	High Performing
4H. School administrators address existing and potential conflicts.	4H1. Efforts to resolve conflicts	School administrators do not or do not always address staff conflicts.	When conflicts arise, school administrators work toward resolution.	School administrators work toward resolution of conflicts, addressing both the immediate concerns and the underlying issues.
	4H2. Anticipation of conflicts	School administrators do not always notice or acknowledge issues that have the potential to cause conflict.	School administrators anticipate where and when conflicts might arise and address issues before they rise to the level of a problem.	School administrators anticipate where and when conflicts, including workplace or community dissatisfaction, might arise and intervene to address both the problems and the underlying issues.

Characteristic 4I: Optimism, Integrity, Fairness, and Respect

Summary of Research

In high-achieving schools, principals can often be found outside of their offices and are "unvaryingly present and approachable in the everyday life of the school . . . a frequent presence in classrooms, observing and interacting with teachers" (Cotton, 2003, p. 14). These principals value and listen carefully to the ideas and insights of others. They "not only share information, but they also listen and take the suggestions of staff and constituents seriously, acknowledging that they do not have all the answers" (p. 16).

The ISLLC (2008) standards call for education leaders to "promot[e] the success of all students" by exhibiting integrity, fairness, and high ethics in all dealings with staff members, students, parents, and the community (Standard 5) and by establishing positive relationships with families and community members (Standard 4). We would expand the wording of the standards to include promoting the success of all *adults* within the school and the greater community through the same actions. Leadership research confirms the importance of these traits, describing effective leaders as treating "all individuals with fairness, dignity, and respect" (Murphy et al., 2006b, p. 18).

Marzano, Waters, and McNulty (2005) refer to optimism as another critical characteristic of an effective school leader and go further to describe an optimizer as one who "inspires others and is the driving force when implementing a challenging innovation" (p. 56).

Staff members in schools who feel valued and respected for their knowledge and experience are much more likely to feel welcome to express their ideas and vision. Leithwood and Riehl (2003) found that successful

> educational leaders enhance the performance of their school by providing oppor-
> tunities for staff to participate in decision-making about issues that affect them and
> for which their knowledge is crucial. In this way, leaders help others to shape the
> school in ways that can accomplish shared goals and address individual concerns
> as well. (p. 7)

Principals in successful schools regularly ask for input from parents and community members and use those ideas in their decision-making processes. These leaders "see parents and themselves as collaborators in the education of the children, and so the schools do everything they can to positively promote this collaboration" (Cotton, 2003, p. 19).

The Rubric

A review team wanting to determine how a school's leadership measures up against the benchmark of Characteristic 4I would look at four traits of that characteristic. The rubric in Table 4.9 describes each trait as it manifests in low-performing, effective, and high-performing schools.

Characteristic 4J: Innovation

Summary of Research

In effective schools, administrators keep current on educational research and instructional theory and practice. Their knowledge and understanding can make the difference between embracing a powerful new tool that results in student learning gains or resisting it and ending up with no gain or, even worse, slipping backwards. Leaders in these schools know that innovation does not entail jumping from one educational idea to another. It begins as they ask staff members to think about effective practice and to engage in a review of current educational theory in an area where improvement is desired. From this grows a conviction to adopt specific practices supported by high-quality research and abandon those practices not supported by results.

Michael Fullan (2001a) has studied and written about change and the change process in schools for more than 20 years. In *Leading in a Culture of Change*, he underscores the importance of choosing innovations carefully and making data-based decisions: "Leading in a culture of change means creating a culture (not just a structure) of change. It does not mean adopting innovations, one after another; it does mean producing the capacity to seek, critically assess, and selectively incorporate new ideas and practices" (p. 44).

Effective leaders encourage innovation and risk-taking in order to improve the effectiveness of instruction. Principals in high-achieving schools support teacher innovation and understand and accept that not all new ideas will be successful. These leaders create a culture in which teachers feel empowered to try new ideas and safe to acknowledge that some of them have failed (Cotton, 2003).

Table 4.9: Rubric for Characteristic 4I

Characteristic	Trait	Effectiveness Continuum		
		Low Performing	Effective	High Performing
4I. School administrators are accessible and model optimism, integrity, fairness, and respect.	4I1. Accessibility of administrators to staff members	It is sometimes or usually difficult to meet with school administrators.	School administrators are accessible to staff members.	School administrators set aside time during each day to meet with staff members.
	4I2. Interactions with staff members, students, and community members	Some staff members, students, and community members do not think that interactions with school administrators are characterized by integrity and fairness.	Staff members, students, and community members believe that interactions with school administrators are characterized by integrity and fairness.	School administrators consistently display integrity and fairness in interactions with staff members, students, and the community and have built a culture of trust schoolwide.
	4I3. Attitudes about reaching goals	Some school administrators are not optimistic that agreed-upon goals can be reached, given the current conditions.	School administrators manifest optimism that staff members and students can and will reach agreed-upon goals.	School administrators ensure that agreed-upon goals are within reach and set a consistent tone of optimism and confidence that the goals can and will be met.
	4I4. Attitudes toward staff members, students, and the community	Staff members, students, and the community do not always feel valued and respected by school administrators.	Staff members, students, and the community feel valued and respected by school administrators.	Staff members, students, and the community feel welcome at the school and valued and respected by school administrators.

The Rubric

A review team wanting to determine how a school's leadership measures up against the benchmark of Characteristic 4J would look at three traits of that characteristic. The rubric in Table 4.10 (page 80) describes each trait as it manifests in low-performing, effective, and high-performing schools.

Table 4.10: Rubric for Characteristic 4J

Characteristic	Trait	Effectiveness Continuum		
		Low Performing	Effective	High Performing
4J. School administrators are adaptable and encourage innovation.	**4J1. Knowledge of current educational research**	School administrators do not keep current on educational research and instructional theory and practice.	School administrators keep current on educational research and instructional theory and practice.	School administrators keep current on educational research and instructional theory and practice, and they routinely share and discuss best practices with staff members.
	4J2. Adaptability to changing circumstances	School administrators resist responding to changing circumstances or respond slowly.	School administrators adapt to changing circumstances.	School administrators anticipate changing circumstances, adapt to meet changing needs, and provide leadership in implementing change efforts.
	4J3. Attitude toward new ideas	School administrators do not always encourage new and innovative ideas.	School administrators encourage new and innovative ideas from staff members.	School administrators encourage new and innovative ideas from staff members and all stakeholders.

Characteristic 4K: Formative Feedback

Summary of Research

Research has demonstrated that "effective principals who are good instructional leaders spend large amounts of time in classrooms, observing teaching and encouraging higher performance" (National Staff Development Council, 2000, p. 3). These principals "are well versed in providing regular 'incidental interventions'—casual conversations and suggestions of ideas—that assist teachers in their efforts to improve instruction" (Murphy et al., 2006b, p. 16). In addition, instructional leaders must have or develop a deep understanding of effective classroom practice so that their observations are valid and the feedback they provide to teachers is useful to them in improving instruction (Lashway, 2003).

Classroom observations are most effective when they occur multiple times a year. In some cases, the observations may be preplanned, with the focus of the observation jointly determined ahead of time. In other cases, the visits may be in the form of drop-ins that take only a few minutes. School administrators and the staff should agree on the purpose of the visits, how often and under what circumstances they will occur, what opportunities will be provided for debriefing, and which data-gathering tools will be used.

Leaders in highly productive schools believe that "feedback about performance is essential to the learning process, and [they] are diligent about providing this information to colleagues on a consistent basis and in a timely manner" (Murphy et al., 2006b, p. 12).

Another crucial way that school leaders ensure that teachers receive frequent, practical feedback is by supporting the practices of peer coaching and lesson study, in which teachers work together to enhance instruction. Peer coaching was first adopted "in the early 1980s as a strategy to improve the degree of implementation of new curriculum and instructional techniques" (Wong & Nicotera, 2003, p. 1). Typically it is a "process of collaborative planning, classroom observation, and feedback, rather than serving as a normal evaluation or review" (p. 1). Leaders in effective schools provide release time for teachers to participate in peer observation, coaching, and lesson study.

The Rubric

A review team wanting to determine how a school's leadership measures up against the benchmark of Characteristic 4K would look at three traits of that characteristic. The rubric in Table 4.11 (page 82) describes each trait as it manifests in low-performing, effective, and high-performing schools.

Characteristic 4L: Formal Staff Evaluation

Summary of Research

In most states, formal, summative evaluation of instructional staff members is governed by state law. These regulations may cover the timing of the evaluations, which may vary based on the years of experience of the staff member; the areas to be reviewed; and specific or general requirements for activities before, during, and after the evaluations. In most school districts, bargaining agreements and district policies further define how such evaluations will be conducted.

Colby, Bradshaw, and Joyner (2002) conducted a large-scale study of both state-mandated and locally developed evaluation systems. While evaluation governed by statewide regulation is still the norm in the great majority of districts, the researchers found that "teacher evaluation as practiced in the majority of school districts is often ineffective with little impact on the quality of education that students receive and often ineffective in facilitating professional development in a meaningful way" (p. 3).

The study concluded that alternative evaluation systems that were

> tightly connected to district priorities and school functions such as school improvement, professional development, and student learning were perceived by both teachers and administrators as having a much stronger impact on school improvement efforts, professional development, and student learning while state mandated teacher evaluation systems were found to have little or no perceived impact in these areas. (p. 6)

The implications that emerged from this study were:

- Teacher evaluation policies and practices can serve as a catalyst for creating connections in practice between school improvement, professional development and student learning; and

Table 4.11: Rubric for Characteristic 4K

Characteristic	Trait	Effectiveness Continuum		
		Low Performing	Effective	High Performing
4K. School administrators ensure that teachers receive constructive feedback through periodic observation, coaching, and lesson study.	**4K1. Administrator observation and feedback**	School administrators occasionally observe teachers informally and provide constructive feedback.	School administrators frequently observe every teacher informally and provide constructive feedback focused on student learning.	School administrators frequently observe every teacher and instructional paraprofessional informally and provide constructive feedback focused on student learning.
	4K2. Support for peer observation, coaching, and lesson study	School administrators give informal support to peer observation, coaching, and lesson study but do not always provide sufficient release time.	Adequate release time is provided for all instructional staff members to participate in frequent, well-planned peer observation, coaching, and lesson study.	Adequate release time is built into the school calendar for all instructional staff members to participate in frequent, well-planned peer observation, coaching, and lesson study.
	4K3. Peer observation and feedback	Teachers observe and are observed by peers infrequently or not at all.	Each teacher frequently observes and is observed by peers and engages in a structured process of feedback.	Each teacher and instructional paraprofessional frequently observes and is observed by peers and engages in a structured process of feedback.

- Developing teacher evaluation systems at the local level is a viable strategy for strengthening teacher evaluation and its connections to school improvement, professional development, and student learning. (pp. 7–8)

The Rubric

A review team wanting to determine how a school's leadership measures up against the benchmark of Characteristic 4L would look at one trait of that characteristic. The rubric in Table 4.12 describes that trait as it manifests in low-performing, effective, and high-performing schools.

Table 4.12: Rubric for Characteristic 4L

Characteristic	Trait	Effectiveness Continuum		
		Low Performing	Effective	High Performing
4L. School administrators provide formal staff evaluations.	4L1. Quality of staff evaluations	School administrators sometimes do not conduct staff evaluations on a timely basis or do not include all components of the evaluation as prescribed by state law and district policy.	School administrators conduct staff evaluations on a timely basis as prescribed by state law and district policy.	School administrators conduct staff evaluations on a timely basis as prescribed by state law and district policy. The evaluations address school improvement goals, professional development, and student learning.

Conclusion

In 2004, Leithwood, Louis, Anderson, and Wahlstrom's review of research on effective leadership concluded that leadership is "second only to classroom instruction among all school-related factors that contribute to what students learn at school," accounting for about 25% of total school effects, and that its impact is even greater in those schools facing the greatest challenges (p. 5). To be sure, student learning should be the foremost priority of every school. However, school administrators must also devote time and attention to ensuring that the culture of the school is positive, that the school community is characterized by collaborative relationships, that high ethical and moral standards are consistently modeled, that innovation is welcomed and risk-taking encouraged, and that when one leader steps down or moves on, there are others at the school ready to lead.

Effectiveness Indicator 5
Strategic Planning

I skate to where the puck is going to be, not where it has been.

—Wayne Gretzky

Effective schools use strategic planning to coordinate improvement initiatives and ensure that they are directed toward a common goal. From this principle, we derive Effectiveness Indicator 5. Certain organizational elements must be in place for the planning process to provide the maximum benefit to the school. An on-site school review examines how the plan is created, what its focus is, who is part of the process, how the plan is implemented, and how it is evaluated.

Eight characteristics define Effectiveness Indicator 5: Strategic Planning:

5A. There is a process in place, and support for, schoolwide strategic planning.

5B. The strategic plan is focused on student learning and refining teaching practices.

5C. As a part of strategic planning, student demographic and achievement data are reviewed and analyzed.

5D. A research-driven approach is used to identify problems and solutions.

5E. Extensive communication ensures that all stakeholders are a part of the decision-making process.

5F. An action plan describes the steps to be taken toward attainment of the goals.

5G. The strategic plan is put into action with fidelity.

5H. The school monitors progress toward attainment of the goals and makes adjustments when appropriate.

Characteristic 5A: Planning Process

Summary of Research

The concept of management as a science made its debut in the 1950s. In more recent decades, we've learned a lot from the private sector and have begun to apply its theories to nonprofit work or to public services such as public education. We learned from Peter Drucker, perhaps the greatest management thinker of the last century, that workers should be treated as assets, not as liabilities. He helped us to understand that the result of a business is a satisfied customer. He states, "The result of a hospital is a healed patient, the result of a school is a student who has learned something and puts it to work ten years later" (Rosenstein, 2001, p. 1). Drucker contends that management needs to start with the intended results and organize the resources of the institution to attain those results.

Mike Schmoker (2001, p. 120) states that "the single most important event of the school year is the time we set aside for annual planning." He advocates for a new and much more direct model of school improvement and outlines the steps that schools can take to make this process successful (pp. 120–22):

- Use simple forms and templates.

- Apply explicit planning procedures.

- Set annual measurable achievement goals.

- Use data to identify areas of strength and challenge.

- Set regular times when teachers will meet in teams to improve instruction to reach the goals.

- Stress productive teamwork.

- Support teacher-conducted research and development.

Researchers from England's National College for School Leadership looked at 23 strategically focused schools to determine their understandings of strategic processes, approaches, and leadership. Examining issues of sustainability and capacity-building, the researchers found that these schools had developed a planning framework based on a balance of short- and long-term planning, as opposed to generating the traditional list of detailed actions or the all-too-familiar vague long-range plans. Strategically focused schools "recognize different approaches to strategic development and deliberately deploy those approaches," all of which are focused on the core purpose of schooling and on meaningful solutions (Davies, Davies, & Ellison, 2005, p. 74).

Organizational-change consultant Jim Collins (2001) writes that we must all make a *"stop-doing* list" (p. 139). We must stop doing anything and everything that doesn't get us the results we want. In a study of 1,435 organizations, Collins set out to identify what separates good companies from great companies. He found that highly focused team efforts create tangible results when conducted with simplicity and diligence.

The Rubric

A review team wanting to determine how a school's strategic planning measures up against the benchmark of Characteristic 5A would look at two traits of that characteristic. The rubric in Table 5.1 describes each trait as it manifests in low-performing, effective, and high-performing schools.

Table 5.1: Rubric for Characteristic 5A

Characteristic	Trait	Effectiveness Continuum		
		Low Performing	Effective	High Performing
5A. There is a process in place, and support for, schoolwide strategic planning.	5A1. Process for strategic planning	No process is in place for the development of strategic plans.	There are explicit procedures in place for the development of schoolwide strategic plans.	There are explicit procedures in place for the development of schoolwide strategic plans, and the process is aligned with district planning processes.
	5A2. Support for strategic planning	The staff does not support schoolwide strategic planning.	The staff supports schoolwide strategic planning.	There is school and district support for schoolwide strategic planning.

Characteristic 5B: Focus on Student Learning and Refining Teaching Practices

Summary of Research

Michael Fullan has spent years studying the power of collaborative work cultures focused on student learning. He argues that collaboration makes a difference only when it is "focused on student performance for all" (Fullan, 2001b, p. 254). He points out that "new policies that promulgate high standards of practice for all teachers invite the possibility of large-scale reform. A corresponding set of policies are required to create many opportunities, in fact requirements, for people to examine their day-to-day practice" (p. 260). These policies need to be formalized to ensure both clarity and the participation of all teachers.

Mike Schmoker (2001) highlights strategies from five dramatically improved school districts. Each of these districts provides a structure that allows teachers to regularly and collaboratively review assessment data in order to improve practice. They focus on results and are obsessive about productive teamwork. Schmoker calls such strategies "organized teacher expertise" (p. 1). He believes that these districts experienced exceptional improvement by "setting goals (few in number); using data to identify areas of lowest performance; and then finding, creating, and continuously refining better ways to teach using a baseline and measuring the number of students who actually learn the specific targeted skills" (Schmoker, 2002, pp. 4–5).

Notably, neither Fullan, Schmoker, nor Collins is a proponent of complex strategic plans. Fullan believes that comprehensive planning often leads to fragmentation and overload. As mentioned earlier, Schmoker advocates for a simple plan that focuses on the structures essential to instructional improvement. Collins (2001) found that companies that went from "good to great" did not invest in long, drawn-out planning processes. In fact, there was "no evidence that the good to great companies spent more time on strategic planning than the comparison companies" (p. 119).

Just as Jim Collins set out to discover what was behind the success of 11 good to great companies, Arizona State University took a close look at 12 high-performing elementary and middle schools in Arizona

(Morrison Institute for Public Policy, 2006). These 12 "beat-the-odds" schools, which had primarily Latino student populations and high percentages of students living in poverty, were compared to similar schools that were performing poorly in reading and mathematics. Two major themes emerged from this research that apply directly to the topics of management and planning: "collaborative solutions" and "built to suit."

The concept of collaborative solutions incorporates the elements of effective work teams and collaboration. Effective teams consist of "people with a wide spectrum of talents who not only tackle projects together, but also engage in real teamwork" (Morrison Institute for Public Policy, 2006, p. 7). Responsibility for school improvement does not rely on a few top leaders but instead is distributed among all staff members, "who are given real ownership and then *buy in* to the idea of candidly identifying problems and actively solving them" (p. 7). The collaborative solution approach includes the following elements:

- Involve teachers and other staff members in the analysis of data.

- Analyze a wide variety of data and other evidence.

- Involve teachers in identifying possible solutions to problems.

- Use data and explore evidence-based practices to decide on solutions.

- Provide targeted training at convenient times.

- Schedule time to allow teachers to meet and work together.

- Assign staff members based on skills and experiences.

- Institutionalize an ongoing change process.

- Engage teachers as problem-solvers.

The concept of built to suit is centered on student-based, targeted, data-driven planning. The 12 successful Arizona schools sought to meet state standards by "placing a relentless focus on individual performance—a vital cycle of instruction, assessment, and intervention, followed by more instruction, assessment, and intervention" (p. 7). These schools put in place a "set of interlocking practices" (p. 40) to address the individual needs of students and kept analyzing the data and tweaking the approach to ensure each student's success. The key here is customizing each student's education and maintaining a structure of flexibility to meet each student's needs.

The Rubric

A review team wanting to determine how a school's strategic planning measures up against the benchmark of Characteristic 5B would look at two traits of that characteristic. The rubric in Table 5.2 describes each trait as it manifests in low-performing, effective, and high-performing schools.

Characteristic 5C: Data Analysis

Summary of Research

The achievement gap is the focus of many federal programs. As performance-based accountability systems are the key to accessing funds and reporting progress, data are critical. Data integrity becomes a make-or-break factor. In planning data collection for school strategic planning, it is important to make

Table 5.2: Rubric for Characteristic 5B

Characteristic	Trait	Effectiveness Continuum		
		Low Performing	Effective	High Performing
5B. The strategic plan is focused on student learning and refining teaching practices.	5B1. Focus of strategic plan	There is no strategic plan, or the plan is not focused on student learning.	The plan is focused on student learning and the implementation of strategies to improve student learning.	The plan is focused on student learning, and identified teacher teams are responsible for implementing explicit strategies for improving student learning.
	5B2. Built-in opportunities for teachers to work collaboratively	The plan does not include structured opportunities for teachers to work collaboratively to refine teaching practices.	The plan includes structured opportunities for teachers to work collaboratively to refine teaching practices.	The plan includes structured opportunities for teachers and paraprofessionals to work collaboratively to refine teaching practices.

sure that the data will be accurate (which means that the data are controlled for variables), reliable (which means that results are similar under similar conditions), valid (which means that the data measure what they are intended to measure), and sufficiently granular (which means that there is an adequate degree of data disaggregation).

As the world gets flatter (according to Thomas Friedman, 2005) and information exchange moves faster and faster, there is too much at risk if important school decisions are made based on hope, intuition, or past practice with no evidence of effectiveness. We've all seen examples of improvement efforts that were inefficient and misguided when soft data or no data were used to establish needs, set goals, and measure progress. In contrast, "real school improvement begins when school administrators use data to address real issues, create realistic goals, and track their progress to support continuous improvement" (Learning Point Associates, 2006a, p. 1).

A longitudinal case study by the Northeast and Islands Regional Educational Laboratory examined how five low-performing, high-poverty urban secondary schools used data to inform school improvement. Researchers Mary Lachat and Stephen Smith found that not having timely access to student performance and demographic data can be a major barrier. This study reaffirmed other research that shows that disaggregating data by student demographics and participation in specific programs or interventions is a key element of improved data use. The study also found that when school staff members discussed and analyzed student performance data together, their comfort level with that work increased, and they began to use data more frequently to inform curriculum decisions (Learning Point Associates, 2006b).

Researchers at the Southwest Educational Development Laboratory (SEDL) looked at the data collected and managed by state education agencies in Arkansas, Louisiana, New Mexico, and Texas and found that "student, school, and district characteristics are available in education databases in all four of the study states and are of critical value in understanding the relative influence of student, school, and district environments on resources and student performance" (Pan et al., 2005, p. vii). Nonetheless, the researchers concluded that

> state education data are underutilized and policy audiences need (a) to expand the use of existing education data to support decision making on instructional resources; (b) to examine data on both resources and student performance to better understand how education inputs and expected outputs relate; and (c) to incorporate data on student, school, and district characteristics when examining education resource issues. (pp. 8–9)

The Data Quality Campaign (DQC) of the National Center for Educational Accountability promotes the effective use of data in schools to improve student learning. In case studies of schools' and districts' use of data, a DQC researcher found that "using both formative and other longitudinal data leads to improved performance at the student, school, and district levels" (Laird, 2006, p. 1). One of the case study schools, which emphasized program evaluation, analyzed student achievement outcomes after implementing a new writing program and found a "68 percentage point improvement over four years" (Laird, 2006, p. 2). This type of long-term data collection and analysis is at the core of effective school improvement. In addition, using detailed data on individual students, preferably over several years, provides educators with information to identify problem areas in instruction.

The DQC report (Laird, 2006, p. 3) recommends that teachers should take the following actions:

- Tailor instructional decisions for individual students based on results of both formative and annual student-level summative assessments, disaggregating data by content area and standard.

- Compare student achievement results by skill and subject with the results of students in other classes in the building to identify and share instructional techniques that increase student achievement.

- Review and ensure the quality of the data being reported on [their] students to account for missing students, students that are counted twice, and so on.

Schools should take the following actions:

- Use data and comparisons with other schools to identify the school's stronger and weaker areas. School comparisons that take students' prior achievement and length of enrollment into account are more informative.

- Base school improvement plans on this analysis and ensure that the data are used to determine areas of focus and resource allocation.

- Ensure that teachers have regular opportunities to access and use data individually and in teams to review and gauge student learning and alter their instruction accordingly.

- Provide ongoing professional development to teachers on how to use data as a tool to improve instruction.

The Rubric

A review team wanting to determine how a school's strategic planning measures up against the benchmark of Characteristic 5C would look at two traits of that characteristic. The rubric in Table 5.3 describes each trait as it manifests in low-performing, effective, and high-performing schools.

Table 5.3: Rubric for Characteristic 5C

Characteristic	Trait	Effectiveness Continuum		
		Low Performing	Effective	High Performing
5C. As a part of strategic planning, student demographic and achievement data are reviewed and analyzed.	**5C1. Analysis of achievement data**	Student achievement data are not analyzed as part of strategic planning.	Overall and disaggregated student achievement data are analyzed as part of strategic planning.	Overall and disaggregated student achievement and program performance data are analyzed as part of strategic planning.
	5C2. Analysis of nonacademic data	Nonacademic data are not reviewed or are not disaggregated and analyzed as part of strategic planning.	Nonacademic data, including discipline, attendance, and graduation rates, are disaggregated and analyzed as part of strategic planning.	Nonacademic data, including trends over time, are disaggregated and analyzed as part of strategic planning.

Characteristic 5D: Research-Driven Identification of Problems and Solutions

Summary of Research

After identifying and studying the 11 most successful companies (organizations that had sustained results) Jim Collins (2001) advocates for a "Council" approach to focus on the basic principle driving the organization. In the case of education, this basic principle is increasing student learning, and the council is the school planning team. Collins describes the features of such a council as follows:

+ It exists to understand important issues.

+ It consists of 5 to 12 people.

+ Each member should be motivated by a search for understanding (not self-interest).

+ Members are respectful toward one another.

+ Membership includes a range of perspectives.

+ Each member has deep knowledge about some aspect of the organization.

+ The team includes management but is not limited to those in leadership roles.

- It is recognized (not ad hoc).

- It meets regularly.

- Final decisions remain with the lead executive.

To know what to do to influence student learning, the planning team must gain an accurate understanding of the school data. Learning Point Associates (2006a) developed an "Action Guide" to give educators direction in using data to improve schools and student achievement. This guide demystifies data analysis and outlines a process that school administrators can use to drive data-based decision-making. After discussing the collection and organization of achievement, demographic, program, and perception data, the guide describes how to analyze data patterns and generate hypotheses. The "guiding questions" at this stage are: "Why are our students performing the way they are? What in our systems and practices is causing our students to have these problems?" (p. 12). It is important to understand why a problem is occurring in order to set about a change process. The Data Quality Campaign recommends following student data over time and "looking at changes and variables to develop better hypotheses about what factors are most likely to be responsible for change" (Laird, 2006, p. 2).

The process of hypothesizing is most commonly associated with science. Before conducting an experiment, the scientist generates hypotheses as possible explanations of a phenomenon or circumstance. A hypothesis may include a prediction. This model is used in school improvement planning in order to focus the work on facts.

In order to generate hypotheses, members of the planning team will look at patterns they have identified in the data and then pose questions to help determine the underlying causes of gaps in student achievement or other problems. For example, they might ask, "Why are our students consistently performing 20 percentage points below our comparison school in mathematics?" "Why are our students getting to class late?" "Why are 68% of our third-graders meeting state reading standards, when only 45% of our fourth-graders are?" "Why are 60% of our white students meeting mathematics standards, when only 23% of our Hispanic students are?" The goal is to understand the root cause of the problem. The team considers several different answers to the questions, and those answers become hypotheses. The planning team selects the hypotheses best supported by the data (Learning Point Associates, 2006a).

If the planning process is well-managed, the hypothesis should lead directly into the development of aligned student learning goals. Goal setting is based on the data about problems and possible explanations. It is not based on a vote by staff members, district directives, or grant opportunities. Goals should reflect the exact needs of the student population. Well-written school improvement goals have the following characteristics: "clear . . . , data-based . . . , few in number . . . , measurable . . . , sustainable . . . , community driven . . . , [and] attainable" (Learning Point Associates, 2004, p. 17).

The current discussion in school improvement circles centers on whether there is a recipe for strategic planning or whether it is better to adopt a less directive approach. Based on the synthesis of five major research studies, Mid-continent Research for Education and Learning (McREL) found strengths in each approach in its publication "Success in Sight: A Comprehensive Approach to School Improvement" (Cicchinelli, Dean, Galvin, Goodwin, & Parsley, 2006). This guide provides a framework to examine issues that influence student success and identifies the first two stages of the school improvement process as taking stock and focusing on the right solution.

Taking stock includes an assessment of readiness for change and a forthright assessment of the factors that influence student needs. The research calls for linking quantitative data with qualitative data to evaluate what's really happening at the school: "Schools must learn to ask the right questions about their situation by examining the wide array of factors that influence student achievement—including district supports (or lack thereof), teachers' knowledge and skills, teachers' attitudes, and other external and internal factors that influence student achievement" (Cicchinelli et al., 2006, p. 10).

While devoting precious time to developing mission and vision statements is controversial, taking time to identify where the school is and where it wants to be in relationship to student achievement is foundational. In this case, vision has more to do with articulating what success looks like and linking goals with energy. Initially, "identifying what people are passionate about and tapping this energy is necessary to help everyone take ownership of the actions they will decide to take later" (p. 11).

Focusing on the right solution means first determining the right problem to solve. We've all seen times when well-meaning educators misidentify the problem and devote time, energy, and resources to what seems like a good solution with little or no positive results to show for their efforts. For example, a school with low student achievement in reading selects a research-based intervention to supplement the core English/language arts program. But if the true cause of low student achievement in reading is that the teachers are not adequately trained to teach reading, the program is unlikely to result in expected gains in student achievement.

The McREL guide recommends focusing on one or two research-based strategies. The researchers write, "Successful schools . . . always keep student learning at the forefront, adopting as their mantra the question, *How are we improving student learning?* They ask themselves whether proposed changes (or resistance to them) are related to improving student learning or making life easier for adults" (p. 12).

The Rubric

A review team wanting to determine how a school's strategic planning measures up against the benchmark of Characteristic 5D would look at two traits of that characteristic. The rubric in Table 5.4 (page 94) describes each trait as it manifests in low-performing, effective, and high-performing schools.

Characteristic 5E: Communication and Shared Decision-Making

Summary of Research

Communication with a wide variety of stakeholders in the school improvement process is important to ensure the generation of diverse ideas, buy-in to the strategies, and sustainability. For example, when student achievement in reading is lagging, there will be a number of hypotheses regarding the cause of the problem and a number of possible solutions. The solutions could be anything from aligning curriculum to the standards to designing a summer school program for students falling behind. Seeking broad stakeholder input and discussing challenges and solutions ensures transparency and can lead to public commitment.

As noted in the discussion of Characteristic 5B, Arizona State University's study of beat-the-odds schools found that in those schools responsibility for school improvement was not concentrated in a few administrators but was shared among the teachers and staff members. One of the "steady climber" schools

Table 5.4: Rubric for Characteristic 5D

Characteristic	Trait	Effectiveness Continuum		
		Low Performing	Effective	High Performing
5D. A research-driven approach is used to identify problems and solutions.	5D1. Depth of solutions	The proposed solutions to identified problems may not address underlying causes.	The planning team studied the problems identified in the data analysis to determine underlying causes and possible solutions.	The planning team studied the problems identified in the data analysis and used internal and external resources to validate its conclusions about underlying causes.
	5D2. Quality of hypothesis	A hypothesis was not developed or did not fully address the identified problems.	A hypothesis was developed that fully addressed the identified problems.	With input from staff members and a wide variety of stakeholders, a hypothesis was developed that fully addressed the identified problems.

identified in that study was Sierra Middle School. Sierra moved from a top-down management style to grassroots leadership in order to design and implement a school improvement process that would be supported by all staff members. Three committees were created in which every staff member was included. The committees were responsible for researching where and how to make instructional improvements, and "the result was a plan that teachers bought into" (Morrison Institute for Public Policy, 2006, p. 34). While eighth-grade math scores on the Arizona Instrument to Measure Standards were steadily declining until 2000, between 2000 and 2004, the years when the collaborative school improvement plan was implemented, eighth-grade math scores increased from 4% proficient to 50% proficient (Arizona Department of Education, 2008).

McREL (2003, p. 2) found that "communicating both the purpose and results of data analysis to all stakeholders is critical for schools that want to sustain improvement efforts." This communication needs to be ongoing and is most effective when it includes "discussions that provide opportunities for stakeholders to participate in decision making" (p. 3). Such an approach results in "sounder strategies and policies and greater understanding and support at all levels" (p. 2). Bringing stakeholders together to accomplish goals has been referred to as creating a "purposeful community" (Cicchinelli et al., 2006, p. 15).

Collins (2001, p. 63) refers to collaborative decision-making as "confronting the brutal facts—yet never losing faith," and he identifies it as one of six distinctive characteristics contributing to breakthrough performance. Collins gives the example of Kroger and A&P, two well-established companies, each in business over 80 years and both with nearly all their assets in traditional grocery stores. Kroger confronted the brutal facts of reality head-on, completely changing its entire system, while A&P stuck to its 100-year-old model of success. Kroger became the number-one grocery store in America in 1999. In that same year, A&P dwindled to a fraction of its former stature.

Collins attributes Kroger's success throughout the three decades from 1970 to 2000 to a "series of good decisions, diligently executed, and accumulated one on top of the other" (p. 69). But the question is, How do you make this happen? Collins' research supports four important strategies that directly apply to improving schools through collaborative decision-making (pp. 74–80):

1. Lead with questions, not answers [use genuine curiosity to search for understanding].

2. Engage in dialogue and debate, not coercion [use a scientific perspective to search for the best answers].

3. Conduct autopsies, without blame [use retrospect to search for learning].

4. Build red flag mechanisms that turn information into information that cannot be ignored [use stakeholder input to establish a climate of truth].

Strategic planning is an inclusive process. In other words, people who have a stake in the work of the organization participate in the planning as appropriate, and "interested individuals have a chance to be heard by the decision-makers" (Alliance for Nonprofit Management, n.d., FAQ 2). An inclusive planning process has the following attributes:

- It builds both internal and external enthusiasm and commitment to the school and its strategies.

- It allows individuals to take on ownership of the goals and efforts to achieve the stated outcomes.

- It ensures that data reflect the needs and perceptions of internal individuals and external constituents.

- It incorporates objectivity into the process so that insiders and outsiders can ask critical questions.

- It develops foundations for future working relationships.

- It develops uniformity of purpose among all stakeholders.

- It establishes a continual information exchange among staff, administrators, families, and other key stakeholders. (Alliance for Nonprofit Management, n.d.)

Ideally, all key stakeholders should be involved in the planning process at some level. Key stakeholders are those persons who can either significantly help or significantly hinder the implementation of the school improvement plan (Alliance for Nonprofit Management, n.d.). They include:

- School board members—responsible for governing and interested in overall district goals, policies, and system success

- District staff members—the link between the school board goals and the activities of the district

- School staff members—most knowledgeable about critical success factors and staff interrelationships and intimately involved with students and families

+ Clients—the students and families served by the school

+ Other external stakeholders—neighborhood leaders, community liaisons, volunteers, and partner agencies

In their study of 23 strategically focused schools, Davies et al. (2005) found a common emphasis on discussion and dialogue. They state that "one of the most powerful insights from the research was the significance of strategic conversations.... Strategic conversations were a central tool in guiding the leaders' own understanding by sharing initial ideas with others. They are also a key element in developing distributed leadership" (p. 73).

Regular dialogue and ongoing conversations consistently reinforce the direction in which the school is headed and the laserlike focus on implementing the school strategic plan.

The Rubric

A review team wanting to determine how a school's strategic planning measures up against the benchmark of Characteristic 5E would look at three traits of that characteristic. The rubric in Table 5.5 describes each trait as it manifests in low-performing, effective, and high-performing schools.

Characteristic 5F: Action Plan

Summary of Research

A discussion of the difference between strategic planning and long-range planning is useful to ensure that the scope of the school improvement plan is indeed strategic. Long-range planning is generally considered to mean the development of "a plan to accomplish a goal or set of goals over a period of several years" (Alliance for Nonprofit Management, n.d., FAQ 1). This way of operating might have been appropriate in the early years of management theory, when the American economy was slower paced and thus more predictable. In the 1950s and 1960s, we knew what jobs to prepare our students for. In the 21st century, we cannot predict what jobs will be available for today's kindergarten students 12 years later. Therefore, it is imperative that schools adopt a strategic planning model that is responsive to changes in the environment.

At this point in the strategic planning process, the data have been collected and analyzed, the critical issues identified, the research into targeted solutions completed, the input from stakeholders integrated, and the goals agreed upon. The next step is to draft a final planning document and to distribute it to all stakeholders for review. Revisions should not drag out over weeks, but any important questions that have been raised should be answered.

Learning Point Associates (2006a) state that "goals are meaningless unless action backs up the commitment" (p. 14). This part of the school improvement process takes forward the accepted hypotheses and identifies a number of actions that will move the school toward its improvement goals. Learning Point Associates offer the following guidelines for selecting strategies while also cautioning that strategies are "commitments to carry out real action" (p. 15). Strategies should be:

• Clear and understandable

• Based on best practice

Table 5.5: Rubric for Characteristic 5E

Characteristic	Trait	Effectiveness Continuum		
		Low Performing	Effective	High Performing
5E. Extensive communication ensures that all stakeholders are a part of the decision-making process.	5E1. Stakeholders' participation in planning discussions	The school does not encourage stakeholders to take part in discussions of school challenges and potential solutions.	The school encourages stakeholders to take part in discussions of school challenges and potential solutions.	A variety of stakeholders take part in discussions of school challenges and potential solutions.
	5E2. Circulation of draft plans	Staff members and families have limited or no opportunities to review and comment on draft plans.	Draft plans are circulated to school staff members and made available to families for review and comment.	Draft plans are circulated to staff members and made available to families for review and comment. Staff members are given time during the school day to provide input on the draft plans.
	5E3. District review of plans	District staff members do not review the plans.	Senior district staff members review and approve the plans to ensure coordination with district efforts.	Senior district staff members review and approve the plans to ensure coordination with district efforts. District staff members who are knowledgeable about the research base on which the plan relies review the plan to ensure consistency with current educational research.

- Observable and measurable

- Directly tied to accomplishing the goal

- Endorsed by planning team members

- Assignable to a person or group

- Doable

The Rubric

A review team wanting to determine how a school's strategic planning measures up against the benchmark of Characteristic 5F would look at two traits of that characteristic. The rubric in Table 5.6 describes each trait as it manifests in low-performing, effective, and high-performing schools.

Table 5.6: Rubric for Characteristic 5F

Characteristic	Trait	Effectiveness Continuum		
		Low Performing	Effective	High Performing
5F. An action plan describes the steps to be taken toward attainment of the goals.	5F1. Identification of sequence and responsibilities	The action plan does not specify the sequence of actions, nor does it identify specific individual or team responsibilities.	An action plan, including a time line and interim checkpoints, lays out a sequence of actions to be completed by specific individuals or teams.	An action plan, including a time line and interim checkpoints, lays out a sequence of actions to be completed by specific individuals or teams, and a monitoring process is in place.
	5F2. Specificity of learning goals	Student learning goals are not specific or measurable or do not address the identified problems.	Student learning goals are specific and measurable and directly address the identified problems.	Student learning goals are specific and measurable and directly address the identified problems. Progress is being made toward reaching the goals.

Characteristic 5G: Fidelity of Implementation

Summary of Research

In this stage of strategic planning, the school planning team moves from analyzing data and planning to action. The planning team must be cognizant of each individual's commitment to taking real action and needs to be aware of how easy it is for school staff members to avoid making waves in a meeting and just as easily avoid accepting their share of the load when it comes to carrying out the work. The McREL guide points out that "agreements only translate into effective action when they are specific and agreed to by all. Therefore, it is vitally important to develop shared agreements that make it clear how everyone in the school will work together to improve student achievement" (Cicchinelli et al., 2006, p. 14). There are three key steps in taking collective action (p. 14):

- Establish shared ownership of the school improvement plan.

- Create shared agreements for accomplishing goals.

- Develop deep knowledge and skills needed to improve student learning.

Shared agreements describe specifically *"what* teachers will do in their classrooms and with their students to move the school toward success and *how* they will be held responsible for living up to their end of the bargain" (p. 14). Will they administer common assessments? Will they analyze the results with their team? Will they revise lessons as a team? Will they group and regroup students every 6 weeks? These agreements make it less likely that people will fall back into familiar routines and impede progress toward goals. The McREL guide stresses that

> it's important to recognize that in order to translate research into action in every classroom, schools must help teachers learn not only what to do, but also how and why to do it. Know-how usually comes with practice, by giving teachers time to apply new research-based practices in their own classrooms and to share what they are learning with one another. (Cicchinelli et al., 2006, p. 14)

Researchers from McREL wanted to determine the common characteristics of schools in which student achievement had dramatically improved. One such school was Alcester-Hudson Elementary School in South Dakota, which had been identified as "in need of improvement" in 2002, leaving the staff members embarrassed and humiliated. They had always thought of their school as a good school. In looking back, however, they realized they needed a wake-up call. They spent 3 years working on school improvement, and on their most recent statewide assessment, 94% of their students reached proficiency on state math tests, and 100% reached proficiency in reading. The researchers (Cicchinelli et al., 2006, p. 16) identified seven keys to their success:

1. Distributing leadership

2. Getting on the same page

3. Getting hooked on data

4. Staying focused

5. Looking to research for answers

6. Building a professional learning community

7. Recognizing that from little things, big things grow

Unless dedicated resources are built into the school strategic plan, there may not be enough fuel to get the work done. Michael Fullan (2001a, p. 64) writes, "Instructional improvement requires additional resources in the form of materials, equipment, space, time, and access to new ideas and expertise." His research in schools leads him to believe that "successful schools are much better at addressing their resource needs" (p. 65).

Fullan's work has been confirmed by Marzano, Waters, and McNulty (2005), who found that garnering resources is a key leadership responsibility. Strategic planning needs to be given a dedicated budget to ensure that this work is on par with other budgeted activities and services.

The Rubric

A review team wanting to determine how a school's strategic planning measures up against the benchmark of Characteristic 5G would look at three traits of that characteristic. The rubric in Table 5.7 (page 100) describes each trait as it manifests in low-performing, effective, and high-performing schools.

Table 5.7: Rubric for Characteristic 5G

Characteristic	Trait	Effectiveness Continuum		
		Low Performing	Effective	High Performing
5G. The strategic plan is put into action with fidelity.	5G1. Agreement on action plan	Schoolwide agreement on how the goals will be accomplished is not reached.	Schoolwide, shared agreements are reached on how the goals will be accomplished.	Schoolwide, shared agreements are reached on how the goals will be accomplished, and each person's role in meeting those goals is clearly articulated in the plan.
	5G2. Adherence to schedule	Planned activities are not completed within the specified time lines.	Planned activities are completed within the specified time lines.	Planned activities are completed before the specified deadlines.
	5G3. Allocation of resources	Resources are not allocated or are not adequate for the activities described in the plan.	Adequate resources are allocated for the activities described in the plan.	Resources are allocated for the activities described in the plan and are monitored for adequacy.

Characteristic 5H: Monitoring and Adjustment Process

Summary of Research

Evaluating progress toward goals is the final step in the ongoing process of strategic planning. Mike Schmoker (2001) recommends that staff members begin each school year by reexamining their strategic plan. Specifically, they should take the following steps:

+ Take stock of the previous year's accomplishments.

+ Review key data, including disaggregated performance data, grade distribution, course completion, attendance, and climate and satisfaction surveys.

+ Select one or two subject area targets.

+ Design measurable goals specifically targeted to improved student achievement.

+ Provide the goals to the district office administration team for feedback.

+ Collect and discuss classroom-tested research relevant to selected goals.

+ Design at least four simple assessments to be administered by all teachers.

+ Set times for short, monthly school improvement meetings to analyze assessment data, discuss activity toward goals, and update quarterly data charts to display progress.

+ Recognize specific goal-oriented efforts and accomplishments by individuals and teams.

Michael Fullan (2001b, p. 101) states that "solving today's educational problems is complex, it *is* rocket science." He advocates for developing a learning organization and a deep understanding of what change is, from the perspective of people experiencing it. Fullan identifies 10 principles of successful educational change (pp. 108–10):

1. Stakeholders must be allowed to exchange and continually develop ideas.

2. Clarification and adjustments should be made through reflective practice.

3. Conflict and disagreement is healthy and valuable for learning.

4. Pressure to change must be coupled with opportunity for discourse and problem-solving.

5. Recognize that innovative change can take 2–3 years and institutional change can take 5–10 years.

6. Resistance to change is not necessarily the reason for lack of implementation.

7. Focus on increasing the number of people actively engaged in the change process.

8. The plan must be evolutionary and based on knowledge of change processes.

9. Action decisions should be based on a combination of knowledge, political considerations, local context, and intuition.

10. The goal is to impact the culture.

Grant Wiggins and Jay McTighe (2007) use an architectural analogy, speaking of schooling as a building and reform as renovation. They identify six pillars upon which the building rests. One of them is

> an overall strategy of reform centered on the constant exploration of the gap between the explicit vision of reform versus the current reality of schooling; in other words, a feedback and adjustment system that is ongoing, timely, and robust enough to enable all teachers and students to change course en route, as needed, to achieve the desired results. (p. 2)

Wiggins and McTighe (pp. 4–5) identify a three-step cycle on which successful school reform efforts rely:

• An increasingly clear and powerful vision of where we want to end up, based on our mission and agreed-upon learning principles.

• A constant and unflinching assessment of where we stand at present against the mission.

• Timely adjustments based on regular analysis of the gap between vision and reality, between goals and results.

They refer to a "backward-design orientation," which "suggests that we think carefully about the evidence we need to show that we have achieved the desired results" (p. 204). They call for using questions to evaluate success, determine the gap between the goal and reality, track progress, and make timely adjustments to the plan. Midcourse corrections are simply part of the process, and "success depends on both thoughtful planning and timely and effective adjustments" (p. 209). Success also depends on avoiding the common temptation to assess actions—such as how much time was spent on professional development or whether curriculum maps were developed—rather than results. They caution that "today's educational leaders must remain vigilant about the confusion between means and ends by constantly reminding staff of the desired results: improved learning" (p. 235).

McREL's guide to school improvement points out that

> to sustain improvement efforts, schools must create a shared vision for success, which helps them work and learn together to improve student outcomes. At the same time, they need to create a culture that relies on data to plan, implement, and sustain reform through ongoing professional learning, thoughtful resource allocation, and effective communication. (Cicchinelli et al., 2006, p. 19)

The goals of this continuous process of identifying new opportunities and building on success are increasing efficacy, increasing capacity, and increasing sustainability (pp. 20–21).

Researchers from McKinsey & Company studied 25 of the world's school systems, including 10 of the top performers, to identify what they had in common and what tools they used to improve student outcomes. They found that the successful systems had three strategies in place: "1) getting the right people to become teachers, 2) developing the teachers into effective instructors, and 3) ensuring the system is able to deliver the best possible instruction for every child" (Barber & Mourshed, 2007, p. 6).

The study also found that the very best systems "set high expectations for what each and every child should achieve, and then monitor performance against the expectations, intervening whenever they are not met" (p. 34). These schools intervene at the level of the individual student to deploy effective instruction. The authors write, "All of the top-performing systems recognize that they cannot improve what they do not measure" (p. 35). The study identifies two mechanisms for monitoring the quality of teaching and learning: examinations that test what students know, understand, and can do, based on an objective measure; and school reviews of performance on a set of indicators that measure both the outcomes and the input processes. They assert that an external review process is critical for struggling schools to make steps toward identifying specific areas that are in need of improvement. Typically as the school system improves, the capacity is built to transfer this function from an external review process to the schools themselves (Barber & Mourshed, 2007, pp. 35–36).

The Rubric

A review team wanting to determine how a school's strategic planning measures up against the benchmark of Characteristic 5H would look at two traits of that characteristic. The rubric in Table 5.8 describes each trait as it manifests in low-performing, effective, and high-performing schools.

Table 5.8: Rubric for Characteristic 5H

Characteristic	Trait	Effectiveness Continuum		
		Low Performing	Effective	High Performing
5H. The school monitors progress toward attainment of the goals and makes adjustments when appropriate.	**5H1. Evaluation of plan's impact**	There is infrequent or no evaluation of the plan's impact on student learning.	At least annually, the staff evaluates the plan's impact on student learning.	The staff frequently evaluates the plan's impact on student learning.
	5H2. Data-based adjustments	There is no process for adjusting the plan in response to student performance data.	Formative and summative student achievement data are used to adjust the plan as needed.	Formative and summative student achievement data and other data, such as attendance, dropout, and discipline data, are used to adjust the plan as needed.

Conclusion

While the strategic planning process may seem linear, it is in reality circular. It requires adopting a mind-set of continuous hypothesizing and analysis and an intense focus on student learning. It is an overlapping, integrated process, much like conducting and playing in a symphony orchestra: the score is the plan, each instrument is tuned and has a part, the musicians know what to do and when, the sections collaborate and synchronize, the group practices and refines, and eventually the piece is performed. It is not performed once, but again and again, and with each iteration, evaluated and improved. The orchestra members have high expectations for excellence, they know exactly what the music should sound like, and they depend on one another to collectively reach the goal. Much like the process that goes into rehearsing and delivering a symphonic masterpiece, strategic planning is a public commitment to purposeful actions.

CHAPTER

6

Effectiveness Indicator 6
Professional Development

Education is not the filling of a pail, but the lighting of a fire.

—William Butler Yeats

The professional development program is centered on ensuring that all children learn to high levels. In effective schools, professional development deepens and refines teachers' knowledge and skills in content and pedagogy. From this principle, we derive Effectiveness Indicator 6. An on-site school review examines the professional development program to find if it is based on student outcome data and is collaborative, sustained, intensive, and closely tied to the classroom. The review also looks at whether the program addresses teacher needs, including those of teachers new to the profession.

Eight characteristics define Effectiveness Indicator 6: Professional Development:

6A. The professional development program is focused on improving student learning by deepening the knowledge and skills of educators in their subject matter and in pedagogy.

6B. The professional development program is based on an analysis of student achievement data and learning needs, is coherent with state standards, and complements the instructional program.

6C. Professional development is collaborative, is job-embedded, and addresses both individual and schoolwide needs.

6D. Professional development is ongoing and sustained over time.

6E. Professional development builds cultural proficiency.

6F. Professional development explicitly addresses the needs of teachers new to the profession.

6G. The professional development program has adequate resources.

6H. An evaluation of program effectiveness is an integral part of professional development.

Characteristic 6A: Emphasis on Knowledge of Subject Matter and Pedagogy

Summary of Research

How important is professional development? In a 1991 study of factors having the greatest impact on student learning, Ronald Ferguson analyzed student achievement in 900 Texas school districts enrolling over 2,000,000 students. He found that among all school-related factors, teacher expertise was the most important element in student achievement, accounting for about 40% of the total effect (Darling-Hammond & Ball, 1997).

In a 1997 literature review, Linda Darling-Hammond and Deborah Ball looked at the Texas research and found that "the effects were so strong, and the variations in teacher expertise were so great, that the large disparities in achievement between black and white students were almost entirely accounted for by differences in the qualifications of their teachers." Taking this one step further, they noted that "every additional dollar spent on more highly qualified teachers netted greater increases in student achievement than did any other use of school resources" (p. 2). In general, they observed, "teacher expertise—or what teachers know and can do—affects . . . how judiciously they select from texts and other materials and how effectively they present material in class . . . and how well they can understand and interpret students' talk and written work" (p. 2).

To be effective in increasing the learning of all students, teachers need considerable knowledge and expertise in their subject matter, general pedagogy, and content-specific pedagogy (Elmore, 2002; Puma & Raphael, 2001; Resnick, 2005).

- Content knowledge is the in-depth knowledge of the subject matter to be taught.

- General pedagogy is the understanding of how children learn and the ability to use that knowledge skillfully.

- Content-specific pedagogy is expertise in effective instructional, assessment, and intervention practices that are specific to an individual subject area.

Knowledge and skill in one area can never make up for deficits in the other two. We sometimes work with schools that have concentrated all of their professional development efforts in only one area, such as subject-matter knowledge, or have designed professional development plans around only pedagogical concerns, such as effective instructional techniques. This narrow focus never nets them the hoped-for results in student learning. It is not sufficient to know everything about a subject if one does not understand how students learn. Conversely, being the very best at instructional strategies is a hollow accomplishment if those strategies are not in aid of delivering high-quality subject-matter knowledge. Again, expertise in assessment will not result in the hoped-for gains if it is not partnered with knowledge about how and when to employ specific interventions that will address the individual or group needs identified by those assessments.

A study that examined the mathematics and science achievement of more than 7,000 eighth-graders who participated in the 1996 National Assessment of Educational Progress (NAEP) confirmed the importance of a fully developed spectrum of teacher professional development. Researchers found that "student achievement was influenced by both (1) teacher content background and (2) teacher education/professional development coursework, especially in how to work with diverse student populations and students with special needs" (National Council for Accreditation of Teacher Education, 2005, p. 2).

A research review by the Committee on Science and Mathematics Teacher Preparation (2000, p. 49) noted similar results, finding that "teachers' subject matter understanding and their pedagogical orientations and decisions critically influence the quality of their teaching." The committee, a part of the National Research Council, also concluded that teachers' "capacity to pose questions, select tasks, evaluate their pupil's understanding, and to make curricular decisions all depend on how they themselves understand the subject matter" (p. 49).

Darling-Hammond and Ball (1997) found that teacher knowledge and skills in content and pedagogy are directly related to teacher effectiveness.

> Reviews of several hundred studies contradict the axiom that "anyone can teach" and that "teachers are born and not made." Teacher education, as it turns out, matters a great deal . . . and those with greater training are found to be more effective than those with less. (p. 5)

Since the late 1990s, there has been a renewed emphasis on content preparation for teachers, and rightly so, as research has shown that the "degree to which professional development was focused on content knowledge has been directly related to teachers' reported increases in pupil knowledge and skills" (Education Alliance, 2005, p. 4). Deep subject-matter knowledge is essential. Yet research is also clear that it is the power of all three dimensions of teacher knowledge taken together (content, pedagogy, and content-specific pedagogy) that leads to the greatest increases in student learning (Elmore, 2002; Resnick, 2005).

In the spring and summer of 1998, Michael Garet and his colleagues studied results from a nationally representative survey that was part of an evaluation of the Eisenhower Professional Development Program. They found that

> both content focus and coherence have substantial positive effects on enhanced knowledge and skills (.33 and .42), indicating that activities that give greater emphasis to content and that are better connected to teachers' other professional development experiences and other reform efforts are more likely to produce enhanced knowledge and skills. (Garet, Porter, Desimone, Birman, & Yoon, 2001, p. 933)

In a study that examined teacher beliefs about professional development, teachers reported that a focus on content knowledge was one of two elements that had "the greatest effect on their knowledge and skills and led to changes in instructional practice" (Resnick, 2005, p. 3).

The Rubric

A review team wanting to determine how a school's professional development program measures up against the benchmark of Characteristic 6A would look at two traits of that characteristic. The rubric in Table 6.1 (page 108) describes each trait as it manifests in low-performing, effective, and high-performing schools.

Characteristic 6B: Support of Student Learning, State Standards, and Instructional Program

Summary of Research

The most effective professional development is designed to be coherent with state standards, to complement the instructional program of the school, and to address student needs such as those identified in

Table 6.1: Rubric for Characteristic 6A

Characteristic	Trait	Effectiveness Continuum		
		Low Performing	Effective	High Performing
6A. The professional development program is focused on improving student learning by deepening the knowledge and skills of educators in their subject matter and in pedagogy.	6A1. Focus on subject matter	The professional development program does not give teachers and instructional staff members opportunities to deepen their knowledge and skills in their subject matter.	The professional development program gives teachers opportunities to deepen their knowledge and skills in their subject matter.	The professional development program gives all teachers and paraprofessionals opportunities to deepen their knowledge and skills in their subject matter.
	6A2. Focus on pedagogy	The professional development program does not give teachers and instructional staff members opportunities to deepen their knowledge and skills in general and content-specific pedagogy.	The professional development program gives teachers opportunities to deepen their knowledge and skills in general and content-specific pedagogy.	The professional development program gives all teachers and paraprofessionals opportunities to deepen their knowledge and skills in general and content-specific pedagogy.

analyses of disaggregated state assessment data, dropout reports, and discipline data (Education Alliance, 2005; Elmore, 2002).

It is important to understand that "the idea of using student outcome data . . . to help set priorities for professional development is linked to the idea that effective professional development has a measurable impact on student performance" (Torgeson et al., n.d., p. 1). This impact increases when teachers can see how professional development provides them with tools and strategies to improve what they already teach. The professional development offerings move from those selected by adults based on their perceptions of what is needed to those that are selected based on student performance. The areas in which students are struggling are targeted as the areas for teacher professional development.

The National Staff Development Council ([NSDC], 2001b) includes the use of data in planning and evaluating professional development as one of its standards for staff development.

> Data on student learning gathered from standardized tests, district-made tests, student work samples, portfolios, and other sources provide important input to the selection of school or district improvement goals and provide focus for staff development efforts. This process of data analysis and goal development typically determines the content of teachers' professional learning in the areas of instruction, curriculum, and assessment (p. 16).

Schools should examine many types of data. These may include results from state and classroom tests, graduation and discipline rates, course-taking patterns (such as which groups of students are enrolled in advanced courses and which groups are enrolled in remedial courses), and disaggregated data, which reveal how various groups of students are performing in relation to the whole. Disaggregated data are commonly reported by race, ethnicity, gender, and program, such as special education, English language learners, Title I, and talented and gifted. This information is used to target professional development to those areas in which all or certain groups of students are not achieving at high levels. The review of disaggregated data may also reveal the need for additional professional development around issues of diversity, equity, and strategies to overcome barriers to the high achievement of all students (NSDC, 2001b).

NSDC is one of many professional organizations that advocate the use of student data to determine teacher professional development needs. For example, the National Science Teachers Association (2008, p. 2) notes in a position statement that "professional development should be based on student learning needs and should help . . . educators address difficulties students have with subject matter knowledge and skills."

One content area that has been at the forefront of using achievement data to target professional development is reading at the early grades. Joseph Torgeson and his colleagues from the Florida Center for Reading Research identify two important ways to use student performance data to guide and focus professional development. First, a school could use "a set of student outcome measures to describe areas of instruction that need to be improved across a broad group of teachers" (Torgeson et al., n.d., p. 1). A review of the data might reveal, for example, that nearly all students at Sandlake Elementary are scoring in the lower two quartiles on the reading comprehension portion of the state assessments at grades 4, 5, and 6. In this example, because students in all of the classes at these grade levels are consistently posting low scores on the same section of the reading assessment, professional development targeted at increasing comprehension should be considered for all teachers in those grades.

"The second way that student data can be used to help guide professional development is to use it as the basis for differentiated training and support" for individuals or smaller groups of teachers whose students are not making adequate progress toward identified learning goals (Torgeson et al., n.d., p. 2). In this example, it might be that students in the classes of only one or two teachers are struggling with reading comprehension, while similar groups of students in other classes are achieving at much higher levels. First, it is important to stress that this comparison must be for similar groups of children. If one teacher has a class in which there are a large number of children for whom English is a new language while her peers do not, that factor must be taken into account when comparing class performance on assessments. However, in those instances when the classes are similar and the results are consistently lower in one classroom than in others, professional development such as peer observation and coaching or assistance with student intervention programs "might then be provided on a differentiated basis to teachers who have the greatest need for improved instructional practices" (p. 2).

In using student outcome measures as the basis for a needs assessment in professional development, schools should consider several factors. First, they should make sure that the assessment is accurate in its measurement of progress toward the goal. We can be fairly confident that large-scale tests such as state assessments and national examinations like NAEP have a reasonably high degree of accuracy. We are probably less sure about Ms. Lee's unit test.

Second, schools should use growth measures rather than static measures. Growth measures provide information on how much a particular student or group of students has improved over time. Such a measure might compare the average score on a fluency assessment that was given at the beginning of the school year to the average score on the same or a similar test halfway through the school year. Growth measures are better for determining professional development needs because

> students assigned to a very effective, hard working teacher might actually achieve lower results on an end-of-year test than students from a less effective teacher, if students of the harder working and more skillful teacher began the year with substantially lower reading or language skills. . . . Only when students in various classes are roughly equal in their talent and preparation for learning can end of year student outcomes be used as an indicator of differences in teacher effectiveness. (Torgeson et al., n.d., pp. 2–3)

Static measures, on the other hand, provide data as to the achievement of individuals or a group against those of a much larger group or an identified goal. An example of this kind of measure would be to compare the average score earned on the state mathematics assessment by Ms. Ruenkle's fourth-grade class to the average score earned by all students statewide on the fourth-grade mathematics assessment. Static measures provide important information about large groups of students but are generally not sensitive enough to use to design professional development at the level of the individual teacher.

To be most effective, professional development must both be targeted and provide teachers with a way to directly apply what they learn to their teaching. Specifically, "professional development leads to better instruction and improved student learning when it connects to the curriculum materials that teachers use, the district and state academic standards that guide their work, and the assessment and accountability measures that evaluate their success" (Resnick, 2005, p. 2).

In a study of California's decade-long effort to change and improve mathematics teaching in the state's public schools, researchers found that teachers "whose learning focused directly on the curriculum they would be teaching were the ones who adopted the practices taught in their professional development" (Resnick, 2005, p. 2). A different study found that

> the things that made a difference to changes in their practice were integral to instruction: curriculum materials for teachers and students to use in class; assessments that enabled students to demonstrate their mathematical performance; . . . and instruction for teachers that was grounded in these curriculum materials and assessments. (Cohen & Hill, 2001, p. 6)

The Rubric

A review team wanting to determine how a school's professional development program measures up against the benchmark of Characteristic 6B would look at three traits of that characteristic. The rubric in Table 6.2 describes each trait as it manifests in low-performing, effective, and high-performing schools.

Table 6.2: Rubric for Characteristic 6B

Characteristic	Trait	Effectiveness Continuum		
		Low Performing	Effective	High Performing
6B. The professional development program is based on an analysis of student achievement data and learning needs, is coherent with state standards, and complements the instructional program.	6B1. Connection to student learning needs	The professional development program does not take into account student achievement data.	The professional development program is based on an analysis of student achievement data and learning needs.	The professional development program is based on an analysis of student achievement data and learning needs, as well as nonacademic data such as discipline, attendance, and dropout rates.
	6B2. Alignment with state standards	The professional development program is not coherent with state standards.	The professional development program is coherent with state standards.	The professional development program is coherent with state standards and includes training in standards-based instruction and assessment strategies.
	6B3. Connection to instructional program	Professional development is disconnected from the school's instructional program.	The professional development program complements the school's instructional program.	The professional development program complements the school's instructional program and includes training in programs used for academic intervention and enrichment.

Characteristic 6C: Collaborative, Job-Embedded, and Need-Based

Summary of Research

Teachers, like other adults, learn best by doing, by participating in activities with other professionals, and by reflecting on and refining their work. In job-embedded professional development, teachers learn how to observe, question, analyze, and modify their teaching in order to provide the kind of instruction necessary for all of their students to meet learning goals. In this model, teachers engage in evaluating their work and examining their daily professional practices.

The Association for Supervision and Curriculum Development (n.d., pp. 1–2) has identified six attributes of effective professional development. Professional development should be:

- Directly focused on helping to achieve student learning goals and supporting student learning needs.

- A collaborative endeavor—teachers and administrators work together in planning and implementation.

- School-based and job-embedded.

- A long-term commitment.

- Differentiated [based on teacher readiness, interest, and preferred ways of learning].

- Tied to the district goals.

In a review of research, Hirsch and Hirsh (n.d.) concluded that job-embedded professional development was not only effective but had "the greatest impact on both teaching and student learning" (p. 5). Most often, professional development addresses the knowledge and skills of groups of teachers. However, even when it is directed at the needs of a single individual, its effectiveness will be enhanced if the teacher has opportunities for practicing and refining skills, coupled with the interaction and collaboration with peers that are hallmarks of job-embedded professional development.

While there is certainly an important place for external professional development in bringing new ideas, research findings, strategies, programs, and practices to schools and teachers, job-embedded professional development has a powerful impact because it takes place at the school and classroom levels and "occurs while teachers and administrators engage in their daily work. While simultaneously performing their job duties, participants learn by doing, reflecting on their experiences and then generating and sharing new insights and learning with one another" (e-Lead, n.d., Sections 1–3). The professional development that teachers experience within this framework builds on existing knowledge and encourages the kind of collaboration in which teachers "observe each other practicing the art of teaching and provide feedback which leads to reflection by the teacher. High-quality professional development should not only focus on the teacher but should also nurture the intellectual and leadership capacities of the teachers" (Education Alliance, 2005, p. 3).

Dennis Sparks (1994) describes job-embedded professional development as systems thinking for educators. This type of professional development moves from a district focus to a school focus, allowing those closest to the students to "address challenges unique to their students' needs" (p. 2). The focus also moves from general instructional skills to a combination of content-specific and pedagogical skills aimed directly at those areas in which student performance is lagging.

Professional development that is collaborative occurs when teachers from the same school, department, or grade level engage in paired or teamed activities, such as observing other teachers' lessons, being observed while teaching, jointly planning lessons or assessments, reviewing and analyzing student work, and mentoring or coaching (Resnick, 2005). These activities are regularly scheduled, intensive, sustained over time, and embedded within the teachers' regular work with students.

To be productive, collaboration cannot be casual or general. Instead, it must include "clear, frequent talk about the concrete details of instruction focused on the attainment of explicit achievement goals," paired with "recognition and celebration of superior practices and their subsequent results" (DuFour, Eaker, & DuFour, 2005, p. 143).

The elements of effective collaboration need to be organized around clear routines and requirements. Time for meetings should be scheduled and structured, with team norms determined in advance of the team time. Teamwork should be dedicated to improving teaching, to attaining improved results on end-of-course assessments, and to developing and refining those assessments, providing a common aligned instructional focus (Schmoker, 2001).

Before undertaking a professional development program that asks teachers to move from an isolated, individual model of teaching to one in which their work is planned, refined, and sometimes evaluated collaboratively, school leaders will have to offer teachers good reasons why they should go down this avenue. Administrators must be prepared for some push-back as they call on teachers to "pursue a common purpose through collaborative activity that is likely to entail great effort, uncertainty and alteration in established norms and habits . . . where most people experience their work as difficult and complex without the additional burden of collaborative effort" (Elmore, 2002, pp. 19–20). The reasons behind this effort are, however, well-supported by the research. Puma and Raphael (2001) found that it is by learning to work together that "teachers break down the isolation of individual classrooms and can begin to transform a whole school" (p. 10). However, "most educators have good reasons to think that they are doing the best work they can under the circumstances. Asking them to engage in work that is significantly different from what they are already doing requires a strong rationale and incentive" (Elmore, 2002, pp. 19–20). Support for collaborative work grows naturally as the leadership capacity across the school expands through training, encouragement, and support for teachers as they take on new roles as mentors, coaches, grade-level team leaders, department heads, and curriculum or content specialists.

The Rubric

A review team wanting to determine how a school's professional development program measures up against the benchmark of Characteristic 6C would look at four traits of that characteristic. The rubric in Table 6.3 (page 114) describes each trait as it manifests in low-performing, effective, and high-performing schools.

Characteristic 6D: Ongoing and Sustained

Summary of Research

An important characteristic of effective professional development is that it is ongoing and sustained:

> Activities which are offered over longer durations tend to have greater impact than those typically classified as one-shot workshops. Longer, focused workshops/training allow the participants to share work, develop new teaching strategies, and collaborate with peers, all of which contribute to robust learning experiences for children. Extended professional development activities promote a richer environment for the participants and allow teachers to develop clear connections between the material presented and their classroom experiences. (Education Alliance, 2005, p. 3)

Table 6.3: Rubric for Characteristic 6C

Characteristic	Trait	Effectiveness Continuum		
		Low Performing	Effective	High Performing
6C. Professional development is collaborative, is job-embedded, and addresses both individual and schoolwide needs.	6C1. Teams focused on improving achievement and learning	Collaborative work teams are informal or do not focus on improving student learning.	Teachers are members of collaborative work teams focused on improving student achievement and learning.	All instructional staff members participate in collaborative work teams focused on improving student achievement and learning.
	6C2. Job-embedded opportunities	Teacher professional development is not embedded in the work of teaching or does not provide opportunities for practice, analysis, and refinement.	Teacher professional development is embedded in the work of teaching, providing opportunities for practice, analysis, and refinement.	All instructional staff members participate in professional development that is embedded in the work of teaching, providing opportunities for practice, analysis, and refinement.
	6C3. Differentiation	Professional development is not or is not consistently differentiated based on knowledge, skills, and experience.	Teacher professional development is differentiated based on knowledge, skills, and experience.	Professional development for all instructional staff members is differentiated based on knowledge, skills, and experience.
	6C4. Attention to individual and school-wide needs	Professional development does not address both individual and schoolwide needs.	Teacher professional development addresses both individual and schoolwide needs.	Professional development for all instructional staff members addresses both individual and schoolwide needs.

Researchers from the Community Training and Assistance Center in Florida (2008, p. 5) found "a positive relationship between teachers' professional development hours in literacy courses and student growth in reading." They report that for every 6-hour day of literacy professional development, student scale scores on the Florida statewide reading assessment increased by half a point. These benefits were found to apply across all levels of teacher experience.

Linda Darling-Hammond and her colleagues, in partnership with NSDC, reported that rigorous research, while limited in quantity, found that "sustained and intensive professional development for teachers is related to student achievement gains" (Darling-Hammond et al., 2009, p. 5). Their meta-analysis of

1,300 research studies, in which nine were identified as "methodologically strong," found that "professional development efforts that offered an average of 49 hours in a year boosted student achievement by approximately 21 percentile points" (p. 9).

Teachers also see a positive benefit in working at a deeper and more in-depth level with new ideas for the classroom. During the 1999–2000 school year, the National Center for Education Statistics of the U.S. Department of Education surveyed more than 52,000 teachers in 12,000 schools across the United States about the professional development in which they had engaged in the previous 12 months. The responses revealed that "the amount of time teachers spent on professional development activities in a particular content area and their perceptions of the usefulness of these activities were strongly related. . . . This pattern held for both public and private school teachers" (Choy, Chen, & Bugarin, 2006, p. 73).

The National Center for Education Statistics also surveyed public school teachers about how the frequency of their participation in various professional development activities affected their perception of the activities' value. The results showed that the greater the frequency of participation, the more teachers felt that the activities improved their teaching (United States Department of Education, 2000).

Of course, while sustained study over time is an essential component of effective professional development, it is what happens within that time that is key to its value. Thomas Guskey speaks of research that has shown that

> simply adding more time for job-embedded activities is insufficient. Doing ineffective things longer doesn't make them any better. Instead, we must ensure that the extended time provided for professional development is structured carefully and used wisely, engaging educators in activities shown to yield improved results. (Harvard Family Research Project, 2005/2006, p. 13)

Conversely, even highly effective activities cannot succeed if they are rushed or if time for professional discussion, practice, and refinement is not available.

The Rubric

A review team wanting to determine how a school's professional development program measures up against the benchmark of Characteristic 6D would look at two traits of that characteristic. The rubric in Table 6.4 (page 116) describes each trait as it manifests in low-performing, effective, and high-performing schools.

Characteristic 6E: Building of Cultural Proficiency

Summary of Research

One important purpose for professional development is to help teachers understand what gets in the way of the achievement of poor and minority students and why. Professional development focused on what is commonly referred to as *cultural proficiency* intends to provide educators with "the knowledge and skills . . . to work well with, respond effectively to, and be supportive of people in cross-cultural settings" (American Academy of Family Physicians, 2009).

Table 6.4: Rubric for Characteristic 6D

Characteristic	Trait	Effectiveness Continuum		
		Low Performing	Effective	High Performing
6D. Professional development is ongoing and sustained over time.	**6D1. Incorporation into routine**	Professional development is seen as external to the real work of the school or regarded as part of teachers' independent responsibilities.	Professional development is a routine part of every teacher's responsibilities and workday.	Ongoing professional development is a routine part of every staff member's responsibilities and workday.
	6D2. Continuity	Professional development is not part of an overall plan or consists primarily of stand-alone activities.	Professional development is ongoing and sustained over time.	Professional development is ongoing, is sustained over time, and seamlessly connects from one year to the next.

When participating in professional development in cultural proficiency, teachers confront beliefs they may have about children, families, and learning that not only have no basis in fact but may actually unintentionally harm children. Ronald Ferguson is the director of the Achievement Gap Initiative at Harvard University. Lewis and Paik (2001, pp. 42–43) reported on his presentation at the Minority Student Achievement Network in 2000, in which he laid out a chronology describing how achievement gaps emerge and grow as children enter and proceed through the grades:

+ Beginning in kindergarten, children come to school with differences in knowledge and skill levels. Children of poverty tend to begin school already behind their more affluent peers. These "patterns are standard enough that teachers learn to expect them."

+ Teachers do not know how to intervene to address existing achievement gaps. When teachers are unfamiliar with the language and culture of the children with whom they are working (in 2008, 10.9 million American school children spoke a language other than English at home [United States Census Bureau, 2008b]), there is an even "greater risk for misjudging children developmentally and teaching them inappropriately."

+ As children grow older, they become more aware of differences in achievement between one child and another and between groups of children. Children may begin to accept stereotypical beliefs about groups of others or about themselves.

+ "Adults' expectations reinforce children's internalization of stereotypes." Teachers' behaviors, such as praising some groups of children more frequently or asking deeper-level questions of some groups of children over others, "may reinforce children's self-perceptions and feelings of superiority or inferiority."

+ Research is clear that children who are labeled as low achievers, as well as low-income and minority children, are much more likely to be taught by teachers who are inexperienced, unlicensed, or not deeply trained in the subject matter.

+ "Children who do poorly even when they work hard may become less preoccupied with scholastic goals and seek other domains in which to excel, such as athletics and social skills. They may accept peer norms that reinforce this inclination to deemphasize schoolwork."

+ Children often begin to lose confidence in themselves and their own abilities. They may "develop anxiety that interferes with their academic performance."

+ Students "who are performing below their potential and who lack confidence, or who have confidence but are ambivalent because they identify with lower-performing groups, may go through cycles of fleeting resolve—working hard at times, but not consistently enough to shift to higher achievement levels and remain there."

+ Leaders fail to publicly support and insist on a schoolwide shared commitment to high levels of achievement for all students and to stress that it is the responsibility of all adults in the school to cultivate that potential.

Professional development can provide the knowledge and skills to help teachers overcome the negative influences identified in Ferguson's chronology. It is particularly important to address teachers' beliefs about the ability of poor and minority students to achieve at high levels, because

> high expectations of student achievement are a well-documented correlate of effective schools, while entrenched low expectations of achievement for children from low-income communities have been identified as a significant barrier to shifting that achievement. . . . When expectations are low, [curricular and instructional] decisions are likely to include non-challenging and non-academic curricula and instructional methods with teachers teaching less to students instead of more. Conversely, when expectations are high, teachers are more likely to assume that they can and will provide whatever programmes and resources are required to meet the needs for the students to succeed. (Timperley, Phillips, & Wiseman, 2003, p. 4).

Investments in professional development are an effective strategy to improve the delivery of the instructional program for all students, particularly those in high-poverty and high-minority schools. In a 2001 review of research drawn primarily from Title I schools, Lewis and Paik concluded:

> Nothing affects the achievement of low-income and/or minority children as much as the quality of the teaching they receive. No curriculum package, test, governance rearrangement, regulation, or special program can equal the impact of a good teacher, one with the knowledge, skills, and commitment to foster student success. (p. 20)

The Rubric

A review team wanting to determine how a school's professional development program measures up against the benchmark of Characteristic 6E would look at three traits of that characteristic. The rubric in Table 6.5 (page 118) describes each trait as it manifests in low-performing, effective, and highly successful schools.

Table 6.5: Rubric for Characteristic 6E

Characteristic	Trait	Effectiveness Continuum		
		Low Performing	Effective	High Performing
6E. Professional development builds cultural proficiency.	6E1. Effect on staff members' cultural proficiency	Few staff members have received training in cultural proficiency or feel culturally proficient.	Staff members engage in professional development that builds cultural understanding and proficiency.	Professional development has increased staff members' confidence in their level of cultural proficiency.
	6E2. Effect on beliefs	Professional development does not address, or does not adequately address, teachers' beliefs about culture, race, and learning.	Professional development addresses teachers' beliefs about and builds insight into culture, race, and learning.	All instructional staff members engage in professional development addressing beliefs about and building schoolwide insight into culture, race, and learning.
	6E3. Effect on equity	Professional development does not address barriers to racial, ethnic, and cultural equity.	Professional development addresses the identification and removal of barriers to racial, ethnic, and cultural equity.	Professional development has resulted in a reduction of the identified barriers to racial, ethnic, and cultural equity.

Characteristic 6F: Support for Teachers New to the Profession

Summary of Research

The knowledge and skills necessary for successful teaching lie in three domains (Elmore, 2002; Resnick, 2005):

1. Subject matter (content)

2. Understanding of how children learn (general pedagogy)

3. Expertise in those instructional, assessment, and intervention practices associated with the specific subjects taught (content-specific pedagogy)

Richard Elmore (2002, p. 17) notes that

> novice teachers differ markedly from expert teachers in their command of these domains and their ability to use them. For example, they differ in the array of examples and strategies they can use to explain difficult concepts to students, in the range of strategies they can employ for engaging students who are at different performance

levels, and in the degree of fluency and automaticity with which they employ the strategies they know.

Professional development for novice teachers should focus on these domains of knowledge. It must also "engage teachers in analysis of their own practice, and provide opportunities for teachers to observe experts and to be observed by and to receive feedback from experts" (Elmore, 2002, p. 17). High-quality induction programs are comprehensive in nature and evolve to meet the needs of new teachers as they gain experience and expertise. These programs typically include a mentoring component in at least the first year and continue over the first several years of a teacher's career (p. 36).

Researchers (Public Education Network, 2003, pp. 26–27; Elmore, 2002) have found that the most successful induction programs have the following features:

* They are coherent with the instructional philosophy and program of the school and have established "professional norms and expectations for all teachers."

* They are "integral to school/district long-term planning for improving teaching and learning."

* They are "aligned with professional standards as well as state and local student learning standards."

* They are strongly supported by administrators, who are involved in their implementation.

* They are required for "all new teachers, whether entering the profession from traditional or alternative pathways."

* They are designed with "input from beginning and veteran teachers."

* They have "adequate time and resources for implementation."

* They are implemented in a way that ensures that new teachers are given "reduced workloads, release time, and placement in classes with less, rather than more, demanding students."

* They are staffed by high-quality mentors who have been carefully selected and well-trained and are supported by the school and district.

* They are frequently evaluated "to determine whether [they are] having [the] desired impact."

* They are in place for new teachers prior to the beginning of the school year and continue through the first years of teaching.

In a 2003 study, researchers from the Public Education Network (PEN) used surveys, focus groups, and interviews to ask more than 200 new teachers in districts with induction and mentoring programs about the effectiveness of the supports they received. New teachers believed that the induction programs could be improved in the following ways (pp. 28–29):

* Start the induction process with a comprehensive orientation before the school year begins.

* Provide clear, comprehensive information on the school system and on building-level policies and procedures.

* Include a well-structured, high-quality mentoring program for all new teachers.

- Provide support in time management, classroom management, and instructional organization.

- Provide ongoing support in curriculum and instruction.

- Establish new teacher networks.

- Establish ongoing on-site opportunities for new teachers to obtain support from experienced teachers.

- Establish common meeting times for teachers in similar grades or disciplines to plan and reflect.

- Provide opportunities for teachers to observe and be observed by experienced teachers.

- Give new teachers more contact with school administrators.

- Give teachers adequate time to participate in on- and off-site induction activities.

As the teachers in the study reported, not all of the support that new teachers most wish for requires a comprehensive professional development program. In fact, simply assembling a new teacher packet with the following 10 items would be extremely helpful (p. 30):

1. A new teacher handbook

2. A copy of the state and local instructional standards for their subject and grade level

3. A statement of their school's philosophy, goals, and values

4. A student handbook

5. A school discipline policy

6. A sample student report card

7. Forms and instructions for ordering books and supplies

8. An organizational chart describing school and district staff and related roles

9. A checklist, designed by veteran teachers, to help them know what to expect on their first day

10. A list of cultural and educational resources available in the community

On the other hand, to meet the needs of challenging students, some new teachers may require support that "goes beyond professional development opportunities and closer supervision. School and district administrators should consider [additional] support strategies . . . when the data indicate the need to improve . . . outcomes in specific classrooms." Examples of such strategies would be providing a trained coach to assist in "implementing targeted student interventions," assigning paraprofessional staff members to the classroom, and reducing student-teacher ratios "through reassignment of selected students to other classrooms" (Torgeson et al., n.d., p. 4).

The Rubric

A review team wanting to determine how a school's professional development program measures up against the benchmark of Characteristic 6F would look at two traits of that characteristic. The rubric in Table 6.6 describes each trait as it manifests in low-performing, effective, and high-performing schools.

Table 6.6: Rubric for Characteristic 6F

Characteristic	Trait	Effectiveness Continuum		
		Low Performing	Effective	High Performing
6F. Professional development explicitly addresses the needs of teachers new to the profession.	6F1. Induction program	There is no formalized teacher induction program for teachers with 3 or fewer years of experience.	A formalized induction program serves the needs of teachers with 3 or fewer years of experience.	A formalized induction program serves the needs of teachers with 3 or fewer years of experience. The program may be extended for those teachers who need additional support.
	6F2. Mentoring	The induction program does not include a formal mentoring component.	Each new teacher works with an assigned mentor throughout his or her first year of teaching.	The induction program includes a formal mentoring component that extends beyond a single year.

Characteristic 6G: Adequate Resources

Summary of Research

Offering the kind of professional development that research shows to be most effective requires dedicating time, funding, and materials to that purpose. Resources are adequate when they are sufficient to provide time for teachers to plan, observe, participate in mentoring and coaching, conduct lesson study, practice and refine lessons, and engage in frequent planned activities that make for meaningful job-embedded professional development. It is hardly surprising that

> teachers, researchers, and policymakers consistently indicate that the greatest challenge to implementing effective professional development is lack of time. Teachers need time to understand new concepts, learn new skills, develop new attitudes, research, discuss, reflect, assess, try new approaches and integrate them into their practice; and time to plan their own professional development. (Abdal-Haqq, 1996, p. 1)

Lack of stable funding has been one of the key barriers to creating long-term professional development programs. Researchers have worked to develop models to help schools and administrators understand how much is actually spent on professional development. A 2005 study of spending on professional development in five large urban districts found that it ranged from 2.3% to 6.9% of the total district budget, averaging 3.6%. Translated into dollars, this equals an average of $4,380 per teacher. The greatest majority (ranging from 21% to 51% of the total overall) of professional development funds were used for teacher stipends and substitute pay. These district totals did not include school-level spending of discretionary funds to pay for professional development (Miles, Odden, Fermanich, & Archibald, 2005, p. 11).

Principals have an important role in garnering and sustaining resources for professional development. In a 2005 study of school leadership, Marzano, Waters, and McNulty concluded that effective school administrators are able to provide "teachers with materials and professional development necessary for the successful execution of their duties" (p. 60).

The Rubric

A review team wanting to determine how a school's professional development program measures up against the benchmark of Characteristic 6G would look at one trait of that characteristic. The rubric in Table 6.7 describes that trait as it manifests in low-performing, effective, and high-performing schools.

Table 6.7: Rubric for Characteristic 6G

| Characteristic | Trait | Effectiveness Continuum | | |
		Low Performing	Effective	High Performing
6G. The professional development program has adequate resources.	6G1. Level of resources	The professional development program lacks adequate resources.	The professional development program has adequate resources.	The professional development program has adequate resources. Funding for professional development is a stable budget item.

Characteristic 6H: Evaluation of Effectiveness

Summary of Research

Evaluation of professional development is essential. Just as with student evaluation, there are two kinds of assessments that are useful for this purpose: formative and summative. One of the clearest descriptions of the difference between the two is Robert Stake's analogy: "When the cook tastes the soup, that's formative evaluation; when the guest tastes it, that's summative evaluation" (Puma & Raphael, 2001, p. 15). As the analogy illustrates, formative assessment is used to sample the professional development program as it exists at that moment, when time still remains to modify it. Summative assessment is used to answer questions about the impact of the professional development. It can't be used to change what has already occurred, but it can be used to modify future renditions of the program.

Thomas Guskey (2002) has developed one of the most widely used strategies for evaluating professional development. His model outlines five levels, beginning with an evaluation of the quality of teachers' initial exposure to new learning and building up to an evaluation of the effect of that professional development on student learning. These five levels are:

1. Participants' reaction

2. Participants' learning

3. Organizational support and change

4. Participants' use of new knowledge and skills

5. Student learning outcomes (pp. 45–49)

Because the ultimate aim of all professional development is the improvement of student learning and achievement, Guskey advocates using an "outcomes" design in evaluating professional development. That is, the first consideration should be the student learning that is the desired outcome of the professional development; then the evaluation can work backwards from step 5 of the model to ensure that the essential elements of the process have been addressed. In using this approach, educators planning professional development and professional development evaluation ask a series of questions (Harvard Family Research Project, 2005/2006):

+ What improvements in student learning do we want to attain, and what evidence will tell us that we have reached our goal?

+ What do we want participants to do with the knowledge and skills they learn?

+ What types of organizational support or change are needed to facilitate that implementation?

+ What new skills or knowledge do we want participants to have as a result of the professional development?

+ How do we want participants to feel about the professional development?

Guskey notes that "this planning process compels educators to plan not in terms of what they are going to do but in terms of what they want to accomplish with their students. All other decisions are then based on that fundamental premise" (Harvard Family Research Project, 2005/2006, p. 12).

Another way to evaluate professional development and to determine how pervasively teachers are applying the new concepts and strategies in their classrooms is to use the Concerns-Based Adoption Model (CBAM), based on the work of Shirley Hord, G. E. Hall, Susan Loucks-Horsley, and others. CBAM is a two-dimensional model (stages of concern and levels of change) that melds participants' reactions to their new learning in professional development with the ways in which teachers are, or are not, incorporating that new learning into their classroom instruction. To use CBAM in evaluation, each participant first identifies his or her stage of concern and then identifies his or her current level of use. There are seven stages of concern and eight levels of use (Horsley & Loucks-Horsley, 1998).

As they adopt a new practice, teachers experience seven stages of concern (North Central Regional Educational Laboratory, n.d.):

1. Awareness. Teachers have little interest in or involvement with the innovation.

2. Informational. Teachers have a general interest in the innovation and would like to know more about it.

3. Personal. Teachers want to learn about the personal ramifications of the innovation—they question how the innovation will affect them.

4. Management. Teachers learn the processes and tasks of the innovation. They focus on information and resources.

5. Consequence. Teachers focus on the innovation's impact on students.

6. Collaboration. Teachers cooperate with other teachers in implementing the innovation.

7. Refocusing. Teachers consider the benefits of the innovation and think of additional alternatives that might work even better.

There are eight levels of teachers' use of their new learning (Horsley & Loucks-Horsley, 1998):

1. Nonuse. Teachers are not yet using what they are learning.

2. Orientation. Teachers seek information about the program or practice.

3. Preparation. Teachers have made a decision to adopt the new practice and are actively preparing for its implementation.

4. Mechanical. Teachers are in the early stages of using new strategies, techniques, and materials.

5. Routine. Teachers have established a satisfactory pattern of behaviors.

6. Refinement. Teachers go beyond the routine by assessing the impact of their efforts and making changes to increase that impact.

7. Integration. Teachers are actively coordinating with others to use the innovation.

8. Renewal. Teachers are seeking more effective alternatives to the established use of the innovation.

Using CBAM to evaluate professional development "can provide baseline and follow-up data for monitoring implementation and determining content of follow-up support . . . [and] can help . . . decision makers stay informed of progress in the crucial processes of early implementation, before impact on student achievement can be shown" (Horsley & Loucks-Horsley, 1998, p. 2).

In using Guskey's model, the Concerns-Based Adoption Model, or any others, evaluation does not end, of course, with the collection of the data. It is what is done with the data that makes evaluation of value. Formative evaluation gives all parties the opportunity to adjust professional development as it is being delivered to make it more useful and meaningful to the participants. Summative evaluation gives the evidence needed to make important decisions about the effectiveness of programs and practices. Taken together, formative and summative evaluations provide the information to ensure that the professional development program is effective for teachers and ultimately improves student learning.

The Rubric

A review team wanting to determine how a school's professional development program measures up against the benchmark of Characteristic 6H would look at one trait of that characteristic. The rubric in Table 6.8 describes that trait as it manifests in low-performing, effective, and high-performing schools.

Table 6.8: Rubric for Characteristic 6H

| Characteristic | Trait | Effectiveness Continuum | | |
		Low Performing	Effective	High Performing
6H. An evaluation of program effectiveness is an integral part of professional development.	6H1. Requirements for program evaluation	Evaluations are not, or not consistently, required for all professional development.	Evaluations are required for all professional development.	Evaluations are required for all professional development, and both formative and summative evaluation data are used to improve the professional development program.

Conclusion

The bottom line of professional development is to help teachers become better at their craft in order to accelerate and deepen the learning and achievement of all students. To accomplish this goal, professional development must address student needs by focusing on both content and pedagogy, and it must give teachers ample opportunities to practice and refine what they have learned in a continuous process of improvement.

Effectiveness Indicator 7

Student Connectedness, Engagement, and Readiness

And those handmade presents that children often bring home from school: They have so much value! To the child the gift is really self, and they want so much for their selves to be acceptable, to be loved.

—Fred Rogers

Effective schools keep students engaged in school both by cultivating caring relationships and by making learning interesting and challenging. From this principle, we derive Effectiveness Indicator 7. Feeling a connection to their school, their peers, and the adults within their school provides an important safety net for students. Students who feel connected are much more likely to stay in school despite obstacles they may face along the way. Extracurricular activities play an important role in these feelings of connection. When student performance begins to falter, there are mechanisms in place to quickly reach out to them with targeted assistance. Students move seamlessly from one school to another in the district because there is a high level of communication and coordination between schools. An on-site school review looks at the extent of all of these efforts to keep students in school until they graduate.

Seven characteristics define Effectiveness Indicator 7: Student Connectedness, Engagement, and Readiness:

7A.   Students feel connected to their school.

7B.   Students have positive, trusting, and caring relationships with adults and peers in the school.

7C.   Extracurricular activities are numerous and varied, providing ample opportunities for all students to participate.

7D.   The school has mechanisms and programs to identify and meet the academic and social service needs of students at risk of not completing school.

7E.   A system of schoolwide, targeted, and intensive interventions meets the needs of students at risk.

7F.   Secondary schools provide alternative options to students in order to increase graduation rates.

7G.   There is coordination and curricular alignment within and among feeder-pattern schools to ensure that students are prepared for transition to the next grade or school.

Characteristic 7A: Connection to School

Summary of Research

Blum (2005, p. 1) defines *school connectedness* as "the belief by students that adults in the school care about their learning and about them as individuals. . . . Research has shown that students who feel connected to school do better academically and also are less likely to be involved in risky health behaviors."

The Learning First Alliance (2001, p. vii) reminds us that

> just a century ago, the average public school enrolled only 40 students; the size of the average school *district* was only 120 students (U.S. Census Bureau, 1900). Safety was easier to ensure, and close, supportive relationships among teachers and students, parents and teachers, and among students themselves were easier to establish. At the same time, schools were more racially, ethnically and economically homogeneous, and society as a whole more ethnocentric; issues of inter-group tolerance, acceptance, and social harmony were evaded through segregation in the schools and neighborhoods.
>
> Today, a typical elementary school enrolls more than 400 students and a high school more than 2,000 students. These students may come from varied cultures and backgrounds, many locales, and a variety of family configurations. As a result, schools must deliberately cultivate and artfully orchestrate a sense of connection, cohesion, and safety.

While school connectedness today may be more challenging to create and maintain, there has never been a time when that effort was more important. There is strong empirical evidence that school connectedness contributes to a variety of important positive educational outcomes, including increases in motivation, classroom engagement, attendance, academic achievement, and school completion rates. School connectedness also reduces negative outcomes, including fighting, bullying, vandalism, substance abuse, emotional distress, disruptive behavior, and school violence (University of Minnesota, 2003).

So exactly what are the conditions students associate with a feeling of connectedness to their school? Heather Libbey (2004) completed a meta-analysis of just this question. She found that while the researchers were using many different terms to describe the elements of connectedness (for example, school bond/school attachment or school involvement/school membership), the descriptions were similar enough to be grouped across the studies. Students feel connected when they are academically engaged and motivated, have a sense of belonging, believe that school rules are fair and enforced consistently and equally, like their school, have a voice in decision-making, participate in extracurricular activities, have friends at school, feel safe in school, and feel close to and valued by teachers and other staff members (pp. 278–82).

Research also helps define what school characteristics must be in place in order to create school connectedness. Although encountering slightly different descriptions, as one would expect from empirical research, Blum (2005, p. 2) has identified six strategies that emerge from the research as key to increasing students' connection to their schools:

- Implement high standards and expectations, and provide academic support to all students.

- Apply fair and consistent disciplinary policies that are collectively agreed upon and fairly enforced.

- Create trusting relationships among students, teachers, staff, administrators, and families.

- Hire and support capable teachers who are skilled in content, teaching techniques, and classroom management to meet each learner's needs.

- Foster high parent/family expectations for school performance and school completion.

- Ensure that every student feels close to at least one supportive adult at school.

School connectedness is important for both academic and social reasons. Academically, it is "highly predictive of success in school" (Blum, 2005, p. 1). Students who are connected with their schools report that they are glad to attend school and enjoy it overall. This enjoyment adds to the diligence with which students pursue learning, the effort they exert on tasks and assignments, and their persistence in working through complex or difficult assignments, all of which result in increased learning and achievement (National Research Council and Institute of Medicine, 2003; Learning First Alliance, 2001). Socially, this sense of belonging is associated with positive outcomes including increased school attendance, higher rates of graduation, reductions in aggression, increased emotional stability, strength in resisting peer pressure, and resilience (Blum, 2005; National Research Council and Institute of Medicine, 2003; Wilson, 2004).

The Rubric

A review team wanting to determine how a school's efforts to foster connectedness measure up against the benchmark of Characteristic 7A would look at two traits of that characteristic. The rubric in Table 7.1 (page 130) describes each trait as it manifests in low-performing, effective, and high-performing schools.

Characteristic 7B: Positive, Trusting, and Caring Relationships

Summary of Research

The significant influence of relationships between students and between students and adults in school has a full and rich evidence base. Students who forge positive school relationships with adults and peers in school have higher educational expectations for themselves and higher rates of participation in and completion of postsecondary education (Wimberly, 2002). The important relationship between children and their teachers and other adults begins with their first encounter. Each subsequent interaction is an opportunity to strengthen or weaken those first impressions.

Table 7.1: Rubric for Characteristic 7A

Characteristic	Trait	Effectiveness Continuum		
		Low Performing	Effective	High Performing
7A. Students feel connected to their school.	7A1. Connection and sense of belonging	Some students feel isolated from adults and from other students at the school.	Students feel a sense of belonging to, and being a part of, the school community.	Guidance and advisory programs build upon students' sense of belonging and their connection to adults and other students at the school.
	7A2. Enjoyment	Some students do not enjoy attending the school.	Students enjoy attending the school.	Students enjoy attending the school, as evidenced by high attendance and low tardy rates.

The importance of positive relationships with teachers and other adults in the school transcends racial, ethnic, and cultural lines. For students who are struggling in school, these relationships can make the difference between staying in or dropping out of school, academic success or academic failure. While it would be absurd to assert that all children of a particular ethnic or cultural group would feel the same way about anything, there are cultural themes that can help in identifying and understanding adult behaviors that are more likely to encourage positive teacher-student relationships.

Despite some recent gains, African American children overall are struggling in our schools. African American 17-year-olds achieve in reading and mathematics at the same level as white 13-year-olds (Haycock, 2007). Connections for these children are critical. What do African American students see as caring behavior? Researchers (Nelson & Bauch, 1997) asked just that question in a study involving African American students attending predominately African American Catholic and magnet schools in Chicago and Washington, D.C. The students described caring teachers as those who:

+ Actively encourage, even push students to succeed

+ Foster meaningful personal relationships with students

+ Create an environment that is educationally and personally challenging

+ Have high expectations for student learning and achievement

+ Actively involve students in the educational experience

+ Demonstrate concern for individual students

+ Make sure students get extra help when they need it

Native American/Alaska Native children, too, face daunting odds for success in school. The Northwest Regional Educational Laboratory reported that the "dropout rate for Native American/Alaska Native students is not just high, it's the highest of any minority group in the school system. Nationally, more than three of every 10 Native students drop out" (McCluskey, 2004, p. 1). In Portland, Oregon, for example, "a study of 408 Native American high school students from 1998 to 2001 revealed that only 40 graduated" (p. 1).

To better understand how to connect with Native American/Alaska Native children, William Demmert (2001) has reviewed the pertinent research. Although there have been few studies to date, Demmert has noted some common themes that suggest methods and teacher behaviors to foster relationships between these students and their teachers:

+ Make personal connections with students.

+ Connect with parents and the Native community.

+ Build trust.

+ Establish family support.

+ Establish cultural relevance in the curriculum.

+ Establish congruency between the culture of the school and the culture of the Native community.

+ Tap intrinsic motivation for learning.

+ Use humor.

+ Provide situations that yield small successes.

+ Use highly engaging, activity-based learning and, in some cases, cooperative learning.

+ Provide role models.

+ Be flexible, fair, and consistent.

+ Provide authentic instruction and assessment practices.

For Latino students, too, there is a strong connection between positive teacher-student relationships and student engagement. Teachers with whom students form bonds build on

> what students already know and can do—their culture, language, and experiences—in ways that provide them with tools for their own academic and social learning. Linking learning to life experiences allows students to see relevance in education, as well as provides incentive for academic engagement. Also crucial to such engagement is knowing what interests and concerns students, and devising instructional plans that fold those interests and concerns into the curriculum. (Rosario, 2006, p. 5)

For Latino students, having respect for and looking up to their teachers translates into motivation to work harder in school. Teachers can help improve student engagement by caring, showing enthusiasm for teaching, being flexible, stimulating curiosity, and allowing students to express themselves creatively and freely (Rosario, 2006).

Pacific Island cultures are widespread and vary significantly. However, they share similar values, such as regarding collective behaviors as more important than individual behaviors and emphasizing compassion, social obligations, and the nurturing of human relationships. Teachers can build positive relationships with Pacific Island students by showing respect for their cultural identity and values (Thaman, 2006).

All students, regardless of background, race, or ethnicity, need to feel safe, respected, and valued if they are to develop a sense of belonging and feel connected to school and to their peers. Teachers who are most successful in forging bonds with students use strategies that satisfy their students' yearning for approval, affection, acceptance, affiliation, and esteem (Rosario, 2006).

Students, like everyone else, remember how adults behave more than what they say. To create strong connections, adults need to model the positive behaviors associated with connectedness and avoid the negative behaviors associated with a lack of connectedness (Learning First Alliance, 2001).

Who children become is strongly influenced by all of those around them, including the other children with whom they spend their days. These relationships have two dimensions: peer acceptance and friendships. The first has to do with a sense of connection to one's peers as a group, such as "The other kids in the choir are a lot like me." The second involves the more personal feelings that grow from individual connections, such as "Nick and Rem are my best friends." Both kinds of relationships become more important as students enter middle school.

Research has shown (Yu, Tepper, & Russell, n.d.) that both peer acceptance and friendships provide some important benefits to children, including:

+ Positive self-image

+ Reduction in aggressive behavior

+ Social competence

+ Enhanced leadership skills

+ Buffering from the negative impact of family problems

+ Reduced likelihood of peer victimization

+ Positive impact on student achievement

In order to be successful in school, children need to feel that they are welcomed, valued, and part of the school community. Sadly, this is not the day-to-day reality for many children who feel alienated, excluded from certain physical spaces, and disadvantaged in the classes and extracurricular activities that are open to them (McNulty, 2004). Children without the protections that peer acceptance and friendship bestow have been shown to be more likely to engage in aggressive behavior, to have low academic achievement, and to experience greater degrees of loneliness and depression (Yu, Tepper, & Russell, n.d.).

Nagle (2001) has identified warning signs that children lack close friends. Some may be seen at school and others are better observed at home or after school. These signs include "being unable to name specific close friends (or naming kids who are not really their friends), lack of incoming calls or invitations from peers, hanging out with friends who are significantly older or younger, and lack of regular peer contacts outside of school" (p. 3).

While for some children, socializing in a positive way seems to come naturally, most children need to be taught important social skills that will increase the likelihood of their forming attachments with their peers. These skills parallel those taught in character education (Yu, Tepper, & Russell, n.d.) and include:

+ Anger management

+ Fairness

+ Sensitivity and empathy

+ Ability to express thoughts, ideas, and emotions in socially acceptable ways

+ Perspective-taking

+ Ability to listen carefully and well

+ Ability to negotiate, resolve conflict, and respectfully disagree

+ Desire to help others

Mobility increases the challenges of establishing strong connections within a school both for the children moving into a school, the children left behind at the old school, and the students at the new school who now must assimilate new peers. For children who change schools frequently throughout their K–12 education, establishing connections becomes increasingly problematic as they move into middle and high school.

For students who remain in a school district over time, mobility among their peers tends to draw them more tightly together, making them less likely to accept new students transferring in to the school (Thorpe, 2003). For mobile children, who often experience the feelings that come with literally being "the new kid on the block, having someone to sit with at lunch, a teacher who helps them catch up with class assignments, or a coach who finds a way to incorporate them into a team—even after the season begins—is vital to their success" (Blum, 2005, Introduction).

The Rubric

A review team wanting to determine how a school's efforts to foster positive relationships measure up against the benchmark of Characteristic 7B would look at two traits of that characteristic. The rubric in Table 7.2 (page 134) describes each trait as it manifests in low-performing, effective, and high-performing schools.

Characteristic 7C: Extracurricular Opportunities

Summary of Research

Despite the lack of a large body of research, there is agreement within the available literature that extracurricular programs offer a wide variety of benefits for students who take part in them. Researchers from Harvard's Family Research Project who were investigating extracurricular programs concluded that the research findings to date "suggest that elementary school children who participated in three or more different activities had higher grades and academic test scores than nonparticipants or youth who participated in only one or two extracurricular activities" (Chaput, 2004, p. 1). The results for children who participated in fewer than three extracurricular activities were "not significantly different than nonparticipants' outcomes."

Table 7.2: Rubric for Characteristic 7B

Characteristic	Trait	Effectiveness Continuum		
		Low Performing	Effective	High Performing
7B. Students have positive, trusting, and caring relationships with adults and peers in the school.	**7B1. Relationships with adults**	Some students have no adult in the school with whom they have a positive, trusting, and caring relationship.	Students have positive, trusting, and caring relationships with one or more adults in the school.	Programs are in place to identify children who are isolated from adults in the school and to help them establish connections with adults.
	7B2. Relationships with peers	Some students are isolated and have limited or no social interactions with peers in the school.	Students have positive, trusting, and caring relationships with peers in the school.	Programs are in place to help students develop positive, trusting, and caring relationships with peers.

For high school students, "the number of activities in which [they] participate . . . was positively associated with numerous indicators, including satisfaction with life, academic achievement, homework completion, beliefs about their abilities, educational and occupational plans, and university enrollment" (Chaput, 2004, p. 2).

Other studies have found that participation in a moderate or large number of extracurricular activities is associated with school connectedness, improved academic achievement, improved behavior, and staying in school through graduation. These benefits are greater for those children who have the greatest challenges (Chaput, 2004). While research is not yet clear on whether there is a level of participation after which no additional benefits occur, or when the benefits even begin to slide backward, it does show that participation in a moderate or large number of extracurricular activities is more advantageous to the student than no or minimal participation.

There is also evidence that participation in extracurricular activities provides greater benefits to children of minority populations and children of poverty. Using SAT data, Everson and Millsap (2005) found that participation in extracurricular activities in high school appears to be one of the few interventions that have more benefits for disadvantaged students than for their more advantaged peers. These findings were similar to those described in other research, in which "involvement in extracurricular activities was linked to decreasing rates of early school dropout for both girls and boys. The outcome was observed primarily among students who were at highest risk of dropping out" (Mahoney & Cairns, 1997, pp. 1–2).

The Rubric

A review team wanting to determine how a school's extracurricular program measures up against the benchmark of Characteristic 7C would look at two traits of that characteristic. The rubric in Table 7.3 describes each trait as it manifests in low-performing, effective, and high-performing schools.

Table 7.3: Rubric for Characteristic 7C

Characteristic	Trait	Effectiveness Continuum		
		Low Performing	Effective	High Performing
7C. Extracurricular activities are numerous and varied, providing ample opportunities for all students to participate.	7C1. Extent of participation	Some students or groups of students do not participate in extracurricular activities.	Most students participate in at least one extracurricular activity.	Most students participate in more than one extracurricular activity.
	7C2. Extent of opportunities	Opportunities for participation in extracurricular activities are limited or not available to all students.	Ample opportunities, extending beyond athletics, exist for all students to participate in extracurricular activities.	There are ample opportunities for all students to participate in extracurricular activities, and students receive public recognition for high performance in all activities.

Characteristic 7D: Attention to the Needs of Students at Risk

Summary of Research

The term *at risk* is used to describe those students whose life experiences put them in the group that is statistically most likely to drop out of school. For these children, negative experiences tend to pile up over time until so many have accumulated that they seem insurmountable. Failure seems inevitable, and remaining in school, not worth the effort or simply too painful.

In interviews of more than 450 young people who left school before graduating, the former students rarely linked their decision to drop out to a single event but instead described a "gradual process of disengagement" from school (National Summit on America's "Silent Epidemic," 2007, p. 2). This withdrawal often begins in middle and even elementary school. Because it occurs over time, there is an opportunity for caring adults to intervene to help students stay in and succeed in school.

For schools that are working to identify the children who have the highest likelihood of dropping out of school, there are a series of warning signs that point to increases in at-risk status (Montes & Lehmann, 2004; Ogle, 1997; Thurlow, Sinclair, & Johnson, 2002). These warning signs include:

+ Excessive absences

+ Low reading skills

+ Low grades

+ Retention in grade

+ Disciplinary issues such as suspensions and expulsions

- Frequent moves from one school to another

- Poverty

- A parent who is not supportive of school

- Lack of participation in school or community extracurricular activities

- Identification for special education

The uneven distribution of these risk factors across racial groups also helps to explain why African American, Hispanic, and Native American children drop out at higher rates than their white and Asian peers (Children's Defense Fund, 2004).

In a multiyear study that examined the relationship between in-grade retention and school dropouts in the Baltimore School District, researchers found that repeating a grade was the single strongest predictor of not completing high school. "Seventy-one percent of students who were retained once dropped out; 80% of students who were retained more than once dropped out; and 94% of those who were retained in both elementary and middle school dropped out" (Children's Defense Fund, 2004, p. 1).

The costs to young people of quitting school are high. Those who do not complete high school are more likely to be unemployed, in poor health, and impoverished; they are also more likely eventually to become the parents of children who themselves later drop out of school. Financially, high school dropouts on average earn $9,200 less per year than high school graduates (Bridgeland, Dilulio, & Morison, 2006).

In a recent study, students across the nation were interviewed about their decision to drop out and how that decision had affected their lives. Students who had dropped out "almost universally expressed great remorse for having left school and expressed strong interest in reentering school with students their age" (Bridgeland, Dilulio, & Morison, 2006, p. iv).

In terms of cost to society, students who drop out of school are eight times as likely to be in jail or prison as high school graduates, half as likely to vote, less likely to volunteer, and more likely to be on public assistance. They represent only 3% of actively engaged citizens in the United States today (Bridgeland, Dilulio, & Morison, 2006; National Conference on Citizenship, 2006).

Dropping out is not inevitable, and schools do not have to wait until it is too late to intervene to help students stay in school. Programs that have been found to be effective in reducing dropouts (Center for Effective Collaboration and Practice, 2000) work to reconnect the student to school by:

- Providing a curriculum that focuses on the individual academic and social needs of each student

- Providing ongoing counseling, including opportunities for students to learn about proper behavior (rather than only punishing inappropriate behavior)

- Encouraging students' active participation in extracurricular activities

- Frequently and systematically monitoring the progress of each student toward graduation

- Encouraging and enabling families to be partners with teachers in educating their children

- Explicitly showing respect for families

+ Calling on the services of community organizations

+ Forming family support groups and assisting parents in connecting with needed services

While the curriculum must include the acquisition of basic skills such as reading, it is also important to give students at risk abundant, meaningful opportunities to use higher-order thinking skills. Tying instruction to the student's life is a key factor in helping him or her stay in school. Yet in many places, "students at risk of educational failure often receive a watered-down curriculum that emphasizes the acquisition of basic academic skills" (Ogle, 1997, p. 1) and is heavily slanted toward memorization and other lower-order thinking skills and away from the kind of engaging, authentic instruction that excites and inspires students.

The emphasis on a basic-skills curriculum for students at risk who are not performing at grade level is based on the belief that learning progresses in a linear sequence; that is, students must first master certain basic skills before they can move up to more challenging and complex tasks. In fact, research on learning has shown that "as students learn, they concurrently use basic skills and higher-level thinking skills" (Ogle, 1997, p. 2). This knowledge has led to the conclusion, especially for children already at risk, that the curriculum must be both richer and deeper in order to reengage students who have previously experienced failure with the linear skills-progression model. Ogle stresses that "all students—especially those at risk—need to be engaged in interesting and challenging learning that goes beyond basic proficiencies" (p. 1).

The Rubric

A review team wanting to determine how a school's efforts to meet the needs of students at risk measure up against the benchmark of Characteristic 7D would look at three traits of that characteristic. The rubric in Table 7.4 (page 138) describes each trait as it manifests in low-performing, effective, and high-performing schools.

Characteristic 7E: System of Interventions

Summary of Research

An important function of the school's discipline or behavior management program is to ensure that students remain and succeed in school. The literature (Balfanz, Herzog, & Mac Iver, 2007) increasingly supports a three-stage model that includes:

1. Schoolwide programs aimed at alleviating approximately 75% of all problem behaviors

2. Individually targeted efforts for the 15% to 20% of students who need additional supports beyond the general schoolwide program

3. Intensive efforts involving specialists (for example, counselors and social workers) for the 5% to 10% of students who need more clinical types of support

For most students, schoolwide programs that look for and recognize positive student behaviors, coupled with programs that trigger consistent responses at the first sign of a problem or misbehavior, provide the support needed to avoid at-risk behaviors.

Table 7.4: Rubric for Characteristic 7D

Characteristic	Trait	Effectiveness Continuum		
		Low Performing	Effective	High Performing
7D. The school has mechanisms and programs to identify and meet the academic and social service needs of students at risk of not completing school.	7D1. Identification of students at risk	There is no systematic process to identify students who are at risk of not completing school.	The school has processes in place to identify students who are at risk of not completing school.	The school examines data on absences, tardies, discipline, and low grades at least quarterly, as part of the process to identify students who are at risk of not completing school.
	7D2. Meeting academic needs of students at risk	There is no systematic process to meet the academic needs of students who are at risk of not completing school.	The school has processes in place to meet the academic needs of students who are at risk of not completing school.	There is a sense of urgency about assisting students at risk when their achievement begins to falter, and there are programs in place to meet their academic needs.
	7D3. Meeting social service needs of students at risk	There is no systematic process to meet the social service needs of students who are at risk of not completing school.	The school has processes in place to meet the social service needs of students who are at risk of not completing school.	The school collaborates with social service agencies and the community to provide needed health and social services to students at risk and their families.

For those 15% to 20% of students who do not respond to the schoolwide program, the school moves on to targeted interventions. Typically, a student is matched with a staff member who works both to build a closer relationship with the student and to keep the student on track. As part of these responsibilities, the adult checks in with the student each day to provide feedback about positive and negative behaviors. Should a student with poor attendance miss school, the staff member calls home to find out why. For a child with behavior problems, the staff member might ask his or her teachers to complete a simple daily checklist describing how the student behaved. Then, at the end of each day, the staff member or the staff member and the student review the reports.

For the remaining 5% to 10% of students, if problems continue despite targeted assistance, more intensive interventions will be required in which the child works individually with counselors or other specialists specifically trained in addressing and alleviating the specific problem behaviors identified (Balfanz et al., 2007).

The effectiveness of programs using a combination of schoolwide, targeted, and intensive interventions was shown through a study of three such projects funded by the Office of Special Education of the U.S. Department of Education in 1990. For 5 years, researchers followed the progress of students who took part in these intervention programs. All three projects shared common characteristics, and researchers found that each was successful in helping students stay in school and graduate. In one of the three programs, for example, "46% of participating students were on track to graduate in four years (68% in five years), compared to 20% of control group students in four years (29% in five years)" (Thurlow et al., 2002, p. 1). Thurlow, Christenson, Sinclair, Evelo, and Thornton (1995) described six interrelated strategies used by all three programs, which, when taken together, were effective in preventing or reducing dropouts among the high-risk population:

1.   Monitoring. An adult was assigned to monitor the behavior of each high-risk student. Individual risk behaviors were identified, including tardies, skipped classes, absences, behavioral referrals, suspensions, and poor academic performance. A way to track these behaviors was designed so that the information was quickly available to the monitor, who then met with the student at least weekly to discuss at-risk behaviors. The monitor also recorded which intervention strategies were tried and whether they resulted in changes in at-risk behaviors.

2.   Relationships. An adult at the school was teamed with each student. That adult was charged to keep track of the student's activities at school. Actions both positive and negative did not go "unnoticed or unremarked" (p. 10). Incremental progress was noted.

3.   Family involvement. Families were seen as key to each student's success. These programs employed multiple strategies to involve family members of students at risk. Strategies included establishing effective and reliable "means of communication, conducting home visits, evening meetings, providing advocacy and problem-solving support, assisting with access to social and community services, sharing ideas regarding home conditions and activities that support student learning" (p. 10).

4.   Affiliation. "A sense of connectedness to the school and belonging to the community of students and staff" was encouraged (p. 10). This was fostered through participation in school-related service learning and in co-curricular and extracurricular activities. Because many students at risk had had previous negative experiences in similar co- and extracurricular activities, staff members had to facilitate participation, sometimes by creating new activities.

5.   Focus on problem-solving skills. Students at risk need the skills to navigate the challenges in their school, community, and home environments. Staff members worked with students to help them learn how and when to use problem-solving skills in their daily lives. Practice helped students to improve their skills and successfully think their way through increasingly difficult problems.

6.   Persistence, continuity, and consistency. Researchers found that successful dropout prevention programs helped students reconnect to school. Persistence refers to the program requirement that an adult be assigned to each student and not give up on the student or allow him or her to lose sight of the importance of school. In all three projects, the school continued to work with students who were "repeatedly truant, suspended, or on the run. Even for students who had made the decision not to return to school, the 'message' was clear from a key person who had connected with the student in the past: *it is important to be in school, and when you [the*

student] are ready I will be available to help you return to school" (p. 12). Continuity refers to a mentoring relationship in which an adult is responsible for knowing the student's needs and is committed to being available to help the student both during the school day and outside of the normal school day and year. Continuity requires that the same adult serve as the student's mentor over a number of years. Consistency means that the message to the student is the same from all concerned adults. The consistent message from the three successful programs was "Do the work, attend classes, be on time, express frustration in a constructive manner, and stay in school!" (p. 12).

The Rubric

A review team wanting to determine how a school's intervention program measures up against the benchmark of Characteristic 7E would look at three traits of that characteristic. The rubric in Table 7.5 describes each trait as it manifests in low-performing, effective, and high-performing schools.

Characteristic 7F: Alternative Options

Summary of Research

The U.S. Department of Education defines an alternative school as a public elementary or secondary school that:

- Addresses needs of students that typically cannot be met in a regular school

- Provides nontraditional education

- Serves as an adjunct to a regular school

- Falls outside the categories of regular, special education, or vocational education (Lehr, Moreau, Lange, & Lanners, 2004, p. 4)

Alternative schools are configured in many ways, but the most common elements include:

- Curriculum leading toward a regular high school diploma

- Policies requiring smaller class sizes than traditional schools

- Opportunities for remedial instruction

- Options for self-paced instruction

- Crisis and behavioral intervention services

- Career counseling (Kleiner, Porch, & Farris, 2002, p. v)

The number of students who are opting for (or would choose to opt for if the choice were available) alternatives to the Monday through Friday, 8:00 to 2:30 school day in a traditional classroom setting is increasing at a rapid pace (Tissington, 2007). As more children, and their parents, seek out alternatives that are a better match for individual needs, interests, strengths, and challenges, the focus of these alternative options is moving from serving children who, for one reason or another, do not fit into traditional classroom settings to providing a placement in which the student will thrive.

Table 7.5: Rubric for Characteristic 7E

Characteristic	Trait	Effectiveness Continuum		
		Low Performing	Effective	High Performing
7E. A system of schoolwide, targeted, and intensive interventions meets the needs of students at risk.	7E1. Schoolwide interventions	There is no schoolwide program to help students avoid at-risk behaviors.	A schoolwide program is in place to help students avoid at-risk behaviors.	A schoolwide program is in place to help students avoid at-risk behaviors, and the program is annually evaluated for effectiveness.
	7E2. Targeted interventions	There are no targeted intervention programs to assist students at risk.	An individually targeted intervention program is in place to assist students at risk who need additional supports beyond the schoolwide program.	An individually targeted intervention program is in place to assist students at risk who need additional supports beyond the schoolwide program, and the program is annually evaluated for effectiveness.
	7E3. Intensive interventions	There are no intensive intervention programs to address specific behavior problems or to reengage students in school.	An intensive intervention program provides assistance from counselors and other specialists in alleviating specific problem behaviors and reengaging students in school.	An intensive intervention program provides assistance from counselors and other specialists in alleviating specific problem behaviors and reengaging students in school, and the program is annually evaluated for effectiveness.

Alternative options include those that are offered at the school site, those that are provided in a self-contained site, those that exist side by side with a traditional school, and, increasingly as technology matures, those that are accessed from wherever a student happens to be at the time. They include pull-out programs for part or all of the school day; schools-within-schools, in which alternative schools exist in tandem with a traditional school, sharing space and resources; private schools; charter schools; home schools; special programs for gifted students; and programs "serving school-aged vulnerable youth who have dropped (or been pushed) out of traditional schools" (Aron, 2003, p. 2). Many alternative options for students combine attention to academic achievement with explicit attention to those factors that engage and connect students to education. These factors include the following (Aron, 2003, p. 3):

1. Physical and psychological safety (e.g., safe facilities, safe ways to handle conflicts between youth, etc.)

2. Appropriate structure (limit setting, clear rules, predictable structure to how program functions, etc.)

3. Supportive relationships (warmth, closeness, etc., with adults and peers)

4. Opportunities to belong (meaningful inclusion)

5. Positive social norms (expectations of behaviors, etc.)

6. Support for efficacy and mattering (empowering youth, challenging environment, chances for leadership, etc.)

7. Opportunities for skill building (e.g., learning about social, communication skills, etc., as well as media literacy, good habits of the mind, etc.)

8. Integration of family, school, and especially community efforts

This is not to say that children who are experiencing difficulty cannot be very well-served by traditional education. But it does underscore the need of schools to be able to individualize instruction in a way that is not yet the norm. To serve all students well, schools must put processes into place that allow them to become more aware of their students' needs, both academic and social, and to address problems before they get out of hand.

In 2006, the Southern Regional Education Board convened a meeting of state legislators and educational leaders from 26 states to examine and discuss strategies that successful schools were employing to increase student achievement and high school graduation rates. A number of recommended strategies emerged from that meeting, including the following (Bottoms, 2006):

1. Schools should take responsibility for "increasing the achievement and graduation rates of all students" (p. 2) by holding all staff members responsible for helping students learn and graduate from high school. Use graduation measures in addition to achievement scores as a frequent gauge of the school's performance. Know which children and which groups of children are graduating and which are not, and then design interventions or modify existing programs and curriculum to address identified needs.

2. Ensure that the curriculum and instruction at the middle school are aligned to that of the high school and that students at the middle grades are being well-prepared academically, especially in language arts, mathematics, and science for "rigorous high school studies" (p. 5). For students who are not performing at grade level, schools should provide tutoring, extended-day or -year instruction, and intervention programs. Use the summer between middle school and high school to provide additional instruction for students who need to catch up in meeting standards so that they do not enter high school already behind.

3. "Create partnerships with employers, community and technical colleges, and shared-time career/technical centers to provide students access to high-quality career/technical studies in high-demand fields. Schools that are raising achievement and holding students in school

have three common elements—a revamped career/technical program that students believe will lead to better jobs; career/technical courses taken along with a challenging set of academic courses; and programs of academic and technical studies that are often aligned with two-year community and technical colleges and with employers" (p. 11).

4. "Develop an extra-help system to provide recovery when students fail a grade or a course and to help them pass high-stakes exams" (p. 12). Include the use of technology to provide catch-up classes that can be accessed outside of regular school hours, extended-day and -year tutoring, and frequent monitoring to ensure that students are not falling behind.

For many students, alternative schools provide a last chance of completing high school, if not on time, then nearly so. For some students, such as those who have been expelled from other schools within the district, their only options are to attend the district alternative school or to receive no schooling at all. For others, alternative schools provide the flexibility missing from traditional schools, more personalized learning, and more acceptance for students who do not fit in with mainstream values and education.

While anecdotal data abound, little is known about the effectiveness of alternative schools (Dynarski, 2000). This inconclusiveness stems from a lack of defining characteristics, which makes generalizations and comparisons problematic; the nature of the obstacles faced by the children who attend these schools; and the individualistic nature of the schools and their missions. Even less is known about alternative schools that reside within traditional school settings (Kleiner et al., 2002). We do know that attendance at alternative schools, and the number of alternative schools themselves, have grown at a rapid pace since the late 1990s and that for those districts reporting, 54% had insufficient capacity to meet student demand (Tissington, 2007, p. 4).

The Rubric

A review team wanting to determine how a school's provision of alternative options measures up against the benchmark of Characteristic 7F would look at one trait of that characteristic. The rubric in Table 7.6 describes that trait as it manifests in low-performing, effective, and high-performing schools.

Table 7.6: Rubric for Characteristic 7F

Characteristic	Trait	Effectiveness Continuum		
		Low Performing	Effective	High Performing
7F. Secondary schools provide alternative options to students in order to increase graduation rates.	7F1. Availability of alternative options	There are few alternative options available to help students complete challenging courses needed for on-time graduation.	Alternative options are available to help students complete challenging courses needed for on-time graduation.	The district offers research-driven alternative options for struggling students and those who have dropped out or been expelled from school.

Characteristic 7G: Support for Transition to Next Grade or School

Summary of Research

In a 2000 literature review, the Oregon Quality Education Commission found that student readiness to progress from one educational level to the next is positively associated with student learning. To ensure such readiness, it is essential to have adequate diagnostic information "for each student so that at any point the school can identify the student's level of functioning and can prescribe a program of improvement, if necessary, to enable the student to be ready to enter the next benchmark level" (p. 44).

Beyond a focus on the individual student, ensuring readiness requires that there be a coordinated curriculum, one in which instruction builds logically from one grade to another. Murphy et al. (2006b, p. 14) note that there must be a "high degree of coordination (a) across subjects within grades, (b) across grade levels and phases of schooling (e.g., from the elementary to the middle school), and (c) among teachers within and across departments and grade levels."

Transitions are almost always difficult for students, particularly those leaving small, personalized elementary learning environments and entering typically larger and more impersonal middle and high schools. Even students "who have had minimal or no problems in school may experience dramatic changes in attendance and performance when making the transition between schools" (Shannon, 2006, p. 36).

Pairing students with adult mentors is one way to ease the disconnect students feel when they progress from one class, grade, or school to another. Because of "societal changes such as increased family mobility, and isolation among families and within communities, many children and youth have fewer opportunities to develop informal caring relationships with adults" (Foster, 2001, p. 8). A high-quality mentoring program matches students to caring adults and aims to create and nurture a supportive relationship that will last over time.

While we know that mentoring is helpful, more research is needed to establish the key elements of effective programs, the optimum duration and intensity of mentoring relationships, and the outcomes that can be expected from mentoring programs (Foster, 2001). Only one large-scale study of mentoring has been conducted to date. In an evaluation of the Big Brothers Big Sisters program, researchers studied more than 1,000 students aged 10–16 over an 18-month period. They found that, compared to a control group, participants in the program "were less likely to begin using drugs and alcohol; less likely to hit someone; and less likely to skip school. Participants reported that they felt more competent about doing schoolwork, skipped one-third fewer classes, and showed modest gains in their grade point averages" (Foster, 2001, pp. 2–3).

Of course, the ultimate transition for which students must be prepared is graduation. Many career and academic guidance programs are aimed at helping students see clearer connections between school, work, and other postsecondary opportunities. Hughes and Karp (2004) drew from more than 50 studies on the effects of school-based career guidance activities and, by extension, school-based academic counseling. They found that, although the studies used different measures and had various limitations, three conclusions did emerge:

1. Academic counseling in which "middle and high school students have regular conferences with counselors to discuss their current and future academic programs" appears to be an effective and cost-efficient strategy (pp. 31–32).

2. "Career development activities that are more experiential in nature," as contrasted with many types of career guidance interventions, "have been found to positively influence such variables as school attendance and completion" (p. 31).

3. "Career guidance and academic counseling [are] potentially very effective with middle school students" (p. 31).

The Rubric

A review team wanting to determine how a school's provisions for ensuring smooth transitions measure up against the benchmark of Characteristic 7G would look at two traits of that characteristic. The rubric in Table 7.7 describes each trait as it manifests in low-performing, effective, and high-performing schools.

Table 7.7: Rubric for Characteristic 7G

Characteristic	Trait	Effectiveness Continuum		
		Low Performing	Effective	High Performing
7G. There is coordination and curricular alignment within and among feeder-pattern schools to ensure that students are prepared for transition to the next grade or school.	**7G1. Level of coordination**	There is little communication or curriculum coordination within and among feeder-pattern schools.	There is communication and coordination between feeder-pattern schools to ensure curriculum alignment.	There is communication, curriculum alignment, and coordination across grade levels and between feeder-pattern schools to improve transitions.
	7G2. Coordination among teachers	Some teachers are not familiar with what will be required of students at the next grade or level.	Teachers know and prepare students for what will be required of them at the next grade or level.	Teachers know and prepare students for what will be required of them at the next grade or level. Teacher teams work together to design communication processes.

Conclusion

As with many components of school improvement, the areas of connectedness, engagement, and readiness are complex and interrelated. Students need to feel a connection to their school, their peers, and the adults within their school. When these connections are in place, students are much more likely to stay in school and value education. The key to creating a school that is characterized by connectedness, engagement, and readiness is to establish a proactive system for identifying students at risk and responding to them with unrelenting assistance. Keeping students in school and engaged in their own learning ensures a higher quality of life, creates lifelong learners, and results in multigenerational socioeconomic improvement.

Effectiveness Indicator 8
School Environment

Students often remember how adults behave more than what they say.

—Learning First Alliance

Effective schools provide students and staff members with a safe and inviting environment that is conducive to working and learning. From this principle, we derive Effectiveness Indicator 8. An on-site school review looks for the combination of warmth and academic challenge that is the key to a positive school environment. Such an environment is strongly associated with student success. There is respect between all stakeholders. Faculty and staff members skillfully meet the needs of culturally and linguistically diverse students. Behavior management systems focus first on instruction and intervention, resulting in an environment that is orderly but not unduly regimented.

Nine characteristics define Effectiveness Indicator 8: School Environment:

8A. School administrators foster a positive school environment in which students and staff members feel valued, students are challenged to grow academically, and staff members are challenged to grow professionally.

8B. The school and its physical environment are safe, welcoming, and conducive to learning.

8C. A culture of trust and respect exists at all levels of the school community.

8D. Staff members work effectively with racially, culturally, and linguistically diverse students.

8E. Positive character traits are taught and reinforced as part of the instructional program.

8F. An effective discipline and behavior management system supports teaching and learning schoolwide.

8G. School administrators and staff members actively support the discipline and behavior management system.

8H.   School rules are fair and are applied consistently and equitably. Consequences are commensurate with the offense.

8I.   Out-of-school suspensions are reserved for only the most serious offenses, and suspended students are allowed to continue the academic program.

Characteristic 8A: Positive School Environment

Summary of Research

The school environment sets the stage for learning and teaching. It projects in overt and subtle ways the expectations for the behavior of both students and staff members—for example, high student achievement, respect between stakeholders, and individualized support for students. So it not surprising that there are differences in environment between high- and low-performing schools.

In effective schools, students are challenged to grow academically in an environment of both support and "academic press." It is the combination of support and press that results in high student achievement (Jerald, 2006). In these same schools, adults are challenged to grow professionally in an atmosphere of trust and respect.

Students attending schools in which there is a co-commitment to academic press and support know what is expected of them both academically and behaviorally and what they in turn can expect to receive in the way of needed supports. Jerald (2006) observes that

> effective schools make sure that even the smallest aspects of daily life align with the core ideology and envisioned future. . . . For example, fifth graders who enter Washington, D.C.'s, Key Academy middle school this fall will be asked to identify themselves as members of the "Class of 2018"—the year their teachers expect them to graduate from *college*. Visitors to the school are encouraged to ask students what class they are in, and students invariably provide their intended college graduation date. Teachers talk frequently about what college they attended and their diplomas hang on the walls of the school. Identification cards outside teachers' classrooms list their alma maters along with their names. . . . Not surprisingly, the school's mostly low-income African American students consistently garner the highest middle school assessment results in the city. (p. 5)

Staff members, too, should know that they are valued at the same time as they are encouraged to excel, and the school's culture communicates strong messages about these beliefs to all stakeholders. A positive culture weds words with actions.

School administrators, as discussed in the leadership chapter, have a key part to play in ensuring that positive conditions, such as those just described, exist at the school. Many of the responsibilities for creating and maintaining a positive school environment can and should be shared; however, there are certain responsibilities that should not be delegated. Because of their unique position in the school and district structures, it is school administrators who must take the reins in setting and maintaining high expectations for themselves, students, teachers, and all others within the school community. Such leadership ensures that the following conditions are established:

•   There is an atmosphere of academic press, in which learning is prioritized as the most important mission of the school.

- Students feel valued by school administrators and challenged to grow academically.

- Schoolwide positive behavior adds to a strong climate for teaching and learning.

- Risks in pursuit of excellence are encouraged.

- New ideas, proposed solutions, and what each individual brings to a discussion are valued and appreciated.

- Success is celebrated.

- Staff members feel simultaneously valued by school administrators and challenged to grow professionally.

- A tone of mutual respect exists at all levels of the organization and between all stakeholders.

- Meaningful relationships are encouraged.

Leaders in schools such as those just described do not give up when faced with difficult issues of climate. They tackle these issues, and in doing so "inspire teachers, staff, [and students] to accomplish things that might seem beyond their grasp" (Waters & Grubb, 2004, p. 10).

The Rubric

A review team wanting to determine how a school's environment measures up against the benchmark of Characteristic 8A would look at four traits of that characteristic. The rubric in Table 8.1 (page 150) describes each trait as it manifests in low-performing, effective, and high-performing schools.

Characteristic 8B: Safe, Welcoming School Environment

Summary of Research

John Mayer (2007, p. 7) notes, "Children are very visual. They delight and thrive in environments that evoke pleasure, comfort and safety." He imagines taking a close look at a school through the eyes of a child:

> Does it convey a sense of adventure, curiosity, fun or excitement? A child should be pulled into the building, curious about what the people inside have in store for them. . . . A bright colour, an expressive face or an interesting object naturally pulls a child toward it. . . . We so desperately want our children to embrace education enthusiastically, yet we do not realize that motionless, unwelcoming buildings may be a child's first impression of learning. (p. 7)

Once inside the school, do students feel a sense of warmth and acceptance? The school atmosphere should project concern for students. In such a school, "teachers and administrators take an interest in the personal goals, achievements, and problems of students and support them in their academic and extracurricular activities" (Cotton, 1990, pp. 3–4).

Marshall (2004, p. 2) reports that

> positive school climate has been associated with fewer behavioral and emotional problems for students. Additionally, specific research on school climate in high-risk

Table 8.1: Rubric for Characteristic 8A

Characteristic	Trait	Effectiveness Continuum		
		Low Performing	Effective	High Performing
8A. School administrators foster a positive school environment in which students and staff members feel valued, students are challenged to grow academically, and staff members are challenged to grow professionally.	8A1. Students' feeling of being valued	Some students do not feel valued by school administrators.	Students feel valued by school administrators.	School administrators provide opportunities within the school day for students to meet with them.
	8A2. Students' feeling of being academically challenged	Some students do not feel academically challenged.	Students feel challenged to grow academically.	School administrators monitor to ensure that an environment of academic challenge is maintained over time.
	8A3. Staff members' feeling of being valued	Some staff members do not feel valued by school administrators.	Staff members feel valued by school administrators.	School administrators regularly meet with and seek the advice of school staff members.
	8A4. Staff members' feeling of being challenged professionally	Some staff members do not feel challenged by school administrators to grow professionally.	Staff members feel challenged by school administrators to grow professionally.	School administrators monitor to ensure that an environment of continuous professional growth is maintained over time.

urban environments indicates that a positive, supportive, and culturally conscious school climate can significantly shape the degree of academic success experienced by urban students. Furthermore, researchers have found that positive school climate perceptions are protective factors for boys and may supply high-risk students with a supportive learning environment yielding healthy development, as well as preventing anti-social behavior.

For adults and students alike, a precondition of teaching and learning is safety. Research has found that when students feel safe in school, they are less likely to be truant and carry weapons to school and more likely to be able to concentrate on schoolwork and achieve at higher levels (Perkins, 2006).

Although much less has been written about teacher safety than about student safety, teachers, too, need to feel safe in order to do their best work. Teachers who do not feel safe are less likely to participate in the social life of the school, attend evening and weekend events at the school, or have a positive attitude toward the school. Moreover, teachers who do not feel safe at school are less likely to remain in either the school or the teaching profession (Luekens, Lyter, & Fox, 2005).

One way to increase safety in schools is to have an up-to-date, well-communicated, and frequently rehearsed emergency plan. Procedures laid out in a school emergency plan should be developed with input from staff members, families, and outside organizations such as law enforcement and social service agencies. The emergency procedures need to be practiced seriously and often. No one should be allowed to opt out of practice drills, which should be as lifelike as possible in order to best prepare staff members and students for what might be experienced should the practice ever become the real thing. Debriefings following each practice are used to improve the processes.

It seems that everything is a little easier in a well-designed and well-kept building. There is no strong research that demonstrates that a building in good repair is a necessity in order for students to achieve, but

> creating an environment in which students thrive is more easily accomplished in a physical plant that promotes safety and community. Unfortunately, three in four U.S. schools need some kind of repair. About one third of all schools—serving 14 million students—need extensive repair or replacement. . . .

> Students can read the message on the walls. When their school has peeling paint, clogged toilets, a leaky roof, dark hallways, littered playgrounds, and poor air quality, the message is that these students and their education are not respected or valued. This concrete evidence of disregard undermines efforts to create a respectful and caring school community.

> The poor condition of many school buildings also has a demonstrable effect on student health, which can in turn affect achievement. Toxic physical conditions such as poor ventilation, environmental contaminants, and lack of daylight harm students' health and hinder their learning. (Learning First Alliance, 2001, p. 12)

The Rubric

A review team wanting to determine how a school's environment measures up against the benchmark of Characteristic 8B would look at five traits of that characteristic. The rubric in Table 8.2 (page 152) describes each trait as it manifests in low-performing, effective, and high-performing schools.

Characteristic 8C: Culture of Trust and Respect

Summary of Research

In late 2003, researchers from the Northwest Regional Educational Laboratory completed a literature review on trust among teachers and administrators in schools. Their review "verified what most educators already know to be true: the quality of the relationships within a school community makes a difference" (Brewster & Railsback, 2003b, p. 2). While the research results do not clearly link increased trust among staff members with trust between staff members and school leaders, the researchers concluded that "while trust alone does not guarantee success, schools with little or no trust have almost no chance of improving" (p. 7).

Table 8.2: Rubric for Characteristic 8B

Characteristic	Trait	Effectiveness Continuum		
		Low Performing	Effective	High Performing
8B. The school and its physical environment are safe, welcoming, and conducive to learning.	8B1. Overall feeling of safety	Some students, staff members, or families do not feel safe at the school.	Students, staff members, and families feel safe at the school.	A safety committee with representation from school administration, staff, families, and students meets regularly to address school safety issues or concerns.
	8B2. Overall atmosphere	Some students, staff members, and families do not view the school as welcoming to students.	Students, staff members, and families view the school as welcoming to students.	School administrators invite student, staff, and family suggestions on ways to improve the school atmosphere.
	8B3. Safety of physical spaces	Classrooms, hallways, or other spaces are not safe for students and adults.	Classrooms, hallways, and other spaces are safe for students and adults.	Classrooms, hallways, and other spaces are safe. Staff members are frequently seen in areas where students congregate and are visible in hallways during passing times.
	8B4. Awareness of safety procedures	Some staff members are unaware of the safety procedures described in the school safety plan.	Staff members are familiar with the safety procedures described in the school safety plan.	Staff members and students are familiar with and practice the safety procedures described in the school safety plan.
	8B5. Condition of building and grounds	The building and grounds need repair or maintenance.	The building and grounds are clean and well-maintained.	The building and grounds are clean and well-maintained, and repairs are made in a timely manner.

Brewster and Railsback cited five components of trusting relationships:

Benevolence: Having confidence that another party has your best interests at heart and will protect your interests is a key ingredient of trust.

Reliability: Reliability refers to the extent to which you can depend upon another party to come through for you, to act consistently, and to follow through.

Competence: Similar to reliability, competence has to do with belief in another party's ability to perform the tasks required by his or her position. For example, if a principal means well but lacks necessary leadership skills, he or she is not likely to be trusted to do the job.

Honesty: A person's integrity, character, and authenticity are all dimensions of trust. The degree to which a person can be counted on to represent situations fairly makes a huge difference in whether or not he or she is trusted by others in the school community.

Openness: Judgments about openness have to do with how freely another party shares information with others. Guarded communication, for instance, provokes distrust because people wonder what is being withheld and why. Openness is crucial to the development of trust between supervisors and subordinates, particularly in times of increased vulnerability for staff.

Finally, it appears from the research "that trust and collaboration are mutually reinforcing: the more parties work together, the greater opportunity they have to get to know one another and build trust" (p. 9).

Each year, North Carolina surveys its teachers about working conditions in schools across the state. An analysis of the 2006 survey found that schools' ability to create and maintain an atmosphere of trust and mutual respect was strongly correlated with employee retention. The factors most strongly associated with trust were "a schoolwide commitment to a shared vision; an effective process for making collaborative decisions and solving problems; and school leadership that consistently supports teachers" (Reeves, Emerick, & Hirsch, 2007, p. 1). The analysis also included the following findings (p. 1):

- Sixty-six percent of North Carolina educators who intend to stay at their school agreed that there was an atmosphere of trust and mutual respect. Conversely, only 22 percent of educators planning to remain in teaching but move to another school agreed that such an atmosphere exists in their school.

- Approximately 20 percent more educators in the state's highest achieving schools agreed there was trust and mutual respect in their school than educators in schools with the lowest student performance. This gap on the question of trust was the largest of all questions on the survey.

- In schools with the lowest teacher turnover rates, about two-thirds of educators agreed that there is an atmosphere of trust, compared to about half of the educators in schools with the highest turnover rates.

In follow-up focus groups, principals and staff members were questioned more deeply about their responses. A principal at one of the schools receiving the highest marks for trust and respect explained that building trust means "helping [staff members] feel like you were listening to them, that they were heard. If they don't feel heard, they will not be as likely to come to you with their ideas" (p. 3). These findings replicate those of earlier studies linking a positive school climate with increased job satisfaction for all school personnel (Marshall, 2004).

In schools that value close relationships, demand respect for others from both staff members and students, and encourage bringing up thoughts and ideas, "students and others in the school community are more likely to feel comfortable voicing concerns—whether about their own experiences at school or home or about the behavior or needs of other students" (Learning First Alliance, 2001, p. 8).

School leaders can also build trust, respect, and positive relationships by giving staff members opportunities and encouragement to participate in professional learning communities. In their foundational book *On Common Ground*, DuFour, Eaker, and DuFour (2005) explore the concept of professional learning communities from the perspectives of 12 educational researchers and practitioners. The concept rests on focused, structured teacher collaboration: "Teachers meet regularly to share, refine, and assess the impact of lessons and strategies to help increasing numbers of students learn at higher levels" (p. xiv). There is also some evidence that participating in well-functioning professional learning communities has a spillover effect: teachers who are active participants in those communities work to provide similar experiences for their students (Learning First Alliance, 2001).

The Rubric

A review team wanting to determine how a school's environment measures up against the benchmark of Characteristic 8C would look at two traits of that characteristic. The rubric in Table 8.3 describes each trait as it manifests in low-performing, effective, and high-performing schools.

Characteristic 8D: Staff Effectiveness With Diverse Students

Summary of Research

Cultural proficiency among staff members contributes to a positive school environment. To be culturally proficient is to work to understand the forces, events, and conditions that mold the lives of our children. It is to consciously strive to acknowledge powerful and often incorrect beliefs that have shaped our understanding of the world around us and the people within it. It is working hard to shed prejudices and stereotypes, knowing that this is a challenging task but accepting that challenge and continuing every day to learn more so that we can better reach every child in our classroom or school. Perhaps most important, it is to understand that many children and their families see the world in very different terms than we might and that as educators it is our responsibility to meet every learner on his or her ground.

For the purposes of this rubric, we looked at many definitions of cultural proficiency (also referred to as *cultural competence*). We selected two: one from the field of medicine and one from the field of education. The first definition is from the *National Standards for Culturally and Linguistically Appropriate Services in Health Care*. It took 5 years to agree on this definition, which reads:

> Cultural and linguistic competence is a set of congruent behaviors, attitudes, and policies that come together in a system, agency, or among professionals that enables effective work in cross-cultural situations. "Culture" refers to integrated patterns of

Table 8.3: Rubric for Characteristic 8C

Characteristic	Trait	Effectiveness Continuum		
		Low Performing	Effective	High Performing
8C. A culture of trust and respect exists at all levels of the school community.	8C1. Level of trust	There is a lack of trust among school staff members or between staff members and school administrators.	Staff members and school administrators trust one another. This trust extends to, and is reciprocated by, students and their families.	A culture of trust exists at all levels of the school community. School administrators listen to and act upon ideas, thoughts, and concerns regarding trust.
	8C2. Level of respect	There is a lack of respect among school staff members or between staff members and school administrators.	Staff members and school administrators respect one another. This respect extends to, and is reciprocated by, students and their families.	A culture of respect exists at all levels of the school community. School administrators listen to and act upon ideas, thoughts, and concerns regarding respect.

human behavior that include the language, thoughts, communications, actions, customs, beliefs, values, and institutions of racial, ethnic, religious, or social groups. "Competence" implies having the capacity to function effectively as an individual and an organization within the context of the cultural beliefs, behaviors, and needs presented by consumers and their communities. (IQ Solutions, 2001, pp. 4–5)

More than 100 education stakeholders gathered at a 2004 summit held by the Oregon Department of Education to consider cultural proficiency. Building on the *National Standards for Culturally and Linguistically Appropriate Services in Health Care,* they further fleshed out the definition, adding:

Cultural competence is based on a commitment to social justice and equity. . . .

Cultural competence is a developmental process occurring at individual and system levels that evolves and is sustained over time. Recognizing that individuals begin with specific lived experiences and biases, and that working to accept multiple world views is a difficult choice and task, cultural competence requires that individuals and organizations:

a. have a defined set of values and principles, demonstrated behaviors, attitudes, policies and structures that enable them to work effectively in a cross-cultural manner;

b. demonstrate the capacity to 1) value diversity, 2) engage in self-reflection, 3) facilitate effectively (manage) the dynamics of difference, 4) acquire and institutionalize cultural knowledge, 5) adapt to the diversity and the cultural contexts of the students, families, and communities they serve, and 6) support actions which foster equity of opportunity and services; and

c. institutionalize, incorporate, evaluate, and advocate the above in all aspects of leadership, policy-making, administration, practice, and service delivery while systematically involving staff, students, families, key stakeholders, and communities. (Oregon Department of Education, 2004, p. 1)

So what does this mean for schools and school systems with students and teachers of widely diverse cultures, races, and backgrounds? Researchers from the Education Trust (2006, p. 2) have found that

schools and school districts that are changing the life opportunities for children of color aren't performing magic, and these high-achieving students aren't the product of "creaming schemes" that teach only the best and brightest. These schools and districts are simply engaged every day in the hard work of teaching all children to high standards. They are giving their students the tools for success:

1. Clear goals

2. High expectations

3. Rigorous coursework

4. Extra instructional help when needed

5. Strong teachers who know their subject matter and how to teach it

To these five tools, we would add four more (Shannon & Bylsma, 2002, pp. 2–3):

1. Changed beliefs and attitudes

2. Cultural responsiveness

3. Extended academic time

4. More family and community involvement

Research has clearly shown a connection between expectations and outcomes. Student performance tends to rise and fall with those expectations. In order to close the achievement gap, teachers, administrators, parents, teaching and nonteaching staff members at the school, coaches, and others must believe in and demand high levels of learning from all students. For some staff and community members, this will mean modifying beliefs and attitudes.

Along with high expectations must come genuine interest in and caring for the children entrusted to us as educators. This caring attitude makes the personal connection possible and communicates to students our positive belief in them.

Teaching and learning are both personal and complex processes: "Teachers provide their instruction from their personal cultural framework, and students learn from within the context of their own experience" (Shannon & Bylsma, 2002, p. 2). A teacher who is culturally competent is able to recognize when instruction or resources are going to be dissonant with his or her students' framework and experience. In these instances, the culturally competent teacher draws on additional resources in order to connect new information to the learner's frame of reference.

Rigorous and challenging coursework must be the curriculum for all students. Although "research tells us that high school students who study advanced math beyond Algebra II—classes like trigonometry and calculus—double their chances of earning a bachelor's degree, . . . less than a third of Black high school graduates are exposed to advanced math in school" (Education Trust, 2006, p. 2).

One of the key pieces of information an on-site school review provides to schools is an analysis of student work. This analysis measures the match of classroom work and homework to the cognitive demands of state or district standards and examines the ratio of higher- to lower-order thinking skills required by each assignment. In higher-performing schools and in higher-level classes, assignments are nearly always more rigorous in relation to state standards, and a much greater percentage of assignments address higher-order thinking skills, than is the case in lower-performing schools and lower-level courses.

The Rubric

A review team wanting to determine how a school's work with diverse students measures up against the benchmark of Characteristic 8D would look at one trait of that characteristic. The rubric in Table 8.4 describes that trait as it manifests in low-performing, effective, and high-performing schools.

Table 8.4: Rubric for Characteristic 8D

Characteristic	Trait	Effectiveness Continuum		
		Low Performing	Effective	High Performing
8D. Staff members work effectively with racially, culturally, and linguistically diverse students.	8D1. Degree of staff effectiveness with diverse students	Not all staff members work effectively with racially, culturally, and linguistically diverse students.	Staff members work effectively with racially, culturally, and linguistically diverse students.	Staff members work effectively with racially, culturally, and linguistically diverse students, resulting in high and equitable achievement levels across all student populations.

Characteristic 8E: Character Education

Summary of Research

In a report on "safe and supportive schools," the Learning First Alliance (2001) notes that "the values of respect, cooperation, responsibility, leadership, helpfulness, and obligation to others are integral to the daily school routine and are taught and reinforced in a variety of ways" (p. 10). Character education is an intentional, proactive effort to instill in students core ethical values that are good both for society as a whole and for each individual within. These values include caring, honesty, fairness, courage, responsibility, equality, generosity, kindness, and respect for self and others. The goal of character education is "to raise children to become morally responsible, self-disciplined citizens" (Berkowitz & Bier, 2005).

In addition to teaching positive behaviors, character education can work to reduce negative ones. Much has been written about school bullying since the late 1990s. Bullying occurs when there

> is an imbalance of power that exists over an extended period of time between two individuals, two groups, or a group and an individual . . . and . . . when the more powerful intimidate or belittle those who are less powerful. It can take both physical and psychological forms, but physical bullying is not as common as the more subtle forms, such as social exclusion, name-calling, and gossip. (Perkins, 2006, p. 15)

Character education can work against both of these forms of intimidation by supporting positive peer relationships and encouraging and empowering students to stop bullying whenever it is observed or encountered.

Students can be taught many of these skills as part of regular classroom instruction. When students are working in groups, for example, teachers have the opportunity to teach and reinforce such skills as listening carefully, disagreeing respectfully, taking responsibility, and working as part of a team. Here, however, actions truly speak louder than words. To be most effective, school staff members "should model these values and behaviors, emphasize them in daily interactions, and discuss them explicitly and directly" (Learning First Alliance, 2001, p. 8).

The Rubric

A review team wanting to determine how a school's efforts to teach positive character traits measure up against the benchmark of Characteristic 8E would look at one trait of that characteristic. The rubric in Table 8.5 describes that trait as it manifests in low-performing, effective, and high-performing schools.

Table 8.5: Rubric for Characteristic 8E

Characteristic	Trait	Effectiveness Continuum		
		Low Performing	Effective	High Performing
8E. Positive character traits are taught and reinforced as part of the instructional program.	8E1. Incorporation of character education into instructional program	The teaching of positive character traits (for example, honesty, fairness, and responsibility) is not part of the instructional program.	The teaching of positive character traits (for example, honesty, fairness, and responsibility) is part of the instructional program.	The teaching of positive character traits (for example, honesty, fairness, and responsibility) is part of the instructional program, and all staff members continually reinforce positive behaviors associated with these traits.

Characteristic 8F: Discipline and Behavior Management System

Summary of Research

Teachers and administrators have an important role in and responsibility for creating and supporting a positive school environment, including a reasonable system of behavior management that supports teaching and learning. In a review of 20 years of research, Kathleen Cotton (1990, p. 6) defined effective classroom managers as "those teachers whose classrooms were orderly, had a minimum of student misbehavior, and had high levels of time-on-task." She found that the following elements have been consistently identified and validated as the hallmarks of an effective behavior management system (pp. 6–7):

- Holding and communicating high expectations for student learning and behavior
- Establishing and clearly teaching classroom rules and procedures
- Specifying consequences and their relation to student behavior
- Enforcing classroom rules promptly, consistently, and equitably
- Sharing with students the responsibility for classroom management
- Maintaining a brisk pace for instruction and making smooth transitions between activities
- Monitoring classroom activities and providing feedback and reinforcement

Other researchers (Gaustad, 1992; Marshall, 2004; Skiba & Peterson, 1999; Tableman, 2004) have identified a number of effective techniques to encourage positive student behavior:

- Increase students' social attachment or connectedness to school.
- Provide a place for kids to blow off steam.
- Provide structured activities during lunchtimes.
- Ensure safety during lunchtimes and between classes.
- Teach students to attribute their successes and failures to personal effort, not to forces beyond their control.
- Teach students to check their own behavior and judge its appropriateness.
- Implement character education or the promotion of fundamental moral values in children.
- Use violence-prevention and conflict-resolution curricula.
- Initiate peer mediation.
- Initiate bullying prevention, and prevent acts of bullying.
- Meaningfully reward students for appropriate behavior.
- Use contracts with students to reinforce behavioral expectations.

The Rubric

A review team wanting to determine how a school's behavior management system measures up against the benchmark of Characteristic 8F would look at three traits of that characteristic. The rubric in Table 8.6 describes each trait as it manifests in low-performing, effective, and high-performing schools.

Table 8.6: Rubric for Characteristic 8F

Characteristic	Trait	Effectiveness Continuum		
		Low Performing	Effective	High Performing
8F. An effective discipline and behavior management system supports teaching and learning schoolwide.	8F1. Impact of discipline and behavior management system on teaching and learning	The school lacks a formal discipline and behavior management system that supports teaching and learning.	The schoolwide discipline and behavior management system supports teaching and learning.	The schoolwide discipline and behavior management system supports teaching and learning and provides meaningful recognition for positive student behavior.
	8F2. Impact of discipline and behavior management system on school safety	The school discipline and behavior management system is ineffective or does not provide for the safety of staff and students.	The school discipline and behavior management system provides for the safety of staff and students.	A representative group of stakeholders periodically reviews and updates the school discipline and behavior management system to ensure a safe environment for staff and students.
	8F3. Interventions for troubled or violent students	The school has few or no processes in place to identify and provide appropriate interventions for the most troubled or violent students.	The school has processes in place to identify and provide appropriate interventions for the most troubled or violent students.	The school, in cooperation with community partners, social service agencies, and law enforcement agencies, has procedures in place to identify and provide appropriate interventions for the most troubled or violent students.

Characteristic 8G: Support for Discipline and Behavior Management System

Summary of Research

Researchers have looked at schools in which discipline is and is not a problem in order to identify those traits associated with schools with few behavior problems and those associated with schools in which discipline is an ongoing struggle. In the most effective schools, one striking difference is the attitude of the staff toward behavior. In effective schools, the staff "is committed to establishing and maintaining appropriate student behavior as an essential precondition of learning" (Cotton, 1990, pp. 3–4). That commitment on the part of teachers, staff, and administrators, in turn, results in a culture of respect that permeates the school and is evident in interactions schoolwide. A number of other differences between well- and poorly disciplined schools have emerged. Cotton (1990, pp. 2–3) notes the following characteristics of effective schools:

- High behavioral expectations. In contrast to poorly disciplined schools, staff in well-disciplined schools share and communicate high expectations for appropriate student behavior.

- Clear and broad-based rules. Rules, sanctions, and procedures are developed with input from students, are clearly specified, and are made known to everyone in the school. Researchers have found that student participation in developing and reviewing school discipline programs creates a sense of ownership and belongingness. Widespread dissemination of clearly stated rules and procedures, moreover, ensures that all students and staff understand what is and is not acceptable.

- Warm school climate. A warm social climate, characterized by a concern for students as individuals, is typical of well-disciplined schools. Teachers and administrators take an interest in the personal goals, achievements, and problems of students and support them in their academic and extracurricular activities.

- A visible, supportive principal. Many poorly disciplined schools have principals who are visible only for "official" duties, such as assemblies, or when enforcing school discipline. In contrast, principals of well-disciplined schools tend to be very visible in hallways and classrooms, talking informally with teachers and students, speaking to them by name, and expressing interest in their activities.

- Delegation of discipline authority to teachers. Principals in well-disciplined schools take responsibility for dealing with serious infractions, but they hold teachers responsible for handling routine classroom discipline problems. They assist teachers to improve their classroom management and discipline skills by arranging for staff development activities as needed.

- Close ties with communities. Researchers have generally found that well-disciplined schools are those which have a high level of communication and partnership with the communities they serve. These schools have a higher-than-average incidence of parent involvement in school functions, and communities are kept informed of school goals and activities.

By contrast, in a study of more than 600 secondary schools across the nation, Johns Hopkins researchers (Gaustad, 1992) found that schools in which discipline was a problem shared the following characteristics:

+ Rules were not understood by students, parents, or staff members.

+ Rules were perceived as unfair.

+ Rules were inconsistently enforced.

+ Students did not support the rules.

+ Teachers and administrators disagreed on the proper responses to student misconduct.

+ Some or all staff members ignored the rules some or all of the time.

+ Teacher-administration cooperation was poor, or the administration did not take a leadership role in behavior management.

+ Teachers tended to want to see students punished for misbehavior.

The role of school administrators is pivotal in setting the tone and climate of the school. Administrators are responsible for carrying out the school discipline program, but that plan should have been developed with broad participation from all stakeholders. It should reflect a shared focus on creating conditions in which all students have opportunities to learn to high standards without undue regimentation.

In supporting school rules, the principals of schools in which discipline is smoothly running maintain a balance of warmth and encouragement coupled with high expectations. They are "liked and respected, rather than feared, and communicate caring for students as well as willingness to impose punishment if necessary" (Gaustad, 1992, p. 2).

As the school leader, the principal must be visible in hallways and classrooms and seen interacting with students and staff members. Marzano, Waters, and McNulty (2005) identify *visibility* as one of 21 specific leadership responsibilities that have a statistically significant correlation with student achievement. Behaviors associated with visibility are "making systematic and frequent visits to classrooms, having frequent contact with students, and being highly visible to students, teachers, and parents" (p. 61). Principals who are regularly seen throughout the school help to send the message of support and clear expectations for behavior.

The Rubric

A review team wanting to determine how a school's support of the discipline program measures up against the benchmark of Characteristic 8G would look at four traits of that characteristic. The rubric in Table 8.7 describes each trait as it manifests in low-performing, effective, and high-performing schools.

Table 8.7: Rubric for Characteristic 8G

Characteristic	Trait	Effectiveness Continuum		
		Low Performing	Effective	High Performing
8G. School administrators and staff members actively support the discipline and behavior management system.	8G1. Staff members' expectations for student behavior	Some staff members do not have high expectations for student behavior.	Staff members have high expectations for student behavior.	Staff members are committed to establishing and maintaining appropriate student behavior.
	8G2. Staff members' support of behavior and discipline management system	Some staff members do not actively support the behavior and discipline system in their classrooms.	Staff members actively support the behavior and discipline system in their classrooms.	Staff members actively support the behavior and discipline system in their classrooms and frequently communicate and discuss the expectations for appropriate student behavior.
	8G3. Division of responsibility for discipline	Neither staff members nor school administrators are satisfied with the current division of responsibility for student discipline.	School administrators take responsibility for dealing with serious infractions and hold teachers responsible for handling routine classroom discipline problems.	School administrators deal with serious infractions and provide professional development to teachers who continue to struggle with classroom discipline to ensure that their classrooms are conducive to learning and teaching.
	8G4. Visibility of school administrators	School administrators are seldom visible in hallways and classrooms or seen talking informally with students or teachers.	School administrators are frequently visible in hallways, classrooms, and the cafeteria and on the building grounds.	School administrators are frequently visible in hallways, classrooms, and the cafeteria and on the building grounds. They talk informally with teachers and students, addressing them by name and expressing interest in their activities.

Characteristic 8H: Consistent and Equitable Application of School Rules

Summary of Research

Gaustad (1992, p. 1) notes that "school discipline has two main goals: (1) ensure the safety of staff and students, and (2) create an environment conducive to learning." Schools with effective behavior management systems work to make sure that the reasons behind the rules, the rules themselves, and the consequences of breaking those rules are clear, easily understood, and communicated to staff members, students, and parents. This communication is much more than simply including lists of rules, consequences, and rewards in a student or parent handbook. To be sure that all stakeholders understand what is expected, behavioral expectations need to be widely shared with students, parents, staff members, and the community through such means as newsletters, student assemblies, updates, and parent and community meetings. Information on the school behavioral system should also be available in the home languages of students attending the school. The Learning First Alliance (2001) points out that

> this emphasis on rules and norms is particularly important at the beginning of the school year, when staff and students can focus systematically on identifying common behavioral problems and helping students identify appropriate alternative behaviors. Staff then can help students display and encourage positive behavior throughout the school year. (p. 14)

In addition, processes need to be in place to ensure that the expectations are communicated to students and families who transfer into the district, new staff members, volunteers, and substitute teachers (Gaustad, 1992, p. 2).

Even in the schools with the best-designed behavior management systems, rules get broken. When that happens, in order for the consequences to be most effective, they must be perceived by all as commensurate with the offense (Cotton, 1990, p. 5). Many schools have succumbed to the temptation to believe that the stiffer the punishment, the more likely it is that students will follow all of the rules, but in fact, researchers have found that "draconian punishments are ineffective" (p. 5). This calls into question the broad application of "zero-tolerance" policies. There is certainly a time and a place for zero-tolerance policies in addressing the most serious and dangerous offenses (such as bringing a lethal weapon to school); however a zero-tolerance policy and the definitions that go with it can also lead to overly severe punishments that far outweigh the offense.

In addition to being commensurate with the offense, to be effective, discipline must be consistently and equitably applied to all students. Yet we are still far from that goal. In a 2007 investigative report, the *Chicago Tribune* noted that in 49 of the 50 states, the percentage of African American students being suspended is higher than the percentage of African American students in the school population, and in 21 states the suspension percentages are nearly double the school population percentages (Witt, 2007).

- In the average New Jersey public school, African American students are almost 60 times as likely as white students to be expelled for serious disciplinary infractions.

- In Minnesota, black students are suspended 6 times as often as whites.

- In Iowa, blacks make up just 5 percent of the statewide public school enrollment but account for 22 percent of the students who get suspended.

- In every state but Idaho, . . . black students are being suspended in numbers greater than would be expected from their proportion of the student population. . . . No other ethnic group is disciplined at such a high rate.

- Hispanic students are suspended and expelled in almost direct proportion to their populations, while white and Asian students are disciplined far less. (Witt, 2007)

Researchers echo these findings. Linda M. Raffaele Mendez and Howard M. Knoff (2003) studied the suspension data from the second-largest school district in Florida. They found that Black males were more than twice as likely as white males to be suspended. During middle school,

almost one-half of all Black males and almost one-third of all Black females experienced at least one suspension. Additionally, it can be seen that the disproportionate percentage of Black students being suspended was evident as early as elementary school, with Black males more than three times as likely as White or Hispanic males to experience a suspension and Black females more than eight times as likely as White or Hispanic females to experience a suspension in elementary school. (p. 38)

This is one reason why, in disaggregating data annually, it is important to analyze discipline data by looking, for example, at the numbers, percentages, and severity of punishments meted out by race, program (such as special education and English as a second language), and income level. When disproportionality is unearthed, staff members in effective schools work together to try to determine reasons and then design new or enhanced features for the behavior management system to address the identified disparities.

The Rubric

A review team wanting to determine how a school's application of its rules measures up against the benchmark of Characteristic 8H would look at four traits of that characteristic. The rubric in Table 8.8 (page 166) describes each trait as it manifests in low-performing, effective, and high-performing schools.

Characteristic 8I: Limits on Out-of-School Suspension

Summary of Research

Of all of the options available for addressing discipline issues, suspension must be limited to only the most serious offenses, because it carries with it so many negative consequences. These include students' loss of instructional time during the suspension, the development of feelings of anger and unfairness, and the real possibility of getting into even more trouble while spending the out-of-school time unsupervised. In addition, suspensions and expulsions lead to disengagement with school and are a predictor of which students will leave school without graduating (Skiba, 2004; Skiba & Peterson, 1999; Skiba et al., 2000). All in all, this amounts to a set of serious consequences added on top of the suspension.

Table 8.8: Rubric for Characteristic 8H

Characteristic	Trait	Effectiveness Continuum		
		Low Performing	Effective	High Performing
8H. School rules are fair and are applied consistently and equitably. Consequences are commensurate with the offense.	8H1. Communication of school rules and consequences	Communications that provide clear explanations of school rules, and the consequences of breaking those rules, are out of date or are not provided to students and families.	School rules and the consequences of breaking those rules are clearly communicated to students and families.	School rules and the consequences of breaking those rules are clearly communicated to students and families in each of the primary languages of the school.
	8H2. Appropriateness of consequences	Consequences for breaches of discipline are sometimes either too lenient or too severe.	Consequences in the discipline and behavior management program are commensurate with the offense.	Staff members, students, and families worked together to develop the discipline and behavior management program, and consequences are commensurate with the offense.
	8H3. Application of school rules	School rules are not fairly, consistently, and equitably applied to all students.	School rules are fairly, consistently, and equitably applied to all students.	School rules are fairly, consistently, and equitably applied to all students. School discipline data are disaggregated annually and analyzed by subgroup for fair, consistent, and equitable application of rules.
	8H4. Academic support for students during in-school suspension	No or limited academic support is provided to students during in-school suspension.	Students receive assignments from missed classes to be completed during in-school suspension.	Students receive assignments from missed classes to be completed during in-school suspension. Licensed teachers are assigned to provide academic support to students placed in in-school suspension.

Johns Hopkins University researchers Gary and Denise Gottfredson found that "in six middle schools in Charleston, South Carolina, students lost 7,932 instructional days—44 years!—to in-school and out-of-school suspension in a single year" (Gaustad, 1992, p. 1). Neil Blomberg (2004, p. 4) notes:

> Perhaps the most important issue related to [out-of-school suspension] is that it tends to push away the very students who need the most support from school. If [out-of-school suspension] is seen from a perspective of learning and learning outcomes, then it rarely functions well. There is little evidence that students learn from their behavior and that students who are suspended avoid further misbehavior. Students most at risk for suspension often have difficult home lives and dangerous peer groups. The act of suspending these students and leaving them at home in a (typically) unsupervised setting can actually create more problems for a student.

Researchers have pointed out that the majority of suspensions nationwide are not for serious or violent offenses (Blomberg, 2004; Skiba & Peterson, 1999). For example, displaying a stunning lack of logic, in the 2001–02 school year, Tennessee recorded almost 30,000 incidents of suspension for attendance issues (Morgan, 2004, p. 3). In fact, in some states, suspension is the most common form of punishment meted out (Blomberg, 2004; Skiba & Peterson, 1999). This practice is particularly troublesome in states such as Texas, which has "criminalized many school infractions, saddling tens of thousands of students with misdemeanor criminal records for offenses such as swearing or disrupting class" (Witt, 2007, p. 28).

In many schools, students are typically assigned to in-school suspension in lieu of out-of-school suspension. In-school suspension has the advantage of keeping the student in school in a well-supervised location. Students assigned to in-school suspension are generally expected to use this time to complete schoolwork. The effectiveness of in-school suspension varies, partly because there are so many models in use. However, just as with out-of-school suspension, there is little evidence that in-school suspension without appropriate behavioral intervention has any positive effect on subsequent behavior (Los Angeles County Office of Education, n.d.).

In-school suspension programs need to avoid the punitive, silent, sit-still model and instead focus on remediation and improving behavior. To help students change their behavior, discipline programs should be well-planned and include:

- Diagnosis and assessment of student behavior problems

- Completion of planned intervention based on the behavior's function

- Completion of a behavior contract

- Follow-up counseling

- Recognition and positive reinforcement

- Evaluation and program modification (Los Angeles County Office of Education, n.d., p. 124)

In cases of either out-of-school or in-school suspension, the school should provide students with classroom assignments, textbooks, or other instructional materials and a way to access teacher support for completing the work during the suspension. This work should be the same or nearly the same as that given to other students in the class and should be closely coordinated with the instructional program of the school.

While most children navigate through school with few or only minor behavioral issues, "all schools should have in place mechanisms for early identification, quick and appropriate early interventions, and intensive interventions for troubled or violent students" (Learning First Alliance, 2001, pp. 18–19).

Crisis intervention plans, developed in coordination with local mental health, law enforcement, and child service agencies, as well as other partners, lay out for school administrators, parents, students, and others what services and options, beyond suspension or expulsion, are available for students whose behavior becomes increasingly disruptive or violent. The plans should include procedures for evaluating the seriousness of warning signs of behavioral or emotional problems and should match those warning signs to appropriate intervention strategies (Skiba et al., 2000).

The Rubric

A review team wanting to determine how a school's handling of suspension measures up against the benchmark of Characteristic 8I would look at three traits of that characteristic. The rubric in Table 8.9 describes each trait as it manifests in low-performing, effective, and high-performing schools.

Table 8.9: Rubric for Characteristic 8I

Characteristic	Trait	Effectiveness Continuum		
		Low Performing	**Effective**	**High Performing**
8I. Out-of-school suspensions are reserved for only the most serious offenses, and suspended students are allowed to continue the academic program.	**8I1. Clarity of policies for suspension and expulsion**	It is not clear which rules, if broken, may result in suspension or expulsion.	School documents explicitly describe which rules, if broken, may result in suspension or expulsion.	School documents, in the school's primary languages, clearly describe which rules, if broken, may result in suspension or expulsion.
	8I2. Limitations on out-of-school suspensions	Out-of-school suspensions are not limited to the most serious offenses.	Out-of-school suspensions are limited to offenses clearly linked to school safety issues.	Out-of-school suspensions are rare and are limited to offenses clearly linked to school safety issues.
	8I3. Credits for courses in alternative settings	Programs for students who are placed in alternative settings do not include credit-earning coursework.	Programs for students who are placed in alternative settings include credit-earning coursework.	Programs for students who are placed in alternative settings are coordinated with the instructional program of the school and include credit-earning coursework.

Conclusion

A positive school environment is characterized by both emotional support and academic challenge. It is dependent on strong, positive relationships between every single person in the school sphere: administrators, teachers, assistants, students, parents, bus drivers, custodians, and the community as a whole. These relationships must be steeped in trust, mutual respect, support, value, safety, challenge, and cultural awareness and acceptance. Behavior management systems are key to an orderly school environment in which students and teachers feel supported and valued. The goal is to create a learning environment that is conducive to effective work and high-quality learning experiences.

CHAPTER

9

Effectiveness Indicator 9

Family and Community Involvement

The voice of parents is the voice of gods, for to their children they are heaven's lieutenants.

—Shakespeare

In effective schools, there are programs in place to engage families and the community in supporting student learning. From this principle, we derive Effectiveness Indicator 9. An on-site school review assesses the commitment of the school, its families, and its community to developing partnerships for the benefit of the students. It examines both the school's outreach efforts and the families' and community's involvement in, and ownership of, the school.

Five characteristics define Effectiveness Indicator 9: Family and Community Involvement:

9A.   Families and the community feel positive about, and welcome at, the school.

9B.   The school maintains high levels of communication with families and the community.

9C.   The school seeks and values family and community involvement.

9D.   The school engages families and the community to support student learning.

9E.   School administrators cultivate shared responsibility for decision-making among families and within the community.

Characteristic 9A: Positive and Welcoming Environment

Summary of Research

Research has clearly demonstrated the benefits of family and community involvement for both students and schools, including improved student behavior, mutual support between parents and teachers, and higher graduation rates. But what are the elements of effective family involvement programs, and what structures need to be in place to support this involvement?

The research reviewed in chapter 8, which focused on the school environment for staff and students, showed the importance of addressing and establishing trust between staff members and administrators in order for lasting, meaningful improvement to take place. This theme of trust recurs in the literature on developing and maintaining effective family and community involvement in schools.

Family attitudes toward the school begin to develop even before the family moves into a school area. Word of mouth is a significant influence on the overall conception new families will form. Often the first personal contact parents have with the school is when they arrive to register their children. What families see and hear when they first walk into the building creates powerful and lasting impressions. Encountering the following features will give them positive feelings about the school:

- Clean and inviting building and grounds

- Colorful, high-quality student work decorating the walls

- Signage in the language of the family

- Forms and handbooks in the parents' home language

- A family center that is comfortable and well-stocked

Being treated in the following ways will add to their positive feelings:

- Being warmly welcomed and treated respectfully

- Having access to someone who speaks the language of the family

- Being invited to tour the school by someone who welcomes the task and can communicate in their home language

- Being invited to meet their children's teachers

- Being told what their children will be learning this year

Successful family involvement programs build trust and positive relationships between parents and the school. But there are other powerful benefits as well, many of them having a direct impact on students' learning. In a survey of 210 schools conducted by the Consortium on Chicago Schools, 30 high-achieving schools were compared with 30 low-achieving schools. Teachers in the top schools reported feeling a great deal of respect in teacher-to-parent relationships. Teachers in the bottom 30 schools felt both a mistrust and a lack of positive relationships between staff and parents (Henderson & Mapp, 2002).

Other researchers have also noted the association of gains in student achievement with trust between parents and school staff members. In 2002, researchers analyzed 100 schools in which students made large gains in standardized mathematics and reading tests over a 5-year period and then compared those schools to 100 schools in which not much improvement was made. They found that schools with high amounts of trust and positive relationships between school staff members and parents were much more likely to see higher student achievement than were schools with poor relationships. "One out of two schools with high trust levels made significant improvements, while only one out of seven schools with low trust levels made such gains. Additionally, the low-trust schools that did see improvements were those that built and strengthened trust over the five-year period [of the study] (Bryk and Schneider, 2002)" (Blank, Melaville, & Shah, 2003, p. 19).

Karen Mapp (2002) conducted a study of the family involvement program at O'Hearn Elementary School in Boston, Massachusetts. O'Hearn had decided to place a priority on increasing family involvement at the school. The O'Hearn staff members knew that they needed help in learning how to successfully reach out to parents. They began by forming a committee of parents and family members who were representative of the very diverse racial and economic makeup of the school population. The committee's particular charge was to increase family involvement and to develop relationships with families who rarely interacted with the school. The committee decided to undertake a series of home visits. These visits were not "designed to lecture parents on how they should be involved in their children's education, but to deliver the message that families were respected and welcomed into the O'Hearn community" (p. 39). The program was so successful that it was expanded to ensure that at the beginning of each school year, home visits were made to every new family.

O'Hearn didn't stop with home visits. The school opened a family center "as a comfortable place for families to come and feel welcome in the school, to gather for refreshments and informal conversation on various social and educational topics" (p. 40). Committee members attended training to improve their skills as outreach volunteers and then put the strategies they learned into place. They thought and planned many ways in which families could be involved in schools and made sure that families were encouraged to participate in whatever way they could. Their successful efforts resulted in more than a 90% participation rate in "one or more of the home- or school-based family engagement activities, despite the school's urban, low socioeconomic setting" (p. 35).

The Rubric

A review team wanting to determine how a school's family and community involvement program measures up against the benchmark of Characteristic 9A would look at two traits of that characteristic. The rubric in Table 9.1 describes each trait as it manifests in low-performing, effective, and high-performing schools.

Table 9.1: Rubric for Characteristic 9A

| Characteristic | Trait | Effectiveness Continuum | | |
		Low Performing	Effective	High Performing
9A. Families and the community feel positive about, and welcome at, the school.	9A1. Parents' attitude toward the school	The attitude of many parents toward the school is indifferent or negative.	Parents have a positive attitude toward the school.	Parents and community members have a positive attitude toward the school.
	9A2. School's effort to make all groups feel welcome	Some families, or families from some groups, do not feel welcome at the school.	Families from all groups feel welcome and comfortable at the school.	Families and community members from all groups feel welcome and comfortable at the school.

Characteristic 9B: Communication

Summary of Research

Communication is the key to trust, positive relationships, and strong family and community involvement. Effective schools communicate frequently and use many strategies to ensure that all parents are engaged. One important strategy is to make sure to start off on a positive note. The very first communication to parents may take many forms. It may be as simple as a short note welcoming the parents and student to a new class, an invitation to parents to visit the school, or a phone call from a child's teacher during the first week of school. These efforts do not have to be formal or complex, but they should be coordinated enough to ensure that every parent's first communication from the school will start building a positive, respectful relationship.

One of the most effective ways to begin to build communication with families is also one of the simplest. At a middle school we worked with, teachers sent home a blank form on the first day of school with a note asking parents to write out, in whatever language they felt most comfortable, what they thought the teacher should know about their child in order for the student to do his or her best in school. Parents were delighted. One teacher laughingly commented to us, "I am going to have to ask parents to limit their responses to 10,000 words." When we later held a parent meeting at the same school and asked about positive communication, the parents immediately mentioned these letters "as a great start to the school year." In middle schools, where students often distance themselves from parents, this gesture gave parents an opportunity to connect with their child's teacher in a way that felt both comfortable and deeply personal.

Early, welcoming communication strategies set a positive tone from the outset. Blank, Melaville, and Shah (2003) found that when schools build "respectful, cooperative relationships among parents, families, teachers, and school administrators, family members feel more capable of contributing to their child's education and connected to their child's school" (p. 26). Of course, this is all predicated on the ability of school staff members to speak the language of the parent and family. Having interpreters available on short notice and on hand for prearranged meetings, conferences, and community events sends a strong signal to parents whose home language is not English that they are both welcome at and valued by the school.

In their project "Parents as School Partners," the National Council of Jewish Women (1996) conducted 33 focus groups with parents and teachers, centered on family involvement in education. One of the areas discussed was school-home communication. For the most part, parents felt positive about schools' efforts to keep them informed; however, they mentioned that students often lost information that was sent home with them. Many parents said they would like more personal, individualized contact—especially positive communication—with their children's teachers. Parents who had received positive phone calls from teachers believed them to be very beneficial. Many parents, however, complained that they heard from their children's teachers only when there was a problem.

Even those parents who normally were not involved with the school wanted to be contacted if their child started to falter academically. They wanted the opportunity to intervene before their child fell too far behind. When parents felt that they were not informed of problems until it was too late, they assumed that "the school did not care about their child's success" (p. 26).

Teachers felt that too many parents failed to attend parent meetings and conferences. Even while acknowledging that many parents had barriers to attending these meetings, teachers believed that parents could get to them if they really wanted to and attributed their not coming to a "lack of interest in their child's education" (p. 36). Teachers overall believed that they communicated regularly and sufficiently with parents. They mentioned sending many written communications home, including corrected homework, portfolios, notes, progress reports, and report cards.

What is especially interesting about these responses is that both parents and teachers assumed that when the other party did not communicate, it was evidence of a lack of caring or support.

In 2005, researchers interviewed a broad array of educators, state officials, parents, and representatives of community-based organizations about "how parental involvement works in public elementary and secondary schools and what still needs to be done" (Coleman, Starzynski, Winnick, Palmer, & Furr, 2006, preface). The message received was that "too many parents fail to receive clear and timely information about their children and their schools." To address this, the researchers made the following recommendation:

> States, districts and schools should ensure that reports of school and district performance are presented in ways that provide clear information and explain their meaning. In particular . . . take steps to provide appropriate interpretations of testing data, which should describe in simple language:
>
> - What the test has covered;
>
> - What scores mean and do not mean;
>
> - How the scores will be used by the school, district or state (including specific consequences associated with the results, if any); and
>
> - What steps parents should take with the data.
>
> Relying on reports produced by test publishers that merely provide data-driven results, without more, will in most cases accomplish little in effectively educating parents about student and school performance. (p. 28)

Coleman and his colleagues found that "poverty, limited English proficiency, and varying cultural expectations are among the biggest barriers to parental involvement" and recommended that "districts and schools must pursue multiple, proactive strategies for communicating with and engaging parents—particularly parents who are low-income or whose first language is not English" (2006, p. 5). They believe that it is critically important to "translate written materials and provide interpreter services in languages that will reach language-minority parents" (p. 5). Many urban districts in fact offer a host of materials targeted to the student/family populations they serve.

The Rubric

A review team wanting to determine how a school's family and community involvement program measures up against the benchmark of Characteristic 9B would look at three traits of that characteristic. The rubric in Table 9.2 (page 176) describes each trait as it manifests in low-performing, effective, and high-performing schools.

Table 9.2: Rubric for Characteristic 9B

Characteristic	Trait	Effectiveness Continuum		
		Low Performing	Effective	High Performing
9B. The school maintains high levels of communication with families and the community.	9B1. Communication about school events and programs	Families are sometimes unaware of school events and programs.	There is frequent and varied communication with families and the community about school events and programs.	Families and community members regularly attend and participate in school events and programs.
	9B2. Communication about student achievement	Families infrequently receive data on the achievement of their children, or the information is presented in a way that is difficult to understand.	Families regularly receive clearly presented data on the achievement of their children.	Families regularly receive clearly presented data in their native languages on both the achievement of their children and overall school performance.
	9B3. Provision of interpreters	Interpreters are only sometimes available to assist in family-staff communications.	Interpreters are readily available to assist in family-staff communications.	Interpreters are readily available to assist in family-staff communications. Interpreters participate in professional development to enhance their effectiveness.

Characteristic 9C: Involvement in the School

Summary of Research

Frequently, the focus on family and community involvement is the work, or passion, of one or two staff members who see its promise. However, effective and lasting family and community involvement cannot depend entirely on the particular interest of a few individuals. Like all other school initiatives, it must be deliberately and systematically carried out, encouraged by administrators, supported by staff, adequately resourced, and monitored and evaluated for continuous improvement.

Few teacher or administrator preparation programs provide training in how to create and sustain positive relationships with parents or how to effectively encourage meaningful parent involvement (Kessler-Sklar & Baker, 2000)—yet so often in low-performing schools, when staff members are asked about why their students are struggling with learning, they point to a lack of parent involvement as a major contributing factor.

Without knowing specifically what to do, school staff members may not be doing what is necessary to build strong school, family, and community partnerships. It is often difficult to understand and overcome barriers to establishing effective family involvement programs when teachers and administrators do not share the economic, cultural, or racial/ethnic backgrounds of their students and their families.

A good way to begin thinking about how to increase the involvement of families and communities in a school or district is to ask parents and community members how they would like to be involved and then work together to make that involvement possible.

Learning what concerns and motivates parents whose experiences may be very different from one's own is key to successfully involving all parents—not just those whose characteristics one shares. For example, Martinez and Velazquez (2000) discuss the perspective of migrant parents. They note the importance of understanding the cultural differences that migrant children experience. They assert that to be effective, "efforts to involve migrant parents must take into account social inequalities, educational ideologies, educational structures, and interpersonal interactions, as well as the interplay of these factors" (p. 2).

With an increasingly diverse population, even engaging parents and families who remain in the neighborhood and at the school over time can be challenging:

> Many schools struggle to actively engage high numbers of parents and other family members in children's schooling. Of those families who do get involved, the majority are white and middle income, typically those whose home culture most closely matches the norms, values, and cultural assumptions reflected in the school. Minority, lower-income, and families who speak limited English, on the other hand, are often highly underrepresented in school-level decision making and in family involvement activities. (Brewster & Railsback, 2003a, p. 2)

Supportive school-based relationships can even help parents "who otherwise would feel vulnerable or ill at ease"—because of language barriers, a lack of social capital, or previous negative school experiences—to overcome their reluctance and take active roles in the school and in their children's education (Learning First Alliance, 2001, p. 15). When students see close collaboration between their parents and the school, their own trust in and support of teachers and administrators increase.

Maintaining supportive communication between school staff members and families has lasting benefits for children: "Students are more likely to bond with their teachers and to learn from them when they see frequent, positive interactions between their family members and school staff" (Blank et al., 2003, p. 28). Such interactions show students that school matters and that parents and teachers are working together to help them succeed.

The Rubric

A review team wanting to determine how a school's parent and community involvement program measures up against the benchmark of Characteristic 9C would look at two traits of that characteristic. The rubric in Table 9.3 (page 178) describes each trait as it manifests in low-performing, effective, and high-performing schools.

Table 9.3: Rubric for Characteristic 9C

Characteristic	Trait	Effectiveness Continuum		
		Low Performing	Effective	High Performing
9C. The school seeks and values family and community involvement.	9C1. Diversity of involvement	Family involvement does not reflect the broad diversity of the community.	Family involvement reflects the broad diversity of the community.	Family and community involvement reflects the broad diversity of the community.
	9C2. Interactions between families and staff members	Some interactions between families and staff members are brusque or discourteous.	Families and school staff members interact positively and respectfully.	Students have frequent opportunities to see families and school staff members interact positively and respectfully.

Characteristic 9D: Support for Student Learning

Summary of Research

Parent and community involvement also appears to pay dividends in terms of student learning. In 2002, Henderson and Mapp examined 51 studies that specifically addressed the connection between student achievement and parent and community involvement activities. They found a "positive and convincing relationship between family involvement and benefits for students, including improved academic achievement. This relationship holds across families of all economic, racial/ethnic, and educational backgrounds and for students at all ages" (p. 24).

In a study of 1,200 New England urban students, researchers found that high-quality parent-teacher interactions are associated with "improvement both in children's behavior and in academic achievement." Through positive and frequent interactions with their child's teachers, parents "gain a greater understanding of the expectations that schools have for students and learn how they can enhance their own child's learning at home" (Blank et al., 2003, p. 27).

The research, although limited, suggests that "programs and interventions that engage families in supporting their children's learning at home are linked to higher student achievement" (Henderson & Mapp, 2002, p. 25). Schools that are effective in encouraging family involvement in homework provide parents and community partners with the necessary knowledge and skills by offering workshop sessions on reading, writing, mathematics, and college and work planning (Epstein & Salinas, 2004).

When we talk with parents and teachers about problems in increasing family involvement, the issues consistently boil down to trust and communication. For example, teachers often tell us that parents do not support the work of the schools. In parent meetings, parents frequently tell us that they feel shut out of their schools. Often, teachers tell us they are not sure how best to use parent volunteers. Parents say they don't know what opportunities there are to get involved. Teachers tell us they sometimes hesitate to ask parents to perform routine or repetitive tasks for fear that such requests will be perceived as demeaning.

Parents often relate that when they do offer to help, either they are never contacted or they feel as if their help is not considered valuable. Sometimes teachers tell us that they need help but too few parents are available during the school day. Parents wonder if there are other ways to help besides working in the classroom, or if there are opportunities to help in the evenings or on weekends, or if there are arrangements for child care if they volunteer time during the school day. This is certainly a case where better communication could result in a powerful source of assistance for both teachers and students.

Of course, parents do not have to come to the school to assist their children academically. In fact, as students get older, parent involvement generally shifts from helping at school to helping at home, but the support parents provide remains critically important to their children's success in school:

> When parents talk about school, encourage studying and learning, guide their children's academic decisions, support their aspirations, and help them plan for college, their children are more likely to earn higher grades and test scores, enroll in higher-level classes, and earn more course credits, regardless of family income and education. (Blank et al., 2003, p. 29)

In 1998, researcher Susan Catsambis looked at the level of parent involvement in 13,500 families whose children had completed their education through grade 12. "Enhancing learning at home" had the strongest effect on student achievement. Other strongly effective strategies included "expressing high expectations, discussing going to college, and helping students prepare for college" (Henderson & Mapp, 2002, pp. 35–36). The same forms of family involvement are most effective in supporting postsecondary attendance.

Researchers studying the relationship between parent involvement and student achievement found that "test scores increased 40% more in schools with high levels of outreach to parents (including in-person meetings, sending materials home, communicating often and in times of difficulty for the child), than in schools with low levels of outreach" (Blank et al., 2003, p. 27). Henderson and Mapp (2002, p. 24) noted that, "although there is less research on the effects of community involvement, it also suggests benefits for schools, families, and students, including improved achievement and behavior."

Another approach that has shown promise for both increasing family involvement and improving student achievement is offering staffed evening or weekend sessions in which parents and their children can work on homework together, with help available to assist with both content and language barriers. Less intense programs can also have positive benefits. Some are as simple, and as important, as helping parents understand how to create a home environment that supports learning (such as a quiet place to study and set times for homework) and giving them information about available community tutoring and before- and after-school learning opportunities (Blank et al., 2003).

For many parents who have not attended college themselves, guiding their children into and through the higher education system can be difficult. Without explicit help from the school system, families frequently do not have the background to advise their children about what courses to take in middle and high school, how to apply to colleges or other postsecondary institutions, or how to apply for scholarships and other tuition-reduction programs. Many schools have programs to counsel students about college and other postsecondary opportunities, but a powerful additional strategy would be to include parents in informational sessions, giving them the tools to help their children make good decisions about their futures. When parents have access to the information, they become advocates for their children.

Other evidence points to the relationship between family involvement in a student's K–12 education and postsecondary success. In their review of research, Blank et al. (2003, p. 28) found that children whose parents are "closely involved in their educational progress throughout elementary and high school are more likely to stay in school and to enter and finish college."

The benefits of involvement are not one-way (the student) or even two-way (the students and their teachers), but are at least four-way (the student, the school, the family, and society as a whole). Research has found that "the more involved parents are in their children's education, the more likely it is that they will continue their own education, thus becoming an even more effective teaching and learning resource and role model for their children" (Blank et al., 2003, p. 28).

The Rubric

A review team wanting to determine how a school's parent and community involvement program measures up against the benchmark of Characteristic 9D would look at four traits of that characteristic. The rubric in Table 9.4 describes each trait as it manifests in low-performing, effective, and high-performing schools.

Characteristic 9E: Shared Responsibility for Decision-Making

Summary of Research

The fact that school systems historically have been governed by elected boards made up of citizens from the community attests to the value families and the community place on their involvement in the decision-making of the school. With the consolidation of smaller schools, it has become more challenging for families and communities to be meaningfully involved in school decision-making, but that has not blunted the public's desire for this involvement. Evidence for this can be seen in the increasing number of charter schools, which have, in effect, returned to the early practice of governance of individual schools by citizen boards that share power and authority with the school leaders and staff members. In these schools, family, and sometimes community, involvement has expanded well beyond that typically found in larger school systems, and there is a sense of shared ownership of the school.

The National Parent Teacher Association (2008) feels so strongly about the importance of parents' participation in the governance and operation of schools that it has made school decision-making and advocacy one of its National Standards for Family-School Partnerships. The PTA's "Standard 5—Sharing Power" states that "families and school staff are equal partners in decisions that affect children and families and together inform, influence, and create policies, practices, and programs" (p. 3).

Research into effective school/family partnerships supports the PTA standard: "Successful partnerships invite parents and community partners to take an active role in decision making at the school level; encourage honest, two-way communication about difficult issues; and create relationships that share power and responsibility" (Blank et al., 2003, p. 28).

In a 2002 meta-analysis, Henderson and Mapp found that families and community members must feel that their involvement in shared decision-making is meaningful and important; they "lose interest when their participation is token" (p. 67). The researchers identified three ways for schools to begin sharing decision-making responsibility:

Table 9.4: Rubric for Characteristic 9D

Characteristic	Trait	Effectiveness Continuum		
		Low Performing	Effective	High Performing
9D. The school engages families and the community to support student learning.	9D1. Connection between family involvement activities and student learning	Family involvement activities are not explicitly linked to student learning.	Family involvement activities are connected to student learning.	Family and community involvement activities are directly linked to the curriculum and student learning.
	9D2. Parent and community involvement in the classroom	Parents and community members are not regularly involved in classroom activities.	Parents and community members are present and involved in classroom activities.	Parents and community members receive training to help them be effective in activities that support learning, such as tutoring.
	9D3. Support for parents' efforts to help their children at home	The school does not provide sufficient information about what their children are learning and how to help them with schoolwork at home.	The school provides information to parents about what their children are learning and how to help them with schoolwork at home.	Frequent, regularly scheduled workshops inform parents about what their children are learning and how to help them with schoolwork at home.
	9D4. School support for family discussions of career and life goals	The school does not encourage families to talk to their children about career and life goals or does not provide adequate information to help all parents to do so.	The school provides information to help families talk to their children about life goals and the importance of education in reaching those goals.	The school has an effective outreach program to help families talk to their children about career and life goals and the importance of education in reaching those goals.

- Explore national school reform initiatives with a comprehensive approach that includes a school, family and community component.

- Provide training for school decision-making groups on how to work effectively.

- Avoid using parents and community members to rubberstamp decisions. (p. 67)

The Rubric

A review team wanting to determine how a school's parent and community involvement program measures up against the benchmark of Characteristic 9E would look at one trait of that characteristic. The rubric in Table 9.5 describes that trait as it manifests in low-performing, effective, and high-performing schools.

Table 9.5: Rubric for Characteristic 9E

Characteristic	Trait	Effectiveness Continuum		
		Low Performing	Effective	High Performing
9E. School administrators cultivate shared responsibility for decision-making among families and within the community.	9E1. Extent of shared decision-making	Families are not actively involved in school decision-making.	School administrators ensure family involvement in school decision-making.	School administrators routinely involve families and the community in school decision-making.

Conclusion

The partnership between home and school boosts the school's ability to help all children reach high learning goals. Schools that have effectively integrated family involvement have moved from a model that engages only a few parents to one that invites all to participate. This model recognizes and values the knowledge and skills of each adult. Parent involvement in these effective schools is not an add-on, but rather a foundational education strategy.

Effectiveness Indicator 10
District Support

I learned that courage was not the absence of fear, but the triumph over it. The brave man is not he who does not feel afraid, but he who conquers that fear.

— Nelson Mandela

The board and district determine the context within which schools function and the culture within which they operate. Effective districts are committed above all else to setting and supporting goals for high levels of student learning, and the board and superintendent work together to emphasize this priority. From this principle, we derive Effectiveness Indicator 10. An on-site school review evaluates the district's leadership in aligning curriculum, instruction, and assessment between and within grade levels, districtwide. It also examines the district's performance in committing resources to its goals and in using data to evaluate progress toward those goals.

Six characteristics define Effectiveness Indicator 10: District Support:

10A. The roles and responsibilities of the board, the district, and the schools are clear and communicated to stakeholders.

10B. The board's, district's, and schools' goals, policies, and resource allocations are aligned and focus on student learning.

10C. The district oversees the development and implementation of curriculum, instruction, and assessment districtwide.

10D. The board's and district's policies and actions reflect the expectation that all children in the district will be engaged in high-quality instruction and assessment.

10E. The board's and district's actions reflect high expectations of staff members.

10F. The board and district use data to monitor school and student performance and intervene if school performance lags.

Characteristic 10A: Clear Roles and Responsibilities

Summary of Research

The Task Force on School District Leadership observed that "an incoherent system causes people to act dysfunctionally" (Institute for Educational Leadership, 2001, p. 6). The members of the task force agreed that when the roles and responsibilities of superintendents, administrators, and board members are ambiguous, the result is

> confusion between governance (the school board's nominal job) and management (the superintendent's). There is consensus that, in an ideal situation, school boards should focus on the "large picture" or "externals" of education: hiring and evaluating the superintendent; developing and popularizing the district's vision for education; setting goals and performance targets; measuring results and reporting them to the public (accountability); engaging the community as a resource for public education; approving and overseeing budgets; and other functions of roughly similar scope. Superintendents, on the other hand, must deal with the daily business of running school systems, which ideally centers on implementing the board's priorities. Unfortunately, it does not always work this way.
>
> The absence of clear definitions of roles and responsibilities frequently results in micromanagement of administrative matters by school boards or, worse, individual members who may intervene inappropriately in aspects of school operations ranging from curriculum design to student transfers. (p. 5)

The task force highlighted a model of *policy governance leadership* with strictly defined roles, in which the board is the policy maker and the superintendent is the administrator. The group concluded that "it is impossible to imagine any community achieving sustained positive results for children unless the adults in charge at the district level are using the same playbook as they work toward shared goals" (p. 11).

In his study of 1,435 organizations, Jim Collins (2001) looked for the key concepts that separate good companies from great companies. He found that the 11 companies that made the leap from good to great and sustained those results for at least 15 years

> first got the right people on the bus, the wrong people off the bus, and the right people in the right seats—and then they figured out where to drive it. The old adage, "People are your most important asset" turns out to be wrong. People are not your most important asset, the *right* people are. (p. 13)

The key point of Collins' theory is that "who" questions come before vision, strategy, and structure, and "what" decisions come after (p. 63). Without clear roles and responsibilities, this process cannot happen.

The Rubric

A review team wanting to determine how a district measures up against the benchmark of Characteristic 10A would look at two traits of that characteristic. The rubric in Table 10.1 describes each trait as it manifests in low-performing, effective, and high-performing schools.

Table 10.1: Rubric for Characteristic 10A

Characteristic	Trait	Effectiveness Continuum		
		Low Performing	Effective	High Performing
10A. The roles and responsibilities of the board, the district, and the schools are clear and communicated to stakeholders.	10A1. Delineation of roles and responsibilities	The roles and responsibilities of the board, the district, and the schools are not clearly delineated.	The roles and responsibilities of the board, the district, and the schools are clearly delineated.	The roles and responsibilities of the board, the district, and the schools are clearly delineated, and processes are in place to evaluate the effectiveness of those divisions.
	10A2. Communication regarding roles and responsibilities	There is limited formalized communication describing the roles and responsibilities of the board, the district, and the schools.	The roles and responsibilities of the board, the district, and the schools are clearly communicated to stakeholders.	The roles and responsibilities of the board, the district, and the schools are clearly communicated to stakeholders. Published documents illustrate areas of sole, shared, limited, and advisory responsibility and authority.

Characteristic 10B: Focus on Student Learning

Summary of Research

In 2006, Waters and Marzano led a team of McREL researchers in conducting a meta-analysis of studies on the effect of school district leadership on student achievement. The researchers initially looked at 200 studies and then whittled them down to 27 that met rigorous research criteria. These 27 studies involved more than 2,700 districts, 4,343 individual ratings of superintendent leadership, and the achievement scores of an estimated 3.4 million students.

The meta-analysis found that effective superintendents focus on creating goal-oriented districts. These superintendents bring together central district staff members, building administrators, board members, and others who will have a part in carrying out the work, and together they establish a small set of goals for their districts. That small set must include one goal in the area of student achievement and one goal in the area of instruction. The authors term these *non-negotiable*, meaning that every staff member districtwide will work toward the realization of these goals.

Effective districts set "specific achievement targets for the district as a whole, for individual schools, and for subpopulations of students within the district. Once agreed upon, the achievement goals are enacted in every school site." Principals are required to explicitly support the goals and action plans through deed and action. No member of the leadership team is permitted to do anything that would "subvert the accomplishment of those goals, such as criticizing district goals or subtly communicating that the goals the district has selected are inappropriate or unattainable" (Waters & Marzano, 2006, p. 12).

The board must also be "aligned with and supportive of the non-negotiable goals for achievement and instruction. The board ensures that these goals remain the top priorities in the district and that no other initiatives detract attention or resources from accomplishing these goals" (p. 12).

Another characteristic of effective superintendents is that they frequently monitor student achievement data to gauge the district's progress toward attainment of the goals. They also ensure that building principals keep a close watch on student achievement and teachers' use of agreed-upon instructional practices and that they take immediate action if they observe slippage in either area. Without such monitoring, "district goals can become little more than pithy refrains that are spoken at district and school events and highlighted in written reports" (p. 12).

Finally, the meta-analysis found that effective superintendents make sure that the district allocates sufficient resources—including funds, personnel, time, materials, and professional development—to support the non-negotiable goals in student achievement and instruction. Doing so "can mean cutting back on or dropping initiatives that are not aligned with district goals for achievement and instruction" (p. 13).

A Massachusetts study that used very different means to research school and district improvement reported similar findings. In this work, the governor appointed a task force of educational leaders from across the state to develop turnaround strategies for low-performing districts. The group began by identifying characteristics of high-performing districts, using a combination of "research, experience, and common sense" (Grogan, 2004, p. 4). The first two characteristics are strikingly similar to those the McREL meta-analysis described:

- Effective school districts own the responsibility for their successes and failures with all learners—they do not excuse or blame. Student achievement is the shared responsibility of both the central office and the individual schools. Effective districts take responsibility for prompt intervention when student achievement or improvement is lagging, whether at the school or classroom level—all the way down to individual students.

- Effective school districts are clear about their mission and goals, and highly focused on achieving their goals. The district identifies a limited set of priorities on which to focus its efforts. (Grogan, 2004, p. 4)

We would add that those priorities must be focused on improving student learning.

The American Institutes for Research conducted a review of the literature on district effectiveness to identify the components of high-performing, high-poverty school districts and the strategies that helped these districts move toward effectiveness. The synthesis of more than 20 significant reports, studies, and policy statements (Dailey et al., 2005) found that successful school districts use the following strategies (pp. 2–5):

- Focus first and foremost on student achievement and learning.

- Have a theory of action for how to effect improvements and then establish clear goals.

- Enact comprehensive, coherent reform policies.

- Expect all staff at all levels to accept personal responsibility for improving student learning [and provide support to help them succeed].

- [Commit to] professional learning at all levels and provide multiple, meaningful learning opportunities.

- Use data to guide improvement strategies.

- Regularly monitor progress and intervene if necessary.

In a 2004 synthesis, researchers from Washington State found that while effective districts all developed goals, they went about the process in very different ways. For example, "in some districts the school board developed goals and then selected superintendents who shared them; in other districts, superintendents and school boards jointly developed goals and shared beliefs" (Shannon & Bylsma, 2004, p. 14). Regardless of how student learning goals were selected, improving districts felt a sense of urgency about meeting them, and everyone, "from central office administrators to principals and teachers, [was] focused on classroom instruction" (p. 32).

The Task Force on School District Leadership, cited in the discussion of Characteristic 10A, stressed that "1) district leaders absolutely must focus their actions on the common goal of improving student learning, and 2) the school system must be organized in such a way as to make this its fundamental priority, the one that matters far more than any other" (Institute for Educational Leadership, 2001, p. 1).

The Rubric

A review team wanting to determine how a district measures up against the benchmark of Characteristic 10B would look at two traits of that characteristic. The rubric in Table 10.2 describes each trait as it manifests in low-performing, effective, and high-performing schools.

Table 10.2: Rubric for Characteristic 10B

Characteristic	Trait	Effectiveness Continuum		
		Low Performing	Effective	High Performing
10B. The board's, district's, and schools' goals, policies, and resource allocations are aligned and focus on student learning.	10B1. Alignment and focus of goals	The board's, district's, and schools' goals are not aligned or do not focus on student learning.	The board's, district's, and schools' goals and policies are aligned and focus on student learning.	The board's, district's, and schools' goals and policies are aligned, focus on student learning, and remain stable over time.
	10B2. Allocation of resources	The board's, district's, and schools' resource allocations do not support a focus on student learning.	The board's, district's, and schools' resource allocations support a focus on student learning.	The board's, district's, and schools' resource allocations fund student learning before all other priorities.

Characteristic 10C: Districtwide Curriculum, Instruction, and Assessment

Summary of Research

Aligning curriculum within and between grade levels is a leadership function that effective districts take very seriously. They also ensure alignment between the essential curriculum supports: instruction, assessment, instructional materials, enrichment and interventions, and the professional development necessary for teachers to deliver the curriculum with expertise (Grogan, 2004).

In an investigation of district efforts that support instruction, the Learning First Alliance studied five school districts that had made substantial improvement in mathematics or reading with all subgroups of students over at least 3 years. The researchers found that in these improving districts,

> central offices drove systemwide change. In each district, the superintendent transformed central office policies, structures, and human resources into forces that guided improvement. . . . Examples of [district] practices included establishing systems to improve principal leadership, coordinating curriculum alignment, establishing and implementing a multimeasure accountability system, and creating systemwide supports for new teachers. (Togneri, 2003, p. 8)

Other research confirms the district's central role in coordinating policies in curriculum, instruction, and assessment to support the implementation of the curriculum. Shannon and Bylsma (2004, p. 25) observe, "In improved districts, curriculum is aligned with standards, assessments, and policies."

In fact, the district leadership role is so important that an evaluation of school districts involved in the Pew Network "did not find any instances in which schools on a widespread basis were able to make significant improvements in classroom practice in the absence of active support and leadership from the district" (David, Shields, Humphrey, & Young, 2001, p. 37).

Waters and Marzano (2006, p. 15) state that the district leadership must ensure that a "preferred instructional program is adopted and implemented." This does not mean that every teacher in every classroom delivers the exact same lesson in the exact same manner at the exact same time. But "it *does* mean that the district adopts a broad but common framework for classroom instructional design and planning, common instructional language or vocabulary, and consistent use of research-based instructional strategies in each school" so that the needs of all students will be met (p. 12).

How districts go about the development and implementation of curriculum, instruction, and assessment varies even among the highest-performing districts:

> Some districts adopt textbooks that are quite prescriptive with lesson plans and pacing guides and monitor teacher adherence to these in implementing the curriculum. Some emphasize the need for particular instructional processes, such as organizing instruction to allow for assessing skills regularly before students move on, providing tutoring or extra help for students who fail to master the skills and enrichment activities for those who have, and frequent practice throughout the year to help students remember what they have learned. Other districts provide explicit expectations for instructional practice and then use "walk-throughs" or other processes to look at classroom instruction. (Shannon & Bylsma, 2004, p. 32)

Effective districts support their aligned curriculum and assessments by providing teachers with the professional development they need to skillfully plan and deliver instruction and evaluate student learning. David et al. (2001, p. iii) found that

> districts that communicate ambitious expectations for instruction, supported by a strong professional development system, are able to make significant changes in classroom practices. . . . *Clear expectations for instruction are as critical as clear expectations for student learning.* Dedicating resources to building the knowledge and skills of educators and to providing additional instructional time for low-performing students is essential if the benefits of standards-based reform are to be realized in increased student achievement.

The Rubric

A review team wanting to determine how a district measures up against the benchmark of Characteristic 10C would look at two traits of that characteristic. The rubric in Table 10.3 describes each trait as it manifests in low-performing, effective, and high-performing schools.

Table 10.3: Rubric for Characteristic 10C

Characteristic	Trait	Effectiveness Continuum		
		Low Performing	Effective	High Performing
10C. The district oversees the development and implementation of curriculum, instruction, and assessment districtwide.	10C1. Responsibility for developing and implementing curriculum and assessment	Responsibility for the development and implementation of curriculum and assessment is school-based.	The district leads the development and implementation of curriculum and assessment districtwide.	The district leads the development and implementation of curriculum and assessment districtwide. Curriculum and assessments are reviewed cyclically, ensuring that at least one subject is reviewed each year.
	10C2. Responsibility for supporting research-based instructional strategies	Responsibility for the support of research-based instructional strategies is school-based.	The district articulates expectations for and leads the dissemination of research-based instructional strategies.	The district articulates expectations for and leads the dissemination of, and professional development in, research-based instructional strategies.

Characteristic 10D: High-Quality Instruction and Assessment

Summary of Research

Districts in which all children are engaged in high-quality instruction and assessment have created and maintained a districtwide commitment to improving learning and support that commitment through action. A key finding from the Learning First Alliance study of five districts with a track record of success was that each of them established a systemwide approach to improving instruction.

> Leaders realized they would need to fundamentally change instructional practice. Teachers would need to be more effective in helping every child succeed, and principals, central office staff, and board members would need to become more effective at supporting teachers in their classrooms.
>
> Before reforms began, the districts had neither clear, well-understood goals nor effective measures of progress. Supports to improve instruction were haphazard. Boards did not make instruction and achievement central to their work. Principals were more likely to focus on administrative duties than on helping teachers to improve their instruction and student outcomes. None of the districts had systemwide curricula to guide instruction. (Togneri, 2003, pp. 3–4)

Common themes existed across the districts that had made substantial and continuing improvement. These districts were focused on student learning, instructional improvement, and systemwide curricula connected to state standards; they gave teachers clear guidance about what to teach; they provided the necessary professional development to implement called-for changes in practice; and they used data to inform practice, monitor progress, and hold schools accountable for results (Togneri, 2003).

The Learning First researchers also found that

> district leaders sought to infuse a reflective and evidence-based approach to teaching practice. This meant that they expected teachers to actively engage students in rigorous content, assess the impact of instructional methods, reflect on their practice, work with colleagues to research and share effective practice, and make appropriate adjustments to help students learn effectively. (Togneri & Anderson, 2003, p. 15)

Districts that have improved substantially over time

> pay close attention to classroom practice and provide guidance and oversight for improving teaching and learning. . . . [They] develop a common vision and understanding of quality teaching and learning. They monitor instruction, curriculum, and changes in instructional practice. Their guidance and improvement efforts require actions such as systemwide approval, interventions and corrective instruction, tutoring, and alignment. (Shannon & Bylsma, 2004, p. 31)

In 1994, Mary Jo Powell studied results of the Eisenhower Math and Science grant program. She concluded that efforts to systemically improve education could succeed only when they addressed the critical and persistent issues of equity. In her definition,

> equity means that each student will be addressed as an individual, with instructional opportunities, content, and approaches that meet his or her specific needs, strengths, and

interests. All students will be engaged in meaningful learning, in a school environment that . . . encourages students to participate actively in the learning process. (p. 3)

This definition, coupled with high expectations and aligned assessments, works equally well for the kind of engaging curriculum that is in place in schools in the most effective districts.

The Rubric

A review team wanting to determine how a district measures up against the benchmark of Characteristic 10D would look at one trait of that characteristic. The rubric in Table 10.4 describes that trait as it manifests in low-performing, effective, and high-performing schools.

Table 10.4: Rubric for Characteristic 10D

Characteristic	Trait	Effectiveness Continuum		
		Low Performing	Effective	High Performing
10D. The board's and district's policies and actions reflect the expectation that all children in the district will be engaged in high-quality instruction and assessment.	10D1. Board and district expectations for instruction and assessment	The board's and district's policies and actions are inconsistent with the expectation that all children will be engaged in high-quality instruction and assessment.	The board's and district's policies and actions emphasize the expectation that all children will be engaged in high-quality instruction and assessment.	The board's and district's policies and actions emphasize the expectation that all children will be engaged in high-quality instruction and assessment. Data on progress toward meeting this expectation are reported to the community annually.

Characteristic 10E: High Expectations of Staff

Summary of Research

The report of the Massachusetts Governor's Task Force on State Intervention in Under-Performing Districts emphasizes the importance of high expectations and accountability at all levels of the system. The group's recommendations address high expectations for *students* but also point to the district-level responsibility to "motivate personnel to raise expectations for themselves and their staff" (Grogan, 2004, p. 11). Clearly, the most effective schools and districts hold high expectations for both *students and adults*. These high expectations are therefore both individual and collective.

Shannon and Bylsma (2004) found that in high-performing districts, these expectations originate at the district level but pervade all levels of the system. They explain that

improved districts hold all adults in the system accountable for student learning, beginning with the superintendent, senior staff, and principals. The districts have clear expectations for instruction and apply consistent pressure on schools for improved outcomes for students. The superintendent expects excellence by all, monitors performance, and provides feedback. High expectations influence hiring decisions and prompt districts and schools to address issues regarding ineffective teachers. (p. 22)

We were fortunate to work with a superintendent who exemplified this model, allowing us to see a great leader in action. His vision, coupled with high expectations for both student and adult performance, made the district come alive, which had a positive impact not only on the school district but on an economically struggling rural community as well. This superintendent's no-excuse but personable leadership turned a historically low-achieving district, with chronically low expectations for students, into one in which students experienced and have sustained substantial academic success, and staff members have created a healthy, productive working environment. Over this superintendent's 6-year tenure, the district's state assessment results went from being some of the lowest in the state to being well above the statewide average, far outperforming comparable school districts. It was through a focus on academics, a declaration of a student-driven imperative, a clear vision of high expectations, the ability to make tough decisions, and an approachable communication style that this leader was able to institutionalize change and dramatically improve student learning.

Effective districts do not shy away from considering discussions with their teacher and classified-staff unions if existing collective bargaining agreements present significant obstacles to the effective implementation of high expectations for adults in the system. Examples of contract provisions that might hinder improvement efforts would be "restrictions on school-day schedules, limits on professional development time, restrictions on teacher evaluations, prohibitions against the use of incentives or bonuses for exceptional performance, [and] constraints on starting salaries for mid-career professionals with little K–12 teaching experience" (Grogan, 2004, pp. 10–11).

Using 26 indicators from the collective bargaining database maintained by the National Council on Teacher Quality, Hess and Loup (2008) studied the labor contracts of the country's 50 largest school districts. The study, conducted for the Fordham Institute, focused specifically on this one "important but solitary thread in the dense tapestry of school management" (p. 12). The authors set out to determine whether labor agreements "provided today's public school administrators with the flexibility that effective organizations routinely provide to accountable managers" (p. 13).

Hess and Loup found that only 5 of the 50 labor agreements met the criteria for "flexible," while 30 others provided flexibility more because they were ambiguous than by design. The authors note that there are three significant components in labor contracts that "hinder management and impede the quality of education for at least some students" (p. 13). These components are:

1. Compensation. Traditional contracts base pay on seniority, credentials, and a rigid pay scale, as opposed to enabling "principals and district leaders to take into account the circumstances, skills, and experience of candidates—and the effectiveness of teachers they already have." This practice has led to a pay system that makes it "virtually impossible to reward teachers for raising student achievement, working hard, [or] possessing rare skills or high-demand expertise" (p. 14).

2. Personnel decisions. School and district managers are often "hobbled by extensive labor rules" when it comes to removing ineffective teachers from the classroom (p. 15). For example, "Illinois school districts, which collectively employ more 95,000 tenured teachers,

had dismissed an average of two teachers a year for poor performance between 1986 and 2004" (p. 15). The report notes that teachers themselves feel frustrated over tenure laws that "protect educators who should not be in the schools" (p. 15). This finding echoes the sentiments expressed in a 2003 survey (underwritten by the Fordham Foundation) of 1,345 public school teachers, in which 78% reported that their school has at least a few teachers who "fail to do a good job and are simply going through the motions" (Farkas, Johnson, & Duffett, 2003, p. 44).

3.   Work rules. Labor agreements often set strict limitations on teachers' day-to-day working conditions, for example: the number of students, the number of preparations, the number of parent conferences, and the exact time the work day begins and ends. This study reports that teachers often "complain of a culture of one-size-fits-all management that inhibits efforts to exercise professional judgment in meeting student needs" (p. 15). These restrictions also often extend to professional development and can reduce the "flexibility that can allow school administrators to forge tight-knit cultures, drive improvement, and respond to unforeseen developments" (p. 16).

We frequently see examples of how restrictions on the instructional leadership of school administrators prevent them from taking the steps that research shows will improve student achievement. For example, in one large district with which we worked, the contract prohibited administrators from asking for and reviewing teacher lesson plans. In another large district, 5 professional development days were provided to teachers. District and school leadership could set the agenda for only one half of one of those 5 days. The remainder of the professional development was selected by a vote of each school's teaching staff. In another district, paraprofessionals attended (with pay) schoolwide professional development only when they chose to do so. In yet a fourth, the school converted to a block schedule, providing every teacher with 90 minutes of preparation time each day (in addition to 30 minutes before and 30 minutes after the end of the school day), no part of which could be used for activities other than those selected by each individual teacher.

This loss of flexibility limits the degree to which school administrators can implement the kind of aligned, job-embedded professional development and collaborative activities that research has found to be most effective.

The Rubric

A review team wanting to determine how a district measures up against the benchmark of Characteristic 10E would look at one trait of that characteristic. The rubric in Table 10.5 (page 194) describes that trait as it manifests in low-performing, effective, and high-performing schools.

Characteristic 10F: Use of Data to Monitor School and Student Performance

Summary of Research

In defining the characteristics of high-performing school districts, the Massachusetts task force noted that "all important decisions in the district—from the classroom to the district office—are based on data, especially data about student achievement. Educators are trained in how to interpret data and how to make decisions based on an analysis of the data" (Grogan, 2004, p. 4). The task force asserted that data-driven decision-making must not rely solely on annual state test results. They recommended instead using quarterly school-level assessments, aligned to the state test, to generate more data.

Table 10.5: Rubric for Characteristic 10E

Characteristic	Trait	Effectiveness Continuum		
		Low Performing	Effective	High Performing
10E. The board's and district's actions reflect high expectations of staff members.	10E1. Board and district expectations of staff members	The board or district does not, or does not always, demonstrate high expectations of staff members.	The board and district demonstrate high expectations of staff members.	The board and district demonstrate high expectations of staff members and publicly recognize those whose efforts have substantially contributed to the attainment of district goals.

Similarly, the Learning First Alliance study of five high-performing districts found that the skillful collection and use of data—whether it was for targeting assistance to individual students, modifying curriculum, planning teacher professional development, or monitoring the instructional program—set such districts apart from their less successful neighbors. Leaders in these districts

> sought to dramatically increase their use of data to drive decision making and improve instruction. . . . Our study revealed that these districts did not just talk about data; they used them to guide important decisions about teaching and learning, particularly at the central office and principal levels. . . . In all five districts staff used data to guide decisions related to instruction, such as budget allocation, staff hiring, and teaching and learning gap identification. (Togneri & Anderson, 2003, pp. 19–20)

While leaders in these districts saw the value of using state test results, they recognized that these assessments alone were not sufficient to provide all of the information they needed. They wanted a deeper, more complete picture of the students, classrooms, and schools across the district. Thus they used an array of student assessment data, including grades, end-of-unit test scores, discipline data, data on attendance and length of time in the district, and diagnostic data. These leaders also gathered valuable contextual data from climate and satisfaction surveys, external evaluations, parent and student surveys, community focus groups and surveys, and principal observations (Togneri & Anderson, 2003).

Several high-performing districts provided teacher professional development on using data for school improvement. Because

> finding time to disaggregate and digest the large reams of data was not possible for most teachers in most schools, . . . districts sought to provide data and data analysis tools that were easy to access and understand. Some districts supplied teachers and principals with interpreted data reports, some assisted schools by funding intermediaries to help interpret school-specific data, and others provided tools to facilitate in-school disaggregation of data. (p. 21)

The value of the data was increased when school administrators and staff members saw that district leaders "were willing to accept the information that data revealed—whether positive or negative" and then "used the information to spur change" (p. 21).

Another study found that, in addition to requiring the use of data in decision-making, effective districts "take responsibility for collecting data, analyzing it, and providing it to schools in manageable, understandable forms. Many districts also provide training to central office and school staff in interpreting and using data in decision making" (Shannon & Bylsma, 2004, p. 36).

The Rubric

A review team wanting to determine how a district measures up against the benchmark of Characteristic 10F would look at two traits of that characteristic. The rubric in Table 10.6 describes each trait as it manifests in low-performing, effective, and high-performing schools.

Table 10.6: Rubric for Characteristic 10F

Characteristic	Trait	Effectiveness Continuum		
		Low Performing	Effective	High Performing
10F. The board and district use data to monitor school and student performance and intervene if school performance lags.	10F1. District use of data to monitor performance	The district uses a limited variety of data to monitor school and student performance.	The district uses a wide variety of student data to monitor school and student performance.	The district uses a wide variety of student data to monitor school and student performance and provides these data to its schools and teachers in an easily understood and manageable format.
	10F2. Accountability for student performance	The district delegates accountability for student performance to school-level leadership.	If school performance begins to lag, the district intervenes, providing additional resources.	If school performance begins to lag, the district intervenes, providing additional resources, including professional development for leaders and staff members in interpreting and using data in decision-making.

Conclusion

The pivotal leadership role of the school district in supporting high levels of learning for all students is only now receiving the necessary attention of researchers. As we have discussed, several studies have begun to identify the characteristics associated with high-performing districts. These districts are clear about the roles and responsibilities of the board, the district, and the schools. They are focused on student learning, and they support this priority by leading the development and implementation of a districtwide curriculum, instructional program, and assessment program. They have high expectations for both students and adults, which they back up with instructional supports and high-quality professional development.

PART 2

The Process: Conducting an On-Site School Review

CHAPTER 11

Leading the Way

"Would you tell me, please, which way I ought to go from here?"

"That depends a good deal on where you want to get to," said the Cat.

—Lewis Carroll

Once a principal has become intrigued with the idea of an external school review, the next step is to discuss the concept with other members of the school leadership team and with the school staff as a whole. Not every school is ready to invite outside eyes into the building to take a close look at how the staff goes about the business of transferring knowledge. Involving others in the decision-making process begins the modeling of collaborative strategies that research has identified as effective in school improvement.

Assessing Readiness

Three sets of questions can help principals evaluate their schools' readiness to benefit from a review. First, principals should ask themselves the following questions:

+ What about a school review do I find intriguing?

+ What advantages would it offer me in leading for improvement?

+ How receptive am I to coaching?

+ Are there roadblocks that I should consider?

+ How willing and able is the staff to commit to new practices and behaviors?

+ How willing am I to lead change efforts and to ensure that agreed-upon changes to existing practices are enacted schoolwide?

Second, in schools where a formally appointed school leadership team is in place, principals should pose the following questions to that team:

+ What is the level of the staff's commitment to improving student achievement?

+ What information do we need most to improve our school?

+ How does the staff react to change?

+ How does the staff respond to coaching?

+ How willing are the leadership team members to lead change efforts and to help to ensure schoolwide commitment to agreed-upon practices?

Third, principals should ask staff members the following questions:

+ Do we believe that all students are challenged in our classes?

+ What percentage of students are not meeting their potential in our classes?

+ Who are these students?

+ What might be holding them back?

+ Are some schools achieving success with kids like those we have described? If so, what might we learn from these other schools?

+ Would we be interested in learning more about what we are doing that research has validated as effective?

+ How receptive are we to coaching?

+ Would we be willing to do things differently if we believed it would result in increased student learning and a better environment for our students?

+ Would we be willing to hold one another accountable for consistently adhering to shared agreements about changes in practice?

If teachers indicate an interest in moving forward with learning about an on-site school review, it is a good time for the principal to introduce this book to them. The research chapters can give staff members a firm grounding in the basis for the review and the areas that a review can cover. We recommend beginning with a study of the first three effectiveness indicators (Written Curriculum, Instructional Program, and Student Assessment). However, if at the outset the staff is more interested in exploring other areas that might be the focus of an on-site school review, Student Connectedness, Engagement, and Readiness (Effectiveness Indicator 7) and School Environment (Effectiveness Indicator 8) are good indicators to use for the initial study and discussions, because they tend to resonate with teachers. The staff members can use one staff meeting to decide which of the research chapters they want to focus on. The principal then invites the staff to read one chapter before the next staff meeting, which will be devoted to discussing what was read.

The following questions will engender interesting discussions at the meetings:

+ What were, to you, the most important ideas in this reading?

+ Were there any ideas that surprised you?

+ Think of a school (and it could be this one) that is embracing the research discussed in this chapter. What school practices reflect this research?

+ How do practices at our school reflect or not reflect this research?

Following the study of the research chapter or chapters, the next step is for the principal and staff to decide if they want to go forward with a review that will look more deeply into one or more of the indicators. Principals handle this decision in a number of ways. Some like to have the staff members vote on, first, whether or not to go forward and then, if they decide to proceed, which indicators should be included in the review. Other principals defer the decision to the leadership team, depending on the team members' decision-making authority.

It is likely that some staff members are used to being observed and will feel comfortable with the review process—particularly those involved in athletics and the visual and performing arts, areas in which coaching for continuous improvement is fundamental. But it is important to ensure that the staff as a whole will be ready for an in-depth look at how the school functions and how its practices align to benchmark standards—standards that research and experience show are in place in high-performing schools. This does not mean that every staff member must enthusiastically embrace the idea of a school review. What the leadership team needs at this point is for teachers to agree to participate fully in the review by answering questions posed by the reviewers, opening their classroom doors to observations, submitting student work, and considering, with an open mind, the recommendations that emerge from the review.

Setting Goals for the Review

Once it has been decided that the school is ready to commit to and benefit from a school review, the school staff must determine the goals of the review. One superintendent we worked with wanted to know how to improve a particular school's instructional program. The school's leadership team, on the other hand, wanted to know more about adult collaboration and where to start in improving those relationships. While we recommended starting with the instructional program, it was possible for the review to meet both goals.

Setting goals with district leaders, school administrators, the leadership team, and staff members helps to create buy-in from all levels. (For example, including key district staff members in these preliminary discussions will help to ensure that the actions the review team ultimately recommends will receive the financial support of the district and will be incorporated into district improvement planning.) The goals that the groups agree upon at the outset will guide every step of the review process and will be carefully addressed in the review team's final report.

Selecting the Effectiveness Indicators for Review

Once the broader goals for the review have been set, the next step is to choose the specific effectiveness indicators to be reviewed. This decision needs to be made early, as it governs all other facets of the review, including the size and makeup of the review team and the materials that will be used during the review.

Selecting Effectiveness Indicators 1–10 will give a full picture of the school. The recommendations that result from this type of review are the strongest in that they grow from a comprehensive assessment of the school and all of its functions in relation to the characteristics of effective schools. Schools may also choose to look at only one or two effectiveness indicators each year. The advantage of looking at fewer areas is that the review requires less time to carry out and can be undertaken with less lead time. The disadvantage of looking at only one or two indicators is that a full picture of the strengths and challenges of the school may not emerge.

Selecting an Academic Focus Area

In addition to choosing the effectiveness indicators to be reviewed, the school needs to select the academic focus area of the review, usually English/language arts, mathematics, or science. The selected academic area should be the one in which the school believes the greatest need exists. This need may be determined based on schoolwide student achievement or based on the achievement of groups of students—for example, English language learners, students from low-income families, or minority students—who are underperforming their peers. The review team will perform an in-depth instructional and data analysis of the selected area. For instance, while every classroom is observed for part of a period during each review, at least one class taught by every teacher in the focus area of the visit will be observed for a full period or lesson.

As another option, the school may decide to request a review of the written curriculum in the focus area and its implementation across classrooms. This would require the addition of one more team member, who would work in this area only during the review. Even without the in-depth curriculum analysis, the selection of the focus area is an important consideration in the makeup of the review team.

The School Review Team, the Team Leader, and the Site Coordinator

The makeup of the team for each school review is customized to include members with expertise in (a) the school's grade range (elementary, middle, or high school), (b) the effectiveness indicators selected, and (c) the academic focus area selected. Team members should also be well-versed in school improvement. Ideally, the team is a well-balanced composite of strengths and knowledge. It is important to have members with diverse backgrounds and educational experiences in order to draw on broad expertise. The decision as to who will serve on the review team is generally made by the principal and other administrators or leadership team members.

Assembling a Team

There are many ways to put together a team. Sometimes a district trades team members with another district that is also interested in on-site school reviews. States may have intermediate service districts that employ staff members who are very knowledgeable about school improvement and are often willing and able to work as review team members. The state department of education, too, can sometimes provide free or nearly free help. Another source of team members is schools of educational administration, some of which require their administrative candidates to engage in school or district improvement initiatives or internships. Retired educators, including teachers, administrators, and specialists, make up a good pool of potential reviewers. Outside consultants often have a broader, sometimes national perspective and are valuable resources. Table 11.1 briefly describes the advantages and disadvantages of the different staffing options.

An additional model would be a mixed team of reviewers from more than one of the groups discussed. It might make a nicely balanced team to bring in a few outside consultants, an intermediate service district specialist, and a few staff members from a neighboring district.

Table 11.1: Review Team Staffing Options

Team Makeup	Advantages	Disadvantages
Staff members, including administrative candidates, from another school in the district	1. Most cost-efficient. Staff costs will consist mainly of pay for substitute teachers, with no food or lodging expenses incurred. 2. The learning occurs both for the school being reviewed and for the staff members conducting the review. That knowledge then stays in the district. 3. Members of the review team are not viewed as outsiders. 4. For administrative candidates, there may be no cost involved, as a review could be part of their program requirements.	1. In addition to the time they spend on-site, reviewers will need to be away from their schools for at least a ½ day of training as well as 1 day at each end of the visit for preparation and report writing. 2. It is difficult for smaller districts to find several qualified substitutes on the same dates. 3. The limited reviewer pool may result in a lack of expertise in some areas. 4. The staff members being reviewed may not be as frank as they would be with outside reviewers. 5. Steps must be taken to ensure that no one in a chain of command interviews others in that chain.
Staff members, including administrative candidates, from a school in a neighboring district	1. Cost-efficient. Staff costs will consist mainly of pay for substitute teachers, with little or no food or lodging expenses incurred. 2. Reviewers are not part of the district and so will not have any "history" to overcome but are still familiar with the region of which the school is a part. 3. For administrative candidates, there may be no cost involved, as a review could be part of their program requirements.	1. In addition to the time they spend on-site, reviewers will need to be away from their schools for at least a ½ day of training as well as 1 day at each end of the visit for preparation and report writing. 2. It is difficult for smaller districts to find several qualified substitutes on the same dates. 3. The limited reviewer pool may result in a lack of expertise in some areas.

(continued)

Team Makeup	Advantages	Disadvantages
Staff members from intermediate service districts and other agencies	1. Reviewers may be available at a reduced cost as part of their regional service agreement. 2. It is likely that sufficient expertise is available. 3. Reviewers are not part of the district and so will not have any "history" to overcome but are still familiar with the region of which the school is a part. 4. The review provides an opportunity for the school staff to get to know the regional staff members and their styles for follow-up professional development consideration.	1. More costly than the first two options because the team will incur food and lodging expenses. 2. In addition to the time they spend on-site, reviewers will need to be away from their regular jobs for at least a ½ day of training as well as 1 day at each end of the visit for preparation and report writing. 3. It is difficult for intermediate service districts to free up staff for several days in a row. 4. The review must be scheduled far in advance.
Outside consultants (such as retired educators)	1. If already trained in the process, team members can accomplish the review at the highest level of expertise. 2. If already trained in the process, team members can accomplish the review in the shortest time. 3. Using outside consultants causes the least disruption to existing school or district schedules. 4. Deep expertise is available in all areas of the review. 5. Reviewers are not part of the district and so will not have any "history" to overcome. 6. The review provides an opportunity for the school staff to get to know consultants with expertise in a variety of areas for future professional development consideration.	1. Depending on experience and makeup of the team, potentially the most expensive of the options because of travel, food, and lodging costs. 2. When the reviewers leave the school, what they have learned leaves with them, except for what they include in the written report. 3. In addition to the time they spend on-site, reviewers will need to be available for at least a ½ day of training as well as 1 day at each end of the visit for preparation and report writing.

When assembling a team, it is essential to make it clear to all members that they must commit to the entire review from beginning to end. It is disruptive to the process when a team member is unavailable in the middle of a project or not fully attending to the work. There should be an agreement with each team member (and his or her principal or supervisor, if necessary) stating that this work cannot be done in conjunction with other work or other responsibilities. Team members will also need to know that they will be working before and after school, into the evenings. These agreements will ensure that everyone is available to work together throughout the review.

Choosing the Team Leader

Selecting the right review team leader is one of the most important decisions to be made. Usually the principal makes this decision. The team leader is key to the value and success of the review. Team leaders typically have broad educational and leadership experience. At a minimum, they should have led or participated in other reviews or should have experience in evaluation, school improvement, mentoring, and interviewing. The leader will be responsible for keeping the team members on track throughout the process, helping them balance their review of the effectiveness indicators, and crafting the final report. The leader should have the skills necessary to maintain good communication with the team and with the school site and to ensure that materials, schedules, and products are ready for the team when needed and returned to the school in a well-organized fashion immediately after the review. He or she must also be able to lead two follow-up sessions with the school staff members as they study the results and plan for next steps. Finally, the team leader must be comfortable with the research and the process.

Selecting a Site Coordinator

While the review team members and team leader come from outside the school, it is essential to designate someone within the school to serve as the site coordinator. If the principal delegates this role, it relieves him or her of much of the organizational work. Principals frequently name an administrative assistant to this position. The site coordinator will be the key point of contact at the school for the leader and members of the review team. He or she will have to have strong organizational and communication skills. The site coordinator will take the lead in communicating with the team leader and organizing the logistics of the visit for the team, including travel arrangements. The site coordinator will also put together interview schedules; collect and organize sample work from all teachers; duplicate, distribute, and collect surveys; and make sure that everyone keeps communicating.

Estimating Time and Costs

Team Size and Number of Days on Site

The size of the review team depends on the number of effectiveness indicators selected for the review and the number of teachers at the school. Once those figures are known, it is possible to determine the number of days the review team should spend at the school. The process is not an exact science, but we have come up with guidelines that are based on past practice and allow for a generous amount of time for team members to collaborate, reflect, and write, as well as perform the on-site work at the school. We know that it is best for the review team to be in the school observing and interviewing at least 2 and not more than 5 days.

Table 11.2 provides an easy way for a school to calculate how many days to schedule for the on-site portion of the visit. The number of days allotted for the different staffing levels gives the team ample time for:

- Completing a ½ day of training at the outset of the review

- Conducting three to four interviews per day per team member

- Observing teachers, taking notes, and reviewing documents

- Reviewing data, discussing what other team members are seeing, and developing initial conclusions

- Using 1 full day at the end of the review for delivering the oral exit report and completing the final written report

Table 11.2: Number of Days On-Site

Number of Team Members*	Number of Teachers on Staff								
	2–12	8–18	19–24	25–30	31–36	37–42	43–48	49–54	55–60
	Number of Days								
2	2–3	4	5						
3		3	4	4	5				
4			3	4	4	5	5		
5			3	4	4	4	5	5	5

*These numbers are based on a review that evaluates Effectiveness Indicators 1–9 but does not include an in-depth review of selected curriculum. To include Effectiveness Indicator 10, add one team member. For an in-depth curriculum review, add one team member per subject area to be reviewed.

As an example of how to use Table 11.2, let us say that a secondary school with 40 teachers is scheduling a review. The shaded boxes in the column for schools with between 37 and 42 teachers indicate that the review team for a school of that size should have no fewer than four members. The box in which the row for the number of team members and the column for the number of teachers intersect indicates that a four-member team would need to spend 5 days on-site in this school.

The estimate derived from the table can be checked by following these steps:

1. To estimate the amount of time it will take to conduct interviews, allot 1 hour to each staff member. In our example of a secondary school with 40 teachers, the interviews will take 40 hours. If the school schedule consists of six 55-minute periods per day, one reviewer would have to spend 7 days on-site for interviews only.

2. For the academic focus area selected (for example, mathematics), reviewers will conduct observations of full lessons. To determine the amount of time required for these observations, allot one full period to each teacher in the focus area. If there are six mathematics teachers in the secondary school in our example, the observations will require 1 day.

3. For teachers outside of the academic focus area, the reviewers will conduct observations of partial lessons. In the secondary school in our example, there are 34 teachers outside of the focus area. Reviewers can conduct two partial-lesson observations per period, for a total of 17 periods, or 3 days.

4. Take the total number of days from steps 1, 2, and 3, and add 25% more time, as schedules will overlap and the team will need time between interviews and observations for reflection and note-taking. In our example, the sum of steps 1, 2, and 3 is 11 days. Add 25% (3 days), for a total of 14 days. Divide 14 days by four people (the number of team members suggested in Table 11.2). It would take 3.5 days for the on-site time, a ½ day to prepare as a team, and 1 day for report writing, for a total of 5 days.

5. Add one more team member if the school selects all 10 effectiveness indicators. Add one more team member for each additional academic focus area selected.

A school should be generous in estimating time for its review to be sure that there is enough time for all of the work to be accomplished before the team disbands.

Estimating Costs

Schools we have worked with have used general, federal, private, or grant funds, or a combination of these funds, to offset the costs of an on-site review. The cost of a school review depends on the number of effectiveness indicators selected for review, the size of the school, the makeup of the review team, and the time the team spends on-site. If the team is coming from a distance, travel, food, and lodging costs will also need to be built into the budget. **Tool 1: Budget Planning** (see CD), provides a template for an itemized budget for a school review.

Basic Time Line

Some on-site school reviews are planned a year in advance, others 3 or 4 months in advance, depending on the circumstances. The time line in Figure 11.1 (pages 208–209) identifies the major milestones of the review process. Because of the nature of school calendars and review team members' calendars, the number of days or weeks for each stage is not specified.

In the first step of the process, the preliminary planning meeting, the principal, site coordinator, and review team leader work together to schedule the major components of the review. **Tool 2: Planning**

Schedule (see CD and appendix, page 260), provides a template for carrying out this task. The scheduling should begin with determining the best time for the on-site portion of the review.

The Planning Stage

The next two steps of the planning stage are (1) identifying the documents that will give the review team essential information about the school and (2) scheduling and holding the first meeting between the team leader and the school leadership team.

Gathering Planning Documents

To assist the review team leader and members in planning for their time on-site, the site coordinator will gather a number of documents and arrange to have them delivered to the team leader before the visit. The review team will need the following documents:

- Master schedule (for each teacher: full name, course/class, class times, prep periods, and room number)
- Teachers' daily instruction times for reading and mathematics (if elementary)
- Daily bell schedule
- Map of school with room numbers
- Staff list (first and last name, role/assignment(s), phone number, email)
- Student achievement data, including trend and disaggregated data, from statewide assessments (last 3 years)
- Comparison school data, if available
- School and district strategic plans

With these documents, the review team will be able to begin analyzing data, planning on-site tasks, and drawing up interview and focus group assignments.

Meeting Between Team Leader and School Leadership Team

About 60 days before the review team's visit, the team leader, principal, and site coordinator should meet with the school leadership team. The principal should ask the site coordinator to find a time that will

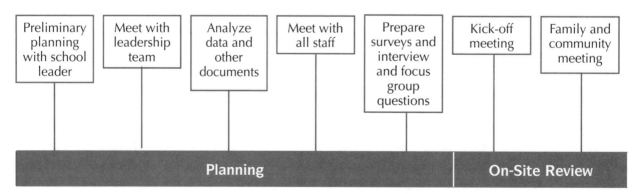

Figure 11.1: The major milestones of the on-site school review process.

work well for all parties and to schedule the meeting. The purposes of this meeting are to:

+ Discuss the review

+ Plan the schedule

+ Determine responsibilities for leadership team members

+ Design a communication plan for the review

This is the first opportunity the team leader has to begin building a relationship with the people at the school. He or she will want to describe the review process, share the plans to date, and provide the leadership team members with the information they will need when they talk to their colleagues about the upcoming visit.

This meeting will set the tone of the work with the school and should explicitly provide time for the surfacing of any questions or concerns. The leadership team is aware of the inner workings of the school and where potential issues may arise. One example of an unanticipated issue in a school in which we worked was the staff members' negative attitude toward the term *research-based*. In discussing their concerns at our first meeting, the members of the leadership team made us aware of this problem. They knew that the staff would literally stop listening if we emphasized the research and instead recommended that we focus on what works for kids in effective schools. Sometimes avoiding hot buttons is simply a matter of using the right vocabulary. As guests in the school, the reviewers need to be sensitive to issues and areas that, if addressed incorrectly, could undermine the success of the review.

The members of the leadership team should leave the meeting feeling knowledgeable about and comfortable with the purpose for the review, the process, and the next steps. When they talk with the staff, they will help to build the energy around this work. The team leader should leave the meeting with additional information about the readiness of the school to undertake this review and a plan for next steps.

At least 2 hours should be allotted for this meeting. The team leader can give a formal PowerPoint presentation using **Tool 3: Leadership Meeting PowerPoint** (see CD) or conduct a more informal discussion covering the same topics as the PowerPoint slides. **Tool 4: Leadership Meeting Agenda** (see CD and appendix, page 261) is based on the main headings of the PowerPoint slides. After the team leader and members of the leadership team introduce themselves and discuss the school's readiness for the review, the team leader explains the effectiveness indicators, the various ways that the review team will gather evidence, and the steps of the review process. The final part of the meeting is devoted to planning. Whether

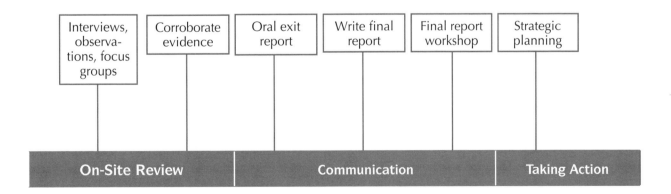

the meeting is formal or informal, the team leader should distribute the following handouts as the topics to which they correspond are discussed:

- **Tool 2: Planning Schedule** (see CD and appendix, page 260)

- Print (handout) version of the 20 slides in **Tool 3: Leadership Meeting PowerPoint** (see CD)

- **Tool 5: Effectiveness Indicator Overview** (see CD and appendix, page 262)

- **Tool 6: On-Site School Review Overview** (see CD and appendix, page 267)

- **Tool 7: Teacher Survey Example** (see CD and appendix, page 270)

- **Tool 8: Collecting Student Work—Letter to Instructional Staff** (see CD)

Working Together

As the school review moves through its different stages, the responsibilities for both leading and carrying out other functions will also shift. For example, in this chapter we have seen that the principal and leadership team carried the primary responsibility for the decision to go forward with the review and for the selection of the effectiveness indicators and an academic focus area. Then the team leader and site coordinator began to take on larger roles. Table 11.3 identifies those who have the primary responsibility for each part of the on-site review process.

Table 11.3: Shared Responsibilities

Chapter Number	Chapter Title	Principal	Site Coordinator	Leadership Team	School Staff	Team Leader	Review Team
11	Leading the Way	✓	✓	✓		✓	
12	Preparing for the On-Site Visit		✓		✓	✓	
13	Examining Data and Other Documents		✓			✓	✓
14	The Process: How to Conduct a Research-Based On-Site School Review					✓	✓
15	Communicating Results	✓				✓	✓
16	Now What? Strategic Planning and Professional Development	✓		✓	✓		

CHAPTER 12

Preparing for the On-Site Visit

Let us put our minds together and see what life we can make for our children.

—Sitting Bull

Now that the school leadership team has met with the review team leader, the stage is set to prepare for the on-site visit. At this point in the process, the team leader, site coordinator, and school staff members take primary responsibility for the work.

Arranging for the Review Team's Visit

It is usually the principal or another school or district administrator who makes initial contact with prospective team members to begin forming the on-site review team. Each person contacted will receive a questionnaire (**Tool 9: Team Member Information Form**, see CD) asking for information about his or her availability and areas of expertise.

As the review team members commit, the team leader sends a follow-up letter welcoming them to the team and informing them of logistical arrangements (**Tool 10: Team Member Welcome Letter**, see CD).

If the team members will be coming from a distance, travel arrangements must be made early on, in order to secure airline reservations and make backup plans in case of inclement weather. If lodging arrangements are necessary, there are several options to consider. The choice depends on how the visit is funded and how team members are compensated. The easiest way to make hotel arrangements is for the site coordinator to select a safe, clean, and comfortable motel or hotel close to the school and ask the hotel to hold the number of rooms needed. A hotel conference room that can serve as the team workroom after school hours is often available at no additional charge if a block of rooms is booked for the visit. The site coordinator should be sure to ask for government rates when inquiring about lodging fees. With advance arrangements through the school district, it is often possible to reserve the rooms under the school district's name, in which case the hotel bills the school district directly via a purchase order process. If the school, for one reason or another, does not want to handle lodging directly, the welcome/logistics letter should let team members know that they need to contact the hotel directly to make or confirm their individual reservations.

Scheduling Interviews and Focus Groups for Staff and Students

During the review team's visit, every staff member will participate in *either* an interview or a focus group, depending on personal preference. (Leadership team members are the only exception, as they participate in both individual interviews and the leadership team focus group.)

Using **Tool 11: Sample Planning Schedule** (see CD), the team leader creates a daily team schedule (based on the school's bell schedule). Each day includes a 1-hour meeting between the principal and the team leader. The rest of the schedule will have blocks of time allocated for interviews or focus groups, but no specific names should be included yet.

The times available for interviews are based on the number of team members and the school schedule. The best way to schedule interviews for a review with two team members is to plan only one interview for any specific time block, ensuring that during each scheduled interview the other team member will be available to observe classrooms or complete other duties. If the team has four members, then two interviews per time block can be scheduled; for a team of six, three interviews; and so on.

Focus group opportunities for teachers and for classified (support) staff members are also included in the daily team schedule. The schedule should allow for a couple of focus group time blocks for teachers who would prefer a group process of communication rather than an individual interview. It is best to separate classified staff members into two focus groups, one for those who give instructional support and one for those whose duties are noninstructional (even if it makes the groups very small). The focus groups for teachers and for classified staff run 45 minutes and are most effective when there are four to eight participants. Teacher focus groups can take place before or after student contact time or during common prep time. Focus groups for classified staff are scheduled at a convenient time during the day.

A leadership team focus group also needs to be scheduled. Because of the diverse makeup of leadership teams, the best time for this focus group is usually just before or right after school. An hour should be blocked out for the leadership team focus group, which will concentrate on issues of school strategic planning.

The team leader sends the site coordinator the daily team schedule showing the times available for interviews, focus groups, and other prescheduled work. The site coordinator reviews the schedule with the principal to make sure that no interview blocks, focus groups, or other meetings are scheduled for times that conflict with other scheduled events. This daily team schedule then becomes the basis of the sign-up form (**Tool 12: Interview and Focus Group Sign-Up Form**, see CD) for the staff interviews and focus groups. The sign-up form should be introduced and circulated at the all-staff meeting with the team leader (described later in this chapter) so that staff members may select the days and times that will work best for them either to be individually interviewed or to participate in a focus group.

In addition to the school staff members, some district staff members are interviewed as part of the review. Depending on the district's communication protocols, the site coordinator may need to ask the principal to contact key district staff members—such as the district superintendent and the directors of curriculum, special education, and Title I—to arrange for these interviews. It is best to schedule district interviews to take place early in the review process, ideally during the first or second on-site day. Interviews with district staff members should take 45–60 minutes, depending on the number of effectiveness indicators selected for the review.

Students are not individually interviewed, but some are selected to participate in focus groups. The student samples should be representative of the school population in terms of grade level, achievement, involvement in school, behavior, and demographic attributes (such as race, income, and English proficiency). Student focus groups should have between 6 and 12 members, and, depending on the size of the school, there should be between one and three such groups set up. The site coordinator should arrange for the students to be absent from class for a period of about 20–25 minutes. The site coordinator will also need to arrange for a location for each meeting. It is sometimes beneficial to use an entire class as a focus group. In this case, the site coordinator simply asks teachers if they are interested in volunteering their class for a 20–25-minute block of time.

When the site coordinator has completed the interview and focus group schedule (every staff member, key district staff members, and selected students have all been scheduled), it is sent to the team leader, who will use it to begin making the review team assignments. If the sign-up form is messy, it is a good idea to ask a clerical staff member to transfer the names onto a clean form.

Planning for the Collection of Student Work

The collection of student work is an important component of the school review process. All teachers will be asked to collect their students' work for a 1- or 2-week period. The review team is looking for a sample of student work that is representative of assignments and projects that are completed during the year. Thus teachers should gather normal, everyday assignments from all students in their classes. The collection must be completed prior to the date the team arrives on-site.

It is common for the review team to run into some initial hesitancy from staff members about submitting their students' work. The best way to handle teachers' misgivings is to provide information about how the team will use the work. The staff should understand that no individual data will ever appear in the review team's final report. Data will be reported by grade level (for elementary schools) or content area (for middle and high schools) when there are three or more teachers at each grade level or in each content area. If there are fewer numbers, elementary classes will be grouped into grade-level spans, such as K–3 and 4–6, and middle and high school subject areas, such as English/language arts and mathematics, social studies and science, or all electives, will be grouped together.

Giving teachers a simplified sample of a review team's student work analysis, as provided in **Tool 13: Sample Student Work Analysis** (see CD and appendix, page 271), commonly turns hesitation into interest. If providing the sample encourages teachers to ask higher-level questions in class or to develop more rigorous lessons for the review, so much the better. Learning and improvement are, after all, the aims of the review.

The team leader will initially explain the logistics of the student work collection to the site coordinator. The teachers will learn about the process at the all-staff meeting with the team leader. One person at the school, either the site coordinator or someone he or she designates, such as an administrative assistant or a school secretary, will set up and oversee the collecting, receiving, and storing of the student work.

The first step is to create and distribute folders in which the teachers will place the work they collect. Secondary teachers should receive separate folders for each class they teach, labeled with the teacher's name, the class period, the course name, and the grade level. Elementary teachers should receive separate folders for each subject they teach during the day (for example, reading, math, science), labeled with the teacher's name, grade, and subject. It is also helpful to provide periodical boxes to each teacher to make it easy to keep his or her folders grouped together. The boxes should not be heavy, because they will be moved frequently as the student work is reviewed.

When the teachers receive their folders, at least one full week before the beginning of the work collection period, they will also be given a letter from the team leader with instructions about how to proceed (**Tool 8: Collecting Student Work—Letter to Instructional Staff,** see CD). The letter explains that teachers should grade their papers as usual, return them to their students for an in-class review, and then pick them back up to put in the folders that will be submitted to the review team. Teachers will not be asked to create additional assignments or documents for the review, but if they have lesson plans or scoring rubrics, those documents should be included in the folders with the student work. Each set of assignments should include submissions from every student, whether or not the students did as well as the teacher had hoped. When a teacher turns in his or her collection of work, it will be checked off and kept in a secure area awaiting the review team's arrival.

All-Staff Meeting With Team Leader

It is important that all the teachers and support staff members have an opportunity to meet the team leader and to discuss the upcoming review prior to the visit. In order to allow sufficient time to prepare for the visit, it is best to hold this meeting around 2 months before the on-site review. This meeting usually runs about 45 minutes. Its purpose is to describe to the staff in more detail exactly how the visit will look and feel. It also gives the staff members a chance to talk about their school, their hopes, and their goals for the review and to become more comfortable with the "outside eyes" that will be visiting their school.

One of the most important messages the team leader conveys during this meeting is that the review is about programs and not about individuals. It looks at patterns across the school, not at individual actions. For example, the fact that the school is engaging in the review is evidence that the staff cares about meeting the needs of all students. The team is looking at *what* is occurring at the school, not *who* is doing what. The team leader stresses that no names will ever appear in the report, nor will any obvious references to any one individual.

The all-staff meeting will set the tone for a successful review. It is important for the team leader to be warm, positive, and inviting and for the principal and other members of the leadership team to explicitly lend their support to the visit throughout this meeting. The idea of a review can be unsettling to some, and successfully communicating that it will not focus on individuals can allay much of that concern. In our experience, even in the most difficult of circumstances, by the end of the second day of the review, staff members will have moved from trepidation about to confidence in the review. In fact, teachers often begin seeking out review team members to request interviews and provide additional data.

The agenda for the all-staff meeting is identical to that for the leadership team meeting (see **Tool 4**), and the handouts are nearly identical (see chapter 11, page 210). The Leadership Meeting PowerPoint is revised to include staff readiness questions but is otherwise the same (**Tool 14: All-Staff Meeting PowerPoint,** see CD). If the staff was not involved in the selection of the effectiveness indicators, the team leader should customize the PowerPoint and the Effectiveness Indicator Overview (**Tool 5**) to present only those effectiveness indicators that will be reviewed during the visit.

Communicating With Team Members After the All-Staff Meeting

After the all-staff meeting has taken place, it is a good time for the team leader to re-contact team members. Using **Tool 15: Team Member Update Letter** (see CD), the team leader reports on recent activities and continues to convey the importance of preparation for the visit.

If the team leader did not furnish them before, he or she should give copies of this book and the accompanying CD to each team member, with chapters containing information relevant to the visit flagged for reading. These sections include:

+ Introduction: Knowing What to Do

+ Chapters on each of the effectiveness indicators the school has selected for the review

+ Chapter 13: Examining Data and Other Documents

+ Chapter 14: The Process: How to Conduct a Research-Based On-Site School Review

+ Chapter 15: Communicating Results

On the CD, team members should look at **Tool 49: Sample Final Report**; **Tools 21–27: Interview Questions**; and **Tools 28–34: Focus Group Questions**. If team members are familiar with these chapters and tools prior to the visit, the training time needed on-site will be greatly reduced.

Using the Master Matrix

The team leader will need to become familiar with **Tool 16: Master Matrix** (see CD) before beginning to create the customized surveys and interview forms. The Master Matrix shows the sources of evidence used to gather data on every trait of every effectiveness indicator. For example, for Effectiveness Indicator 2 (Instructional Program), Characteristic 2A, Trait 2A1, there are three Xs along the 2A1 row of the matrix. There is an X in each of the following columns: school administrator interview, teacher interview, and classroom observation. Each X directs the user to a tool that will include a question aligned with and keyed to Trait 2A1. This matrix is used both as an overview of the evidence collection system and as a double-check when creating the surveys and interview forms to be sure that all questions are included and therefore all evidence is being gathered for the effectiveness indicators selected for the review.

Preparing and Administering Surveys

The surveys can be prepared as soon as the effectiveness indicators have been selected. The team leader and site coordinator can complete this task jointly. The team leader generally assembles the surveys, and the site coordinator then reproduces them and distributes or administers them to the appropriate groups. The surveys are unique to the school in that the questions they contain depend on the effectiveness indicators selected for review. There will be different surveys for teachers, classified staff, students, and parents.

Tools 17, 18, 19, and 20: Surveys for Teachers, Classified Staff, Parents, and Students (see CD) provide preassembled surveys for those schools that decide to review all 10 effectiveness indicators. Surveys are also easily created for schools using only some of the effectiveness indicators. For example, because each question is directly associated with an effectiveness indicator and trait number (indicated by the number/

letter code preceding the question on the survey form), to assemble a customized survey, the team leader simply deletes the questions aligned with the effectiveness indicators *not* being reviewed. Then he or she renumbers the questions (leaving the trait number in place) and checks for formatting. This process is used for all four surveys. Once the surveys are copy-ready, the team leader sends them to the site coordinator electronically or as hard copy. The surveys will need to be copied, distributed to each group being surveyed, completed, collected, and returned to the site coordinator no later than 2 weeks prior to the site visit for tallying. Results of the surveys will be used as a source of evidence for team members and disseminated to the school staff as part of the final report.

Parent surveys should be mailed out or otherwise distributed to all parents and guardians about 3 weeks before the visit, along with an invitation to attend the family and community meeting (discussed on the next page).

Teachers and classified staff members should take the survey during a staff meeting or some other meeting time. It is best not to share the surveys prior to the staff meeting. The site coordinator should make sure that sufficient time is set aside at the meeting (probably 20–30 minutes) to allow the staff members to complete the surveys carefully enough to reflect their individual thoughts. When a school has selected all 10 indicators for review, it is best to divide the teacher survey into two parts and to administer the first half in one staff meeting and the second half in a following meeting.

The student surveys are to be completed in class by every student and are best administered during homeroom, English/language arts, or other classes taken by all students. The surveys are appropriate for students in grades 5–12 and usually take between 5 and 10 minutes to complete. For some English language learners and special education students, as well as for younger students, it is better to use focus groups and interviews to obtain the information asked for on the survey.

Preparing Interview and Focus Group Questions

As with the surveys, the interview and focus group questions are assembled by the team leader based on the Master Matrix and the effectiveness indicators that the school has selected for the review. There are separate sets of interview questions and focus group questions for the following groups:

+ District administrators (interview)

+ School administrators (interview)

+ Curriculum administrators (interview)

+ Board members (interview)

+ Teachers (interview and focus group)

+ School leadership team (focus group)

+ Counselors (interview)

+ Classified instructional staff (focus group)

+ Classified noninstructional staff (focus group)

+ Elementary students (focus group)

+ Secondary students (focus group)

- ◆ Family/community members (focus group)

- ◆ Community members (interview)

Tools 21–34 (the question templates for each group in the preceding list; see CD), provide pre-assembled sets of interview and focus group questions for those schools that decide to review all 10 effectiveness indicators. Question templates are also easily created for schools using only some of the effectiveness indicators. For example, because each question is directly associated with an effectiveness indicator and trait number (indicated by the number/letter code preceding the question on the template), to assemble a customized template, the team leader simply deletes the questions aligned with the effectiveness indicators *not* being reviewed. Then he or she renumbers the questions (leaving the trait number in place).

Once the focus group and interview questions have been assembled, the team leader will make enough hard copies for the team to use for note-taking when interviewing and conducting focus groups. The team leader should also make an electronic copy of all survey, interview, and focus group questions and keep a backup set on a flash drive. The questions can then be shared electronically with team members, who should be encouraged to take notes using a laptop. Because team members will have their own flash drives and will be using their own laptop computers during this work, all the notes they take electronically can be easily shared.

Planning for the Family and Community Meeting

Probably the first focus group the review team conducts will be the family and community meeting. In order to result in a high turnout by families, this event needs to be planned well in advance. The principal and site coordinator take the lead in planning for and advertising the family and community meeting. If only one family and community meeting is held, it is generally scheduled for the evening of the first day of the visit. This timing allows the team to use the following evenings for assembling collected data and planning. Of course, the meeting should be set when there are no conflicts with the school schedule or activities, when the principal can be present to welcome the parents, and at a time that the principal believes will be best for parents. It may be possible to coordinate a convenient meeting time before an at-home game, a choir concert, or even an open house.

It also works well to schedule a second family and community meeting during a morning or an afternoon for parents who may drop off or pick up their children at school or who for other reasons, such as work schedules, may prefer to meet during the day.

The evening meetings ideally include a light dinner beforehand. Whether or not a meal is served, there should be light refreshments such as cookies and punch or coffee. We have found the PTA to be especially supportive of these meetings, and its members have often volunteered to prepare and serve a meal or even conduct a raffle at the conclusion of the evening, which helps encourage parents to stay for the whole meeting.

The actual focus group (which will be discussed in more detail in chapter 14 under "Family and Community Meeting") should be planned for 1 hour, with an additional ½ hour's access to the building so that guests don't feel rushed out. The meeting will be more convenient for parents of small children if child-care arrangements, such as a supervised playroom in the gymnasium, are provided. Another effective strategy is to schedule a movie for the kids while the parents attend the focus group.

Finally, if it is likely that parents' or community members' home language is not English, the site coordinator should make sure that interpreters will be present at the meeting. It is best to find interpreters who are not staff members at the school. Using outside interpreters will ensure that parents feel safe in answering the questions posed to them and that the interpretation is accurate and remains confidential.

Once the family and community meeting location, time, and date have been decided, the principal should send an invitation letter (**Tool 35: Family and Community Meeting Invitation Letter**, see CD), along with the parent survey (**Tool 19**), to the home of each family. The upcoming meeting should be announced through every venue possible—school newsletters, outdoor signs, the school website, the local newspaper, school email lists, and PTA and booster clubs meetings. The site coordinator and principal should consider having both the letter and the parent survey translated into the major languages of the school community and making them available to parents whose home language is not English.

One of the best-attended family and community meetings we've seen occurred when the school sent the invitation and survey along with grade reports. One of the best returns on the survey was obtained when parents filled out and turned in the surveys as they waited their turn for a parent-teacher conference.

Scheduling Team Interviews and Observations

When the review team leader schedules the interviews with school staff members, he or she should consider individual team members' expertise. For example, it is best to have a member who has administrative experience conduct the interviews with school and district administrators. Similarly, when the team leader schedules observations, it works best if team members observe the classrooms of the same teachers they interview. It will not always work out perfectly, but whenever observations can be arranged this way, they should be. **Tool 36: Interview/Observation Schedule Template (Secondary)** and **Tool 37: Interview/Observation Schedule Template (Elementary)** (see CD) show examples in which a team member has been scheduled to interview and observe the same staff member.

The team leader should begin by assigning team members to interview the English/language arts and mathematics staff. After the English/language arts, mathematics, and science interviews have been assigned, the rest of the interviews should be assigned. The team leader should try to balance the load so that each team member has roughly the same number of interviews. This system will then allow team members to have approximately an equal number of observations as well, in addition to time to reflect on and organize their notes, observe other school areas, analyze student work, and complete other assigned tasks. The team leader will create a master schedule with all interviews scheduled and assigned and then pencil in possible observations for each team member.

In secondary schools with departmentalized classes, the school's master schedule will be used to schedule observations (**Tool 36**). In elementary schools with self-contained classes, the class times in which reading and mathematics are taught will be used to schedule observations (**Tool 37**).

Scheduling observations is never an exact science. Because of this, the review team does not usually share the classroom observation schedule with the school staff. Team members need the flexibility to drop into classrooms and observe based on their availability. From our experience, even though in every communication and conversation about the observations the reviewers stress that they will be observing *students—not teachers*, there is trepidation about "being observed." Scheduling an exact time frame can put too much pressure on both the teachers and the team members. For some teachers, however, it is more stressful not to know when they will be observed. If a teacher requests that the observation be at a certain time, the team leader should attempt to accommodate that request.

Work and Interview Spaces

Attention to a few details prior to the on-site visit will make a difference in how the team members function and how efficiently they use their limited on-site time. The site coordinator needs to identify a team workroom that can be reserved for the exclusive use of the team during the visit. This room must be secluded enough for team members to plan and to discuss their progress without disrupting school activities or being overheard as they begin to share information gleaned from the visit. It must be large enough for the team members to use as they write up their notes, review curriculum, and analyze student work, and it must be configured so that they can work in pairs or as a full group. Other considerations include sufficient work surfaces for all team members, adequate electrical outlets for laptops, and security so that valuables such as purses and computer equipment can be left in the room while team members come and go.

The team will also need two small rooms in which they can conduct interviews and one room large enough to hold a focus group. The interview and focus group rooms do not have to be dedicated to review team use during the entire visit but must be empty during the interview times and free at least 10 minutes before and 10 minutes after each focus group meeting.

It may seem trivial, but it is important for team members to be physically comfortable and to have access to food and drink. They will work long hours and have very short breaks for lunch and dinner. It is best to identify in advance a person and a system for providing food and beverages for the team room. This simply means that the workroom will be stocked with snacks based on team member preferences, along with coffee and bottles of water; that lunch orders either at the school cafeteria or at a local restaurant are placed; and that a location for dinner each night is selected and car pooling arranged if the team is from out of town.

Equipment and Supply Needs

One of the final preparation steps is an equipment and supply check. The team leader needs to discuss with the site coordinator what equipment and supplies the school will furnish and then arrange for the team to bring the rest. **Tool 38: Equipment, Supplies, and Materials Checklist** (see CD) spells out what is needed for an on-site visit.

Communicating With the Team as the On-Site Visit Nears

As the date of the visit gets close, the team leader should again communicate with the team to discuss final details. It is helpful to provide electronic copies of the interview and focus group templates via email for the team members to review prior to the visit (see "Preparing Interview and Focus Group Questions," page 216). Team members will want to load these materials onto their laptops. The team leader should check with the team members to ensure that no snags have developed in their plans to participate or in their arrival or departure times. This is also an opportunity to remind them of their homework assignment to read the flagged chapters from this book and become familiar with the effectiveness indicators and interview and focus group questions prior to the visit. Now is the time to provide directions regarding check-in procedures at the school and to announce the location and time for the team planning meeting. Finally, it is a good idea to remind team members to bring with them pens, pencils, notepads, laptop computers, and flash drives.

The Week and Day Before the Visit

The team leader will set up two final contacts with the principal and site coordinator. One week before the visit, the team leader should call the principal and site coordinator to confirm the time and location of the review kick-off meeting (described in chapter 14). This conversation also includes updates on any last-minute preparations such as schedule or staffing changes. The site coordinator should share with the principal and review team leader any logistical or other concerns that have arisen during the planning, as this is an opportunity to quickly address and overcome those obstacles.

The team leader should also call the principal and site coordinator one day before the visit. In most cases, because the visit has been well-planned and communicated, this call is to thank the site coordinator for his or her efforts in preparing for the visit and to express the team's preparedness and enthusiasm to both the principal and site coordinator.

Reminders to the School Staff

At the staff meeting nearest to the beginning of the visit, the principal should remind the staff members of the upcoming review and request that they remind their students to ask their parents to complete the survey and attend the family and community meeting. This meeting is also a good time to give the teachers the handout provided in **Tool 39: Student Announcement** (see CD) so that they can distribute it to their students on the first day of the review. This announcement briefly explains what the review entails, asks for the students' cooperation, and generates excitement about the review team's visit.

CHAPTER 13

Examining Data and Other Documents

Too often we forget that genius, too, depends upon the data within its reach, that even Archimedes could not have devised Edison's inventions.

—Ernest Dimnet

An important component of the school review process is looking at and evaluating the school's data reports and other written documentation—the policies, procedures, agreements, and communications that underpin the school's activities and beliefs. The documents also provide a sort of mirror that shows us how well those beliefs are reflected and formalized in writing.

The team leader and site coordinator share the responsibility of assembling the data. Generally, the team leader collects the information that is available from public sources, such as the websites of the state department of education, the school, and the district. He or she then puts together a list of other documents and materials for the site coordinator to collect. The checklist on page 222 is a good start at specifying what the team will need. The first column is a list of documents that the team leader can review prior to the visit. On the first day of the visit, the team leader will provide a packet containing these materials to each team member as part of the team briefing. The second column is a list of reference documents and materials that should be available in the team workroom.

Collecting and Analyzing State Achievement Data

The team leader, or a team member designated by the team leader, completes an initial analysis of the data on student achievement as measured by state assessments. There are four analyses that should be performed using state achievement data:

1. Current-year analysis in all content areas at each grade level

2. Current-year analysis disaggregated by ethnicity and by participation in programs such as gifted and special education, English as a second language, and specialized grant programs

3. Three- to five-year trends in all content areas at each grade level

4. Comparison of the school's disaggregated achievement data to those of schools with similar characteristics

Data and Documents Checklist

Prior to the Visit (Team Data Packet)	On-Site Reference
❑ Student achievement data from state assessments (last 3 years)	❑ Written curriculum
	❑ Scope and sequence documents
❑ Student achievement trends from state assessments (last 3 years)	❑ Pacing charts
	❑ List of textbooks and classes in which they are used
❑ Disaggregated student achievement data	
❑ Comparison schools data, if available	❑ List of supplemental and intervention materials
❑ School strategic plan	❑ Local student data collections (such as intervention assessments)
❑ District strategic plan	
❑ Survey results (teacher, classified staff, student)	❑ Student attendance data
	❑ Student behavior data
	❑ Behavior or discipline plan
	❑ Student, parent, and staff handbooks
	❑ Recent newsletters
	❑ Extracurricular opportunities
	❑ Grant awards
	❑ Recent district, state, or federal reports
	❑ Survey results (parent)
	❑ Student work

In selecting and analyzing data, the team leader should consider that the analyses will be used for two purposes. First, they will provide key information to the review team about the school's central mission—student learning. Second, they will be highlighted in the review team's final report to the school staff. The team leader should provide brief summary statements of the achievement data and include graphs to illustrate the analyses. He or she will often be able to copy these graphs directly from the website of the state department of education or the district's website. It is not necessary to include a summary and graph for every analysis; instead the team leader should report achievement trends and highlight areas in which the school is doing well and areas where achievement is lagging. These summaries and graphs will ultimately be included in the data packet that will be delivered to the staff along with the final report. Section I of **Tool 40: Sample Data Packet** (see CD) provides examples of the presentation of achievement data.

When incorporating the analysis into the final report to the school staff, the team leader should keep in mind that providing too much data lessens the impact. Providing too little lessens the significance. The report should include the information that the school needs in order to make good decisions and to understand which students are achieving and which are not. It is also important that the report show how similar children achieve across the state and how children in similar schools perform (see "Similar Schools Comparison," page 224). For example, in one school with which we worked, the data clearly illustrated that while only 68% of the school's eighth-grade students overall were meeting the state mathematics standards, among schools with similar demographics, this school's percentages were among the highest in the state.

Team Member Data Brief

Once the team leader has completed the initial analysis, he or she should prepare a student achievement brief for the team members. This brief should focus only on state assessment results and trends, as shown in **Tool 41: Sample Team Member Data Brief** (see CD). The information presented in the brief will increase the team members' knowledge of the school and will help to focus them on the school's results, documents, and communications as they start the process of inquiry.

Collecting, Preparing, and Analyzing Survey Data

The team will also work with the data from the four surveys: teacher, classified staff, parent, and student. With the exception of the parent surveys, the site coordinator will collect the completed surveys, tally the results, and return them to the team leader at least 2 weeks before the on-site visit. This allows time for the team leader to begin building the data displays. If careful and trusted students or other workers at the school are available, enlisting their assistance in this task will be a time- and money-saver.

While there are services that will analyze and display survey data for a fee, it is easy to compile the data and create reports using a spreadsheet program such as Excel. First, the site coordinator or an assistant will tally the responses using a copy of the original survey form and then transfer the questions along with the data into the spreadsheet. Then he or she will use the chart-making function (which is a part of almost all spreadsheet programs) to create a bar graph for each question. Each graph should include the number and percentage of responses in each of the five possible response categories. If this seems too complicated, the data can simply be reported in a table format by creating two tables for each survey—one to display the number of responses in each category and the second to display the percentage of responses in each category. Section III of **Tool 40: Sample Data Packet** (see CD) provides illustrations of these two tables.

Analyzing Student Work

For 1 to 2 weeks before the on-site visit, teachers collect their students' work to submit for review. The procedures for the collection were described in detail in chapter 12. Depending on the number of classes, two or more team members are assigned the responsibility of reviewing all submissions and tabulating the results during the on-site visit. The interview and observation schedule will need to be lighter for these team members to allow them to have substantial blocks of time to complete the review. If the team is large enough, one way to capture time during the visit is to divide the team into two groups during the family and community night and have one group conduct the meeting while the other group scores student work in the team workroom at the school. The team size needed for the family and community night is two team members per each group of 12–14 parents. Any team members not needed for the parent focus group can work on the analysis.

The team members who review the collection of work prepare a summary of the number of teachers who submitted work, the content areas, the grade levels, and the number of unique assignments. A unique assignment is one that is given in one or more classes by the same teacher. Thus, an identical assignment given in two or more classes counts as a single unique assignment. An example of how these data were reported for a grade K–7 school appears in Section II of **Tool 40: Sample Data Packet** (see CD).

Using **Tool 42: Student Work Taxonomy and Rigor Analysis Worksheet** (see CD), the team members analyze each assignment to determine its level of cognitive demand, that is, whether it is targeted to higher- or lower-order thinking skills, according to Bloom's Taxonomy. They also calculate each assignment's level of rigor, that is, its degree of academic challenge in relation to the demonstrations of knowledge and skills called for in state grade-level standards and benchmarks.

Similar Schools Comparison

The review team may be asked to perform a similar schools comparison. Similar schools comparisons are powerful motivators. They reveal how well the school's students are performing in relation to schools with similar demographics, and they provide intriguing information about programs, practices, and strategies to consider adopting.

Comparison data enable the school to look at its own assessment scores alongside those of schools that are like them. Whenever possible, the review team should include in its report to the school a list of top comparable schools in each content area—the highest-performing schools in the state with demographics similar to the selected school. The school can use these data to make decisions about improvement efforts as part of its strategic action plan. For example, the similar schools comparison may report data showing that students who qualify for free or reduced-price lunch at Casper Elementary are lagging behind similar students in other schools that have many of the same characteristics as Casper in terms of size, grade levels, and student demographics.

Many states, districts, and a number of organizations also provide information on comparable schools. Each state uses a somewhat different definition of similar schools, and the data provided range from simple to complex. For example, Kansas uses just four indicators, while New York uses a complex set of indicators that can be assembled in any number of ways. Indicators may include the percentage of students who qualify for free or reduced-price lunch, school size, number of students, experience of the teachers, funding levels, and demographic data. In some states, sophisticated databases allow comparisons of schools and districts in terms of community support, demographics, instructional programs, instructional time, parent involvement, personnel, professional development, resource allocation, school safety, student-teacher ratios, summer and after-school programs, and technology investment.

The federal government, state education agencies, and nonprofit agencies (such as the Education Trust, Education Commission of the States, and Council of Chief State School Officers) collect a wide variety of information about how schools do business. Another source is Just for the Kids (www.just4kids .org), which offers well-organized comparison data for more than 30 states.

Analyzing the School Strategic Plan

A key piece of information in looking at overall school performance is how well the school plans its future work. For most schools there is a ready-made vehicle for school planning: the school strategic plan.

Many schools, however, view this plan as a paperwork burden to be completed only to fulfill a state or federal requirement and then filed away to be reviewed again only when the next plan is due. This attitude is due partly to the bureaucratic constraints and requirements that states have crafted around these plans and partly to the fact that planning is not something that seems to come naturally to schools. Few schools of education and programs of school administration include strategic planning in their training of teachers and administrators, and those that do rarely take the next step of teaching how to effectively implement and evaluate strategic plans.

While most schools have some type of school improvement plan, seldom does the plan come alive in the school. This is a shame, because written planning documents are for the school much like written curriculum is for teachers: Schools can use the school strategic plan as a road map in day-to-day decision-making in order to ensure arrival at an agreed-upon place at the agreed-upon time.

Effective schools know where they are, where they are going, and how they are going to get there—this is the essence of a strategic plan. As part of the review, the team carefully analyzes school planning documents on two fronts. The first is the process used to develop the plan, and the second is the way in which the plan is being implemented. As with everything else in the review, it is research on the practices of effective schools, not mandated or political processes, that is the basis for the analysis of school strategic plans. (For a summary of the research on effective strategic planning, see chapter 5.)

The team will use Effectiveness Indicator 5: Strategic Planning to evaluate both the development and the implementation of the plan. See chapter 5 and **Tool 5: Effectiveness Indicator Overview** (CD and appendix, page 262) for a breakdown of the eight characteristics of strategic planning that are associated with effective schools and that the reviewers will be looking for during their visit.

The team leader should obtain a copy of the school's strategic plan early in the review process in order to be familiar with it prior to the on-site visit. A copy should also be available to team members during the on-site visit for reference. The team will gather and analyze the evidence that is linked to each of the traits of the effectiveness indicator and determine where on the effectiveness continuum the policies, practices, and procedures of the school fall. The results will be included in the final report.

Analyzing the School's Curriculum

The school's curriculum is the core, some say the *soul*, of the instructional program. A well-designed and -implemented curriculum gives the school a foundation from which teachers then apply their instructional skills. Research on increasing levels of student learning clearly supports the importance and effectiveness of developing a high-quality, rigorous curriculum aligned to classroom instruction and assessment. It is these components and their coordination that are analyzed when reviewing the school's written curriculum.

The written curriculum is aligned to and organizes the delivery of the content standards. It is the structure from which the instructional materials and assessments grow. Instructional materials, including textbooks, enrichment materials, and research-driven intervention materials, should be aligned to and identified within the written curriculum. State-developed summative assessments measure attainment of the standards that guide the curriculum. Formative assessments are frequently locally developed and are designed to lead up to the summative assessments. Finally, grade-level pacing charts provide an instructional plan that is aligned to the standards and expectations, describe the classroom lessons and activities, and establish their sequence throughout the year.

When the school selects a content area for deep review, usually reading/English, mathematics, or science, the team reviews all materials and documents in this area. Thus one team member should be a specialist in the chosen curricular area, and his or her primary role will be to study the focus area deeply. In addition, the team will review all written curriculum documents, both from the school and from the district, to determine the strength of the overall curricular system.

The team will use Effectiveness Indicator 1: Written Curriculum to evaluate the quality of the curricular system in all instructional areas. See chapter 1 and **Tool 5: Effectiveness Indicator Overview** (CD and appendix, page 262) for a breakdown of the five characteristics that are associated with the written curriculum of effective schools and that the reviewers will be looking for during their visit.

The written curriculum documents and their related instructional materials (textbooks, supplemental materials, and enrichment and intervention materials) should be collected and made available to the team during the on-site visit. The team will gather and analyze the evidence that is linked to each of the traits of the effectiveness indicator and determine where on the effectiveness continuum the policies, practices, and procedures of the school fall. The results will be included in the final report.

The Process:
How to Conduct a Research-Based
On-Site School Review

The best way to observe a fish is to become a fish.

—Jacques Cousteau

The review team's on-site visit runs between 2 and 5 days, with time built in at the end for writing the final report. Should additional training for team members be necessary, it should be conducted near the beginning of the site visit so that the concepts are fresh in the members' minds as they begin the review. Table 14.1 shows what a general schedule for the on-site portion of a school review might look like.

Table 14.1: On-Site Schedule

Day 1	In-Between Days	Last Day	Post-Review
Team planning meeting: 2 hours	Interviews and observations	One or more team members may return to the school, if necessary, to ask specific questions of staff members to obtain more data	Finalize report
Kick-off meeting with all staff: 30 minutes	Document review	Document review	
Interviews	Report writing	Report writing	
Possible family/community meeting: 1 hour (evening), plus dinner and setup	Team meeting: 2–4 hours (after school)	Oral exit report	

Check-In

When the team first arrives at the school, each member needs to check in with the school office and follow any procedures in place for visitors. These usually include signing in and wearing a visitor badge. Some schools want the teams to check in and out every day. Some schools will give the team visitor badges to use for the duration of the visit and may not require daily sign-in and -out. If possible, the second option is preferable, as the team often arrives and departs before and after the office staff.

When to ask team members to arrive depends on the distance they will be traveling, the number of days in the visit, and how much training is needed. Table 14.2 summarizes some of the considerations involved in setting the start time.

Table 14.2: Determining Team Arrival Times for On-Site Review

Circumstance	Arrival Time: Team Members	Arrival Time: Team Leader	Notes
The team members all live nearby.	Meet at the team work-room at 8:00 a.m. on the first day of the visit.	Team leader should be at the school by 2:00 p.m. the day *before* the visit.	This schedule gives the team leader a little while to meet and greet and still have time to set up the team room for the next day. Training in the school review process and planning for the visit can be completed before the staff kick-off meeting.
The team members are arriving from a driving distance of 1–3 hours away.	Meet at the team work-room on the first day of the visit at a time set between 9:00 a.m. and 10:30 a.m.	Team leader should be at the school by 8:00 a.m. on the first day of the visit.	The starting time depends on how long it takes the driver coming the longest distance to arrive at the school. Lunch should be brought in. Beginning later may require the team to meet after the staff kick-off meeting.
Some team members have already been fully trained in the on-site school review process.	New team members arrive for training early in the day. Experienced members arrive after the training for a 2-hour planning meeting or for the kick-off meeting if that occurs first.	Team leader should be at the school by 2:00 p.m. the day *before* the visit.	Previously trained members may want a refresher in the procedures. For others, joining the team later works best and will save the district money in contract and per diem expenses.

Preparing the Team for the Review

Preparing team members for the on-site review consists of two parts:

+ Training in the on-site school review process

+ Planning for the review

Team members who have already been trained or who have participated in a previous review using this process do not need to attend the training, although giving them the option to do so is a good idea. Sometimes trained team members benefit from a refresher.

Training in the on-site review process is straightforward and consists of taking the team members through the portions of this book that were flagged for them to read in advance (see "Communicating With Team Members After the All-Staff Meeting," page 215). The time needed for team training is greatly reduced if team members have completed the reading before the visit.

The planning meeting prior to the review is used to focus the team on the unique nuances of the visit, confirm assignments, distribute and go over materials, discuss questions, and get to know one another's areas of expertise. Because the team needs to use the time at the school literally from bell to bell, the team will also meet and plan after the end of each school day. Team members, even those commuting to and from the site, should plan to work long days.

Taking the Proper Approach

A school review measures the way work is done at the school, the results of the work, and how members of the school act and interact. However, the review will not be successful if it is approached as a mechanistic organizational evaluation. A school review is an interactive process of analysis, and it is important that it be conducted with professionalism, empathy, and integrity.

The team must approach this work through the lens of a learner. Members must be organized and detail oriented, but they must also be curious, gathering evidence as if they were systematically trying to solve a mystery.

Most important, the reviewers must be cognizant of the school as a human system. While the school is an organization, the functions within are 100% human. As a leader or member of a school review team, it is essential to acknowledge and be sensitive to the feelings and emotions of the school staff members and the students. The school is their home, and the review team members are invited guests. They must remember to tread lightly and listen respectfully.

Kick-Off Meeting With Staff

The kick-off meeting is a very informal 20- to 30-minute meeting to introduce the team to the staff members and the staff members to the team. The team leader, principal, and site coordinator go over the schedule for the visit, including the day, date, and time for both the family and community meeting and the oral exit report.

This meeting is also an opportunity for the team to ask for help in encouraging parents and community members to attend the family and community meeting if the meeting is not being held that night.

The team should ask teachers to announce the date and time of the family and community meeting in their classes and again in the morning announcements if possible. We have seen increased attendance when teachers offer small incentives, such as community service credit, to students whose parents attend the meeting.

One of the main purposes for the meeting is to give the staff the final interview schedule (including focus groups and all-staff meetings). The team leader asks if there are any changes to the schedule so that the whole staff is aware of any rescheduled interviews. This is important, because staff members have often coordinated their class coverage in order to attend interviews. As mentioned earlier, the tentative observation schedule—unlike the interview schedule—is not meant for distribution to the staff, because the team members need the flexibility to observe classes without setting a schedule.

Finally, staff members appreciate being given the team leader's contact information, such as a cell phone number and email address. This enables them to get in touch with the team leader if they want to follow up regarding an interview. Giving only the team leader's contact information relieves the rest of the team from the need to watch cell phones and emails during the visit.

The team leader should also let the staff members know that they can communicate with the team in writing at any time. It is a good idea to tape a large envelope to the door of the team workroom so that any notes, comments, or messages can be left and kept confidential. The team leader will need to check this envelope frequently throughout the visit in order to rapidly address any concerns or scheduling conflicts.

Data Squared

Review team members must primarily be listeners. They must not make any sort of judgmental or evaluative statements when interviewing or facilitating focus groups, nor can they offer advice, even when asked. This is a time to look and listen intently, giving all of their attention to what is going on in the school environment. There is much to learn, and a short time to do so.

To ensure that the scoring of characteristics within each rubric is accurate, the team must collect sufficient data and corroborate the data's accuracy before the scoring. We call this system *Data Squared* (hereafter Data²), and it is best understood by looking at the Master Matrix (**Tool 16**). As the Master Matrix shows, data are gathered for each trait and characteristic from multiple sources and in different ways. For example, to obtain information about a particular trait, one team member might collect data from an interview with a district staff member. A second team member might collect corroborating data from a classroom observation. Only after evidence is collected from at least two different sources and reported by at least two team members (and not contradicted by the findings of any other team member) is it deemed sufficient.

To recap, the evidence sources include:

+ Interviews with school administrators, district administrators, community members, school counselors, and teachers

+ Focus groups with the school leadership team, classified instructional and noninstructional staff members, family and community members, students, and teachers

+ Surveys of classified staff members, parents, students, and teachers

+ Observations of classrooms and common areas

+ Documents and materials such as attendance records, course syllabi, pacing charts, curriculum documents, discipline procedures and reports, formative and summative assessments, meeting records, safety reports, schedules, school strategic plan, state and district assessments, student and parent handbooks, and textbooks

While the Master Matrix prescribes specific sources of evidence to use to assess each characteristic, team members sometimes want to pursue answers for themselves to questions that may not be tied directly to the matrix. For example, when observing a class, a team member might witness a student being sent to in-school detention for being late to class. This incident might cause the team member to wonder about the school's discipline procedures and to seek out and review the document outlining the behavior policies. Such a question-and-answer process builds a rich collection of evidence to support the team's assessment of the school's effectiveness in different areas. Giving team members the freedom to follow "leads" is one of the reasons extra time and flexibility need to be built into their schedules.

Survey Data

Prior to the on-site portion of the school review, parents, staff members, and students completed customized surveys, and the results were tabulated for use by the team. The questions are keyed to specific characteristics and traits of each effectiveness indicator selected for the review. The team leader may wish to report to the rest of the team those statements with which high percentages of respondents either agreed/strongly agreed or disagreed/strongly disagreed. Surveys are a powerful data source, and each team member should review the results as part of the Data^2 process. One caveat: If only a few parent surveys come in, the team must beware of generalizing the results to all parents. Enough surveys must be returned to result in a reasonable sample size before any conclusions can be drawn.

For more details on surveys, see chapter 12, "Preparing and Administering Surveys," pages 215–216.

Interviews

Sets of interview questions are also customized for each individual school review, based on the selected effectiveness indicators. Each question is keyed to a specific trait that is being evaluated, so that asking and obtaining answers to these questions will yield the information the team needs to score the rubrics. Usually the interviews are conducted one-on-one. There are instances, however, when it is a good idea to have two team members present during an interview. An example would be an interview with a district leader who might address multiple areas, such as district policies and curriculum. The team leader decides the interview configurations on a case-by-case basis.

Based on the number of effectiveness indicators selected for review, there may be a large number of interview questions for one group (such as teachers or counselors). In these cases, the questions should be divided so that every team member asks a set number of questions on set days. For example, the first third of the questions are asked on day 2, the second third on day 3, and the final questions on day 4. This procedure keeps the interviews from being rushed, allows time for the interviewees to respond fully to each question, and ensures that the interviewers cover the array of questions.

It is of paramount importance that every team member ask the questions assigned to him or her during the review. This is not to say that *only* the assigned questions may be asked, but covering the assigned questions is the only way that Data² can be guaranteed. We have been at visits in which information we thought was very important could not be included in the evaluation because some team members did not complete their interview questions, and we did not have the evidence to meet the stringent Data² requirements.

Interviews with teachers are scheduled for 45 minutes, and administrator interviews are scheduled for 1 hour. It is very important to start and stop on time. Should an educator being interviewed request that the interview continue past the scheduled time, it is up to the team member to decide whether or not to go on. In no case, however, should a team member request that an educator stay beyond the scheduled time. If more time is needed, the interviewer should ask if there is another time that would be convenient to meet to finish up—and be ready to take "no" for an answer.

It is preferable for team members to take notes on laptop computers. Team members for whom this is not feasible will need to transcribe their handwritten notes onto a computer each evening for sharing with the rest of the team the next morning. When the time comes for evaluating the evidence and writing reports, word-processed notes will be easier to collate and to organize around the specific traits. They can also be more easily read by other team members. Each day the team leader should make sure that copies of the notes are available to all team members.

For more details on interviews, see chapter 12, "Scheduling Interviews and Focus Groups for Staff and Students," pages 212–213, and "Preparing Interview and Focus Group Questions," pages 216–217.

Focus Groups

Focus groups are scheduled with:

+ Teachers who request a focus group rather than an individual interview (45 minutes)

+ Classified instructional and classified noninstructional staff members (45 minutes)

+ Students in grades 5 through 12 (20–25 minutes)

+ The school leadership team (45–60 minutes)

The family and community meeting is also a focus group, but because it involves more complicated arrangements, it will be discussed in a separate section of this chapter.

Ideally, at least two team members should be present at each focus group, one to ask questions and one to record the answers. If a focus group is small, one person may conduct it alone if he or she is skilled at interviewing and simultaneously recording responses electronically.

Every focus group question is keyed to a specific trait that the team will be evaluating. The teacher and school leadership team focus groups will be asked the most questions (all questions appear in **Tool 28: Teacher Focus Group** and **Tool 33: School Leadership Team Focus Group**). The questions for the leadership team center on the development and implementation of the school strategic plan.

If it looks like a focus group will be large, it may be advantageous to split it into two or more groups, with each group having no fewer than four members. This arrangement will help to ensure there will be adequate time for all members to participate and for all of the questions to be fully answered.

Classified staff members are scheduled into focus groups rather than one-on-one interviews primarily because experience has shown that they prefer to be interviewed as a group. The instructional and noninstructional staff members are separated because while many of the questions are the same for both groups, questions relating to instruction are asked only of the instructional staff.

One to three student focus groups of 6–12 students each are held during the visit, depending on the size of the school. Normally, one interviewer can facilitate a student focus group. With six to eight questions, a student focus group will take about 20–25 minutes. For secondary student focus groups, a 5-minute writing assignment in which students respond to three questions, each keyed to a specific trait (**Tool 32: Student Focus Group [Secondary]**, see CD), is helpful to garner additional input. If the focus group is made up of an entire class, it is often preferable for a teacher to remain in the room to ensure good student behavior. However, if the class is well-behaved and taking the activity seriously, the teacher may wish for the students to provide confidential feedback and will step outside of the room but remain nearby.

For more information on focus groups, see chapter 12, "Scheduling Interviews and Focus Groups for Staff and Students," pages 212–213, and "Preparing Interview and Focus Group Questions," pages 216–217.

Observations

Team members conducting observations use **Tool 43: Classroom Observation Form** (see CD) as a guide to what to look for as they gather evidence on the specific traits that are being evaluated. For example, to evaluate Trait 8C2, Level of Respect, the team member will note whether students are respectful toward the teacher. Observers position themselves facing the students, because the focus of the observation is the students, not the teacher. For classes that fall within the academic focus area selected by the school, observations will take place for a full period or a full lesson for at least one class per teacher. The exception to this rule is blocked classes. In these cases, the observer should plan on staying for about 45 minutes. For all other classes, observers spend a minimum of 15 minutes per class. If students are taking a test or silently reading, the observers should plan to return and observe the class at another time. Over the course of the review, the team should observe at least one class taught by every teacher.

Each team member should have several copies of the Classroom Observation Form and complete one copy for each observation. Using the tool, observers gather evidence on what the students are hearing, saying, doing, and learning. Whenever possible, without interrupting instruction, observers casually talk with students, asking the questions that appear at the bottom of the form.

Level of Engagement

An important component of classroom observations is determining the students' level of engagement. The team member makes this determination by first counting the number of students in the class and then, at a certain point after the lesson is under way, scanning the room and carefully counting the number of students who are *not* engaged or not paying attention to the instruction. The reason for counting the students who are not engaged rather than those who are is that there are usually fewer students in the former category, and thus they are easier to count. If the observer is not sure if a student is engaged or not, the student should be considered engaged.

Next, the team member subtracts the number of students counted as not engaged from the number of students in the class. This gives the number of students who are engaged. For example, if 2 out of 20 students are not engaged, 18 students are. The data on engagement are reported out to the team in the form of a ratio, 18/20. The ratios submitted from all the observations can be aggregated to determine and report a schoolwide, grade-level, or subject-area level of engagement. Team members should be careful to record exactly how many observations, in which grades and subjects, the data represent. The data on engagement will be collected at the end of each day and recorded on **Tool 44: Daily Tally of Interactions** (see CD) under the section "Classroom Observations."

For more information on observations, see chapter 12, "Scheduling Team Interviews and Observations," pages 218–219.

Document Review

The more comprehensive the document review, the more deeply the team will understand the school. A checklist of the documents that should be collected both prior to the visit and during the visit appears in chapter 13, "Examining Data and Other Documents" (page 222).

As team members have available time, they should look through the documents and take notes in reference to specific characteristics and traits. For example, if a reviewer is analyzing the mathematics curriculum and benchmarking it to Characteristic 1B, "The written curriculum is vertically and horizontally aligned," he or she will want to thoroughly look through the curriculum documents and determine to what degree (a) the curriculum is aligned vertically between grade levels and sequential courses and (b) the curriculum is aligned horizontally within each grade level and course (Traits 1B1 and 1B2). Writing some notes while reviewing the documents allows the reviewer to use the notes, together with evidence collected by other team members, to determine where the school's current performance falls on the effectiveness continuum. The team will also use the notes to write the commentary on the effectiveness indicator in the final report.

Family and Community Meeting

The family and community meeting is usually held on the evening of the first day of the visit. The details of scheduling and organizing the family and community meeting were presented in chapter 12, "Planning for the Family and Community Meeting," pages 217–218.

The agenda for the meeting, a version of which can be found in **Tool 45: Family and Community Meeting Agenda** (see CD and appendix, page 273) should be distributed to all attendees. The principal opens the meeting by introducing the team and describing the purpose of the meeting and the school review. Then he or she should leave the room, in order for the participants to feel completely free to express their opinions and feelings. Confidentiality is essential in this process, and family and community members need to feel comfortable providing honest input and sharing concerns. When team members report that input, they must always avoid associating individual names with it. While data are collected individually, they are reported collectively and anonymously.

The family and community meeting is organized as one or more focus groups, each ideally led by one team member who asks most of the questions and a second team member who takes notes. Groups should be formed based on both the number and the primary languages of the attendees. This arrangement allows for more personalized conversations. If school staff members who are also parents or other relatives of students at the school attend the meeting, it is best that they be organized into their own focus group. Separating staff members from the other attendees results in more open discussions. The ideal focus group size is 8 to 10, not counting the team members. Questions asked of family and community members (**Tool 34: Family/Community Focus Group**) are, like the questions in the surveys and interviews, keyed to the traits and characteristics of the effectiveness indicators selected for the review, so it is vital that every question be asked and answered.

A Typical Day On-Site

The team gathers each morning before the beginning of the school day. The team leader will go over the schedule for the day, update the team regarding any changes, and ask if there are any foreseeable conflicts. This is also the time for team members who will be collaborating on interviews or focus groups to verify details such as time, location, and roles. In going over the day's schedule, it is important to set a time and location for the team to meet and debrief at the end of the school day. The team leader should also confirm lunch orders and plans. Because of time constraints, it is best not to leave campus for lunch but instead to eat the school lunch or place orders and designate one team member to pick up lunch at a nearby restaurant. Often a staff member from the school will be assigned this duty, freeing up another hour for interviews and observations.

The team leader will meet with the principal each day of the visit to ask questions from **Tool 22: School Administrator Interview** (see CD) and to discuss emerging findings from the visit. The principal will be asked if these findings seem to be accurate and if not, where the team members should look for additional information. The principal talks with the team leader about the review to date from his or her perspective and discusses any pertinent issues. This daily meeting is key to ensuring that the school staff members see the school leader as an integral part of the school review.

Based on the master schedule, team members will carry out their assigned duties (scheduled interviews and planned observations). However, there are several informal observations that should take place during the visit. For example, each team member should take an opportunity to observe the lunchroom by having lunch with the students one day. Hallway observations during passing times also provide a great deal of information about student interactions, discipline, and safety, as will observing the rooms used for time-outs, in-school suspension, and lunchtime detention. The bus loading area or the parking lot is another interesting place to observe student interactions and look for staff visibility and safety. An opportunity not to be missed during the visit is lunch in the staff room. Team members should be sure that they are welcome and invited to take this opportunity to interact casually with staff members at least one day during the visit. Finally, after-school activities such as athletic meets or practices, study club, or chess club should also receive drop-in visits, allowing team members to observe such characteristics as how many students attend and whether they represent a cross-section of the school population.

Unscheduled times are opportunities for conducting classroom observations outside of the focus area. The site coordinator should be asked to post a map of the school in the team workroom. During lunch and after school each day, team members can update the map by initialing the classrooms they have observed. This system will help to ensure that observations occur in all classrooms.

Each day, each team member keeps a tally of his or her interviews, focus groups, and observations. When all team members have completed their last observations or interviews for the day, it is good to take an hour to debrief and plan for the next day. This meeting starts by using **Tool 44: Daily Tally of Interactions** to record each team member's number of interviews, number of observations, and level-of-engagement data from the observations. Then the team members record the number of focus groups and the number of attendees in each. The master schedule is reviewed briefly to ensure that the day's plans were carried out and to look at the plans for the next day. Finally, each team member gives a brief (5–10-minute) report of what he or she learned that day. Team members should organize their notes by effectiveness indicator number and print copies for distribution at the meeting. Beginning on the second day of the visit, the team will use a facilitated communication model (see the following section) to begin the scoring process. These meetings frequently extend into the early evening.

Facilitated Communication

The team's goal while on-site is to gather evidence around the characteristics and traits. The time at the school is limited, and managing the evidence-gathering is critical. It requires facilitation and discussion both as a group and, oftentimes, between the team leader and individual team members.

The most efficient way to go about organizing the data being collected is to assign particular team members to be in charge of individual effectiveness indicators based on their experience and expertise. For example, one member may take responsibility for Written Curriculum (Effectiveness Indicator 1) and Instructional Program (Effectiveness Indicator 2). Then as the other team members individually collect data on these two effectiveness indicators, they turn the information over to the person in charge. As the process evolves, this person becomes the "expert" in these areas and will be responsible for carrying out the initial evaluation of the school's performance on the associated characteristics and for writing a commentary on the findings. It is important to be sure that team members are all collecting the full gamut of evidence during their interviews and observations and then transferring the data to the team member responsible for assembling the evidence around each effectiveness indicator. This procedure must be followed, because to meet the Data^2 requirement for scoring a characteristic, at least two team members must report evidence gathered in two different ways.

By the end of the second day, the team will have spent enough time at the school to begin corroborating the evidence. The effectiveness indicator *experts* will begin the process of evaluation. Using the effectiveness indicator rubrics, the team starts the iterative process by making an initial selection of the column containing the statement for each trait that best matches what has been seen, heard, and read so far. As explained earlier, each statement describes performance at one of three levels on the effectiveness continuum. Each team member will briefly present his or her rationale and test his or her initial evaluation through discussion with the team. This process needs to be efficiently facilitated so that the team remains focused.

In many areas, there may not yet be enough evidence to determine where to place the school's performance on the effectiveness continuum. Throughout this discussion, the team members will use **Tool 46: Effectiveness Indicator Map** (see CD and appendix, page 274) to keep track of the characteristics for which ample evidence has been collected. A large master copy, preferably on colored paper, of the Effectiveness Indicator Map is always left in a specific place in the team workroom. As each trait is initially scored, members place a check mark, their initials, and a notation of how evidence was gathered (using initials only, for example, "I" for interview, "O" for observation) in the appropriate box on the Effectiveness Indicator Map. The result of this honing process is the identification of specific areas in which additional evidence is needed to meet the Data² requirement. This collaborative communication process will occur each evening during the visit and will prepare the team for the next day. As the meeting ends each day, some rubrics will be well along, and others will require collecting more information.

Once the evidence gaps have been identified, the team leader and other members who may be further along in the evidence-gathering process can assist the team members who need additional information. At this point in the review, team members begin to ask specific questions in follow-up interviews, in order to corroborate or set aside initial evidence.

Each evening, team members put forth their ideas on the most important strengths and challenges that appear to be emerging from the evidence collection. All team members participate in a discussion of the tentatively identified challenges and strengths, helping to home in on those few that will become the basis of the overarching recommendations growing out of the review.

The Last Day of Interviews and Observations

At the beginning of the last day of the on-site portion of the visit, there will be traits that have not been scored. The team members should take some time in the morning to be sure that they will be able to collect all of the data they need. They also need to be sure that all observations and interviews have been completed or will be completed that day. Documents that require review should be studied, and any last questions answered.

Team members who have completed their interviews and observations or who have free time during the day will help the team gather the last pieces of missing evidence for specific traits and characteristics. If there are any remaining traits on the Effectiveness Indicator Map that need to be scored, the team as a whole shares its evidence, and the placement is made. At this time, any team member may suggest higher or lower scoring of specific traits. The group as a whole discusses these suggestions. If there is evidence that the scoring should be changed, it will be amended. If consensus cannot be reached, it is better to move higher on the effectiveness continuum. At the end of the last day of the visit, the scoring on the rubrics is set.

Finally, it is important for the team to consolidate the quantitative data (for example, number of observations, number of students interviewed, and level of engagement) and to reflect on the school's strengths or emerging strengths. This information will be shared with the school staff at the oral exit presentation.

Meeting With the Principal

Because the team leader and the principal have been meeting each morning of the visit, the principal has helped in troubleshooting and has assisted the team with clarifications and locating information. He or she has also received daily updates of emerging strengths and possible areas of concern. Before the team delivers the oral exit report to the staff, the team leader should meet with the principal to give a general overview of the upcoming report. Because of the ongoing communication, it is unlikely that the principal will be surprised by any of the findings, but he or she needs to have an opportunity to process the information that will be shared. This discussion will go a long way in both helping the principal and team leader present a united message to the staff and empowering the principal to lead the next steps.

Oral Exit Report

At the end of the school day on the last day of the visit, the team presents an oral exit report to the school staff. At this meeting, the team communicates only the broadest findings of the review. Specifics will be shared later, when the final report is written and delivered at a follow-up inservice workshop. The oral exit report should last only 30 minutes or so, and it is best if all team members can be present. It is not necessary for each team member to be a part of the presentation, but should questions arise, it is a good idea to defer to the effectiveness indicator experts for any detailed responses.

By this time, the team members know the school so well that they most likely feel a connection with the staff, and each staff member has had personal contact with at least one team member. The staff is always very interested in hearing an overview of what transpired during the visit and what the next steps will be.

A sample agenda for this meeting appears in **Tool 47: Oral Exit Report Agenda** (see CD and appendix, page 315). Following a brief thank-you, the report is delivered. The presentation can be made by the team leader or shared among the team members. The team will want to report on the quantitative components of the review (items 4 and 5 on the agenda) so that the staff members understand the comprehensive nature of the work now that they have personally experienced the visit. Because the final report will take some time to prepare, the staff members will want to know how that occurs and when the final report will be delivered. The team should be sure to allow time for questions and answers.

Above all, the team leader and members should recognize the staff and administrators for the trust, time, and energy they have invested in working to meet the needs of all students through this review. This work could not be accomplished without the support and openness of school staff members. It is important to validate the effort it took for them to invite in an external team to take a deep look at their school and their classrooms. This especially goes for the site coordinator and principal, who have made the largest commitment to this process in terms of time and resources.

Evaluation

The team leader should ask the staff to evaluate the review, using the form provided in **Tool 48: On-Site School Review Evaluation Form** (see CD). Staff members should fill out the form and return it to the site coordinator. This evaluation gives the team members important feedback regarding the review process and allows them to address any concerns. In addition, it is a modeling activity that shows the staff that the team is interested in continuous improvement and *walks the talk*. The site coordinator tallies the evaluations and provides the data to the principal to share with the staff and to the team leader to share with the team.

Parting Remembrances

It leaves a positive impression if the team can find a tangible way to thank the staff members for their willingness to take on a school review. Small mementos might include paperback books for the library, school supplies for students who may not be able to purchase supplies on their own, supplies for the teachers' lunchroom, and individual thank you notes to each staff member.

Communicating Results

For time and the world do not stand still. Change is the law of life. And those who look only to the past or the present are certain to miss the future.

—John F. Kennedy

Communicating the results of a school review begins with the team's delivery of the oral exit report, discussed in the previous chapter. Then, when the team has completed the Data² process, the team members and leader collaborate to write a comprehensive final report. This final report will include the scored rubrics, the data packet, commentary, and recommendations. It will become the basis of the next steps in the process: the final report workshop, strategic planning, and implementation.

Final Report

The purpose of an on-site school review is, first, to objectively determine the current status of a school in relation to what research tells us is in place in the most effective schools and, second, to use the data gathered to identify what actions the school should take to bring about the greatest increases in student achievement and learning. In order for schools to use the data to guide their next steps, the final report must be accurate, concise, and provide powerful recommendations. **Tool 49: Sample Final Report** (see CD and appendix, page 316) provides a model.

Some team leaders prefer to both write the final report and put together a finished data packet while the team is still on-site, while others prefer to complete the written portion on-site and then finish the data packet after the team disbands. Whichever method is selected, the team leader can construct the report by using the format and guidelines provided in **Tool 50: Final Report Template** (see CD) and completing the following steps:

- Summarizing the visit based on daily and cumulative quantitative data

- Summarizing state assessment data and the student work analysis

- Bringing together the scored rubrics for each effectiveness indicator, along with commentary from the team experts

- Reiterating the school's strengths, as reported in the oral exit report and substantiated through high scores on the rubrics

- Writing the recommendations

- Completing the data packet

- Editing the text for grammar and continuity

- Formatting the report for reproduction

General Guidelines

The final report needs to be an evaluation of the effectiveness of the programs, practices, and procedures of the school and not of *individuals* at the school. Individuals are never named, even in a positive context. The review looks at trends and practices across the school, not the attributes of an administrator, a teacher, a parent, or a student.

It is also important, whenever possible, to cast statements in a positive rather than a negative way. It is much easier for the school to hear what needs to be done than it is to hear that what is currently being done should not be. In addition, what the school is doing well should receive equal billing to the programs or actions that are not as effective. This does not mean that the report should include praise that is not genuine in order for the message to be balanced; it does, however, mean that identifying strengths is a fundamental component of the review process. The concept of asset-building, in which existing strengths are recognized and used to leverage continued improvement, is a powerful strategy.

Finalizing the Status of the Effectiveness Indicators

The final report will contain a section titled "Mapping of Effectiveness Indicators and Commentary." The team members write this section on the last 2 days of the visit, usually beginning immediately after the oral exit meeting and continuing into the next day. The section consists of two pieces: (a) the scored rubrics for each effectiveness indicator and (b) the commentary. This section is drafted by the team members who have become the experts in each area and who will now translate the team's findings into a written format.

The final scored rubrics appear with shaded boxes, which indicate the team's placement (referred to as "mapping") of each trait on the effectiveness continuum. If, by the time the team meets to work on the final report, there are still traits that have not been scored, there are two options. Depending on the time available, either a team member can return to the school during the report-writing day to collect specific information upon which to base a final determination, or a trait can be marked as "could not determine" and all three boxes in its row left unshaded.

The Writing Process

On the day before the report-writing day, the team leader should give the team members the homework assignment of reading through **Tool 49: Sample Final Report** and drafting outlines of their sections in order to be ready to begin writing the next day. He or she should also set a time and location to meet.

The team writing process for the final report begins in earnest first thing on the last day of the visit. At this time each member should have his or her draft commentary ready to share. Writing is usually both an individual and a team effort. The team leader, or a designated team member, will act as an editor and help the team members think through and draft their sections. He or she roves around during the writing sessions and keeps the writing on track. Sometimes, the team members may wish to write in teams. The system really depends on the team leader's style and the team members' preferences. When the first draft of the report is complete, a single copy of each section is circulated in round-robin fashion to all team members to read and edit. One edited version of each section is returned to the author(s) for a second draft and then submitted to the team leader to be put into the report. Ideally, team members also each read and final-edit the second draft before heading home. The team leader then finalizes the report and takes responsibility for polishing and formatting.

Summarizing the Evidence for Each Effectiveness Indicator

Each team member approaches writing from a unique perspective and with his or her own writing style and preference. Some will write using an inductive model (reasoning from specific to general), and some will write using a deductive model (reasoning from general to specific). This means that the inductive people will gather together all of the evidence and details and then organize them according to the trait statements. The deductive people will use the trait statements to gather together the evidence. Either way, the notes and data should be organized around each characteristic or each effectiveness indicator to write a summary. It is not necessary to write a statement for each trait. A sentence or two for each characteristic is sufficient. When writing, the team members should be sure to be descriptive, use the active voice, avoid opinions, and balance the use of data (including quotes) with commentary. All quotes should be generalized—the report should never mention names or even roles if they would result in the identification of an individual. The commentary should be easy to read, include clear transitions, be free of jargon, and ultimately paint a picture of the characteristics as seen and heard by the review team.

Recognizing Strengths

The team as a whole identifies the school's strengths that will be listed in the report. Because this activity builds on the strong communication that team members have established during the visit, it should take little more than 30 minutes. It can occur either at the end of the last day of observations and interviews at the school or during the report-writing day. The team reviews the rubrics to find traits that have been scored in the "effective" and "high-performing" columns of the effectiveness continuum. The descriptions of these traits at those levels become the phrases used to describe the school's strengths, such as "strong community support" or "building-wide focus on student learning." The strength statements will form the first part of the Conclusions section of the report (see **Tool 49: Sample Final Report**). It is important that the team identify at least as many strengths as recommendations.

Determining Recommendations

Recommendations emerge from the evidence that has been collected and evaluated during the on-site visit. They are central to the school review process and are designed to provide specific guidance to the school about what to do next. Some recommendations can be carried out by the school ("Provide students with assignments that are rigorous, are engaging, and extend learning" or "Develop a clear behavior and discipline program"), while others may require districtwide coordination ("Develop or adopt a coordinated PK–12 written curriculum in mathematics"). It is most common to have a mix of school and district recommendations, but it needs to be a very small, targeted mix.

Each recommendation is made up of a goal statement, usually at the level of the effectiveness indicator, followed by specific steps the school should take to reach that goal. The recommendations grow directly from the mapping of the effectiveness indicators. Because each characteristic and trait is research-based, the team can confidently determine recommendations from the evidence collected. In reviewing the Effectiveness Indicator Map, which by the end of the visit will be marked to indicate the evaluation of the school for each trait, the team looks for those effectiveness indicators in which the greatest percentage of traits have been mapped at the lower end (low performing) of the effectiveness continuum. These areas will be where the recommendations emerge. For example, if Effectiveness Indicator 2: Instructional Program has a greater percentage of traits mapped in the low-performing column than do other effectiveness indicators, a recommendation should be made in the area of the instructional program. The bullets for the recommendation grow from the characteristics but are personalized to reflect the specifics of what the team saw, heard, and read during the visit.

The recommendations are the final section of the final report and the last step in the team's report-writing process. The best way to arrive at the recommendations is to regroup the team following the drafting and editing of the report. In a brainstorming process, the team members pose possible recommendations, come to consensus, and draft the specific steps to meet the recommendations. This exercise allows the team to bring closure to the review while also having a part in focusing the school on the most important next steps.

The recommendations in the report need to be limited to those that are the most important and foundational in order for the school to make the next improvement steps. For example, recommendations about teacher coordination of instruction require that the school first have a written curriculum in place that describes that instruction. The recommendation in the written report would thus discuss developing or adopting a written curriculum that is aligned across grade levels. In order to avoid overloading the staff with so many things to do that they simply seem out of reach, the team should limit the recommendations to four or fewer at the school level and two or fewer at the district level (see the "Recommendations" section in **Tool 49: Sample Final Report**).

Submitting a Draft Copy of the Report to the Principal

When the report is ready, the team leader sends a copy (marked "Draft") to the principal and asks him or her to review the work for accuracy and feel. No matter how careful the team has been, it is possible that the report will contain small errors. These could be such details as the number of years the school has been using a certain textbook or the specifics of how a schedule works. "Feel" relates to how well the staff will be able to hear and internalize the report. For example, we have worked with principals who have requested that we prepare two reports—one for school administrators and one for the staff. For some staff members, especially in very low-performing schools, seeing too many traits at the lower-performing end of the continuum can reinforce their feelings of demoralization rather than galvanize them into action. In these cases, the report for the staff may need to be focused on only a limited number of effectiveness indicators, while the leadership version reflects all effectiveness indicators reviewed.

Before sending the draft report to the principal, the team leader should call to let him or her know the report will be arriving and to schedule a time to discuss it shortly after it has been received. Because the principal has been intimately involved with this process from the very beginning, it is unusual for anything in the report to be totally unexpected. However, it is helpful in the delivery of the report for the principal to identify any *hot topics* or concerns that might call for special handling. For example, topics that may be politically sensitive or personnel issues of which the review team is unaware may call for the principal's advice on wording. This information will help in designing the final report workshop and in disseminating the report and data.

Final Report Inservice Workshop

It is always a high-energy moment when the staff has the opportunity to read and understand the final report. At the final report workshop, the team transfers ownership of the data and recommendations to the school staff members, enabling them to design and implement new practices to improve student learning.

The staff may be apprehensive when first looking at the final report, so the team should begin by spending time talking about the strengths of the school. Whenever possible, the team should present the recommendations in the context of an asset-building model, in which existing skills and capacity are identified. In this way, the school can call upon its strengths as it works toward the goals identified in the report. If internal capacity is limited, then the team should spend some time discussing where the school could locate the expertise to assist it in implementing the review's recommendations.

The inservice workshop should be scheduled for a 6-hour block of time, with all staff members present (including classified staff members). It is important for the team leader and at least one or two team members, depending on the size of the school staff, to facilitate this workshop, because they are deeply knowledgeable about the process, the indicators, the data, and the visit. Often school staff members will have questions, even some pushback. When there are individuals at the workshop who have the expertise to address any concerns right away, it provides more time for the important work of helping the staff move toward internalizing the report and recommendations.

Depending on the number of sections in the report and the size of the staff, it works well to divide the meeting into groups of three to eight people and to give each group a part of the report to discuss. To more easily ensure that the groups are well-mixed, the staff counts off. For example, to form five small groups, the staff counts off in several series of one through five. If there are more effectiveness indicators than groups, it is fine to ask each group to work with more than one indicator. It is ideal to have all but one group review one or more of the effectiveness indicators and one group review the recommendations.

Tool 51: Final Report Workshop Agenda (see CD and appendix, page 331) shows the steps of a meeting in which a final report with nine effectiveness indicators, plus the recommendations section, is delivered to a staff of 40. The group is divided into five smaller groups, with eight staff members in each group. Four of the groups are assigned two effectiveness indicators to study, and one group is assigned a single effectiveness indicator and the recommendations section. Following the study, the large group reconvenes, and each small group reports out to the large group and facilitates discussion around its topic. After this general session, there is another round of breakout sessions, in which the small groups each discuss one component of the data packet, for example, the student work analysis. Again, the large group reconvenes for reports from the smaller groups. After these reports and a general discussion that centers on the review team's recommendations, each participant chooses the recommendation that most interests him or her and joins a new group that will discuss the recommendation and brainstorm how to implement it. The workshop ends with another general session, in which these new small groups report out and facilitate a final discussion, after which the next steps are planned.

The workshop should be paced to ensure that all of the steps are adequately covered without anyone feeling rushed. The staff members need plenty of time to *digest* this material and design solutions that they are committed to and willing to support.

Evaluation

As with all professional development offerings, it is important to give participants the opportunity to provide feedback about the inservice workshop. The facilitator distributes the form provided in **Tool 52: Professional Development Evaluation Form** (see CD), which includes a brief survey and questionnaire. The evaluation will help the facilitator address any concerns and determine if changes should be made in any subsequent inservices. As with the on-site review evaluation, this is also a modeling activity, in which the facilitator demonstrates that continuous improvement is a foundational principle.

Now What?
Strategic Planning and
Professional Development

I have learned over the years that when one's mind is made up, this diminishes fear; knowing what must be done does away with fear.

—Rosa Parks

The concept of strategic planning comes to education from the effective practices of business. The theory behind strategic planning is twofold:

+ Organizations must select from competing goals by staying focused on their core mission.

+ Actions undertaken to achieve the selected goals must be those that will be the most powerful and have the greatest impact.

Strategic thinking is deciding on the most important actions to affect the organization. These decisions have to do with what an organization is and why it exists; the actions have to do with what it does. While this chapter focuses on how to move forward with strategic planning after completing a school review, readers might want to review the summary of research on strategic planning in chapter 5. As detailed in the discussion there, the key characteristics of strategic planning in effective schools are:

5A. There is a process in place, and support for, schoolwide strategic planning.

5B. The strategic plan is focused on student learning and refining teaching practices.

5C. As a part of strategic planning, student demographic and achievement data are reviewed and analyzed.

5D. A research-driven approach is used to identify problems and solutions.

5E. Extensive communication ensures that all stakeholders are a part of the decision-making process.

5F. An action plan describes the steps to be taken toward attainment of the goals.

5G. The strategic plan is put into action with fidelity.

5H. The school monitors progress toward attainment of the goals and makes adjustments when appropriate.

Initial Considerations

Focusing on Student Learning

In high-performing schools, the foundational mission and actions have to do with student learning. Successful schools always keep student learning at the forefront of their decision-making process, adopting as their constant refrain the question "*How are we improving student learning?*" They ask themselves whether proposed changes (or resistance to them) are related to improving student learning or to other issues. Strategic planning for schools must always center on the reason the school exists—to advance learning. Once this fundamental value is firmly in place in the ethos of the school, then the cyclical process of planning, implementing, and evaluating can become integral to the functioning of the school.

Addressing Critical Issues

Strategic planning will only be as strong as the work described in the plan. Failure or unwillingness to put critical issues on the table for discussion and resolution will not lead to the desired results, because these issues are frequently the very ones that are impeding progress. School improvement plans often fail to address the real issues at the school. They contain lofty goals or are simply boilerplates, completed only to meet district, state, or national policy and serving no other purpose. In fact, such plans can lead staff members and stakeholders to challenge the credibility of the school's priorities, leadership, and future planning efforts.

While addressing critical issues can be uncomfortable at first, there is usually a feeling of relief once these subjects are on the table for discussion and resolution. The review itself provides the necessary impetus to confront these issues, because its recommendations are directly tied to the research-based effectiveness indicators and to evidence that was gathered and corroborated at the school. The key henceforward is commitment, determination, and follow-through. It really means setting the school's sights on the right goals and not allowing distractions.

Leadership for Planning

The strategic plan will not move forward without leadership and advocacy. For example, while the whole staff is included in the final report workshop, it will be a team of selected staff members (or in some cases an individual) who must then take responsibility for coordinating the strategic planning process. If a leadership team is not already in place, this is a good time for the principal to name and officially appoint its members. Key to their efforts will be clearly defined and understood roles and responsibilities and the authority to make decisions. Creating a decision-making matrix that identifies who makes what decisions and who carries out specific activities can be of great help. **Tool 53: Decision-Making Matrix** (see CD) provides a partially filled-in sample.

As discussed in chapter 4, research has found that leadership is second only to instruction in its effect on student achievement. This is a fundamental concept and emphasizes the impact of school administrators on how well students learn. Research supports the notion that the school leader's roles of determining who will oversee different parts of the planning and implementation, scheduling routine evaluation meetings to review progress, ensuring that adequate time and resources are available, and holding all staff members accountable for working together are critical to both the strategic planning process and student learning.

Ultimately, the school principal must be the driving force behind strategic planning and implementation. This is not to say that the principal should do this work alone; in fact all staff members are obligated to be a part of these processes in one way or another. This is what DuFour, Eaker, and DuFour (2005, p. xii) mean when they say, "If there is anything the research community agrees on, it is this: The right kind of continuous, structured teacher collaboration improves the quality of teaching and pays big, often immediate, dividends in student learning and professional morale in virtually any setting." Collaboration focused on the evaluation of student learning goals is key to successful strategic planning.

Hypotheses: The Process of Scientific Inquiry

To effectively address any concerns that surfaced during the on-site review process or that arise during the strategic planning process or school improvement implementation process, the leadership team must try to understand why the problems are occurring. Thus, throughout the strategic planning process, the team should routinely engage in hypothesizing. Questions to start this process include, for example, "Why are certain groups of students performing poorly?" and "Why do some students seem disconnected from the school?"

The team then considers possible causes of these problems, researches the issues using the effectiveness indicator chapters and the references in this book, and suggests possible solutions based on that research. Team members routinely bring these concerns and possible solutions forward to the staff. As they continually seek more data to test their hypotheses and communicate their questions and findings to the staff, these actions begin to create an environment and instill a culture of inquiry and improvement.

Getting Started on the School Strategic Plan

The strategic planning inservice workshop follows the final report workshop. It allows the staff members to step back and take stock of their belief systems before committing to school improvement goals. Where to start depends to a certain extent on what experience the school has had in collaborative strategic planning. If the staff members have not engaged in much group process work in the past or are new at setting goals based on data, it is helpful for the leadership team to start out by familiarizing them with some basic tools for conducting team planning and decision-making activities. Preliminary agreements and common knowledge can help a group move forward together. **Tool 54: How Teams Function** (see CD) provides a good introduction to what it means to work as a team. **Tool 55: Group Facilitation Models** (see CD) gives step-by-step directions for a number of basic teamwork strategies (for example, brainstorming) that staff members will be using as they collaborate in the planning process.

Members of the leadership team, school administrators, district professional development specialists, review team members, or others skilled in working with strategic planning and group facilitation can lead the strategic planning inservice workshop. **Tool 56: Strategic Planning Workshop Agenda** (see CD and appendix, page 333) outlines an all-day (6-hour) session. After a few preliminaries, the all-staff group breaks into five smaller groups. Each of the smaller groups is assigned one set of questions (referred to as a

"Discussion Set") and instructed to develop a plan for facilitating a large-group discussion of those questions. The small groups can use one of the facilitation models provided (**Tool 55**) or choose another model with which they are familiar and comfortable. The questions help the staff look at current school practices and how they might be improved.

Writing the School Strategic Plan

The staff members have now spent a fair amount of time coming together around their work. They know more about their students, the school, and themselves; they have identified critical issues based on the review team's final report; and they have discussed issues using a hypothesis/inquiry model. Now it's a matter of putting it all down on paper.

In the next all-staff inservice session, the faculty will use **Tool 57: Action-Planning Template** (see CD) to develop the final pieces to complete the school strategic plan. The action plans must clearly describe *what* teachers will do in their classrooms and with their students to move the school toward success, as well as *how* implementation will be monitored and *by whom*. In addition, it must be clear *how* all staff members can contribute to implementing the plans and, finally, *how* progress toward the goals will be evaluated. Once these specific agreements are in place, no staff member will be allowed to opt out or to decide on his or her own not to participate.

Tool 58: Designing School Strategic Plan Workshop Agenda (see CD and appendix, page 335) outlines the steps for this 3-hour inservice session. First, the large group decides which of the recommendations from the review team's final report should be included as the goals of the school strategic plan. Then the group splits into smaller groups, one for each goal. The small groups use the Action-Planning Template to brainstorm how the school might reach the goals. The large group reconvenes, and each small group presents a report on its action plan and asks for input.

Identifying Resources

The final step to completing the Action-Planning Template is the identification of the resources that will be necessary to implement the actions. The school may need to develop curriculum, purchase instructional materials, arrange for professional development, access assessment tools, or even purchase staff time or substitute time for collaboration. Depending on decision-making procedures, either the principal or the leadership team identifies what resources are needed for each action step. It is helpful to identify the existing resources (both internal and external) that are available and the additional resources (both internal and external) that will be required. The last two columns in the Action-Planning Template are used to record the existing and additional resources needed for each action.

Professional Development

As is common with school improvement work, the staff will most likely need professional development to acquire the skills and knowledge to complete the actions and reach the goals of the strategic plan. Not all professional development activities need to occur schoolwide. For example, if students are randomly assigned to a grade-level team of four teachers, and the students from three classes are consistently meeting their learning targets while students from the fourth class are consistently lagging behind, the situation may indicate the need for individual professional development for a single teacher. At other times, an entire grade-level team or the entire staff will need specific professional development, for example, training in the use of a newly selected formative assessment system in mathematics. The principal or leadership team should identify the needs and funding sources and document the agreements and time lines. The selection of professional development providers should be captured on the last two columns of the Action-Planning Template. Whether to use internal or external professional development providers depends on whether the existing school staff has the needed experience and skill to provide professional development in the targeted area.

Time for Professional Development

Ideally, the principal or leadership team should develop a yearlong plan for all professional development and team meetings. **Tool 59: Sample Professional Development and Team Meeting Calendar** (see CD) provides an example of what such a schoolwide plan might look like.

Time is always an issue in planning professional development. Because solid amounts of time have already been dedicated to this planning, much of the follow-up work can be accomplished within the regular school day. For example, time can be captured from regularly scheduled staff or team meetings and refocused to address staff development and strategic planning. Staff meeting time should be used for face-to-face training and to focus on student achievement. It is important to keep critical issues in front of the staff and to discuss progress regularly. Most administrative issues can be left to email or staff newsletters.

Bringing It All Together

When all staff members have been involved in the strategic planning process and shared in the resulting decision-making, there is promise that the school will move forward in a cohesive fashion. Once the action plans have been drafted, the principal or leadership team brings them together into one document and adds an evaluation schedule. Then the school strategic plan is ready to guide the school forward.

The highest level of accountability is public accountability, so the school should not hesitate to share its plan with the PTA and the school board and to post it on the school website. All staff members should hold one another individually and collectively responsible for implementing the plan and should be proud of the work that happens on a daily basis in their school.

Monitoring and Adjusting

Are we doing what we said we would do? Because implementation is often where school improvement efforts get off track, it is important to monitor progress on how well improvement strategies are being put into effect. If the work appears to be sliding off track, it may be helpful to bring the review team leader, a team member, or another outside consultant to the school to work with the leadership team periodically to analyze the progress toward meeting the school's improvement goals.

Quick progress checks to ensure that the staff remains committed to the plan and is meeting the time lines should be a part of every staff meeting. One way to accomplish these checks is to ask each team that is working on a goal to deliver a status report. Status reports are simply based on the measures of success that the plan specifies for each action. In light of the progress reports, adjustments to the plan will need to be made and communicated. These adjustments are evidence of a dynamic process, as opposed to letting a plan stagnate on a shelf, gathering dust.

On a frequent basis, the leadership team needs to review and revise the school strategic plan and identify resources to support the school staff members as they implement the activities in the plan. A frequent review is the key difference between typical school improvement plans and strategic plans. Strategic plans are nimble and form the basis for ongoing discussion, analysis, and adaptation. At least annually, the team should review current student achievement data and follow the same processes that have been described in this chapter to update the school strategic plan.

Periodically, every 3 to 4 years, it would be beneficial for the school to arrange for an external team to conduct an on-site review to once again gather evidence both on current practice and on progress.

At the End of the Day

The result of undertaking this work is that the school experiences—maybe for the first time—a research-based continuous improvement process. Cicchinelli et al. (2006, pp. 14–15) sum it up nicely:

> The goal of continuous improvement is to create a purposeful community—a group of learners that works together to use all available assets, manage the implications of change, and establish structures and processes that support them in finding solutions to the challenges they face. It's important for school improvement efforts to strike the right balance between telling teachers *what* to do and respecting their intelligence, professionalism, and ability to create their own solutions for improving student performance. This means giving teachers enough guidance to make changes in their classrooms and providing them with opportunities to create their own demand for learning.

Because of this work, all stakeholders come to have a deep understanding about:

- What high-quality research has identified as the key characteristics in the most effective schools across the nation

- How current practice in their school matches up in those key areas

- What actions need to occur to efficiently and effectively move student and adult performance to the next level

- How action plans will be implemented, when, and by whom

Interest in a school review grows from a curiosity about how effectively a school or district is currently functioning and a desire to use that knowledge to take the next steps to improve performance. We applaud those educators who are inspired by and act on this curiosity.

CONCLUSION

Sustaining and Nurturing a Student-Focused School

An organization's ability to learn, and translate that learning into action rapidly, is the ultimate competitive advantage.

—Jack Welch

As we move further into the information age, the demand for higher levels of knowledge and skills from our students, our teachers, our school administrators, and our workforce becomes greater. We feel its pressures daily in ways that are both positive and negative. We enjoy new technologies that improve our lives. New understandings in medicine ease suffering across the world. At the same time, we see a worrying shift away from our connections with one another and an eroding of trust in traditional public institutions such as public education. As John Kotter of the Harvard Business School, an authority on business and leadership, notes:

> We are in the midst of great social change. The transition from the industrial age to the information age is a huge shift. In all of human history, there have only been two other socioeconomic revolutions of this magnitude: the move from hunting and gathering to agriculture and from agriculture to industry. (Blagg & Young, 2001, p. 1)

While we have only limited information to help us understand what the change from hunting/gathering to agriculture meant to those who were in the midst of it, we have a very good understanding of the profound changes the industrial revolution brought to all facets of society. We know that those organizations that did not, or were not able to, adapt to those changes became casualties of the revolution. In what seemed like the blink of an eye, technology rendered centuries-old skills, often painstakingly acquired over a lifetime, obsolete. New knowledge, skills, and attitudes were swept into dominance. Those organizations that attempted to hold on to the status quo—to resist change—were eventually swept away by the unstoppable forces of technological evolution. Those organizations that emerged from the industrial revolution did so because they met the needs of a changing society; they embraced new ways of thinking, transforming to meet the challenges confronting them. And they were stronger for it.

In the shift from the industrial to the information age we, in education, have several important assets to help us successfully navigate the changes. First, unlike our less fortunate predecessors who were part of great societal revolutions, we have research to guide us and tools and processes to help us meet and overcome the challenges that confront us. Second, as a group, we are familiar with the concept of continuous improvement, and we know how to take on new strategies, programs, and practices as part of that process. What we haven't been so sure about until now is exactly what it is we should be doing and in what order.

In retooling for the information age, the first step for a school is to learn how it is currently operating, compared to what research tells us is happening in highly effective schools. This is a practice that Jim Collins (2001) found to be a common thread among American businesses that had gone from "good to great" despite rapidly changing consumer demands, new technologies, and adverse economic conditions. Each of these highly successful companies routinely looked searchingly at every facet of its organization and operations to help identify its strengths and resources and to find where and how it could improve. Then it created a tightly aligned strategic plan to address areas for improvement, and then it put that plan into action.

The on-site review—with its attention to the research-based characteristics and traits, measured through observation, surveys, interviews, and analysis—provides the data Jim Collins talks about, only for schools.

The rubrics for each of the effectiveness indicators and the research summary that supports each effectiveness indicator provide schools with the ability to look deeply at the degree to which its programs and practices match the characteristics and traits of the most effective schools. The evidence-gathering process of the on-site review, in which each data element is corroborated by multiple sources, ensures accuracy. The rubrics provide a picture of what each research-based trait and characteristic looks like in schools on a performance continuum from least to most effective.

When a school knows in which areas it is performing at high levels and where improvements could be made, it has the information it needs to discuss and create a plan that addresses the most urgent needs first. This knowledge also ensures that new programs, practices, or strategies will move the school in the right direction—toward meaningful, second-order change.

For each effectiveness indicator, rubrics provide a visual image of how improvement efforts will change what is happening in classrooms and in school and district offices. They describe how those improvements will look to staff members, students, parents, and community members. The research that accompanies each rubric provides clear guidance in why and how to take those next steps. As one of the principals we worked with said, "When the review was over, the work began, but this time we knew what to do."

By using the tools we have provided with this book, schools can also conduct their own formative assessments. For example, they can periodically survey staff members or parents, or they can analyze how student work changes over time. Because the data are keyed directly to the rubrics, a new picture can be developed at any time that will clearly show where improvement is being made and where additional effort is required.

Throughout this book, we have made a strong and, we hope, compelling argument that student learning is the core mission of every school and thus must be the beginning point for all improvement efforts. For those not involved in the field of education, this assertion might not seem controversial, but the debate over the central purpose of school has gone on for many decades and has both fueled and stymied educational innovations. There are still many educators, especially in lower-performing schools, whose highest priority is making allowances for children's home lives, or recognizing student effort rather than student learning, or ensuring that the school has a pleasant and collegial working environment (Jerald,

2006). None of these purposes, however, can be the top priority if schools are going to be survivors of the information revolution. Student learning must be that priority, and all else becomes support for that priority, creating an environment in which both students and adults thrive.

Start Here: Curriculum, Instruction, Assessment, and Leadership

With 10 effectiveness indicators, where should schools begin? Effective schools must have their instructional houses in order. In undertaking improvement efforts, schools begin by attending to the characteristics of the first four effectiveness indicators: Written Curriculum, Instructional Program, Student Assessment, and School Leadership. Of course, curriculum, instruction, assessment, and leadership are not the only important, even vital, components of effective schools. In fact, research is clear that the characteristics in the remaining six effectiveness indicators must be attended to in order to both successfully reach all children and sustain and accelerate learning gains for all students.

End Up Here: Schools in the Information Age

Effectiveness Indicator 1: Written Curriculum. Because student learning is the central mission of schools, improvement grows from public statements describing what that learning will entail. Effective schools and districts develop a written curriculum for each course and subject, aligned to state and national standards and articulated from pre-K through grade 12. Instructional materials, assessments, interventions, and enrichment programs are aligned with and included as part of the written curriculum.

Effectiveness Indicator 2: Instructional Program. Instruction is governed by the written curriculum, as evidenced by what occurs in every classroom, every day. Teachers have organized instruction to support clearly articulated and communicated learning targets. Assignments are rigorous and engaging and extend student learning. Teachers have high expectations of their students and pair those expectations with both challenging instruction and support.

Effectiveness Indicator 3: Student Assessment. While assessments for grading are still an important element, assessment for learning takes center stage. Formative assessments give teachers and students information about current levels of learning, provide guidance on which steps to take next, and help teachers in designing instruction. Data from state assessments are disaggregated and used to improve the school's instructional program.

Effectiveness Indicator 4: School Leadership. Effective school administrators have an essential role in creating and sustaining an effective instructional program. Through distributed leadership, they widely share authority and responsibility. They encourage and promote collaborative relationships and address conflict that could potentially harm those relationships. Through frequent teacher observations, they ensure that teachers receive the constructive feedback they need to continuously improve. They provide support for a schoolwide culture of high expectations for students and adults, and they ensure that while student needs remain the unarguable priority of the school, the school is also a place in which adults thrive.

Effectiveness Indicator 5: Strategic Planning. Like the written curriculum, strategic planning is a public commitment to both a goal and the actions that will be taken toward attaining that goal. Schoolwide decision-making aligns the strategic plan, which is, in turn, supported with resources from the district level.

Effectiveness Indicator 6: Professional Development. Professional development focuses on deepening and refining teachers' knowledge and skills and grows out of an assessment of student needs. Primarily job-embedded, professional development addresses both schoolwide and individual needs. Some professional development is specialized to build staff members' cultural proficiency.

Effectiveness Indicator 7: Student Connectedness, Engagement, and Readiness. Students feel connected to their school, even when faced with obstacles that place them at risk of not graduating. Students find the academic program challenging and engaging. Supports are in place to ensure that students are ready to progress from one grade level or phase of schooling to the next. The school uses effective practices for encouraging students to stay in school, such as promoting healthy relationships between students and adults in the school and providing opportunities for involvement in extracurricular activities. If students begin to show signs of disconnection from school, a system of interventions is in place to rapidly respond to reconnect them.

Effectiveness Indicator 8: School Environment. In a positive school environment, students and staff members feel both valued and challenged to grow either academically or professionally. The school environment is safe and welcoming, creating a sense of trust at all levels. Staff members work effectively with a diverse student body. School rules are fair and consistent. Suspensions are rare and meted out only for the most serious of offenses.

Effectiveness Indicator 9: Family and Community Involvement. Families and community members are involved in the activities of the school in many ways. They feel welcome at the school and feel positive about it and about its work with children. Families and the community support and are involved in the instructional program of the school and are committed to working with students to ensure high levels of student achievement.

Effectiveness Indicator 10: District Support. The board and district, like the school, focus on student learning as their first priority. They support this priority by targeting funds; by leading in the development and implementation of curriculum, instruction, and assessment; and by providing professional development.

Together, these 10 effectiveness indicators form a complete picture of a high-performing school. The information revolution provides the imperative for education to change. The research provides the assurance that the changes schools undertake will be the correct and most important ones. The effectiveness indicators, tools, and processes provide the path. Breakthrough schools that are doing today what others said, just yesterday, couldn't be done—moving all students to high levels of learning in spite of significant challenges—provide the inspiration.

Victor Hugo once commented that "there is nothing like a dream to create the future." All children wish for a future in which they can reach their dreams. All teachers dream of encountering their students as successful adults and hearing them say proudly, "I am who I am today, in part, because of what I learned from you." We have a responsibility to make those dreams a reality for every student and every teacher. We know what to do and how to do it. How can we wait?

Selected Tools

The CD that accompanies this book is a complete toolkit for conducting an on-site school review. It includes evidence-gathering tools, planning tools, and communication tools. The tools are numbered according to their order of appearance in the book. Table A.1 (page 256) lists all the tools and indicates where they are first mentioned in the text.

This appendix provides a sample of 13 tools:

Tool 2: Planning Schedule (page 260)

Tool 4: Leadership Meeting Agenda (page 261)

Tool 5: Effectiveness Indicator Overview (page 262)

Tool 6: On-Site School Review Overview (page 267)

Tool 7: Teacher Survey Example (page 270)

Tool 13: Sample Student Work Analysis (page 271)

Tool 45: Family and Community Meeting Agenda (page 273)

Tool 46: Effectiveness Indicator Map (page 274)

Tool 47: Oral Exit Report Agenda (page 315)

Tool 49: Sample Final Report (page 316)

Tool 51: Final Report Workshop Agenda (page 331)

Tool 56: Strategic Planning Workshop Agenda (page 333)

Tool 58: Designing School Strategic Plan Workshop Agenda (page 335)

Table A.1: Tools in Order of Appearance in Book

Tool Number	Tool Name	Chapter Number	Section Where First Mentioned
1	Budget Planning	11	Estimating Costs
2	Planning Schedule	11	Basic Time Line
3	Leadership Meeting PowerPoint	11	Meeting Between Team Leader and School Leadership Team
4	Leadership Meeting Agenda	11	Meeting Between Team Leader and School Leadership Team
5	Effectiveness Indicator Overview	11	Meeting Between Team Leader and School Leadership Team
6	On-Site School Review Overview	11	Meeting Between Team Leader and School Leadership Team
7	Teacher Survey Example	11	Meeting Between Team Leader and School Leadership Team
8	Collecting Student Work—Letter to Instructional Staff	11	Meeting Between Team Leader and School Leadership Team
9	Team Member Information Form	12	Arranging for the Review Team's Visit
10	Team Member Welcome Letter	12	Arranging for the Review Team's Visit
11	Sample Planning Schedule (Secondary)	12	Scheduling Interviews and Focus Groups for Staff and Students
12	Interview and Focus Group Sign-Up Form	12	Scheduling Interviews and Focus Groups for Staff and Students
13	Sample Student Work Analysis	12	Planning for the Collection of Student Work
14	All-Staff Meeting PowerPoint	12	All-Staff Meeting With Team Leader

Tool Number	Tool Name	Chapter Number	Section Where First Mentioned
15	Team Member Update Letter	12	Communicating With Team Members After the All-Staff Meeting
16	Master Matrix	12	Using the Master Matrix
17	Teacher Survey	12	Preparing and Administering Surveys
18	Classified Staff Survey	12	Preparing and Administering Surveys
19	Parent Survey	12	Preparing and Administering Surveys
20	Student Survey	12	Preparing and Administering Surveys
21	District Administrator Interview	12	Preparing Interview and Focus Group Questions
22	School Administrator Interview	12	Preparing Interview and Focus Group Questions
23	Curriculum Administrator Interview	12	Preparing Interview and Focus Group Questions
24	Teacher Interview	12	Preparing Interview and Focus Group Questions
25	Counselor Interview	12	Preparing Interview and Focus Group Questions
26	Community Interview	12	Preparing Interview and Focus Group Questions
27	Board Member Interview	12	Preparing Interview and Focus Group Questions
28	Teacher Focus Group	12	Preparing Interview and Focus Group Questions
29	Classified Staff (Instructional) Focus Group	12	Preparing Interview and Focus Group Questions

(continued)

Tool Number	Tool Name	Chapter Number	Section Where First Mentioned
30	Classified Staff (Noninstructional) Focus Group	12	Preparing Interview and Focus Group Questions
31	Student Focus Group (Elementary)	12	Preparing Interview and Focus Group Questions
32	Student Focus Group (Secondary)	12	Preparing Interview and Focus Group Questions
33	School Leadership Team Focus Group	12	Preparing Interview and Focus Group Questions
34	Family/Community Focus Group	12	Preparing Interview and Focus Group Questions
35	Family and Community Meeting Invitation Letter	12	Planning for the Family and Community Meeting
36	Interview/Observation Schedule Template (Secondary)	12	Scheduling Team Interviews and Observations
37	Interview/Observation Schedule Template (Elementary)	12	Scheduling Team Interviews and Observations
38	Equipment, Supplies, and Materials Checklist	12	Equipment and Supply Needs
39	Student Announcement	12	Reminders to the School Staff
40	Sample Data Packet	13	Collecting and Analyzing State Achievement Data
41	Sample Team Member Data Brief	13	Team Member Data Brief
42	Student Work Taxonomy and Rigor Analysis Worksheet	13	Analyzing Student Work
43	Classroom Observation Form	14	Data Squared: Observations
44	Daily Tally of Interactions	14	Data Squared: Observations—Level of Engagement

Tool Number	Tool Name	Chapter Number	Section Where First Mentioned
45	Family and Community Meeting Agenda	14	Family and Community Meeting
46	Effectiveness Indicator Map	14	Facilitated Communication
47	Oral Exit Report Agenda	14	The Last Day of Interviews and Observations: Oral Exit Report
48	On-Site School Review Evaluation Form	14	The Last Day of Interviews and Observations: Evaluation
49	Sample Final Report	15	Final Report
50	Final Report Template	15	Final Report
51	Final Report Workshop Agenda	15	Final Report Inservice Workshop
52	Professional Development Evaluation Form	15	Evaluation
53	Decision-Making Matrix	16	Leadership for Planning
54	How Teams Function	16	Getting Started on the School Strategic Plan
55	Group Facilitation Models	16	Getting Started on the School Strategic Plan
56	Strategic Planning Workshop Agenda	16	Getting Started on the School Strategic Plan
57	Action-Planning Template	16	Writing the School Strategic Plan
58	Designing School Strategic Plan Workshop Agenda	16	Writing the School Strategic Plan
59	Sample Professional Development and Team Meeting Calendar	16	Professional Development: Time for Professional Development

Tool 2

Planning Schedule

For each of the individual tasks listed, agree on a time line and identify the person responsible for the activity and who will participate. This schedule should be designed by the principal, site coordinator, and team leader, with input from the leadership team.

Start Date	End Date	Time	Activity	Lead	Participants
			Leadership team planning meeting		
			Provide planning documents to team leader		
			All-staff planning meeting		
			Provide survey templates to site coordinator		
			Mail parent survey and meeting notice		
			Finalize focus groups and interviews		
			Provide student work collection folders to teachers		
			Collection of student work		
			Administer staff surveys		
			Administer student surveys		
			Provide completed surveys to team leader		
			On-site review		
			Kick-off meeting		
			Family and community meeting		
			Oral exit report		
			Final report inservice		
			Strategic planning inservice		
			Designing strategic plan inservice		

Leadership Meeting Agenda

1. Intended outcomes for today's meeting

2. Getting to know one another

3. Assessing readiness

4. Effectiveness indicators (handout: *Effectiveness Indicator Overview* [Tool 5])

5. School review tools

6. Elements of the on-site school review process (handout: *On-Site School Review Overview* [Tool 6])

7. The planning process

8. Documents the team will review

9. Survey creation and dissemination (handout: *Teacher Survey Example* [Tool 7])

10. Collecting student work (handout: *Collecting Student Work—Letter to Instructional Staff* [Tool 8])

11. On-site process

12. Communicating results

13. Strategic planning

14. Benefits of an external review

15. Discuss concerns/clarify questions

16. Create planning schedule

Effectiveness Indicator Overview

The 10 Effectiveness Indicators are the foundation of the on-site school review process. These indicators have been validated by research and by more than 5 years of reviews in schools at all grade levels. Each effectiveness indicator is defined by between 5 and 12 Characteristics. Research-based rubrics enable the review team to determine the extent to which each characteristic of each indicator is, or is not, in place within a school. Every rubric is tied to specific questions asked during the review and to evidence and documentation gathered before and during the visit.

Effectiveness Indicator 1: Written Curriculum

The written curriculum is the foundation of the school's instructional program. An on-site school review examines the written curriculum to gauge its alignment with state content standards; its horizontal and vertical alignment; its alignment with instructional materials; the supports available for it, such as assessments and interventions; and the degree to which it is implemented in classrooms every day.

Five characteristics define Effectiveness Indicator 1: Written Curriculum:

1A. The written curriculum is aligned to state standards or the standards of national disciplinary organizations.

1B. The written curriculum is vertically and horizontally aligned.

1C. Textbooks and other instructional materials are aligned with the written curriculum.

1D. Formative and summative assessments are identified in the written curriculum.

1E. Intervention and enrichment materials are identified in the written curriculum.

Effectiveness Indicator 2: Instructional Program

The instructional program is clearly the reason for which the school exists—its core mission. An on-site school review looks at the instructional program as a whole, focusing on its rigor (access, challenge, and support for all students), its flexibility (individualized tools, strategies, and assessments for all students), and the supports it provides for teachers (curriculum cohesion, professional collaboration, and instructional leadership).

Ten characteristics define Effectiveness Indicator 2: Instructional Program:

2A. Teachers integrate content standards into classroom instruction.

2B. The instructional program is rigorous and provides access, challenge, and support for all students.

2C. Teachers expect all students to make substantial learning gains each year, and students have high expectations of themselves.

2D. Teachers organize instruction to support clearly articulated and communicated learning targets.

2E. Teachers provide students with activities and assignments that are rigorous and engaging and that extend their learning.

2F. Teachers have deep knowledge of their subject matter, possess expertise in a wide range of effective instructional strategies, and are committed to closing achievement gaps.

2G. Teachers plan together to ensure that instruction and assessment meet the needs of all learners.

2H. Instructional time is fully and effectively used.

2I. School administrators support and promote effective instructional practices, program coordination, and resource allocation.

2J. School administrators ensure that the taught curriculum reflects the written curriculum and aligns with the pacing charts.

Effectiveness Indicator 3: Student Assessment

Student assessment can be used to determine individual students' levels of specific knowledge and skills; to improve classroom instruction; to adapt instruction or prescribe interventions for individuals or groups of students; to evaluate and improve larger instructional programs; and to measure and compare schools, districts, and states for broad public accountability. An on-site school review examines the range and quality of a school's assessment system.

Six characteristics define Effectiveness Indicator 3: Student Assessment:

3A. Local assessments are aligned to the cognitive demand of the standards and to the written curriculum.

3B. Teachers employ a variety of formative and summative assessment strategies.

3C. Diagnostic assessments are used to identify student skill levels and to determine appropriate interventions or remediations.

3D. Data from diagnostic assessments are used to place, group, and regroup students.

3E. Aggregated and disaggregated data from state assessments are used to improve the school's curriculum and instructional program.

3F. State and local student assessment data are collected, disseminated, and readily available.

Effectiveness Indicator 4: School Leadership

Effective leaders create a school climate in which academic achievement is the primary goal, and they ensure that policies, procedures, and resources support that goal. An on-site school review examines the role of school administrators in developing, implementing, and maintaining improvement efforts that are focused on student learning.

Twelve characteristics define Effectiveness Indicator 4: School Leadership:

4A. School administrators provide leadership in strategic planning.

4B. School administrators create a culture of high expectations for student and adult success and support those beliefs schoolwide.

4C. School administrators see student learning as the foremost priority for the school.

4D. School administrators ensure that adequate resources are allocated to achieve school improvement goals.

4E. School leadership is distributed schoolwide.

4F. School administrators recognize staff members' accomplishments, expertise, and leadership potential.

4G. School administrators encourage and promote collaborative relationships.

4H. School administrators address existing and potential conflicts.

4I. School administrators are accessible and model optimism, integrity, fairness, and respect.

4J. School administrators are adaptable and encourage innovation.

4K. School administrators ensure that teachers receive constructive feedback through periodic observation, coaching, and lesson study.

4L. School administrators provide formal staff evaluations.

Effectiveness Indicator 5: Strategic Planning

Certain organizational elements must be in place for the planning process to provide the maximum benefit to the school. An on-site school review examines how the plan is created, what its focus is, who is part of the process, how the plan is implemented, and how it is evaluated.

Eight characteristics define Effectiveness Indicator 5: Strategic Planning:

5A. There is a process in place, and support for, schoolwide strategic planning.

5B. The strategic plan is focused on student learning and refining teaching practices.

5C. As a part of strategic planning, student demographic and achievement data are reviewed and analyzed.

5D. A research-driven approach is used to identify problems and solutions.

5E. Extensive communication ensures that all stakeholders are a part of the decision-making process.

5F. An action plan describes the steps to be taken toward attainment of the goals.

5G. The strategic plan is put into action with fidelity.

5H. The school monitors progress toward attainment of the goals and makes adjustments when appropriate.

Effectiveness Indicator 6: Professional Development

The professional development program is centered on ensuring that all children learn to high levels. In effective schools, professional development deepens and refines teachers' knowledge and skills in content and pedagogy. An on-site school review examines the professional development program to find if it is based on student outcome data and is collaborative, sustained, intensive, and closely tied to the classroom. The review also looks at whether the program addresses teacher needs, including those of teachers new to the profession.

Eight characteristics define Effectiveness Indicator 6: Professional Development:

6A. The professional development program is focused on improving student learning by deepening the knowledge and skills of educators in their subject matter and in pedagogy.

6B. The professional development program is based on an analysis of student achievement data and learning needs, is coherent with state standards, and complements the instructional program.

6C. Professional development is collaborative, is job-embedded, and addresses both individual and schoolwide needs.

6D. Professional development is ongoing and sustained over time.

6E. Professional development builds cultural proficiency.

6F. Professional development explicitly addresses the needs of teachers new to the profession.

6G. The professional development program has adequate resources.

6H. An evaluation of program effectiveness is an integral part of professional development.

Effectiveness Indicator 7: Student Connectedness, Engagement, and Readiness

Feeling a connection to their school, their peers, and the adults within their school provides an important safety net for students. Students who feel connected are much more likely to stay in school despite obstacles they may face along the way. Extracurricular activities play an important role in these feelings of connection. When students begin to falter, there are mechanisms in place to quickly reach out to them with targeted assistance. Students move seamlessly from one school to another in the district because there is a high level of communication and coordination between schools. An on-site school review looks at the extent of all of these efforts to keep students in school until they graduate.

Seven characteristics define Effectiveness Indicator 7: Student Connectedness, Engagement, and Readiness:

7A. Students feel connected to their school.

7B. Students have positive, trusting, and caring relationships with adults and peers in the school.

7C. Extracurricular activities are numerous and varied, providing ample opportunities for all students to participate.

7D. The school has mechanisms and programs to identify and meet the academic and social service needs of students at risk of not completing school.

7E. A system of schoolwide, targeted, and intensive interventions meets the needs of students at risk.

7F. Secondary schools provide alternative options to students in order to increase graduation rates.

7G. There is coordination and curricular alignment within and among feeder-pattern schools to ensure that students are prepared for transition to the next grade or school.

Effectiveness Indicator 8: School Environment

An on-site school review looks for the combination of warmth and academic challenge that is the key to a positive school environment. Such an environment is strongly associated with student success. There is respect between all stakeholders. Faculty and staff members skillfully meet the needs of culturally and linguistically diverse students. Behavior management systems focus first on instruction and intervention, resulting in an environment that is orderly but not unduly regimented.

Nine characteristics define Effectiveness Indicator 8: School Environment:

8A. School administrators foster a positive school environment in which students and staff members feel valued, students are challenged to grow academically, and staff members are challenged to grow professionally.

8B. The school and its physical environment are safe, welcoming, and conducive to learning.

8C. A culture of trust and respect exists at all levels of the school community.

8D. Staff members work effectively with racially, culturally, and linguistically diverse students.

8E. Positive character traits are taught and reinforced as part of the instructional program.

8F.   An effective discipline and behavior management system supports teaching and learning schoolwide.

8G.   School administrators and staff members actively support the discipline and behavior management system.

8H.   School rules are fair and are applied consistently and equitably. Consequences are commensurate with the offense.

8I.   Out-of-school suspensions are reserved for only the most serious offenses, and suspended students are allowed to continue the academic program.

Effectiveness Indicator 9: Family and Community Involvement

In effective schools, there are programs in place to engage families and the community in supporting student learning. An on-site school review assesses the commitment of the school, its families, and its community to developing partnerships for the benefit of the students. It examines both the school's outreach efforts and the families' and community's involvement in, and ownership of, the school.

Five characteristics define Effectiveness Indicator 9: Family and Community Involvement:

9A.   Families and the community feel positive about, and welcome at, the school.

9B.   The school maintains high levels of communication with families and the community.

9C.   The school seeks and values family and community involvement.

9D.   The school engages families and the community to support student learning.

9E.   School administrators cultivate shared responsibility for decision-making among families and within the community.

Effectiveness Indicator 10: District Support

The board and district determine the context within which schools function and the culture within which they operate. Effective districts are committed above all else to setting and supporting goals for high levels of student learning, and the board and superintendent work together to emphasize this priority. An on-site school review evaluates the district's leadership in aligning curriculum, instruction, and assessment between and within grade levels, districtwide. It also examines the district's performance in committing resources to its goals and in using data to evaluate progress toward those goals.

Six characteristics define Effectiveness Indicator 10: District Support:

10A.   The roles and responsibilities of the board, the district, and the schools are clear and communicated to stakeholders.

10B.   The board's, district's, and schools' goals, policies, and resource allocations are aligned and focus on student learning.

10C.   The district oversees the development and implementation of curriculum, instruction, and assessment districtwide.

10D.   The board's and district's policies and actions reflect the expectation that all children in the district will be engaged in high-quality instruction and assessment.

10E.   The board's and district's actions reflect high expectations of staff members.

10F.   The board and district use data to monitor school and student performance and intervene if school performance lags.

Tool 6

On-Site School Review Overview

Interest in a school review grows from a curiosity about how effectively a school or district is currently functioning and a desire to use that information to take the next steps to improve performance. A school review provides school administrators and staff with comprehensive information in three key areas:

1. What has high-quality research identified as essential elements of effective schools?

2. How can we tell the extent to which those characteristics and traits are present in our school?

3. What are the next steps for our school to take in becoming a more effective school?

The On-Site School Review Process

Figure 1 shows the main steps of the on-site school review process.

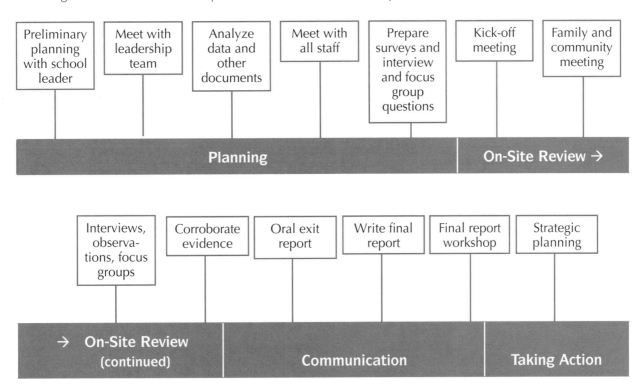

Figure 1: The major milestones of the on-site school review process.

The Effectiveness Indicators

The 10 Effectiveness Indicators have emerged from studies of schools in which all groups of students are performing at high levels. They are used to create a detailed picture of what an effective school looks like.

1. Written Curriculum
2. Instructional Program
3. Student Assessment
4. School Leadership
5. Strategic Planning
6. Professional Development
7. Student Connectedness, Engagement, and Readiness
8. School Environment
9. Family and Community Involvement
10. District Support

The Tools

The review team uses a variety of tools to collect and validate evidence, to communicate the results of the on-site review, and to plan for school improvement.

- Data analysis
- Interviews
- Focus groups
- Student, parent, teacher, and staff surveys
- Document review
- Curriculum analysis
- Student work analysis
- Classroom observation
- Strategic planning
- Professional development

The Rubrics

The rubrics (scoring guides) are the basic tool of the school review process. They provide a systematic way to determine the extent to which each characteristic of each effectiveness indicator is, or is not, in place within a school. Table 1 is an example of the rubric for one characteristic.

Communication

Communication between the review team and the school is well-planned and ongoing. Planning for the review consists of selecting the effectiveness indicators, setting the schedule, communicating with staff members, and administering the surveys. A kick-off meeting is held with the staff on the first day of the on-site visit. Every day during the on-site visit, the team leader meets with the principal. The visit concludes with an all-staff exit briefing.

Strategic Planning

Strategic planning begins with an all-staff inservice to discuss the results of the final report, including data, commentary on the effectiveness indicator review, and recommendations. A second inservice involves examining current instructional practices and deciding on the most important actions to affect the school. The third inservice results in a strategic plan that sets goals, establishes the time line, and identifies current and needed resources.

Table 1: Rubric for Characteristic 1A

Characteristic	Trait	Effectiveness Continuum		
		Low Performing	Effective	High Performing
1A. The written curriculum is aligned to state standards or the standards of national disciplinary organizations.	1A1. Extent of written curriculum	Some or all classes for which there are state standards lack written curriculum.	There is written curriculum for all subjects and classes for which there are state standards.	There is written curriculum for all subjects and classes.
	1A2. Alignment to content of standards	The written curriculum is not aligned to the content of state standards.	The written curriculum is aligned to the content of state standards.	The written curriculum is aligned to the content of state standards in those subjects for which there are state standards and the content of the standards of national disciplinary organizations for other subjects.
	1A3. Alignment to cognitive demands of standards	The written curriculum is not aligned to the cognitive demands of state standards.	The written curriculum is aligned to the cognitive demands of state standards.	The written curriculum is aligned to or exceeds the cognitive demands of state standards in those subjects for which there are state standards and the cognitive demands of the standards of national disciplinary organizations for other subjects.

Tool 7

Teacher Survey Example

Please think about each statement below. For each statement, decide to what degree you believe the statement to be true, and mark the appropriate box. Please answer every question. Your answers will be anonymous. Thank you for taking the time to share your thoughts about your school.

NA = Not Applicable or No Answer

Question #	Trait	Question	Always True	Most Often True	Sometimes True	Never True	NA
1	1A2	Our school's curriculum is aligned to state standards or national disciplinary standards (in subjects for which there are state or national disciplinary standards).					
2	1B2	The curriculum in the subject(s) I teach builds logically from one level to the next.					
3	1C2	There are sufficient quantities of instructional materials available for me to use with my classes.					
4	1E2	I have sufficient quantities of intervention and enrichment materials for my students' needs.					
5	2B1	Students find my classes rigorous and challenging.					
6	2C1	I believe all students in my classes can make substantial learning gains.					
7	2C2	My students express high expectations for their own learning.					
8	2D2	As I start every new unit, I tell my students exactly what they will be expected to know and be able to do at the conclusion of the unit.					
9	2E1	Students are attentive during classroom instruction.					

Note: Number of questions on survey depends on the selection of effectiveness indicators.

Comments: _____

_____

Thank you!

<u>Tool 13</u>

Sample Student Work Analysis

Prior to the on-site school review, teachers were asked to collect student work from each of their classes for a 2-week period. Teachers were also asked to include corresponding lesson plans, any scoring guides used, and a description of each assignment if available. In this sample, student work was received from 13 teachers in a K–7 school in the following content areas/classes: language arts, science, social studies, mathematics, special education, physical education, technology, and art. A total of 243 unique assignments were received and reviewed (Table 1). A "unique assignment" is one that is given in one or more classes. Thus an identical assignment given in three classes counts as a single unique assignment.

Table 1: Number of Assignments by Grade Level and Specialist Grouping

Grade Level and Specialist Grouping	Number of Unique Assignments
K, 1, 2, and 1–2 split	76
3, 4, and 2–3 split	31
5, 6, 7	51
Special education, physical education, technology, and art	85
Grade level could not be determined	5
Total	**243**

Cognitive Demand

To determine the level of cognitive demand, assignments were analyzed using Bloom's Taxonomy (Table 2, next page). This classification system divides tasks into two orders representing higher- and lower-order thinking skills, with three progressively more complex levels in each of the orders. The cognitive demands from the lower order progress from recall to comprehension to application. Within the higher order, the cognitive demands progress from analysis to synthesis to evaluation.

This analysis of student work reviewed during the 2-week window revealed that the majority of assignments (90%) were targeted to lower-order thinking skills. However, within that majority, the highest percentage of assignments were at the application level, which is the highest level in the lower order.

Level of Rigor

Academically rigorous content leads students beyond the acquisition of knowledge. An academically rigorous curriculum teaches analytical thinking, learning skills, comprehension skills, and writing skills. The rigor of each assignment reviewed was calculated based on the degree of academic challenge present in the assignment in relation to state grade-level standards (Table 3, next page).

Table 2: Cognitive Demand

Level	Number of Assignments at Level
Higher Order	
Evaluation	3
Synthesis	0
Analysis	21
Total Higher Order	**24**
Lower Order	
Application	115
Comprehension	31
Knowledge/recall	68
Total Lower Order	**214**
Could not be determined	5

Table 3: Level of Rigor

Level	Number at Level	Percentage at Level
Higher than state standard/benchmark	23	10
Match to state standard/benchmark	168	69
Below standard/benchmark	44	18
Could not be determined	8	3
Total	243	100

Tool 45

Family and Community Meeting Agenda

1. Welcome by the principal

2. Goals of the on-site school review

3. Purpose of the family and community meeting

4. Introduction of the review team

5. Interpretation and child-care arrangements

6. Where the focus groups will meet

7. Group separates into focus groups

8. Introductions

    • How many children do you have at the school/in the district?

    • How long have you lived in the district?

    • What interests you in tonight's conversation?

9. Facilitated questions [from Tool 34: Family/Community Focus Group]

10. [Possible closing activity]

11. Meeting ends at _____

Thank you for coming tonight!

Tool 46

Effectiveness Indicator Map

Effectiveness Indicator 1: Written Curriculum

Characteristic	Trait	Effectiveness Continuum		
		Low Performing	Effective	High Performing
1A. The written curriculum is aligned to state standards or the standards of national disciplinary organizations.	1A1. Extent of written curriculum	Some or all classes for which there are state standards lack written curriculum.	There is written curriculum for all subjects and classes for which there are state standards.	There is written curriculum for all subjects and classes.
	1A2. Alignment to content of standards	The written curriculum is not aligned to the content of state standards.	The written curriculum is aligned to the content of state standards.	The written curriculum is aligned to the content of state standards in those subjects for which there are state standards and the content of the standards of national disciplinary organizations for other subjects.
	1A3. Alignment to cognitive demands of standards	The written curriculum is not aligned to the cognitive demands of state standards.	The written curriculum is aligned to the cognitive demands of state standards.	The written curriculum is aligned to or exceeds the cognitive demands of state standards in those subjects for which there are state standards and the cognitive demands of the standards of national disciplinary organizations for other subjects.

Characteristic	Trait	Effectiveness Continuum		
		Low Performing	Effective	High Performing
1B. The written curriculum is vertically and horizontally aligned.	**1B1. Vertical alignment**	The curriculum is not aligned vertically between grade levels or sequential courses.	The curriculum is aligned vertically between grade levels and sequential courses.	The curriculum is aligned vertically between grade levels and sequential courses, and periodic analyses are conducted to review the appropriateness of grade-level curriculum loads.
	1B2. Horizontal alignment	The curriculum is not aligned horizontally within grade levels and courses.	The curriculum is aligned horizontally within each grade level and course.	The curriculum is aligned horizontally within each grade level and course, and periodic analyses are conducted to review the appropriateness of the pacing charts.
1C. Textbooks and other instructional materials are aligned with the written curriculum.	**1C1. Identification of instructional materials**	The written curriculum does not identify aligned instructional materials.	The written curriculum identifies aligned instructional materials.	The written curriculum identifies specific pages or units from instructional and supplemental materials that address each learning objective or standard.
	1C2. Availability of instructional materials	The instructional materials identified in the written curriculum are not available or are not being used in all classrooms.	The identified instructional materials are available in sufficient quantities and are being used in all classrooms.	The identified instructional materials are available in sufficient quantities, are being used in all classrooms, and are in excellent condition.

Characteristic	Trait	Effectiveness Continuum		
		Low Performing	Effective	High Performing
1D. Formative and summative assessments are identified in the written curriculum.	1D1. Identification of assessments	Formative and summative assessments are not identified in the written curriculum.	Formative and summative assessments are identified in the written curriculum.	Formative and summative assessments are identified in the written curriculum, and result ranges are keyed to interventions and enrichments.
1E. Intervention and enrichment materials are identified in the written curriculum.	1E1. Identification of intervention and enrichment materials	The written curriculum does not identify intervention and enrichment materials.	The written curriculum identifies intervention and enrichment materials.	The written curriculum identifies intervention and enrichment materials keyed to specific learner needs.
	1E2. Availability of intervention and enrichment materials	Intervention and enrichment materials either are not available or are not available in sufficient quantities to meet identified student needs.	Intervention and enrichment materials are available in sufficient quantities to meet student needs.	Intervention and enrichment materials are available in sufficient quantities to meet student needs and are available in the major languages of the school.

Effectiveness Indicator 2: Instructional Program

Characteristic	Trait	Effectiveness Continuum		
		Low Performing	Effective	High Performing
2A. Teachers integrate content standards into classroom instruction.	2A1. Integration of standards	Instruction in those subjects for which state content standards exist does not reflect, or is only loosely coupled with, the content standards.	State content standards are explicitly integrated into instruction in those subjects for which state content standards exist.	State content standards or those of national disciplinary organizations are explicitly integrated into instruction in all classes.

Characteristic	Trait	Effectiveness Continuum		
		Low Performing	Effective	High Performing
2B. The instructional program is rigorous and provides access, challenge, and support for all students.	2B1. Access to rigorous program	Students do not have access to an instructional program that is rigorous and provides challenging opportunities to extend their learning.	Students have access to an instructional program that is rigorous and provides challenging opportunities to extend their learning.	Students have access to an instructional program that is rigorous and provides challenging opportunities to extend their learning. Enrollment patterns in advanced and honors classes reflect the demographics of the student population.
	2B2. Availability of intervention, support, and enrichment programs	Students are not systematically matched with intervention, support, and enrichment programs based on individual student needs.	Teachers have access to a variety of intervention, support, and enrichment programs to address individual student needs.	Teachers have access to a variety of research-based intervention, support, and enrichment programs to address individual student needs.
2C. Teachers expect all students to make substantial learning gains each year, and students have high expectations of themselves.	2C1. Teacher expectations	Some teachers convey low or modest academic expectations of students or high expectations of some, but not all, students.	Teachers express confidence in the ability of their students to make substantial learning gains.	Instructional goals and activities, teacher talk, and the classroom environment all convey high expectations of all students.
	2C2. Student expectations	Some students express low or modest academic expectations of themselves.	Students express confidence in their ability to make substantial learning gains.	Students express confidence in their ability to make substantial learning gains, and student academic achievement supports that confidence.

Characteristic	Trait	Effectiveness Continuum		
		Low Performing	Effective	High Performing
2D. Teachers have organized instruction to support clearly articulated and communicated learning targets.	2D1. Student understanding of importance of content	Some students cannot explain why what they are learning is important.	Students know why what they are learning is important.	Students know why what they are learning is important and can explain how it might be used outside of school.
	2D2. Student awareness of progress	Some students do not know where they are in the progression of steps to meet their learning targets.	Students know where they are in the progression of steps to meet their learning targets.	All students know where they are in the progression of steps to meet their learning targets and what evidence will be required to demonstrate mastery of the next step.
	2D3. Student access to additional help	Some students do not know where to access additional help when they need it.	Students know how and where to access additional help when they need it.	Procedures are in place to ensure that all students who need extra help have access to and are using that assistance.
2E. Teachers provide students with activities and assignments that are rigorous and engaging and that extend their learning.	2E1. Student engagement	Some students are not attentive during instruction, not on task, or not engaged in classroom activities.	Students are actively engaged in classroom activities.	Students are attentive during instruction and engaged in classroom activities. Activities are varied for the range of student skill levels, and enrichment activities are readily available.
	2E2. Rigor of activities and assignments	Activities and assignments lack rigor or do not extend student learning.	Activities and assignments are rigorous and contribute to student understanding or extend concepts addressed in the lesson.	Activities and assignments are rigorous and extend concepts addressed in the lesson. Assistance and supports are readily available to enable all students to complete assignments.

		Effectiveness Continuum		
Characteristic	**Trait**	**Low Performing**	**Effective**	**High Performing**
2F. Teachers have deep knowledge of their subject matter, possess expertise in a wide range of effective instructional strategies, and are committed to closing achievement gaps.	**2F1. Teacher content knowledge**	Some teachers make or fail to correct content errors.	Teachers demonstrate strong content knowledge in the subjects taught.	Teachers demonstrate strong content knowledge in the subjects taught and are adept at diagnosing student gaps in understanding and knowledge.
	2F2. Repertoire of instructional strategies	Teachers demonstrate a limited number of instructional strategies or use strategies that are not well-matched to the needs of their students.	Teachers use a variety of instructional strategies matched to the needs of their students.	Teachers differentiate instruction to meet the diverse needs of students by varying content, processes, products, or the learning environment.
	2F3. Teacher commitment to closing achievement gaps	Teachers do not convey a commitment to raising achievement or closing achievement gaps between groups of students.	Teachers are committed to raising achievement and closing achievement gaps between groups of students.	Teachers' commitment to raising achievement has narrowed or closed achievement gaps between groups of students.
2G. Teachers plan together to ensure that instruction and assessment meet the needs of all learners.	**2G1. Extent of collaborative planning**	Most teachers do not meet or infrequently meet together to plan common lessons or assessments.	Teams of grade-level or content-area teachers frequently meet together to review student work and plan common lessons and assessments.	A formalized process exists and sufficient time is allocated for teams of grade-level or content-area teachers to plan common lessons and assessments. Planning time is used effectively, and teams document strategies and results.

Characteristic	Trait	Effectiveness Continuum		
		Low Performing	Effective	High Performing
2G (continued)	2G2. Scheduled collaboration	The daily schedule does not support instructional collaboration.	The school schedule provides time for joint planning or collaboration within grade levels and content areas.	The school schedule fosters collaboration and planning within and across grade levels, content areas, and programs (for example, ELL, special education).
2H. Instructional time is fully and effectively used.	2H1. Use of instructional time	Some teachers do not use instructional time effectively, losing time to behavior problems, classroom management, attendance, and noninstructional activities.	Teachers use instructional time effectively and lose little time to behavior problems, classroom management, attendance, and noninstructional activities.	Teachers use instructional time effectively with minimal time lost to behavior problems, classroom management, attendance, and noninstructional activities. Schoolwide interruptions such as announcements and assemblies during class time are rare.
	2H2. Clarity of instruction and procedures	Instruction and procedures in some classes are not clear to students, and instructional time is lost as clarifications are made.	Instruction and directions are clear to students, and little time is spent on clarifying directions, reteaching, or repeating previously described procedures.	In all classes, the teachers' directions and procedures are clear to students. Teachers anticipate areas of possible student misunderstanding and proactively address those areas in their instruction.
2I. School administrators support and promote effective instructional practices, program coordination, and resource allocation.	2I1. Administrator support of effective instructional practices	School administrators provide little instructional guidance.	School administrators support and promote effective instructional practices.	School administrators provide instructional leadership, support effective instructional practices, and actively seek out and acknowledge high-quality instructional strategies.

Characteristic	Trait	Effectiveness Continuum		
		Low Performing	Effective	High Performing
2I (continued)	2I2. Administrator efforts to coordinate instructional program	School administrators do not, or do not always, ensure coordination of the instructional program.	School administrators ensure coordination of the instructional program.	School administrators ensure coordination of the instructional program and ensure that new initiatives are coordinated with existing instructional efforts.
	2I3. Administrator provision of time and resources	School administrators do not, or do not always, ensure that sufficient time and resources are available to support the instructional program.	School administrators ensure that sufficient time and resources are available to support the instructional program.	School administrators ensure that sufficient time and resources are available to support the instructional program and ensure that new initiatives are fully resourced prior to implementation.
2J. School administrators ensure that the taught curriculum reflects the written curriculum and aligns with the pacing charts.	2J1. Match between taught and written curriculum and pacing charts	School administrators do not observe, or infrequently observe, classroom instruction to ensure that the taught curriculum matches the written curriculum and pacing charts.	School administrators ensure that the taught curriculum matches the written curriculum and pacing charts.	School administrators and all instructional staff members hold one another accountable to ensure that the taught curriculum matches the written curriculum and pacing charts.

Effectiveness Indicator 3: Student Assessment

Characteristic	Trait	Effectiveness Continuum		
		Low Performing	Effective	High Performing
3A. Local assessments are aligned to the cognitive demand of the standards and to the written curriculum.	3A1. Alignment to cognitive demand and to written curriculum	Local assessments are not aligned to the cognitive demand of the standards and to the written curriculum.	Local assessments are aligned to the cognitive demand of the standards and to the written curriculum.	Local assessments, aligned to the cognitive demand of the standards and to the written curriculum, are sufficient to measure attainment of all standards.
3B. Teachers employ a variety of formative and summative assessment strategies.	3B1. Repertoire of assessment strategies	Teachers do not employ a variety of formative and summative assessment strategies.	Teachers employ a variety of formative and summative assessment strategies.	Teachers employ a common set of formative and summative assessments and use the results to improve instruction within grade levels or courses.
3C. Diagnostic assessments are used to identify student skill levels and to determine appropriate interventions or remediations.	3C1. Assessment of knowledge and skill levels	Diagnostic assessments are not used to identify student knowledge and skill levels.	All students participate in diagnostic assessments to identify current knowledge and skill levels in reading and mathematics.	All students participate in diagnostic assessments to identify current knowledge and skill levels in reading, mathematics, science, and social studies.
	3C2. Assessment for interventions or remediations	Diagnostic assessments are not used to determine needed interventions or remediations.	Diagnostic assessments are used in reading and mathematics to determine needed interventions or remediations.	Diagnostic assessments are administered in reading, mathematics, science, and social studies throughout the year to determine needed interventions or remediations.

Characteristic	Trait	Effectiveness Continuum		
		Low Performing	Effective	High Performing
3D. Data from diagnostic assessments are used to place, group, and regroup students.	3D1. Assessment for grouping	Data from diagnostic assessments are not used to place, group, and regroup students.	Data from diagnostic assessments are used to place, group, and regroup students across grade levels based on knowledge and skills.	Data from diagnostic assessments are used to group and regroup students, student progress is monitored closely, and a continual remixing of assigned groups occurs throughout the year.
3E. Aggregated and disaggregated data from state assessments are used to improve the school's curriculum and instructional program.	3E1. Analysis of data	Aggregated and disaggregated data from state assessments are not analyzed by school staff.	Aggregated and disaggregated data from state assessments are analyzed by school staff.	Aggregated and disaggregated data, including state assessment, local assessment, and student demographic data, are analyzed at least annually by school staff.
	3E2. Use of data for school improvement	The school's curriculum and instructional program are not reviewed and refined based on disaggregated data from state assessments.	Disaggregated data from state assessments are used as a basis to review and refine the school's curriculum and instructional program.	Teachers meet as a faculty and in grade-level or content-area teams at least annually to discuss possible modifications to the curriculum and instructional program based on disaggregated results from state assessments.
3F. State and local student assessment data are collected, disseminated, and readily available.	3F1. Availability of assessment data	Student-level state assessment data are not readily available to teachers and staff members.	State and local student assessment data are collected, disseminated, and readily available to teachers and staff members.	State and local student assessment data are collected, disseminated, and readily available to teachers, staff members, families, and students.

Characteristic	Trait	Effectiveness Continuum		
		Low Performing	Effective	High Performing
3F (continued)	3F2. Reporting of assessment data	State assessment data are not communicated in a way that is understandable.	State assessment data are communicated in a way that is understandable to staff, members, students, families, and the public.	State assessment data are communicated in a clear and concise manner to all stakeholders. Trends over time are included in the communication.

Effectiveness Indicator 4: School Leadership

Characteristic	Trait	Effectiveness Continuum		
		Low Performing	Effective	High Performing
4A. School administrators provide leadership in strategic planning.	4A1. Development of strategic plan	The school lacks a current strategic plan, or the plan was developed without significant staff input.	The school has a current strategic plan that was developed with significant staff participation.	The school has a current strategic plan that was developed by school leadership and staff members and approved by district leadership or the school board.
	4A2. Focus of strategic plan	The school lacks a strategic plan, or the plan is not focused on student learning.	The school strategic plan is focused on student learning.	The school strategic plan is focused on student learning and includes disaggregated student achievement data and analysis supporting the goals and action plans.
	4A3. Relationship of strategic plan to decision-making	School decisions are made without regard to the strategic plan.	The strategic plan guides school decision-making.	The strategic plan is the pivotal factor in school decision-making.

		Effectiveness Continuum		
Characteristic	**Trait**	**Low Performing**	**Effective**	**High Performing**
4A (continued)	**4A4. Responsibility for strategic plan**	School administrators do not take responsibility for implementing the strategic plan.	School administrators take personal responsibility for the strategic plan.	School administrators take personal responsibility for the strategic plan and lead its implementation.
4B. School administrators create a culture of high expectations for student and adult success and support those beliefs schoolwide.	**4B1. Expectations for students**	School administrators do not have high expectations for the success of all students.	School administrators have high expectations for the success of all students.	School administrators have high expectations for student success and consistently reinforce that belief in interactions with students, staff members, and parents.
	4B2. Expectations for staff members	School administrators do not have high expectations for the success of all staff members.	School administrators have high expectations for the success of all staff members.	School administrators have high expectations for the success of all staff members and consistently reinforce that message in interactions with staff members, students, parents, and the community.
4C. School administrators see student learning as the foremost priority for the school.	**4C1. Priority assigned to student learning**	School administrators do not see student learning as the highest priority in decision-making.	School administrators see student learning as the highest priority in all decision-making.	School administrators see student learning as the highest priority for the school and take direct responsibility for the quality of the school's instructional program.

Characteristic	Trait	Effectiveness Continuum		
		Low Performing	Effective	High Performing
4D. School administrators ensure that adequate resources are allocated to achieve school improvement goals.	4D1. Sufficiency of resources for school improvement	School administrators have not ensured that sufficient resources have been allocated to support school improvement goals.	School administrators ensure that sufficient resources are allocated to support school improvement goals.	School administrators allocate sufficient resources to support implementation of the school improvement efforts and actively seek additional resources that support school goals.
4E. School leadership is distributed schoolwide.	4E1. Sharing of leadership	School leadership is restricted to those in administrative positions.	School leadership is shared among staff members based on knowledge, skills, and interests.	School leadership is widely shared among staff members based on knowledge, skills, and interests. There is formalized acknowledgment of staff members' leadership roles.
4F. School administrators recognize staff members' accomplishments, expertise, and leadership potential.	4F1. Recognition of staff accomplishments	Staff accomplishments receive little or no recognition.	School administrators informally recognize and acknowledge staff accomplishments.	School administrators formally and informally recognize staff members' individual and group accomplishments.
	4F2. Recognition and utilization of staff members' expertise	No processes exist to identify or utilize staff members' expertise.	School administrators identify and utilize internal staff members' expertise.	School administrators identify and utilize internal staff members' expertise and ensure that professional development is targeted to continue to build these internal resources.

		Effectiveness Continuum		
Characteristic	**Trait**	**Low Performing**	**Effective**	**High Performing**
4F (continued)	**4F3. Professional development for staff leadership**	Staff members with an interest in leadership roles pursue that interest without school or district assistance.	Staff members are encouraged to seek professional development to build their leadership capacities.	A formal professional development program exists to identify and prepare staff members for shared leadership opportunities and to provide them with ongoing support.
4G. School administrators encourage and promote collaborative relationships.	**4G1. Provision of opportunities to collaborate**	Opportunities for staff members to communicate, plan, and work with one another are limited, informal, and self-organized or primarily occur outside of the school day.	School administrators ensure that there are ample organized opportunities for staff members to communicate, plan, and work with one another.	The school calendar provides specific and frequent opportunities for grade-level, content-area, and other team meetings. Contract hours provide paraprofessionals with the opportunity and responsibility to participate as appropriate.
	4G2. Focus of collaborative efforts	Collaborative efforts are not focused on student learning.	School administrators ensure that collaborative efforts are focused on student learning.	School administrators ensure that collaborative efforts are focused on student learning, and instructional teams document and communicate strategies and results.
4H. School administrators address existing and potential conflicts.	**4H1. Efforts to resolve conflicts**	School administrators do not or do not always address staff conflicts.	When conflicts arise, school administrators work toward resolution.	School administrators work toward resolution of conflicts, addressing both the immediate concerns and the underlying issues.

Characteristic	Trait	Effectiveness Continuum		
		Low Performing	**Effective**	**High Performing**
4H (continued)	**4H2. Anticipation of conflicts**	School administrators do not always notice or acknowledge issues that have the potential to cause conflict.	School administrators anticipate where and when conflicts might arise and address issues before they rise to the level of a problem.	School administrators anticipate where and when conflicts, including workplace or community dissatisfaction, might arise and intervene to address both the problems and the underlying issues.
4I. School administrators are accessible and model optimism, integrity, fairness, and respect.	**4I1. Accessibility of administrators to staff members**	It is sometimes or usually difficult to meet with school administrators.	School administrators are accessible to staff members.	School administrators set aside time during each day to meet with staff members.
	4I2. Interactions with staff members, students, and community members	Some staff members, students, and community members do not think that interactions with school administrators are characterized by integrity and fairness.	Staff members, students, and community members believe that interactions with school administrators are characterized by integrity and fairness.	School administrators consistently display integrity and fairness in interactions with staff members, students, and the community and have built a culture of trust schoolwide.
	4I3. Attitudes about reaching goals	Some school administrators are not optimistic that agreed-upon goals can be reached, given the current conditions.	School administrators manifest optimism that staff members and students can and will reach agreed-upon goals.	School administrators ensure that agreed-upon goals are within reach and set a consistent tone of optimism and confidence that the goals can and will be met.
	4I4. Attitudes toward staff members, students, and the community	Staff members, students, and the community do not always feel valued and respected by school administrators.	Staff members, students, and the community feel valued and respected by school administrators.	Staff members, students, and the community feel welcome at the school and valued and respected by school administrators.

Characteristic	Trait	Effectiveness Continuum		
		Low Performing	Effective	High Performing
4J. School administrators are adaptable and encourage innovation.	4J1. Knowledge of current educational research	School administrators do not keep current on educational research and instructional theory and practice.	School administrators keep current on educational research and instructional theory and practice.	School administrators keep current on educational research and instructional theory and practice, and they routinely share and discuss best practices with staff members.
	4J2. Adaptability to changing circumstances	School administrators resist responding to changing circumstances or respond slowly.	School administrators adapt to changing circumstances.	School administrators anticipate changing circumstances, adapt to meet changing needs, and provide leadership in implementing change efforts.
	4J3. Attitude toward new ideas	School administrators do not always encourage new and innovative ideas.	School administrators encourage new and innovative ideas from staff members.	School administrators encourage new and innovative ideas from staff members and all stakeholders.
4K. School administrators ensure that teachers receive constructive feedback through periodic observation, coaching, and lesson study.	4K1. Administrator observation and feedback	School administrators occasionally observe teachers informally and provide constructive feedback.	School administrators frequently observe every teacher informally and provide constructive feedback focused on student learning.	School administrators frequently observe every teacher and instructional paraprofessional informally and provide constructive feedback focused on student learning.

Characteristic	Trait	Effectiveness Continuum		
		Low Performing	Effective	High Performing
4K (continued)	4K2. Support for peer observation, coaching, and lesson study	School administrators give informal support to peer observation, coaching, and lesson study but do not always provide sufficient release time.	Adequate release time is provided for all instructional staff members to participate in frequent, well-planned peer observation, coaching, and lesson study.	Adequate release time is built into the school calendar for all instructional staff members to participate in frequent, well-planned peer observation, coaching, and lesson study.
	4K3. Peer observation and feedback	Teachers observe and are observed by peers infrequently or not at all.	Each teacher frequently observes and is observed by peers and engages in a structured process of feedback.	Each teacher and instructional paraprofessional frequently observes and is observed by peers and engages in a structured process of feedback.
4L. School administrators provide formal staff evaluations.	4L1. Quality of staff evaluations	School administrators sometimes do not conduct staff evaluations on a timely basis or do not include all components of the evaluation as prescribed by state law and district policy.	School administrators conduct staff evaluations on a timely basis as prescribed by state law and district policy.	School administrators conduct staff evaluations on a timely basis as prescribed by state law and district policy. The evaluations address school improvement goals, professional development, and student learning.

Effectiveness Indicator 5: Strategic Planning

Characteristic	Trait	Effectiveness Continuum		
		Low Performing	Effective	High Performing
5A. There is a process in place, and support for, schoolwide strategic planning.	5A1. Process for strategic planning	No process is in place for the development of strategic plans.	There are explicit procedures in place for the development of schoolwide strategic plans.	There are explicit procedures in place for the development of schoolwide strategic plans, and the process is aligned with district planning processes.
	5A2. Support for strategic planning	The staff does not support schoolwide strategic planning.	The staff supports schoolwide strategic planning.	There is school and district support for schoolwide strategic planning.
5B. The strategic plan is focused on student learning and refining teaching practices.	5B1. Focus of strategic plan	There is no strategic plan, or the plan is not focused on student learning.	The plan is focused on student learning and the implementation of strategies to improve student learning.	The plan is focused on student learning, and identified teacher teams are responsible for implementing explicit strategies for improving student learning.
	5B2. Built-in opportunities for teachers to work collaboratively	The plan does not include structured opportunities for teachers to work collaboratively to refine teaching practices.	The plan includes structured opportunities for teachers to work collaboratively to refine teaching practices.	The plan includes structured opportunities for teachers and paraprofessionals to work collaboratively to refine teaching practices.
5C. As a part of strategic planning, student demographic and achievement data are reviewed and analyzed.	5C1. Analysis of achievement data	Student achievement data are not analyzed as part of strategic planning.	Overall and disaggregated student achievement data are analyzed as part of strategic planning.	Overall and disaggregated student achievement and program performance data are analyzed as part of strategic planning.

Characteristic	Trait	Effectiveness Continuum		
		Low Performing	Effective	High Performing
5C (continued)	5C2. Analysis of nonacademic data	Nonacademic data are not reviewed or are not disaggregated and analyzed as part of strategic planning.	Nonacademic data, including discipline, attendance, and graduation rates, are disaggregated and analyzed as part of strategic planning.	Nonacademic data, including trends over time, are disaggregated and analyzed as part of strategic planning.
5D. A research-driven approach is used to identify problems and solutions.	5D1. Depth of solutions	The proposed solutions to identified problems may not address underlying causes.	The planning team studied the problems identified in the data analysis to determine underlying causes and possible solutions.	The planning team studied the problems identified in the data analysis and used internal and external resources to validate its conclusions about underlying causes.
	5D2. Quality of hypothesis	A hypothesis was not developed or did not fully address the identified problems.	A hypothesis was developed that fully addressed the identified problems.	With input from staff members and a wide variety of stakeholders, a hypothesis was developed that fully addressed the identified problems.
5E. Extensive communication ensures that all stakeholders are a part of the decision-making process.	5E1. Stakeholders' participation in planning discussions	The school does not encourage stakeholders to take part in discussions of school challenges and potential solutions.	The school encourages stakeholders to take part in discussions of school challenges and potential solutions.	A variety of stakeholders take part in discussions of school challenges and potential solutions.
	5E2. Circulation of draft plans	Staff members and families have limited or no opportunities to review and comment on draft plans.	Draft plans are circulated to school staff members and made available to families for review and comment.	Draft plans are circulated to staff members and made available to families for review and comment. Staff members are given time during the school day to provide input on the draft plans.

Characteristic	Trait	Effectiveness Continuum		
		Low Performing	Effective	High Performing
5E (continued)	5E3. District review of plans	District staff members do not review the plans.	Senior district staff members review and approve the plans to ensure coordination with district efforts.	Senior district staff members review and approve the plans to ensure coordination with district efforts. District staff members who are knowledgeable about the research base on which the plan relies review the plan to ensure consistency with current educational research.
5F. An action plan describes the steps to be taken toward attainment of the goals.	5F1. Identification of sequence and responsibilities	The action plan does not specify the sequence of actions, nor does it identify specific individual or team responsibilities.	An action plan, including a time line and interim check points, lays out a sequence of actions to be completed by specific individuals or teams.	An action plan, including a time line and interim check points, lays out a sequence of actions to be completed by specific individuals or teams, and a monitoring process is in place.
	5F2. Specificity of learning goals	Student learning goals are not specific or measurable or do not address the identified problems.	Student learning goals are specific and measurable and directly address the identified problems.	Student learning goals are specific and measurable and directly address the identified problems. Progress is being made toward reaching the goals.

Characteristic	Trait	Effectiveness Continuum		
		Low Performing	Effective	High Performing
5G. The strategic plan is put into action with fidelity.	5G1. Agreement on action plan	Schoolwide agreement on how the goals will be accomplished is not reached.	Schoolwide, shared agreements are reached on how the goals will be accomplished.	Schoolwide, shared agreements are reached on how the goals will be accomplished, and each person's role in meeting those goals is clearly articulated in the plan.
	5G2. Adherence to schedule	Planned activities are not completed within the specified time lines.	Planned activities are completed within the specified time lines.	Planned activities are completed before the specified deadlines.
	5G3. Allocation of resources	Resources are not allocated or are not adequate for the activities described in the plan.	Adequate resources are allocated for the activities described in the plan.	Resources are allocated for the activities described in the plan and are monitored for adequacy.
5H. The school monitors progress toward attainment of the goals and makes adjustments when appropriate.	5H1. Evaluation of plan's impact	There is infrequent or no evaluation of the plan's impact on student learning.	At least annually, the staff evaluates the plan's impact on student learning.	The staff frequently evaluates the plan's impact on student learning.
	5H2. Data-based adjustments	There is no process for adjusting the plan in response to student performance data.	Formative and summative student achievement data are used to adjust the plan as needed.	Formative and summative student achievement data and other data, such as attendance, dropout, and discipline data, are used to adjust the plan as needed.

Effectiveness Indicator 6: Professional Development

Characteristic	Trait	Effectiveness Continuum		
		Low Performing	Effective	High Performing
6A. The professional development program is focused on improving student learning by deepening the knowledge and skills of educators in their subject matter and in pedagogy.	6A1. Focus on subject matter	The professional development program does not give teachers and instructional staff members opportunities to deepen their knowledge and skills in their subject matter.	The professional development program gives teachers opportunities to deepen their knowledge and skills in their subject matter.	The professional development program gives all teachers and paraprofessionals opportunities to deepen their knowledge and skills in their subject matter.
	6A2. Focus on pedagogy	The professional development program does not give teachers and instructional staff members opportunities to deepen their knowledge and skills in general and content-specific pedagogy.	The professional development program gives teachers opportunities to deepen their knowledge and skills in general and content-specific pedagogy.	The professional development program gives all teachers and paraprofessionals opportunities to deepen their knowledge and skills in general and content-specific pedagogy.
6B. The professional development program is based on an analysis of student achievement data and learning needs, is coherent with state standards, and complements the instructional program.	6B1. Connection to student learning needs	The professional development program does not take into account student achievement data.	The professional development program is based on an analysis of student achievement data and learning needs.	The professional development program is based on an analysis of student achievement data and learning needs, as well as nonacademic data such as discipline, attendance, and dropout rates.

Characteristic	Trait	Effectiveness Continuum		
		Low Performing	Effective	High Performing
6B (continued)	6B2. Alignment with state standards	The professional development program is not coherent with state standards.	The professional development program is coherent with state standards.	The professional development program is coherent with state standards and includes training in standards-based instruction and assessment strategies.
	6B3. Connection to instructional program	Professional development is disconnected from the school's instructional program.	The professional development program complements the school's instructional program.	The professional development program complements the school's instructional program and includes training in programs used for academic intervention and enrichment.
6C. Professional development is collaborative, is job-embedded, and addresses both individual and schoolwide needs.	6C1. Teams focused on improving achievement and learning	Collaborative work teams are informal or do not focus on improving student learning.	Teachers are members of collaborative work teams focused on improving student achievement and learning.	All instructional staff members participate in collaborative work teams focused on improving student achievement and learning.
	6C2. Job-embedded opportunities	Teacher professional development is not embedded in the work of teaching or does not provide opportunities for practice, analysis, and refinement.	Teacher professional development is embedded in the work of teaching, providing opportunities for practice, analysis, and refinement.	All instructional staff members participate in professional development that is embedded in the work of teaching, providing opportunities for practice, analysis, and refinement.

Characteristic	Trait	Effectiveness Continuum		
		Low Performing	Effective	High Performing
6C (continued)	6C3. Differentiation	Professional development is not or is not consistently differentiated based on knowledge, skills, and experience.	Teacher professional development is differentiated based on knowledge, skills, and experience.	Professional development for all instructional staff members is differentiated based on knowledge, skills, and experience.
	6C4. Attention to individual and schoolwide needs	Professional development does not address both individual and schoolwide needs.	Teacher professional development addresses both individual and schoolwide needs.	Professional development for all instructional staff members addresses both individual and schoolwide needs.
6D. Professional development is ongoing and sustained over time.	6D1. Incorporation into routine	Professional development is seen as external to the real work of the school or regarded as part of teachers' independent responsibilities.	Professional development is a routine part of every teacher's responsibilities and workday.	Ongoing professional development is a routine part of every staff member's responsibilities and workday.
	6D2. Continuity	Professional development is not part of an overall plan or consists primarily of stand-alone activities.	Professional development is ongoing and sustained over time.	Professional development is ongoing, is sustained over time, and seamlessly connects from one year to the next.
6E. Professional development builds cultural proficiency.	6E1. Effect on staff members' cultural proficiency	Few staff members have received training in cultural proficiency or feel culturally proficient.	Staff members engage in professional development that builds cultural understanding and proficiency.	Professional development has increased staff members' confidence in their level of cultural proficiency.

Characteristic	Trait	Effectiveness Continuum		
		Low Performing	Effective	High Performing
6E (continued)	6E2. Effect on beliefs	Professional development does not address, or does not adequately address, teachers' beliefs about culture, race, and learning.	Professional development addresses teachers' beliefs about and builds insight into culture, race, and learning.	All instructional staff members engage in professional development addressing beliefs about and building schoolwide insight into culture, race, and learning.
	6E3. Effect on equity	Professional development does not address barriers to racial, ethnic, and cultural equity.	Professional development addresses the identification and removal of barriers to racial, ethnic, and cultural equity.	Professional development has resulted in a reduction of the identified barriers to racial, ethnic, and cultural equity.
6F. Professional development explicitly addresses the needs of teachers new to the profession.	6F1. Induction program	There is no formalized teacher induction program for teachers with 3 or fewer years of experience.	A formalized induction program serves the needs of teachers with 3 or fewer years of experience.	A formalized induction program serves the needs of teachers with 3 or fewer years of experience. The program may be extended for those teachers who need additional support.
	6F2. Mentoring	The induction program does not include a formal mentoring component.	Each new teacher works with an assigned mentor throughout his or her first year of teaching.	The induction program includes a formal mentoring component that extends beyond a single year.
6G. The professional development program has adequate resources.	6G1. Level of resources	The professional development program lacks adequate resources.	The professional development program has adequate resources.	The professional development program has adequate resources. Funding for professional development is a stable budget item.

Characteristic	Trait	Effectiveness Continuum		
		Low Performing	Effective	High Performing
6H. An evaluation of program effectiveness is an integral part of professional development.	6H1. Requirements for program evaluation	Evaluations are not, or not consistently, required for all professional development.	Evaluations are required for all professional development.	Evaluations are required for all professional development, and both formative and summative evaluation data are used to improve the professional development program.

Effectiveness Indicator 7: Student Connectedness, Engagement, and Readiness

Characteristic	Trait	Effectiveness Continuum		
		Low Performing	Effective	High Performing
7A. Students feel connected to their school.	7A1. Connection and sense of belonging	Some students feel isolated from adults and from other students at the school.	Students feel a sense of belonging to, and being a part of, the school community.	Guidance and advisory programs build upon students' sense of belonging and their connection to adults and other students at the school.
	7A2. Enjoyment	Some students do not enjoy attending the school.	Students enjoy attending the school.	Students enjoy attending the school, as evidenced by high attendance and low tardy rates.
7B. Students have positive, trusting, and caring relationships with adults and peers in the school.	7B1. Relationships with adults	Some students have no adult in the school with whom they have a positive, trusting, and caring relationship.	Students have positive, trusting, and caring relationships with one or more adults in the school.	Programs are in place to identify children who are isolated from adults in the school and to help them establish connections with adults.

Characteristic	Trait	Effectiveness Continuum		
		Low Performing	Effective	High Performing
7B (continued)	7B2. Relationships with peers	Some students are isolated and have limited or no social interactions with peers in the school.	Students have positive, trusting, and caring relationships with peers in the school.	Programs are in place to help students develop positive, trusting, and caring relationships with peers.
7C. Extracurricular activities are numerous and varied, providing ample opportunities for all students to participate.	7C1. Extent of participation	Some students or groups of students do not participate in extracurricular activities.	Most students participate in at least one extracurricular activity.	Most students participate in more than one extracurricular activity.
	7C2. Extent of opportunities	Opportunities for participation in extracurricular activities are limited or not available to all students.	Ample opportunities, extending beyond athletics, exist for all students to participate in extracurricular activities.	There are ample opportunities for all students to participate in extracurricular activities, and students receive public recognition for high performance in all activities.
7D. The school has mechanisms and programs to identify and meet the academic and social service needs of students at risk of not completing school.	7D1. Identification of students at risk	There is no systematic process to identify students who are at risk of not completing school.	The school has processes in place to identify students who are at risk of not completing school.	The school examines data on absences, tardies, discipline, and low grades at least quarterly, as part of the process to identify students who are at risk of not completing school.

Characteristic	Trait	Effectiveness Continuum		
		Low Performing	Effective	High Performing
7D (continued)	7D2. Meeting academic needs of students at risk	There is no systematic process to meet the academic needs of students who are at risk of not completing school.	The school has processes in place to meet the academic needs of students who are at risk of not completing school.	There is a sense of urgency about assisting students at risk when their achievement begins to falter, and there are programs in place to meet their academic needs.
	7D3. Meeting social service needs of students at risk	There is no systematic process to meet the social service needs of students who are at risk of not completing school.	The school has processes in place to meet the social service needs of students who are at risk of not completing school.	The school collaborates with social service agencies and the community to provide needed health and social services to students at risk and their families.
7E. A system of schoolwide, targeted, and intensive interventions meets the needs of students at risk.	7E1. Schoolwide interventions	There is no schoolwide program to help students avoid at-risk behaviors.	A schoolwide program is in place to help students avoid at-risk behaviors.	A schoolwide program is in place to help students avoid at-risk behaviors, and the program is annually evaluated for effectiveness.
	7E2. Targeted interventions	There are no targeted intervention programs to assist students at risk.	An individually targeted intervention program is in place to assist students at risk who need additional supports beyond the schoolwide program.	An individually targeted intervention program is in place to assist students at risk who need additional supports beyond the schoolwide program, and the program is annually evaluated for effectiveness.

Characteristic	Trait	Effectiveness Continuum		
		Low Performing	Effective	High Performing
7E (continued)	7E3. Intensive interventions	There are no intensive intervention programs to address specific behavior problems or to reengage students in school.	An intensive intervention program provides assistance from counselors and other specialists in alleviating specific problem behaviors and reengaging students in school.	An intensive intervention program provides assistance from counselors and other specialists in alleviating specific problem behaviors and reengaging students in school, and the program is annually evaluated for effectiveness.
7F. Secondary schools provide alternative options to students in order to increase graduation rates.	7F1. Availability of alternative options	There are few alternative options available to help students complete challenging courses needed for on-time graduation.	Alternative options are available to help students complete challenging courses needed for on-time graduation.	The district offers research-driven alternative options for struggling students and those who have dropped out or been expelled from school.
7G. There is coordination and curricular alignment within and among feeder-pattern schools to ensure that students are prepared for transition to the next grade or school.	7G1. Level of coordination	There is little communication or curriculum coordination within and among feeder-pattern schools.	There is communication and coordination between feeder-pattern schools to ensure curriculum alignment.	There is communication, curriculum alignment, and coordination across grade levels and between feeder-pattern schools to improve transitions.
	7G2. Coordination among teachers	Some teachers are not familiar with what will be required of students at the next grade or level.	Teachers know and prepare students for what will be required of them at the next grade or level.	Teachers know and prepare students for what will be required of them at the next grade or level. Teacher teams work together to design communication processes.

Effectiveness Indicator 8: School Environment

Characteristic	Trait	Effectiveness Continuum		
		Low Performing	Effective	High Performing
8A. School administrators foster a positive school environment in which students and staff members feel valued, students are challenged to grow academically, and staff members are challenged to grow professionally.	8A1. Students' feeling of being valued	Some students do not feel valued by school administrators.	Students feel valued by school administrators.	School administrators provide opportunities within the school day for students to meet with them.
	8A2. Students' feeling of being academically challenged	Some students do not feel academically challenged.	Students feel challenged to grow academically.	School administrators monitor to ensure that an environment of academic challenge is maintained over time.
	8A3. Staff members' feeling of being valued	Some staff members do not feel valued by school administrators.	Staff members feel valued by school administrators.	School administrators regularly meet with and seek the advice of school staff members.
	8A4. Staff members' feeling of being challenged professionally	Some staff members do not feel challenged by school administrators to grow professionally.	Staff members feel challenged by school administrators to grow professionally.	School administrators monitor to ensure that an environment of continuous professional growth is maintained over time.
8B. The school and its physical environment are safe, welcoming, and conducive to learning.	8B1. Overall feeling of safety	Some students, staff members, or families do not feel safe at the school.	Students, staff members, and families feel safe at the school.	A safety committee with representation from school administration, staff, families, and students meets regularly to address school safety issues or concerns.
	8B2. Overall atmosphere	Some students, staff members, and families do not view the school as welcoming to students.	Students, staff members, and families view the school as welcoming to students.	School administrators invite student, staff, and family suggestions on ways to improve the school atmosphere.

Characteristic	Trait	Effectiveness Continuum		
		Low Performing	Effective	High Performing
8B (continued)	8B3. Safety of physical spaces	Classrooms, hallways, or other spaces are not safe for students and adults.	Classrooms, hallways, and other spaces are safe for students and adults.	Classrooms, hallways, and other spaces are safe. Staff members are frequently seen in areas where students congregate and are visible in hallways during passing times.
	8B4. Awareness of safety procedures	Some staff members are unaware of the safety procedures described in the school safety plan.	Staff members are familiar with the safety procedures described in the school safety plan.	Staff members and students are familiar with and practice the safety procedures described in the school safety plan.
	8B5. Condition of building and grounds	The building and grounds need repair or maintenance.	The building and grounds are clean and well-maintained.	The building and grounds are clean and well-maintained, and repairs are made in a timely manner.
8C. A culture of trust and respect exists at all levels of the school community.	8C1. Level of trust	There is a lack of trust among school staff members or between staff members and school administrators.	Staff members and school administrators trust one another. This trust extends to, and is reciprocated by, students and their families.	A culture of trust exists at all levels of the school community. School administrators listen to and act upon ideas, thoughts, and concerns regarding trust.
	8C2. Level of respect	There is a lack of respect among school staff members or between staff members and school administrators.	Staff members and school administrators respect one another. This respect extends to, and is reciprocated by, students and their families.	A culture of respect exists at all levels of the school community. School administrators listen to and act upon ideas, thoughts, and concerns regarding respect.

Characteristic	Trait	Effectiveness Continuum		
		Low Performing	Effective	High Performing
8D. Staff members work effectively with racially, culturally, and linguistically diverse students.	8D1. Degree of staff effectiveness with diverse students	Not all staff members work effectively with racially, culturally, and linguistically diverse students.	Staff members work effectively with racially, culturally, and linguistically diverse students.	Staff members work effectively with racially, culturally, and linguistically diverse students, resulting in high and equitable achievement levels across all student populations.
8E. Positive character traits are taught and reinforced as part of the instructional program.	8E1. Incorporation of character education into instructional program	The teaching of positive character traits (for example, honesty, fairness, and responsibility) is not part of the instructional program.	The teaching of positive character traits (for example, honesty, fairness, and responsibility) is part of the instructional program.	The teaching of positive character traits (for example, honesty, fairness, and responsibility) is part of the instructional program, and all staff members continually reinforce positive behaviors associated with these traits.
8F. An effective discipline and behavior management system supports teaching and learning schoolwide.	8F1. Impact of discipline and behavior management system on teaching and learning	The school lacks a formal discipline and behavior management system that supports teaching and learning.	The schoolwide discipline and behavior management system supports teaching and learning.	The schoolwide discipline and behavior management system supports teaching and learning and provides meaningful recognition for positive student behavior.
	8F2. Impact of discipline and behavior management system on school safety	The school discipline and behavior management system is ineffective or does not provide for the safety of staff and students.	The school discipline and behavior management system provides for the safety of staff and students.	A representative group of stakeholders periodically reviews and updates the school discipline and behavior management system to ensure a safe environment for staff and students.

Characteristic	Trait	Effectiveness Continuum		
		Low Performing	Effective	High Performing
8F (continued)	8F3. Interventions for troubled or violent students	The school has few or no processes in place to identify and provide appropriate interventions for the most troubled or violent students.	The school has processes in place to identify and provide appropriate interventions for the most troubled or violent students.	The school, in cooperation with community partners, social service agencies, and law enforcement agencies, has procedures in place to identify and provide appropriate interventions for the most troubled or violent students.
8G. School administrators and staff members actively support the discipline and behavior management system.	8G1. Staff members' expectations for student behavior	Some staff members do not have high expectations for student behavior.	Staff members have high expectations for student behavior.	Staff members are committed to establishing and maintaining appropriate student behavior.
	8G2. Staff members' support of behavior and discipline management system	Some staff members do not actively support the behavior and discipline system in their classrooms.	Staff members actively support the behavior and discipline system in their classrooms.	Staff members actively support the behavior and discipline system in their classrooms and frequently communicate and discuss the expectations for appropriate student behavior.
	8G3. Division of responsibility for discipline	Neither staff members nor school administrators are satisfied with the current division of responsibility for student discipline.	School administrators take responsibility for dealing with serious infractions and hold teachers responsible for handling routine classroom discipline problems.	School administrators deal with serious infractions and provide professional development to teachers who continue to struggle with classroom discipline to ensure that their classrooms are conducive to learning and teaching.

Characteristic	Trait	Effectiveness Continuum		
		Low Performing	Effective	High Performing
8G (continued)	8G4. Visibility of school administrators	School administrators are seldom visible in hallways and classrooms or seen talking informally with students or teachers.	School administrators are frequently visible in hallways, classrooms, and the cafeteria and on the building grounds.	School administrators are frequently visible in hallways, classrooms, and the cafeteria and on the building grounds. They talk informally with teachers and students, addressing them by name and expressing interest in their activities.
8H. School rules are fair and are applied consistently and equitably. Consequences are commensurate with the offense.	8H1. Communication of school rules and consequences	Communications that provide clear explanations of school rules, and the consequences of breaking those rules, are out of date or are not provided to students and families.	School rules and the consequences of breaking those rules are clearly communicated to students and families.	School rules and the consequences of breaking those rules are clearly communicated to students and families in each of the primary languages of the school.
	8H2. Appropriateness of consequences	Consequences for breaches of discipline are sometimes either too lenient or too severe.	Consequences in the discipline and behavior management program are commensurate with the offense.	Staff members, students, and families worked together to develop the discipline and behavior management program, and consequences are commensurate with the offense.

Characteristic	Trait	Effectiveness Continuum		
		Low Performing	Effective	High Performing
8H (continued)	8H3. Application of school rules	School rules are not fairly, consistently, and equitably applied to all students.	School rules are fairly, consistently, and equitably applied to all students.	School rules are fairly, consistently, and equitably applied to all students. School discipline data are disaggregated annually and analyzed by subgroup for fair, consistent, and equitable application of rules.
	8H4. Academic support for students during in-school suspension	No or limited academic support is provided to students during in-school suspension.	Students receive assignments from missed classes to be completed during in-school suspension.	Students receive assignments from missed classes to be completed during in-school suspension. Licensed teachers are assigned to provide academic support to students placed in in-school suspension.
8I. Out-of-school suspensions are reserved for only the most serious offenses, and suspended students are allowed to continue the academic program.	8I1. Clarity of policies for suspension and expulsion	It is not clear which rules, if broken, may result in suspension or expulsion.	School documents explicitly describe which rules, if broken, may result in suspension or expulsion.	School documents, in the school's primary languages, clearly describe which rules, if broken, may result in suspension or expulsion.
	8I2. Limitations on out-of-school suspensions	Out-of-school suspensions are not limited to the most serious offenses.	Out-of-school suspensions are limited to offenses clearly linked to school safety issues.	Out-of-school suspensions are rare and are limited to offenses clearly linked to school safety issues.

Characteristic	Trait	Effectiveness Continuum		
		Low Performing	Effective	High Performing
8I (continued)	8I3. Credits for courses in alternative settings	Programs for students who are placed in alternative settings do not include credit-earning coursework.	Programs for students who are placed in alternative settings include credit-earning coursework.	Programs for students who are placed in alternative settings are coordinated with the instructional program of the school and include credit-earning coursework.

Effectiveness Indicator 9: Family and Community Involvement

Characteristic	Trait	Effectiveness Continuum		
		Low Performing	Effective	High Performing
9A. Families and the community feel positive about, and welcome at, the school.	9A1. Parents' attitude toward the school	The attitude of many parents toward the school is indifferent or negative.	Parents have a positive attitude toward the school.	Parents and community members have a positive attitude toward the school.
	9A2. School's effort to make all groups feel welcome	Some families, or families from some groups, do not feel welcome at the school.	Families from all groups feel welcome and comfortable at the school.	Families and community members from all groups feel welcome and comfortable at the school.
9B. The school maintains high levels of communication with families and the community.	9B1. Communication about school events and programs	Families are sometimes unaware of school events and programs.	There is frequent and varied communication with families and the community about school events and programs.	Families and community members regularly attend and participate in school events and programs.
	9B2. Communication about student achievement	Families infrequently receive data on the achievement of their children, or the information is presented in a way that is difficult to understand.	Families regularly receive clearly presented data on the achievement of their children.	Families regularly receive clearly presented data in their native languages on both the achievement of their children and overall school performance.

Characteristic	Trait	Effectiveness Continuum		
		Low Performing	Effective	High Performing
9B (continued)	**9B3. Provision of interpreters**	Interpreters are only sometimes available to assist in family-staff communications.	Interpreters are readily available to assist in family-staff communications.	Interpreters are readily available to assist in family-staff communications. Translators participate in professional development to enhance their effectiveness.
9C. The school seeks and values family and community involvement.	**9C1. Diversity of involvement**	Family involvement does not reflect the broad diversity of the community.	Family involvement reflects the broad diversity of the community.	Family and community involvement reflects the broad diversity of the community.
	9C2. Interactions between families and staff members	Some interactions between families and staff members are brusque or discourteous.	Families and school staff members interact positively and respectfully.	Students have frequent opportunities to see families and school staff members interact positively and respectfully.
9D. The school engages families and the community to support student learning.	**9D1. Connection between family involvement activities and student learning**	Family involvement activities are not explicitly linked to student learning.	Family involvement activities are connected to student learning.	Family and community involvement activities are directly linked to the curriculum and student learning.
	9D2. Parent and community involvement in the classroom	Parents and community members are not regularly involved in classroom activities.	Parents and community members are present and involved in classroom activities.	Parents and community members receive training to help them be effective in activities that support learning, such as tutoring.

Characteristic	Trait	Effectiveness Continuum		
		Low Performing	Effective	High Performing
9D (continued)	9D3. Support for parents' efforts to help their children at home	The school does not provide sufficient information about what their children are learning and how to help them with schoolwork at home.	The school provides information to parents about what their children are learning and how to help them with schoolwork at home.	Frequent, regularly scheduled workshops inform parents about what their children are learning and how to help them with schoolwork at home.
	9D4. School support for family discussions of career and life goals	The school does not encourage families to talk to their children about career and life goals or does not provide adequate information to help all parents to do so.	The school provides information to help families talk to their children about life goals and the importance of education in reaching those goals.	The school has an effective outreach program to help families talk to their children about career and life goals and the importance of education in reaching those goals.
9E. School administrators cultivate shared responsibility for decision-making among families and within the community.	9E1. Extent of shared decision-making	Families are not actively involved in school decision-making.	School administrators ensure family involvement in school decision-making.	School administrators routinely involve families and the community in school decision-making.

Effectiveness Indicator 10: District Support

Characteristic	Trait	Effectiveness Continuum		
		Low Performing	Effective	High Performing
10A. The roles and responsibilities of the board, the district, and the schools are clear and communicated to stakeholders.	10A1. Delineation of roles and responsibilities	The roles and responsibilities of the board, the district, and the schools are not clearly delineated.	The roles and responsibilities of the board, the district, and the schools are clearly delineated.	The roles and responsibilities of the board, the district, and the schools are clearly delineated, and processes are in place to evaluate the effectiveness of those divisions.

Characteristic	Trait	Effectiveness Continuum		
		Low Performing	Effective	High Performing
10A (continued)	**10A2. Communication regarding roles and responsibilities**	There is limited formalized communication describing the roles and responsibilities of the board, the district, and the schools.	The roles and responsibilities of the board, the district, and the schools are clearly communicated to stakeholders.	The roles and responsibilities of the board, the district, and the schools are clearly communicated to stakeholders. Published documents illustrate areas of sole, shared, limited, and advisory responsibility and authority.
10B. The board's, district's, and schools' goals, policies, and resource allocations are aligned and focus on student learning.	**10B1. Alignment and focus of goals**	The board's, district's, and schools' goals are not aligned or do not focus on student learning.	The board's, district's, and schools' goals and policies are aligned and focus on student learning.	The board's, district's, and schools' goals and policies are aligned, focus on student learning, and remain stable over time.
	10B2. Allocation of resources	The board's, district's, and schools' resource allocations do not support a focus on student learning.	The board's, district's, and schools' resource allocations support a focus on student learning.	The board's, district's, and schools' resource allocations fund student learning before all other priorities.
10C. The district oversees the development and implementation of curriculum, instruction, and assessment districtwide.	**10C1. Responsibility for developing and implementing curriculum and assessment**	Responsibility for the development and implementation of curriculum and assessment is school-based.	The district leads the development and implementation of curriculum and assessment districtwide.	The district leads the development and implementation of curriculum and assessment districtwide. Curriculum and assessments are reviewed cyclically, ensuring that at least one subject is reviewed each year.

Characteristic	Trait	Effectiveness Continuum		
		Low Performing	Effective	High Performing
10C (continued)	10C2. Responsibility for supporting research-based instructional strategies	Responsibility for the support of research-based instructional strategies is school-based.	The district articulates expectations for and leads the dissemination of research-based instructional strategies.	The district articulates expectations for and leads the dissemination of, and professional development in, research-based instructional strategies.
10D. The board's and district's policies and actions reflect the expectation that all children in the district will be engaged in high-quality instruction and assessment.	10D1. Board and district expectations for instruction and assessment	The board's and district's policies and actions are inconsistent with the expectation that all children will be engaged in high-quality instruction and assessment.	The board's and district's policies and actions emphasize the expectation that all children will be engaged in high-quality instruction and assessment.	The board's and district's policies and actions emphasize the expectation that all children will be engaged in high-quality instruction and assessment. Data on progress toward meeting this expectation are reported to the community annually.
10E. The board's and district's actions reflect high expectations of staff members.	10E1. Board and district expectations of staff members	The board or district does not, or does not always, demonstrate high expectations of staff members.	The board and district demonstrate high expectations of staff members.	The board and district demonstrate high expectations of staff members and publicly recognize those whose efforts have substantially contributed to the attainment of district goals.

Characteristic	Trait	Effectiveness Continuum		
		Low Performing	Effective	High Performing
10F. The board and district use data to monitor school and student performance and intervene if school performance lags.	10F1. District use of data to monitor performance	The district uses a limited variety of data to monitor school and student performance.	The district uses a wide variety of student data to monitor school and student performance.	The district uses a wide variety of student data to monitor school and student performance and provides these data to its schools and teachers in an easily understood and manageable format.
	10F2. Accountability for student performance	The district delegates accountability for student performance to school-level leadership.	If school performance begins to lag, the district intervenes, providing additional resources.	If school performance begins to lag, the district intervenes, providing additional resources, including professional development for leaders and staff members in interpreting and using data in decision-making.

Oral Exit Report Agenda

1. Thank teachers for participation and hospitality.

2. Recognize the staff and leadership for their help and openness to the visit.

3. Recognize the site coordinator.

4. Report numbers of:

   - Surveys

   - Interviews

   - Observations

   - Student focus groups

5. Report on:

   - Student work collection

   - Family and community meeting

   - Documents reviewed

6. Identify emerging strengths.

7. Identify emerging challenges.

8. Share next steps for review team.

9. Announce date and time for the final report workshop.

10. Distribute On-Site School Review Evaluation forms [Tool 48].

11. Question/answer session

Sample Final Report

The on-site school review provides a school with an in-depth analysis of areas strongly tied to increasing student learning and achievement. The review team extends its appreciation to Harrison School District and Harrison Middle School (pseudonyms) administrators, staff members, students, and parents for the opportunity to work together on this on-site school review, which took place January 13–16, 2009.

Section I: The Process

Effectiveness Indicators

The heart of the school review process is the Effectiveness Indicators. These research-based indicators provide the organizational structure for the review. In addition to being used for more than 5 years in on-site reviews of schools at all grade levels, these indicators have recently been re-validated and updated based on a synthesis of current research (see *The High-Performing School: Benchmarking the 10 Indicators of Effectiveness,* 2009, for this research).

The effectiveness indicators that Harrison Middle School (HMS) selected to be reviewed were:

- Effectiveness Indicator 1: Written Curriculum

- Effectiveness Indicator 2: Instructional Program

- Effectiveness Indicator 3: Student Assessment

- Effectiveness Indicator 4: School Leadership

- Effectiveness Indicator 5: Strategic Planning

- Effectiveness Indicator 7: Student Connectedness, Engagement, and Readiness

- Effectiveness Indicator 8: School Environment

Tools and Processes

The effectiveness indicators are used to compare current school performance to that which is found in effective schools. Each effectiveness indicator is broken down into components called "characteristics" and "traits." To determine where on the effectiveness continuum a school is currently performing, the review team collects evidence from various sources, including surveys, documents, and observations conducted during the on-site review. The different sources yield information about different characteristics and traits of the effectiveness indicators. For example, each question on a survey is tied to a specific trait.

Document Review

Documents from which data were drawn include:

- School strategic plan

- State assessment data

- STAR mathematics data

- Read 180 data

- Accelerated Reader reports

- Textbooks and supplemental materials

- Discipline data and forms

- Student handbooks

- Newsletters

- Healthy Youth Survey

Student Work

Student work provides valuable insights into the school's instructional program. Teachers were asked to collect all student work from their classes for a 2-week period. As part of the on-site review, this work was analyzed to determine its level of cognitive demand and its rigor in relation to state standards. Work was received from 18 teachers in the following content areas/classes: language arts, science, social studies, mathematics, art, home economics, physical education, skills for adolescents, and computers.

The Visit

Central to the school review is the time the review team spends at the school site. At HMS, three team members spent 3 full days on-site and 1 additional day while writing the final report. The team has an extensive background in curriculum, instruction, pedagogy, and professional development, coupled with a deep knowledge of the effectiveness indicators and on-site review processes.

During the on-site portion of the review, the review team:

- Collected and analyzed surveys from:

  - Eleven (11) classified staff members

  - Thirteen (13) parents

  - Twenty-three (23) teachers/administrators

  - Two hundred ninety-nine (299) students

- Conducted structured interviews with:

  - Twenty-six (26) teachers, administrators, and classified staff members

  - Forty-three (43) students during classroom observations

  - The district superintendent

- Conducted 22 classroom observations, allowing a member of the review team to be present for at least one class taught by every teacher at HMS, including 10 full-period observations in language arts

- Met with 24 students in two focus groups

- Held three evening parent focus groups attended by 27 parents, including 6 parents whose primary language was Spanish

Section II: What We Found

The findings from our review are organized as follows:

Highlights From the Data: In this section, highlights from state assessments are displayed, and highlights from student work are discussed. The data packet that accompanies this report includes the detailed information from which the highlights were drawn.

Mapping of Effectiveness Indicators: Based on our analyses of assessment data, survey data, and student work, as well as information drawn from interviews, reviews of documents, and classroom observations, we determined the school's position on the effectiveness continuum for each trait. This process is referred to as "mapping" the effectiveness indicators. Examples, evidence, and comments help in understanding these placements.

Highlights of State Assessment Data

The detailed analysis of state assessment data from which these highlights are drawn is included as Section I of the data packet that accompanies this report. Below are highlights from the 2007–08 state assessment results:

- Both seventh- and eighth-grade students achieved below the state average in reading, writing, and mathematics.

- The percentage of eighth-grade students meeting standards in science was above the statewide average.

- HMS low-income students were meeting standards in all areas at lower rates than that of low-income students statewide.

- There was a wide gap between the percentage of HMS low-income students meeting standards and their HMS higher-income peers.

- Hispanic students were experiencing a persistent and widening achievement gap in mathematics and reading but had made gains in writing and science.

Highlights of Student Work Analysis

Prior to the visit, all teachers were asked to collect and score student work from every class for 2 weeks. Student work was received from 18 teachers. A total of 91 unique assignments were reviewed. A "unique assignment" is one that is given in one or more classes. Thus an identical assignment given in three classes counts as a single unique assignment. The detailed analysis of the student work from which the following highlights are drawn is included as Section II of the data packet that accompanies this report.

- Ninety-one (91) unique assignments were reviewed:

  - Forty-six (46) from grade 7

  - Thirty-two (32) from grade 8

  - Three (3) from combined grade levels

  - Ten (10) for which the grade level was not specified (reviewed as grade 7)

- The cognitive demand of each assignment was determined based on Bloom's Taxonomy. Of the 91 assignments, 5 were targeted to higher-level thinking skills, and 86 were targeted to lower-level thinking skills:

  - One (1) assignment was at the evaluation level.

  - Four (4) assignments were at the analysis level.

  - No assignment was at the synthesis level.

- Twenty-seven (27) assignments were at the application level.

- Fifteen (15) assignments were at the comprehension level.

- Forty-four (44) assignments were at the recall level.

- The rigor of each assignment was calculated based on the degree of academic challenge present in the assignment in relation to grade-level expectations:

  - Four (4) assignments were higher than the state standard/benchmark.

  - Thirty (30) assignments matched the state standard/benchmark.

  - Fifty-seven (57) assignments were below the state standard/benchmark.

Mapping of Effectiveness Indicators and Commentary

(Note: This sample includes only Effectiveness Indicator 4.)

The review team uses rubrics to assess the school's performance on each of the effectiveness indicators. Each indicator is broken down into the components most closely associated with increased student performance, which are referred to as "characteristics." Each characteristic is further broken down into "traits."

Based on effective schools research, the rubrics display a continuum of school effectiveness and describe each trait as it would appear at three different points along that continuum. The review team shades the box containing the trait description that most closely matches current practice at the school. A shaded box in the middle ("effective") column of the effectiveness continuum indicates that observed school practices are in line with practices found in schools in which nearly all students are meeting state standards. A shaded box in the left-hand ("low-performing") column indicates that the school's practices—many of which in the past might have been acceptable—will not result in the increases in student learning that would be necessary for nearly all students to reach standards. A shaded box in the right-hand ("high-performing") column indicates that the school's practices correspond to those found in schools that are the most effective learning environments.

To determine which box on the continuum would be shaded, we collected evidence of the school's performance from various sources. Every characteristic and trait is linked to specific sources of evidence that will yield information about it: questions asked in surveys, focus groups, and interviews; our review of student work; our analysis of documents; and observations conducted during the on-site review. We collected evidence by the following methods:

- Teacher interviews

- Guidance counselor interviews

- School administrator interviews

- District administrator interviews

- Student interviews

- Teacher surveys

- Classified staff surveys

- Parent surveys

- Student surveys

- Classified staff focus groups

- Parent/community focus group

- Student focus groups

- Classroom observations

- Analysis of student work

- Review of documents

Mapping of Effectiveness Indicator 4: School Leadership

School leadership exerts a powerful influence on student learning. Recognizing student learning as the foremost priority of the school and its teachers, school leaders ensure that a culture of high expectations nurtures student and teacher efficacy. School leaders maximize their influence by increasing leadership capacity schoolwide and widely distributing leadership responsibilities. Effective leaders model the characteristics they expect of staff members and students, including optimism, fairness, respect, collaboration, and an openness to constructive feedback. They are learners themselves who recognize and acknowledge staff expertise. They provide the foundation upon which school improvement is built, including the provision of adequate resources.

Table 1 presents the mapped (shaded) rubric for Effectiveness Indicator 4. The shaded boxes indicate our evaluation of the school's performance on each trait.

Table 1: Mapped Rubric for Effectiveness Indicator 4: School Leadership

Characteristic	Trait	Effectiveness Continuum		
		Low Performing	Effective	High Performing
4A. School administrators provide leadership in strategic planning.	4A1. Development of strategic plan	The school lacks a current strategic plan, or the plan was developed without significant staff input.	The school has a current strategic plan that was developed with significant staff participation.	The school has a current strategic plan that was developed by school leadership and staff members and approved by district leadership or the school board.
	4A2. Focus of strategic plan	The school lacks a strategic plan, or the plan is not focused on student learning.	The school strategic plan is focused on student learning.	The school strategic plan is focused on student learning and includes disaggregated student achievement data and analysis supporting the goals and action plans.

Characteristic	Trait	Effectiveness Continuum		
		Low Performing	Effective	High Performing
4A (continued)	**4A3. Relationship of strategic plan to decision-making**	School decisions are made without regard to the strategic plan.	The strategic plan guides school decision-making.	The strategic plan is the pivotal factor in school decision-making.
	4A4. Responsibility for strategic plan	School administrators do not take responsibility for implementing the strategic plan.	School administrators take personal responsibility for the strategic plan.	School administrators take personal responsibility for the strategic plan and lead its implementation.
4B. School administrators create a culture of high expectations for student and adult success and support those beliefs schoolwide.	**4B1. Expectations for students**	School administrators do not have high expectations for the success of all students.	School administrators have high expectations for the success of all students.	School administrators have high expectations for student success and consistently reinforce that belief in interactions with students, staff members, and parents.
	4B2. Expectations for staff members	School administrators do not have high expectations for the success of all staff members.	School administrators have high expectations for the success of all staff members.	School administrators have high expectations for the success of all staff members and consistently reinforce that message in interactions with staff members, students, parents, and the community.
4C. School administrators see student learning as the foremost priority for the school.	**4C1. Priority assigned to student learning**	School administrators do not see student learning as the highest priority in decision-making.	School administrators see student learning as the highest priority in all decision-making.	School administrators see student learning as the highest priority in all decision-making.

Characteristic	Trait	Effectiveness Continuum		
		Low Performing	Effective	High Performing
4D. School administrators ensure that adequate resources are allocated to achieve school improvement goals.	**4D1. Sufficiency of resources for school improvement**	School administrators have not ensured that sufficient resources have been allocated to support school improvement goals.	School administrators ensure that sufficient resources are allocated to support school improvement goals.	School administrators ensure that sufficient resources are allocated to support school improvement goals.
4E. School leadership is distributed schoolwide.	**4E1. Sharing of leadership**	School leadership is restricted to those in administrative positions.	School leadership is shared among staff members based on knowledge, skills, and interests.	School leadership is widely shared among staff members based on knowledge, skills, and interests. There is formalized acknowledgment of staff members' leadership roles.
4F. School administrators recognize staff members' accomplishments, expertise, and leadership potential.	**4F1. Recognition of staff accomplishments**	Staff accomplishments receive little or no recognition.	School administrators informally recognize and acknowledge staff accomplishments.	School administrators formally and informally recognize staff members' individual and group accomplishments.
	4F2. Recognition and utilization of staff members' expertise	No processes exist to identify or utilize staff members' expertise.	School administrators identify and utilize internal staff members' expertise.	School administrators identify and utilize internal staff members' expertise and ensure that professional development is targeted to continue to build these internal resources.

Characteristic	Trait	Effectiveness Continuum		
		Low Performing	Effective	High Performing
4F (continued)	4F3. Professional development for staff leadership	Staff members with an interest in leadership roles pursue that interest without school or district assistance.	Staff members are encouraged to seek professional development to build their leadership capacities.	A formal professional development program exists to identify and prepare staff members for shared leadership opportunities and to provide them with ongoing support.
4G. School administrators encourage and promote collaborative relationships.	4G1. Provision of opportunities to collaborate	Opportunities for staff members to communicate, plan, and work with one another are limited, informal, and self-organized or primarily occur outside of the school day.	School administrators ensure that there are ample organized opportunities for staff members to communicate, plan, and work with one another.	The school calendar provides specific and frequent opportunities for grade-level, content-area, and other team meetings. Contract hours provide paraprofessionals with the opportunity and responsibility to participate as appropriate.
	4G2. Focus of collaborative efforts	Collaborative efforts are not focused on student learning.	School administrators ensure that collaborative efforts are focused on student learning.	School administrators ensure that collaborative efforts are focused on student learning, and instructional teams document and communicate strategies and results.
4H. School administrators address existing and potential conflicts.	4H1. Efforts to resolve conflicts	School administrators do not or do not always address staff conflicts.	When conflicts arise, school administrators work toward resolution.	School administrators work toward resolution of conflicts, addressing both the immediate concerns and the underlying issues.

Characteristic	Trait	Effectiveness Continuum		
		Low Performing	Effective	High Performing
4H (continued)	4H2. Anticipation of conflicts	School administrators do not always notice or acknowledge issues that have the potential to cause conflict.	School administrators anticipate where and when conflicts might arise and address issues before they rise to the level of a problem.	School administrators anticipate where and when conflicts, including workplace or community dissatisfaction, might arise and intervene to address both the problems and the underlying issues.
4I. School administrators are accessible and model optimism, integrity, fairness, and respect.	4I1. Accessibility of administrators to staff members	It is sometimes or usually difficult to meet with school administrators.	School administrators are accessible to staff members.	School administrators set aside time during each day to meet with staff members.
	4I2. Interactions with staff members, students, and community members	Some staff members, students, and community members do not think that interactions with school administrators are characterized by integrity and fairness.	Staff members, students, and community members believe that interactions with school administrators are characterized by integrity and fairness.	School administrators consistently display integrity and fairness in interactions with staff members, students, and the community and have built a culture of trust schoolwide.
	4I3. Attitudes about reaching goals	Some school administrators are not optimistic that agreed-upon goals can be reached, given the current conditions.	School administrators manifest optimism that staff members and students can and will reach agreed-upon goals.	School administrators ensure that agreed-upon goals are within reach and set a consistent tone of optimism and confidence that the goals can and will be met.
	4I4. Attitudes toward staff members, students, and the community	Staff members, students, and the community do not always feel valued and respected by school administrators.	Staff members, students, and the community feel valued and respected by school administrators.	Staff members, students, and the community feel welcome at the school and valued and respected by school administrators.

Characteristic	Trait	Effectiveness Continuum		
		Low Performing	Effective	High Performing
4J. School administrators are adaptable and encourage innovation.	**4J1. Knowledge of current educational research**	School administrators do not keep current on educational research and instructional theory and practice.	School administrators keep current on educational research and instructional theory and practice.	School administrators keep current on educational research and instructional theory and practice, and they routinely share and discuss best practices with staff members.
	4J2. Adaptability to changing circumstances	School administrators resist responding to changing circumstances or respond slowly.	School administrators adapt to changing circumstances.	School administrators anticipate changing circumstances, adapt to meet changing needs, and provide leadership in implementing change efforts.
	4J3. Attitude toward new ideas	School administrators do not always encourage new and innovative ideas.	School administrators encourage new and innovative ideas from staff members.	School administrators encourage new and innovative ideas from staff members and all stakeholders.
4K. School administrators ensure that teachers receive constructive feedback through periodic observation, coaching, and lesson study.	**4K1. Administrator observation and feedback**	School administrators occasionally observe teachers informally and provide constructive feedback.	School administrators frequently observe every teacher informally and provide constructive feedback focused on student learning.	School administrators frequently observe every teacher and instructional paraprofessional informally and provide constructive feedback focused on student learning.

Characteristic	Trait	Effectiveness Continuum		
		Low Performing	Effective	High Performing
4K (continued)	4K2. Support for peer observation, coaching, and lesson study	School administrators give informal support to peer observation, coaching, and lesson study but do not always provide sufficient release time.	Adequate release time is provided for all instructional staff members to participate in frequent, well-planned peer observation, coaching, and lesson study.	Adequate release time is built into the school calendar for all instructional staff members to participate in frequent, well-planned peer observation, coaching, and lesson study.
	4K3. Peer observation and feedback	Teachers observe and are observed by peers infrequently or not at all.	Each teacher frequently observes and is observed by peers and engages in a structured process of feedback.	Each teacher and instructional paraprofessional frequently observes and is observed by peers and engages in a structured process of feedback.
4L. School administrators provide formal staff evaluations.	4L1. Quality of staff evaluations	School administrators sometimes do not conduct staff evaluations on a timely basis or do not include all components of the evaluation as prescribed by state law and district policy.	School administrators conduct staff evaluations on a timely basis as prescribed by state law and district policy.	School administrators conduct staff evaluations on a timely basis as prescribed by state law and district policy. The evaluations address school improvement goals, professional development, and student learning.

Effectiveness Indicator 4: School Leadership—Evidence and Commentary

The review team found that school leaders had just begun to work with the staff on developing a strategic plan. There was, as yet, no written plan. A comprehensive District Improvement Plan has been written, which included goals for HMS. However, responses to our question "What are the schoolwide improvement goals?" varied widely. Some staff members thought the goals were about reading and literacy, some thought they were about science, and some thought they were about math. Many thought the goal was to be respectful, responsible, and safe, but no one came up with the HMS improvement goals contained in the district plan. It would benefit the staff members, students, and community to have a collaboratively developed school strategic plan that includes a comprehensive data analysis; agreed-upon, well-communicated, and measurable goals; and an implementation plan, including an ongoing evaluation plan. (See recommendation #1.)

There are clear and shared high expectations for student and adult success among teachers, administrators, and staff members of HMS. This belief translates into every interaction we observed both in and out of class. HMS is a positive environment in which teachers acknowledge their responsibility for student learning. At HMS, 100% of teachers and 90% of classified staff members surveyed agreed with the statement "School administrators believe all students can do well in school." This was echoed by students, 72% of whom agreed with the statement "The principal believes I can do well in school." Eighty-nine percent (89%) of parents agreed with the statement "School administrators believe that my child can do well in school." In the comments section of the survey, one parent wrote, "We love the school's administration team and their firm, loving approach with the students—refreshing and rare." Another parent wrote:

> As a parent, it is our responsibility to train our children to be good students and model citizens in our community. We are thankful to say that Harrison MS has been thus far very instrumental and a positive influence in helping us achieve this goal. I applaud the principal for his interest in the students, not just by word but by deed. The teachers and staff also need to be commended—for on a daily basis they build up our children. Our society today presents many challenges for many, especially our young people. I just want to take the opportunity now to thank the teachers, the staff, and administrators for doing their part in providing a positive educational experience for my children.

As can be seen from the placements on the effectiveness continuum in Table 1, HMS excels in many areas of leadership, and one of the ways this is demonstrated is through a consistent focus on student learning. This is evidenced by the comments of one staff member who said, "The principal is unconditionally supportive of students; he knows every student by name." Eighty-five percent (85%) of teachers and 80% of classified staff members surveyed agreed with the statement "School administrators see student learning as the number-one priority for the school."

Another area in which HMS leadership is highly effective is in ensuring that sufficient resources are allocated to instruction. It was common to hear teachers say, "The superintendent asks if there is anything I need in order to be an effective teacher, and then I get what I ask for." Several teachers said that there is nothing that they need that they don't have. Considering the economic constraints public education has faced over the last several years, this is strong evidence of an unusually high degree of district support for the HMS instructional program.

As indicated on surveys and in focus groups, teachers (100%), classified staff members (90%), and parents (84%) agreed that the principal has high expectations of staff members. In surveys, 85% of teachers and 100% of classified staff members also agreed with the statement "School administrators convey a sense of confidence in the knowledge and skills of our staff members." Parents echoed this belief.

Conflict can derail improvement efforts. Seventy-five percent (75%) of certificated staff members and 80% of classified staff members agreed with the statement "School administrators work to resolve conflicts between staff members." Eighty percent (80%) of teachers and 70% of classified staff members agreed with the statement "School administrators defuse negative situations before they get out of hand."

Shared leadership is foundational to effective schools. In interviews and focus groups, teachers commented that the principal looked "for ways to involve staff members in leadership roles," and that there were opportunities for both teachers and classified staff members to "take on leadership responsibilities." Classified staff members commented that they wished there were a way for them to take on more leadership responsibility. Noninstructional classified staff members felt that there was untapped potential among them in areas from safety issues to helping disengaged students reconnect with the school.

Staff members acknowledged the efforts of the principal to be available when needed. In surveys, 85% of certificated staff reported that the principal was accessible to staff.

Collaborative efforts in school improvement require integrity and trust among staff members and administrators. At HMS, 95% of teachers and 90% of classified staff members surveyed indicated that they believed that the principal and superintendent "demonstrate integrity and fairness in their dealings with staff members."

The area of administrative support for peer observation, coaching, and lesson study was perceived less favorably. Only 15% of teachers agreed with the statement "Adequate release time is provided for me to participate in frequent, well-planned peer observation, coaching, and lesson study."

Section III: Conclusions and Recommendations

In this section, we identify the school's strengths and offer our recommendations. The recommendations focus on actions that have the promise to result in the greatest gains in student learning and achievement or that will need to be in place before other improvement efforts can be successfully undertaken.

Prior to the on-site portion of the review, the review team analyzed student achievement data and other documents. Following the 3-day on-site portion of the review, the team sifted through the data, reviewed evidence from interviews and observations, and followed up on data collection in the preparation of this report.

The meticulous evidence-gathering and -corroboration processes give us confidence in the validity of both the findings we reported in the previous section and the conclusions and recommendations we will offer in this section. We have made three recommendations for implementation by HMS and one recommendation for implementation by the Harrison School District.

(Note: The strengths and recommendations are derived from the full report on HMS, in which Effectiveness Indicators 1–5 and 7–8 were reviewed.)

Strengths Identified at Harrison Middle School

- Mathematics, reading, and science scores have improved over the last 3 years.
- The faculty genuinely cares about the kids.
- Faculty members trust one another and trust the school and district administration.
- Staff members appreciate and respect the community, and the parents respect and support the school, the teachers, and the administration.
- Administrators, faculty, and staff clearly believe that all students can learn to high levels.
- Students at HMS believe that the teachers care about them both as students and as individuals.
- Classified staff members perform at high levels. They are part of the team in every way.
- Administrators at HMS are supported by staff members, and staff members believe that HMS administrators empower and support them.
- The school provides double-dosing in mathematics and language arts for struggling students.
- Students know how to access extra help from teachers when they need it and feel teachers go out of their way to help them.
- A variety of programs are available to assist students needing additional help with schoolwork.
- The school provides a "tutoring bus" that makes it possible for students who take the bus to school to take advantage of the early-release Friday session.

- The school offers extracurricular programs, particularly sports, that provide a positive venue for kids.

- The building is open for children from 7:00 a.m. to 7:00 p.m. every day.

- Building-wide interruptions during instructional time are very rare.

- The building is well-kept and reflects pride of ownership.

Recommendations for Harrison Middle School

1. Design and implement a school strategic plan that is focused on student learning and includes the following components:

   - Review and analysis of student achievement and demographic data

   - Research-driven process of identifying problems and solutions

   - Communication with stakeholders in the decision-making process

   - An action plan describing the specific steps to be taken toward attainment of plan goals

   - Progress monitoring and adjustments when appropriate

2. Develop a research-based, integrated English/language arts program that includes the following components:

   - Direct and systematic instruction in reading for every emerging reader and nonreader

   - Professional development for all English/language arts, reading, and writing teachers in explicit and systematic instruction in reading. This includes instruction in phonemic awareness, phonics, fluency, guided oral reading, independent silent reading, vocabulary, and comprehension.

   - A communication plan to ensure that data on the reading level of every student are conveyed to all teachers and that every teacher has received the professional development necessary to use that information to differentiate instruction

   - Continuation of the double-period daily instruction in reading for those students whose reading levels are lagging behind expected levels

   - Selection and implementation of research-based intervention and enrichment reading programs

   - A procedure for determining which students should enter the intervention programs and when they should exit the program

   - Training for staff in the intervention and enrichment programs, including the use of diagnostic assessments to ensure student reading levels are increasing at expected rates

3. Redesign the student discipline system with a laserlike focus on providing an environment that is conducive to student learning. Make sure that the following conditions are in place:

   - The school discipline and behavior management system supports teaching and learning schoolwide.

   - The school discipline and behavior management system ensures the safety of staff and students.

   - School leaders take responsibility for dealing with serious infractions, and they hold teachers responsible for handling routine classroom discipline problems.

- There are high expectations for appropriate student behavior.

- The school discipline system minimizes the loss of instructional time.

- Teachers and administrators consistently cooperate in reporting and follow-through on student misconduct.

Recommendation for Harrison School District

1. Develop a research-based, K–12 coordinated grade-level curriculum that will provide the instructional program necessary to ensure academic growth and success for all students. Make sure that the following components are in place:

   - There is a written curriculum for each subject.

   - There is vertical alignment between grade levels, and there is a logical skills and process flow.

   - The written curriculum includes guidelines for instructional pacing.

   - The written curriculum is aligned to textbooks and other instructional materials.

   - The written curriculum identifies shared formal and informal assessments.

   - The written curriculum identifies enrichment and intervention materials.

   - There is a process to ensure that the written curriculum is the taught and tested curriculum.

Acknowledgments

The members of the review team extend their sincere thanks to the district administrators and the administrators, faculty, staff, students, and parents at Harrison Middle School for generously giving of their time to answer our sometimes difficult questions; graciously inviting us into their offices and classrooms; and cheerfully attending meetings, completing surveys, and collecting and providing student work for our review. This report owes its quality and usefulness to their support of the process and their assistance.

Tool 51

Final Report Workshop Agenda

Note: This example is based on a workshop with 40 participants discussing a review for which nine effectiveness indicators were selected. Ideally, this workshop is scheduled for 6 hours.

1. **Team leader delivers overview of report**

2. **Form five small groups of eight each** *(One group is assigned the "Conclusions and Recommendations" section of the report and one effectiveness indicator. The other four groups are assigned two effectiveness indicators each.)*

   Small-group instructions:

   - Describe the effectiveness indicator.

   - Describe the characteristics.

   - Describe the written commentary.

   - Report out to large group and facilitate discussion.

3. **Small groups review components of the data packet**

   Group 1. State Assessment Data Highlights

   - All students

   - Low-income students

   Group 2. State Assessment Data Highlights

   - Disaggregated by ethnicity

   - Disaggregated by program

   Group 3. Comparable Schools Data

   - Comparable criteria

   - Identification of comparison schools

   - Student achievement data

   Group 4. Survey Data

   - Teacher/administrator survey

   - Classified staff survey

   - Student survey

   - Parent survey

   Group 5. Student Work Analysis

   - Taxonomic analysis: cognitive demand

   - Level of rigor

   - Results

   - Summarize as a small group.

- Report out to large group.

4. **Large-group discussion**

   - Do the recommendations support the research and the data?

   - Should the recommendations be revised in any way?

   - Prioritize the recommendations by those that can be addressed immediately and those that need to wait for the appropriate timing.

5. **Action planning: Participants select the recommendation in which they are most interested and regroup** *(one small group for each recommendation)*.

   Discuss the recommendation:

   - Does it accurately capture an essential need at our school?

   - Should bullets (actions) be added or removed?

   - Brainstorm: How could we implement the recommendation?

   - What resources are needed outside of current resources?

   - Report out to large group and facilitate discussion.

6. **Next steps**

   - Set next meeting or action.

   - Think-pair-share: What is your take-away from today's session?

   - Professional development evaluation [Tool 52]

Thank you!

Tool 56

Strategic Planning Workshop Agenda

(6-hour time block)

Note: If the total staff is fewer than 20, then regroup the discussion sets into fewer sets with more questions.

1. **Gearing up** (30 minutes)

   - Review agenda for the day

   - Review notes and recommendations from final report workshop

   - Questions/clarifications

   - Overview of teamwork [Tool 54] and facilitation models [Tool 55] (*handouts*)

2. **Small-group planning** (30 minutes)

   Break into five groups *(each group will facilitate one Discussion Set [detailed under items 3, 5, and 7] with the large group)*

   Small-group instructions:

   - Think about the questions assigned to your team for facilitation.

   - Using the facilitation models described earlier or another model, develop a plan to best elicit answers to your Discussion Set from the whole staff. The plan must ensure that:

     - Every person/small group has an opportunity and is expected to add comments and ideas to the discussion.

     - As part of the activity, the responses are collected and sorted, and some consensus ideas emerge.

     - The consensus ideas are captured on paper.

     - The process is completed within the times listed on the agenda.

     - Lingering issues are captured on a parking lot for future consideration.

3. **Large group reconvenes for Discussion Sets**

   Discussion Set 1: Achievement Gaps (45 minutes)

   - Are all students learning to their highest levels?

   - Which groups of students are not achieving?

   - What could we do differently to help those students achieve at higher levels?

   - What will we need?

   Discussion Set 2: Expectations for Academic Rigor (45 minutes)

   - Should we have common expectations for all student work in terms of academic rigor?

   - How can we determine what that level should be?

   - What collaborative processes are in place now in terms of common expectations?

   - What collaborative processes need to be in place?

4. **Lunch**

5. **Large group reconvenes to continue Discussion Sets**

   Discussion Set 3: Student Engagement (45 minutes)

   - How do we engage all students in their own learning?

   - What specific strategies are we currently using that are working?

   - What strategies could we add to our repertoire?

   Discussion Set 4: Interventions and Enrichment (45 minutes)

   - How do we respond when a student struggles with learning?

   - What systems (both recommended and required) are in place for struggling students?

   - What do we have in place for a student who has met expectations and is ready for enrichment?

   - What systems (both recommended and required) are in place for enrichment?

6. **Break**

7. **Large group reconvenes for final Discussion Set**

   Discussion Set 5: Wrap-up (45 minutes)

   - Review what we have identified as future needs.

   - Have we missed anything today (parked issues)?

   - What can we give up to make time to work on these areas?

   - What were the themes that emerged today?

8. **Next steps** (15 minutes)

   - Set next meeting or action.

   - Think-pair-share: What is your take-away from today's session?

   - Professional development evaluation [Tool 52]

Thank you!

Designing School Strategic Plan Workshop Agenda

(3-hour time block)

Notes: (1) Request participants to bring their materials from the final report workshop and strategic planning workshop. (2) List the recommendations carried over from the final report workshop on poster paper.

1. **Large-group selection of school improvement goals** (30 minutes)

   - Based on the final report workshop, which recommendations should be included as goals in the next school strategic plan? (Note that these may not all be accomplished in just one year.)

   - Identify why these goals are the most important (review notes from two previous workshops).

   - Using three dots (three votes) each, indicate on the poster paper which recommendations you individually believe should form the foundation of the new school strategic plan.

2. **Small-group design of action plans (implementation strategies)** (1 hour, 30 minutes)

   - Divide into the number of groups that equal the number of school improvement goals.

   - Join the group working on the goal that interests you most.

   - Using the Action-Planning Template [Tool 57], brainstorm how our school might reach these goals:

     - What actions need to be completed?

     - What evidence indicates the actions have worked in similar schools?

     - What steps are necessary to carry out each action?

     - When will each step begin and end?

     - Who will be responsible for each step and in what way?

     - What existing resources (including time and professional development) are available?

     - What additional resources (including time and professional development) are necessary?

     - How will we evaluate/measure our success?

     - Who will be responsible for and who will be involved in the evaluation of progress toward the goals?

3. **Large-group share-out** (30 minutes)

   - Small groups present their action plans to whole staff.

   - Invite additional comments and add to plans.

4. **Next steps** (30 minutes)

   - Ensure that every staff member is part of a group and has a role.

   - Determine communication process and schedule.

   - Think-pair-share: What is your take-away from today's session?

   - Professional development evaluation [Tool 52]

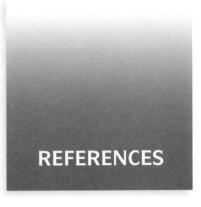

REFERENCES

Abdal-Haqq, I. (1996). *Making time for teacher professional development: ERIC Digest.* Washington, DC: ERIC Clearinghouse on Teaching and Teacher Education. (ERIC Document Reproduction Service No. ED400259). Accessed at www.ericdigests.org/1997–2/time.htm on August 11, 2008.

Achieve, Inc. (2009). *Closing the expectations gap.* Washington, DC: Author.

Alliance for Nonprofit Management. (n.d.). *Frequently asked questions: Strategic planning.* Washington, DC: Author. Accessed at www.allianceonline.org/FAQ/strategic_planning on August 11, 2008.

Allington, R. (2005). Urgency and instructional time. *Reading Today, 23*(1), 17.

American Academy of Family Physicians. (2009). *Cultural proficiency (definition).* Accessed at www.aafp.org/online/en/home/clinical/publichealth/culturalprof/cultprofdef.html on February 20, 2009.

American Educational Research Association. (2004). Closing the gap: High achievement for students of color. *Essential Information for Education Policy, 2*(3), 1–4.

Appalachia Educational Laboratory at Edvantia. (2005a). *Research brief: Aligned curriculum and student achievement.* Charleston, WV: Edvantia, Inc.

Appalachia Educational Laboratory at Edvantia. (2005b). *Research digest: Effective instructional strategies.* Charleston, WV: Edvantia, Inc.

Arizona Department of Education. (2008). *School report cards.* Accessed at www10.ade.az.gov/reportcard on August 11, 2008.

Aron, L. Y. (2003). *Towards a topology of alternative education programs: A compilation of elements from the literature.* Washington, DC: Urban Institute. Accessed at www.urban.org/UploadedPDF/410829_alternative_education.pdf on February 25, 2009.

Association for Supervision and Curriculum Development. (n.d.). *Design your professional development program: Where to start.* Alexandria, VA: Author. Accessed at http://webserver3.ascd.org/ossd/planning_definitions.html on August 11, 2008.

Baker, D., & LeTendre, G. (2005). *National differences, global similarities: World culture and the future of schooling.* Palo Alto, CA: Stanford University Press.

Baker, E. L. (2004). *Aligning curriculum, standards, and assessments: Fulfilling the promise of school reform* (CSE Report 645). Los Angeles: National Center for Research on Evaluation, Standards, and Student Testing.

Balfanz, R., Herzog, L., & Mac Iver, D. J. (2007). *Preventing student disengagement and keeping students on their graduation track in high poverty middle-grades schools: Early identification and effective interventions.* Baltimore: Johns Hopkins University, Center for Social Organization of Schools; Philadelphia Education Fund.

Ball, D. L., & McDiarmid, G. W. (1990). *The subject matter preparation of teachers.* New York: Macmillan. Accessed at http://ncrtl.msu.edu/http/ipapers/html/pdf/ip894.pdf on August 11, 2008.

Bamburg, J. D. (1994). *NCREL monograph: Raising expectations to improve student learning.* Naperville, IL: North Central Regional Educational Laboratory.

Barber, M., & Mourshed, M. (2007). *How the world's best-performing school systems come out on top.* New York: McKinsey & Company. Accessed at www.mckinsey.com/clientservice/socialsector/resources/pdf/Worlds_School_Systems_Final.pdf on August 11, 2008.

Barley, W., Bolt, S., & Greathouse, S. M. (2006). *MASP position statement on response-to-intervention.* Traverse City: Michigan Association of School Psychologists. Accessed at www.maspweb.com/about/RTI_position_paper.pdf on April 28, 2009.

Barth, R. S. (2001). Teacher leader. *Phi Delta Kappan, 82*(6), 443–449.

Bempechat, J. (1999, May/June). Learning from poor and minority students who succeed in school: Children's views on success and failure have a big impact on their learning. *Harvard Education Letter.* Accessed at www.edletter.org/past/issues/1999-mj/learning.shtml on August 11, 2008.

Bennett, N., Wise, C., & Woods, P. (2003a). *Distributed leadership: Full report.* London: National College for School Leadership.

Bennett, N., Wise, C., & Woods, P. (2003b). *Distributed leadership: Summary report.* London: National College for School Leadership.

Berkowitz, M. W., & Bier, M. (2005). *What works in character education: A research-driven guide for educators.* Washington, DC: Character Education Partnership.

Berliner, D. (1990). *What's all the fuss about instructional time?* New York: Teachers College Press.

Black, P., & Wiliam, D. (1998). Inside the black box: Raising standards through classroom assessment. *Phi Delta Kappan, 80*(2), 139–148. Accessed at www.pdkintl.org/kappan/kbla9810.htm on August 11, 2008.

Blagg, D., & Young, S. (2001, April). What makes a good leader? *Harvard Business School Bulletin.* Accessed at http://hbswk.hbs.edu/item/2141.html on August 11, 2008.

Blank, M. J., Melaville, A., & Shah, B. P. (2003). *Making the difference: Research and practice in community schools.* Washington, DC: Coalition for Community Schools; Institute for Educational Leadership.

Blomberg, N. (2004). *Effective discipline for misbehavior: In school vs. out of school suspension.* Villanova, PA: Villanova University, Department of Education and Human Services.

Bloom, B., & Krathwohl, D. (1956). *Taxonomy of educational objectives: The classification of educational goals, by a committee of college and university examiners.* New York: Longman, Green.

Blum, R. (2005). *School connectedness: Improving students' lives.* Baltimore: Johns Hopkins Bloomberg School of Public Health.

Bottoms, G. (2006). *10 Strategies for improving high school graduation rates and student achievement.* Atlanta: Southern Regional Education Board.

Bottoms, G., Presson, A., & Han, L. (2005). *Rigor, relevance and relationships improve achievement in rural high schools: High school reform works when schools do the right things.* Atlanta: Southern Regional Education Board.

Brewster, C., & Fager, J. (2000). *Increasing student engagement and motivation: From time-on-task to homework.* Portland, OR: Northwest Regional Educational Laboratory.

Brewster, C., & Railsback, J. (2003a). *Building trust with schools and diverse families: A foundation for lasting partnerships.* Portland, OR: Northwest Regional Educational Laboratory.

Brewster, C., & Railsback, J. (2003b). *Building trusting relationships for school improvement: Implications for principals and teachers.* Portland, OR: Northwest Regional Educational Laboratory.

Bridgeland, J., Dilulio, J., Jr., & Morison, K. (2006). *The silent epidemic: Perspectives of high school dropouts.* Washington, DC: Civic Enterprises; Peter D. Hart Research Associates.

Carter, S. (2002). *The impact of parent/family involvement on student outcomes: An annotated bibliography of research from the past decade.* Eugene, OR: Consortium for Appropriate Dispute Resolution in Special Education.

Center for Effective Collaboration and Practice. (2000). *Preventing school dropouts.* Washington, DC: Author.

Center for Public Education. (2007). *Research review: What research says about the value of homework.* Alexandria, VA: Author. Accessed at www.centerforpubliceducation.org/site/c.kjJXJ5MPIwE/b.2479409/k.BF59 on August 11, 2008.

Chappuis, S., & Stiggins, R. (2002). Classroom assessment for learning. *Educational Leadership, 60*(1), 40–43. Accessed at http://curriculum.risd41.0rg/commitee/best_practices/files/mod2_day1/Nov1%20Mag Article.doc on August 11, 2008.

Chaput, S. S. (2004, Spring). Characterizing and measuring participation in out-of-school time programs. *The Evaluation Exchange, X*(1), 2–3. Accessed at www.hfrp.org/evaluation/the-evaluation-exchange/issue-archive/evaluating-out-of-school-time-program-quality on August 11, 2008.

Children's Defense Fund. (2004). *The road to dropping out: Minority students and academic factors correlated with failure to complete high school.* Washington, DC: Author.

Choy, S. P., Chen, X., & Bugarin, R. (2006). *Teacher professional development in 1999–2000: What teachers, principals, and district staff report* (NCES 2006–305). Washington, DC: National Center for Education Statistics. Accessed at http://nces.ed.gov/pubs2006/2006305.pdf on August 11, 2008.

Cicchinelli, L., Dean, C., Galvin, M., Goodwin, B., & Parsley, D. (2006). *Success in sight: A comprehensive approach to school improvement.* Aurora, CO: Mid-continent Research for Education and Learning.

Cohen, D. K., & Hill, H. C. (2001). *Learning policy: When state education reform works.* New Haven, CT: Yale University Press. Accessed at http://yalepress.yale.edu/yupbooks/pdf/0300089473.pdf on January 6, 2008.

Colby, S., Bradshaw, L., & Joyner, R. (2002). *Perceptions of teacher evaluation systems and their impact on school improvement, professional development and student learning.* Washington, DC: American Educational Research Association.

Coleman, A. L., Starzynski, A. L., Winnick, S. Y., Palmer, S. R., & Furr, J. E. (2006). *It takes a parent: Transforming education in the wake of the No Child Left Behind Act.* Washington, DC: Appleseed Foundation.

Collins, J. (2001). *Good to great: Why some companies make the leap . . . and others don't.* New York: Harper-Collins.

Committee on Science and Mathematics Teacher Preparation. (2000). *Educating teachers of science, mathematics, and technology: New practices for a new millennium.* Washington, DC: National Research Council; National Academies Press.

Community Training and Assistance Center. (2008). *Focus on literacy: Professional development audit.* Boston: Author.

Corallo, C., & McDonald, D. H. (2002). *What works with low-performing schools: A review of research.* Charleston, WV: Appalachian Regional Education Laboratory.

Corley, M. A. (2005, March). Differentiated instruction: Adjusting to the needs of all learners. *Focus on Basics: Connecting Research and Practice, 7*(C). Accessed at www.ncsall.net/?id=736 on August 11, 2008.

Cotton, K. (1989). *Expectations and student outcomes.* Portland, OR: Northwest Regional Educational Laboratory.

Cotton, K. (1990). *Schoolwide and classroom discipline.* Portland, OR: Northwest Regional Educational Laboratory. Accessed at www.nwrel.org/scpd/sirs/5/cu9.html on August 11, 2008.

Cotton, K. (2003). *Principals and student achievement: What the research says.* Alexandria, VA: Association for Supervision and Curriculum Development.

Crooks, T. (2001). *The validity of formative assessments.* Paper presented at the annual conference of the British Educational Research Association, Leeds, United Kingdom.

Cuban, L. (1988). *Perspectives on research and practice.* Richmond, CA: McCutchan.

Dailey, D., Fleishman, S., Gil, L., Holtzman, D., O'Day, J., & Vosmer, C. (2005). *Toward more effective school districts: A review of the knowledge base.* Washington, DC: American Institutes for Research.

Darling-Hammond, L. (1998). Teacher learning that supports student learning. *Educational Leadership, 55*(5), 6–11.

Darling-Hammond, L. (2005). Thoughts on teacher preparation. *Edutopia.* Accessed at www.edutopia.org/linda-darling-hammond-teacher-preparation on August 11, 2008.

Darling-Hammond, L., & Ball, D. L. (1997). *Teaching for high standards: What policymakers need to know and be able to do.* Washington, DC: National Education Goals Panel.

Darling-Hammond, L., & Bransford, J. (Eds.). (2005). *Preparing teachers for a changing world: What teachers should learn and be able to do.* San Francisco: Jossey-Bass.

Darling-Hammond, L., Wei, R. C., Andree, A., Richardson, N., & Orphanos, S. (2009). *Professional learning in the learning profession: A status report on teacher development in the United States and abroad.* Dallas, TX: National Staff Development Council.

David, J. L., Shields, P. M., Humphrey, D. C., & Young, V. M. (2001). *When theory hits reality: Standards-based reform in urban districts.* Philadelphia: Pew Charitable Trusts.

Davies, B., Davies, B. J., & Ellison, L. (2005). *Success and sustainability: Developing the strategically-focused school.* Nottingham, England: National College for School Leadership.

Demmert, W. G., Jr. (2001). *Improving academic performance among Native American students: A review of the research literature.* Charleston, WV: ERIC Clearinghouse on Rural Education and Small Schools. (ERIC Document Reproduction Service No. ED-99-CO-0027) Accessed at www.sfu .ca/mpp/aboriginal/colloquium/pdf/Improving_Performance.pdf on August 11, 2008.

DuFour, R., DuFour, R., & Eaker, R. (2008). *Revisiting professional learning communities at work: New insights for improving schools.* Bloomington, IN: Solution Tree.

DuFour, R., DuFour, R., Eaker, R., & Karhanek, G. (2004). *Whatever it takes: How professional learning communities respond when kids don't learn.* Bloomington, IN: Solution Tree (formerly National Educational Service).

DuFour, R., & Eaker, R. (1998). *Professional learning communities at work: Best practices for enhancing student achievement.* Bloomington, IN: Solution Tree (formerly National Educational Service).

DuFour, R., Eaker, R., & DuFour R. (Eds.). (2005). *On common ground: The power of professional learning communities.* Bloomington, IN: Solution Tree (formerly National Educational Service).

Dynarski, M. (2000). *Making do with less: Interpreting the evidence from recent federal evaluations of dropout-prevention programs.* Princeton, NJ: Mathematica Policy Research.

e-Lead: Leadership for Student Success. (n.d.). *Job embedded learning.* Washington, DC: Author. Accessed at www.e-lead.org/resources/resources.asp?ResourceID=15 on August 21, 2008.

Education Alliance. (2005). *Bridging the achievement gap: The role of professional development for teachers.* Providence, RI: Author.

Education Commission of the States. (2002). *No child left behind issue brief: Data-driven decision making.* Denver, CO: Author.

Education Trust. (2000). *Honor in the boxcar: Equalizing teacher quality.* Washington, DC: Author.

Education Trust. (2003). *African American achievement in America.* Washington, DC: Author.

Education Trust. (2006). *Key education facts and figures: Achievement, attainment and opportunity from elementary school through college.* Washington, DC: Author.

Education Trust. (2007). *2007 NAEP reading and math grades 4 and 8* [PowerPoint]. Accessed at www2 .edtrust.org/NR/rdonlyres/1A369201-F4B6–45D1-A93A-0FDA0954E4CF/0/NAEP2007 ReadingMath4and8.ppt on February 19, 2009.

Education Week. (2008, June 5). *Diplomas count 2008: School to college—Executive summary.* Accessed at www .edweek.org/ew/articles/2008/06/05/40execsum.h27.html on February 19, 2009.

Ellis, E., & Worthington, L. (1994). *Research synthesis on effective teaching principles and the design of quality tools for educators.* Eugene, OR: National Center to Improve the Tools of Educators.

Elmore, R. (2000). *Building a new structure for school leadership.* Washington, DC: Albert Shanker Institute.

Elmore, R. (2002). *Bridging the gap between standards and achievement: The imperative for professional development in education.* Washington, DC: The Albert Shanker Institute.

Elmore, R. (2003). *Knowing the right thing to do: School improvement and performance-based accountability.* Washington, DC: National Governors Association; Consortium for Policy Research in Education.

Epstein, J. L., & Salinas, K. C. (2004). Partnering with families and communities. *Educational Leadership, 61*(8), 12–18.

Everson, H. T., & Millsap, R. E. (2005). *Everyone gains: Extracurricular activities in high school and higher SAT scores.* New York: College Board.

Farkas, S., Johnson, J., & Duffett, A. (2003). *Stand by me: What teachers really think about unions, merit pay and other professional matters.* New York: Public Agenda.

Finkelstein, N. D., & Fong, A. B. (2008). *Course-taking patterns and preparation for postsecondary education in California's public university systems among minority youth* (Issues & Answers Report, REL 2008-No. 035). Washington, DC: U.S. Department of Education. Accessed at http://ies.ed.gov/ncee/edlabs/ projects/project.asp?id=86 on February 19, 2009.

Florida Literacy and Reading Excellence Center. (n.d.). *Vygotsky, scaffolding and the zone of proximal development.* Orlando: University of Central Florida.

Foster, L. (2001). *Effectiveness of mentor programs: Review of the literature from 1995 to 2000.* Sacramento: California State Library, California Research Bureau.

Fouts, J. T. (2003). *A decade of reform: A summary of research finds on classroom, school, and district effectiveness in Washington State.* Seattle: Washington School Research Center.

Friedman, T. L. (2005). *The world is flat: A brief history of the twenty-first century.* New York: Farrar, Straus and Giroux.

Fullan, M. (2001a). *Leading in a culture of change.* San Francisco: Jossey-Bass.

Fullan, M. (2001b). *The new meaning of educational change.* New York: Teachers College Press.

Garet, M. S., Porter, A. C., Desimone, L., Birman, B. F., & Yoon, K. S. (2001). What makes professional development effective? Results from a national sample of teachers. *American Educational Research Journal, 38*(4), 915–945. Accessed at http://aztla.asu.edu/ProfDev1.pdf on August 11, 2008.

Gaustad, J. (1992). *School discipline: ERIC Digest 78.* Eugene, OR: Clearinghouse on Educational Policy and Management. (ERIC Document Reproduction Service No. ED-99-CO-0011). Accessed at http://eric.uoregon.edu/publications/digests/digest078.html on August 11, 2008.

Good, R. H., Kaminski, R. A., Smith, S., Simmons, D., Kame'enui, E., & Wallin, J. (2002). Reviewing outcomes: Using DIBELS to evaluate a school's core curriculum and system of additional intervention in kindergarten. In S. R. Vaughn & K. L. Briggs (Eds.), *Reading in the classroom: Systems for observing teaching and learning.* Baltimore: Paul H. Brookes.

Grogan, P. S. (2004). *Partners in progress: A framework for raising student achievement in under-performing school districts.* Boston: State of Massachusetts, Governor's Task Force on State Intervention in Under-Performing Districts.

Guskey, T. R. (2002). Does it make a difference? Evaluating professional development. *Educational Leadership, 59*(6), 45–49.

Hallam, S. (2004). *Homework: The evidence.* London: Institute of Education.

Haycock, K. (2007, October). *Raising achievement and closing gaps for all groups of kids: Lessons from schools on the performance frontier.* Paper presented at the OELA Sixth Annual Celebrate Our Rising Stars Summit, Washington, DC.

Harvard Family Research Project. (2005/2006, Winter). A conversation with Thomas R. Guskey. *Evaluation Exchange, 11*(4), 12–14.

Henderson, A. T., & Mapp, K. L. (2002). *A new wave of evidence: The impact of school, family and community connections on student achievement.* Austin, TX: National Center for Family and Community Connections with Schools; Southwest Educational Development Laboratory.

Hess, F. M., & Loup, C. (2008). *The leadership limbo: Teacher labor agreements in America's fifty largest school districts.* Washington, DC: Thomas B. Fordham Institute.

Hirsch, E., & Hirsh, S. (n.d.). *Making the case for quality professional development.* Washington, DC: National Conference of State Legislatures. Accessed at www.ncsl.org/programs/educ/TProDev.htm on August 11, 2008.

Hirsh, S. (2002, October). Together, you can do more. *National Staff Development Council Results.*

Hollifield, J. (1987). *Ability grouping in elementary schools: ERIC Digest.* College Park, MD: ERIC Clearinghouse on Assessment and Evaluation. (ERIC Document Reproduction Service No. ED290542). Accessed at http://ericae.net/edo/ED290542.htm on August 11, 2008.

Horsley, D. L., & Loucks-Horsley, S. (1998). CBAM brings order to the tornado of change. *Journal of Staff Development, 19*(4). Accessed at www.nsdc.org/library/publications/jsd/horsely194.cfm on February 23, 2009.

Hughes, K. L., & Karp, M. M. (2004). *School-based career development: A synthesis of the literature.* New York: Institute on Education and the Economy.

Institute for Educational Leadership. (2001). *Leadership for student learning: Restructuring school district leadership.* Washington, DC: Author.

Interstate School Leaders Licensure Consortium. (2008). *Educational leadership policy standards: ISLLC 2008*. Washington, DC: Council of Chief State School Officers.

IQ Solutions. (2001). *National standards for culturally and linguistically appropriate services in health care: Final report*. Washington, DC: The Office of Minority Health, National Standards on Culturally and Linguistically Appropriate Services.

Jackson, D. (2002). *Distributed leadership: Spaces between the pebbles in the jar*. Nottingham, United Kingdom: National College for School Leadership.

Jerald, C. D. (2006). *School culture: The hidden curriculum*. Washington, DC: Center for Comprehensive School Reform and Improvement. Accessed at www. centerforcsri.org on August 11, 2008.

Kessler-Sklar, S. L., & Baker, A. J. L. (2000). School district parent involvement policies and programs. *Elementary School Journal, 101*(1), 101–118.

Kleiner, B., Porch, R., & Farris, E. (2002). *Statistical analysis report: Public alternative schools and programs for students at risk of education failure—2000–01*. Washington, DC: National Center for Education Statistics; U.S. Department of Education, Office of Educational Research and Improvement.

Knapp, M., Copland, M., & Talbert, J. (2003). *Leading for learning*. Seattle: Center for the Study of Teaching and Policy.

Kotter, J. P. (1996). *Leading change*. Boston: Harvard Business School Press.

Kuykendall, C. (1989). *Improving black student achievement by enhancing students' self image*. Chevy Chase, MD: The Mid-Atlantic Equity Center. Accessed at www.maec.org/pdf/kuykendall.pdf on December 2, 2008.

Laird, E. (2006). *Data use drives school and district improvement*. Austin, TX: National Center for Educational Accountability; Data Quality Campaign.

LaMarca, P. M., Redfield, D., Winter, P. C., Bailey, A., & Handsche-Despriet, L. (2000). *State standards and state assessment systems: A guide to alignment*. Washington, DC: Council of Chief State School Officers.

Lashway, L. (2003). *Role of the school leader*. Eugene, OR: Clearinghouse on Educational Policy and Management.

League of Women Voters of California. (2005). *Education positions of the League of Women Voters of California*. Sacramento: Author. Accessed at http://ca.lwv.org/lwvc/issues/socpol/edu.html on August 11, 2008.

Learning First Alliance. (2001). *Every child learning: Safe and supportive schools*. Washington, DC: Author.

Learning Point Associates. (2004). *Guide to using data in school improvement efforts: A compilation of knowledge from data retreats and data use at Learning Point Associates*. Naperville, IL: Author.

Learning Point Associates. (2006a). *Using data as a school improvement tool: NCREL quick key 11 action guide*. Naperville, IL: Author. Accessed at www.learningpt.org/pdfs/qkey11.pdf on December 2, 2008.

Learning Point Associates. (2006b). *Research brief: Practices that support data use in urban high schools*. Washington, DC: Center for Comprehensive School Reform and Improvement.

Lehr, C. A., Moreau, R. A., Lange, C. M., & Lanners, E. J. (2004). *Alternative schools: Findings from a national survey of the states—Research report 2*. Minneapolis, MN: Institute on Community Integration.

Leithwood, K., Louis, K., Anderson, S., & Wahlstrom, K. (2004). *How leadership influences student learning*. New York: The Wallace Foundation.

Leithwood, K., & Riehl, C. (2003). *What we know about successful school leadership*. Philadelphia: Laboratory for Student Success.

Lewis, A., & Paik, S. (2001). *Add it up: Using research to improve education for low-income and minority students*. Washington, DC: Poverty & Race Research Action Council.

Libbey, H. P. (2004). Measuring student relationships to school: Attachment, bonding, connectedness and engagement. *Journal of School Health, 74*(7), 274–283.

LoGerfo, L. (2006). Research: Climb every mountain. *Education Next, 3*, 68–75.

Los Angeles County Office of Education. (n.d.). *Teaching alternative behaviors schoolwide: A resource guide to prevent discipline problems*. Los Angeles: L.A. County Office of Education, Division of Student Support Services.

Louisiana Department of Education. (2005). *2005 comprehensive curriculum*. Baton Rouge, LA: Author.

Luekens, M. T., Lyter, D. M., & Fox, E. E. (2005). Teacher attrition and mobility: Results from the teacher follow-up survey, 2000–01. *Education Statistics Quarterly, 6*(3), Table B.

Mahoney, J. L., & Cairns, R. D. (1997). Do extracurricular activities protect against early school dropout? *Developmental Psychology, 33*(2), 241–253. Accessed at www.nwrel.org/scpd/re-engineering/rycu/ReferenceDetailas.asp?RefID=411 on August 10, 2008.

Mapp, K. L. (2002, April). *Having their say: Parents describe how and why they are involved in their children's education*. Paper presented at the annual meeting of the American Educational Research Association, New Orleans, LA.

Marshall, M. L. (2004). *Examining school climate: Defining factors and educational influences* [White paper]. Atlanta: Georgia State University, Center for Research on School Safety, School Climate and Classroom Management. Accessed at http://education.gsu.edu/schoolsafety on August 11, 2008.

Martinez, Y. G., & Velazquez, J. A. (2000). *Involving migrant families in education*. Denver, CO: Centennial Board of Cooperative Educational Services. Accessed at www.cboces.org/assets/docs/federalprograms/InvolvingMigrantfamiliesineducation.doc on February 22, 2009.

Marzano, R. J., Pickering, D. J., & Pollock, J. E. (2001). *Classroom instruction that works: Research-based strategies for increasing student achievement*. Alexandria, VA: Association for Supervision and Curriculum Development.

Marzano, R. J., Waters, T., & McNulty, B. A. (2005). *School leadership that works: From research to results*. Alexandria, VA: Association for Supervision and Curriculum Development.

Mayer, J. E. (2007). *Creating a safe and welcoming school*. Paris: United Nations Educational, Scientific and Cultural Organization, International Academy of Education, International Bureau of Education.

McCluskey, I. (2004). In their element: Urban youth find more than just tutoring in an after-school program. *Northwest Education, 9*(3). Accessed at www.nwrel.org/nwedu/09–03/element.php on August 11, 2008.

McDiarmid, G. W., Ball, D. L., & Anderson, C. W. (1989). Why staying one chapter ahead doesn't really work: Subject-specific pedagogy. In M. Reynolds (Ed.), *Knowledge base for the beginning teacher* (pp. 193–205). New York: Pergamon Press. Accessed at http://ncrtl.msu.edu/http/ipapers/html/pdf/ip886.pdf on August 10, 2008.

McNulty, J. (2004, March). Peers are an untapped positive influence on Latino high school students, researcher says. *UC Santa Cruz Currents Online.* Accessed at http://currents.ucsc.edu/03-04/03-22/gibson.html on August 11, 2008.

Mendez-Morse, S. (1992). *Leadership characteristics that facilitate change.* Austin, TX: Southwest Educational Development Laboratory.

Mid-continent Research for Education and Learning. (2003). *Sustaining school improvement: Data-driven decision making.* Aurora, CO: Author. Accessed at www.mcrel.org/PDF/LeadershipOrganizationDevelopment/5031TG_datafolio.pdf on December 2, 2008.

Miles, K. H., Odden, A., Fermanich, M., & Archibald, S. (2005). *Excerpts from* Inside the black box: School district spending on professional development in education—Lessons from five urban districts. Washington, DC: The Finance Project.

Mitchell, K., Shkolnik, J., Song, M., Uekawa, K., Murphy, R., Garet, M., et al. (2005). *Rigor, relevance, and results: The quality of teacher assignments and student work in new and conventional high schools.* Washington, DC: American Institutes for Research.

Montes, G., & Lehmann, C. (2004). *Who will drop out from school? Key predictors from the literature* (Series No. T04–001). Pittsburgh: The Children's Institute.

Morgan, J. G. (2004). *Truant, teaching to empty desks: The effects of truancy in Tennessee schools.* Nashville: Tennessee Office of Education Accountability.

Morrison Institute for Public Policy. (2006). *Why some schools with Latino children beat the odds and others don't.* Phoenix: Author.

Murphy, J., Elliott, S. N., Goldring, E., & Porter, A. C. (2006a, October). *Leadership for learning: A research-based model and taxonomy of behaviors.* Paper presented at the Wallace Foundation State Action for Educational Leadership Conference, St. Louis, MO. Accessed at www.vanderbilt.edu/lsi/valed/leadershipforlearning.pdf on August 11, 2008.

Murphy, J., Elliott, S. N., Goldring, E., & Porter, A. C. (2006b). *Learning-centered leadership: A conceptual foundation.* Nashville: Vanderbilt University.

Nagle, M. (2001, October-November). One best friend: Children's friendships are training grounds for adult relationships. *UMaine Today Magazine.* Accessed at www.umainetoday.umaine.edu/Issues/v1i1/friend.html on August 11, 2008.

National Association of School Psychologists. (2005). *Position statement on ability grouping and tracking.* Bethesda, MD: Author.

National Association of State Directors of Special Education & Council of Administrators of Special Education. (2006). *Response to intervention: NASDE and CASE* [White paper]. Alexandria, VA: Authors. Accessed at www.nasdse.org/documents/RTIAnAdministratorsPerspective1–06.pdf on August 11, 2008.

National Conference of State Legislatures. (2006). *School leadership: Licensure and certification.* Denver, CO: Author. Accessed at www.ncsl.org/programs/educ/schleadercert.htm on August 11, 2008.

National Conference on Citizenship. (2006). *America's civic health index: Broken engagement.* Washington, DC: Author. Accessed at www.civicenterprises.net/pdfs/2006civichealth.pdf on August 11, 2008.

National Council for Accreditation of Teacher Education. (2005). *High quality teacher/educator preparation makes a difference in student achievement: Student performance increases when teachers are prepared.* Washington, DC: Author. Accessed at www.ncate.org/public/conc1.asp?ch=48 on August 11, 2008.

National Council of Jewish Women. (1996). *Parents as school partners: Dissemination kit.* New York: Author.

National Council of Teachers of Mathematics. (2000). *Curriculum and evaluation standards for school mathematics.* Reston, VA: Author.

National Education Association. (2002). *2002 instructional materials survey.* Washington, DC: Author.

National Education Commission on Time and Learning. (1994). *Prisoners of time.* Washington, DC: Author.

National Institute on Educational Governance, Finance, Policymaking, and Management. (1998). *What the Third International Mathematics and Science Study (TIMSS) means for systemic school improvement.* Washington, DC: U.S. Department of Education, Office of Educational Research and Improvement.

National Joint Committee on Learning Disabilities. (2005, June). Responsiveness to intervention and learning disabilities. *LD Online.* Accessed at www.ldonline.org/article/11498 on August 11, 2008.

National Literacy Trust. (2005). *Self-efficacy, self-esteem and literacy: Research abstracts.* London: Author.

National Parent Teacher Association. (2008). *National standards, goals, and indicators for family-school partnerships.* Chicago: Author. Accessed at www.pta.org/national_standards.asp on February 22, 2009.

National Research Council and Institute of Medicine. (2002). *Community programs to promote youth development.* Washington, DC: National Academy Press.

National Research Council and Institute of Medicine. (2003). *Engaging schools: Fostering high school students' motivation to learn.* Washington, DC: National Academies Press.

National Science Teachers Association. (2008). *NSTA position statement: Professional development in science education.* Arlington, VA: Author. Accessed at www.nsta.org/about/positions/profdev.aspx on August 11, 2008.

National Staff Development Council. (2000). *Learning to lead, leading to learn.* Oxford, OH: Author.

National Staff Development Council. (2001a). *NSDC standards: Quality teaching.* Oxford, OH: Author. Accessed at www.nsdc.org/standards/qualityteaching.cfm on August 11, 2008.

National Staff Development Council. (2001b). *Standards for staff development* (Rev. ed.). Oxford, OH: Author. Accessed at www.nsdc.org/standards/datadriven.cfm on August 11, 2008.

National Staff Development Council. (2005, November/December). Transform your group into a team. *Tools for Schools, 9*(2).

National Summit on America's "Silent Epidemic." (2007). *Ending the silent epidemic: A blueprint to address America's high school dropout crisis.* New York: MTV Press. Accessed at www.silentepidemic.org/pdfs/take-away.pdf on August 11, 2008.

Neill, M. (1996, April). *How the principles and indicators for student assessment systems should affect practice.* Paper presented at the annual meeting of the American Educational Research Association, New York.

Nelson, M. D., & Bauch, P. A. (1997, March). *African-American students' perceptions of caring teacher behaviors in Catholic and public schools of choice.* Paper presented at the annual meeting of the American Educational Research Association, Chicago.

Newmann, F. M., & Wehlage, G. G. (1995). *Successful school restructuring: A report to the public and educators.* Madison: Wisconsin Center for Education Research.

North Central Regional Educational Laboratory. (n.d.). *Stages of concern.* Chicago: Learning Point Associates (formerly North Central Regional Educational Laboratory).

Northwest Regional Educational Laboratory. (2005). *Research you can use to improve results: Section 3—Instruction and instructional improvement.* Accessed at www.nwrel.org/scpd/sirs/rycu/3classroom.html on April 28, 2009.

Ogle, D. M. (1997). *Critical issue: Rethinking learning for students at risk.* Chicago: Learning Point Associates (formerly North Central Regional Educational Laboratory).

Ohio Department of Education. (2006). *Ohio ninth-grade proficiency tests citizenship.* Columbus, OH: Author.

Ohio Department of Education. (2008). *Stats show minorities don't pursue STEM courses.* Columbus, OH: Author. Accessed at www.ode.state.oh.us/GD/Templates/Pages/ODE/ODEDetail.aspx?page=363 on February 19, 2009.

Oregon Department of Education. (2004). *Working definition of cultural competency.* Salem, OR: Author. Accessed at www.ode.state.or.us/search/page/?=656 on August 11, 2008.

Oregon Quality Education Commission. (2000). *Report to the governor and superintendent of public instruction on the Oregon quality education model.* Salem, OR: Author.

Orfield, G., Losen, D., Wald, J., & Swanson, C. B. (2004). *Losing our future: How minority youth are being left behind by the graduation rate crisis.* Boston: Harvard University, The Civil Rights Project.

Pan, D., Smith-Hanson, L., Jones, D., Rudo, Z., Alexander, C., & Kahlert, R. (2005). *Investigation of education databases in four states to support policy research on resource allocation.* Austin, TX: Southwest Educational Development Laboratory.

Pellegrino, J. W., Chudowsky, N., & Glaser, R. (Eds.). (2001). *Knowing what students know: The science and design of educational assessment.* Washington, DC: National Academy Press.

Perkins, B. K. (2006). *Where we learn: The CUBE survey of urban school climate.* Alexandria, VA: National School Boards Association.

Porter, A. (2004). Curriculum assessment [Pre-publication draft]. In J. Green, G. Camilli, & P. Elmore (Eds.), *Handbook of complementary methods for research in education.* New York: Routledge. Accessed at www .secsupport.org/pdf/curricassess.pdf on August 11, 2008.

Powell, M. J. (1994). *Equity in the reform of mathematics and science education: A look at the issues and solutions—Executive summary.* Austin, TX: Southwest Educational Development Laboratory; Southwest Consortium for the Improvement of Mathematics and Science Teaching.

President's Commission on Excellence in Special Education. (2002). *A new era: Revitalizing special education for children and their families.* Washington, DC: U.S. Department of Education.

Public Education Network. (2003). *The voice of the new teacher.* Washington, DC: Author.

Puma, M., & Raphael, J. (2001). *Teaching teachers: Evaluating standards-based professional development for teachers—A handbook for practitioners.* Washington, DC: The Urban Institute.

Raffaele Mendez, L. M., & Knoff, H. M. (2003). Who gets suspended from school and why: A demographic analysis of schools and disciplinary infractions in a large school district. *Education and Treatment of Children, 26*(1), 30–51.

Reeves, C., Emerick, S., & Hirsch, E. (2007). *Creating an atmosphere of trust: Lessons from exemplary schools.* Hillsborough, NC: Center for Teaching Quality; North Carolina Professional Teaching Standards Commission.

Resnick, L. (Ed.). (2005). *Professional development to improve student achievement: Research points.* Washington, DC: American Educational Research Association.

Rosario, J. (2006). *On engaging Latino students in their education: A resource guide to research and programs.* Indianapolis: Indiana University-Purdue University Indianapolis, Center for Urban and Multicultural Education.

Rosenstein, B. (2001). All about Drucker. *Information Outlook, 5*(12). Accessed at www.sla.org/content/shop/ information/infoonline/2001/dec01/drucker.cfm on August 21, 2008.

Schlechty, P. C. (2001). *Shaking up the school house: How to support and sustain educational innovation.* San Francisco: Jossey-Bass.

Schmoker, M. (2001). *The results fieldbook: Practical strategies from dramatically improved schools.* Alexandria, VA: Association for Supervision and Curriculum Development.

Schmoker, M. (2002, Spring). Up and away. *Journal of Staff Development, 23*(2). Accessed at www.nsdc.org/ library/publications/jsd/schmoker232.cfm on January 10, 2008.

Schmoker, M. (2006). *Results now: How we can achieve unprecedented improvements in teaching and learning.* Alexandria, VA: Association for Supervision and Curriculum Development.

Senge, P. (1990). *The fifth discipline: The art and practice of the learning organization.* New York: Doubleday.

Shannon, G. S. (2006). *Helping students finish school: Why students drop out and how to help them graduate.* Olympia, WA: Office of Superintendent of Public Instruction.

Shannon, G. S., & Bylsma, P. (2002). *Addressing the achievement gap: A challenge for Washington State educators.* Olympia, WA: Office of Superintendent of Public Instruction.

Shannon, G. S., & Bylsma, P. (2004). *Characteristics of improved school districts: Themes from research.* Olympia, WA: Office of Superintendent of Public Instruction.

Sharp, C., Keys, W., Benefield, P., Flannagan, N., Sukhnandan, L., Mason, K., et al. (2001). *Recent research on homework: An annotated bibliography.* Berkshire, United Kingdom: National Foundation for Educational Research.

Simpson, M. (2005). *The art and science of professional teaching.* Kenmore, WA: Education Resource Network.

Skiba, R. (2004). Zero tolerance: The assumptions and the facts. *Education Policy Briefs, 2*(1), 1–8. Accessed at http://ceep.indiana.edu/ChildrenLeftBehind/pdf/ZeroTolerance.pdf on August 10, 2008.

Skiba, R., Boone, K., Fontanini, A., Wu, T., Strassel, A., & Peterson, R. (2000). *Preventing school violence: A practical guide to comprehensive planning.* Bloomington: Indiana Education Policy Center. Accessed at www.unl.edu/srs/pdfs/PrevSchViol.pdf on August 10, 2008.

Skiba, R., & Peterson, R. (1999). The dark side of zero tolerance: Can punishment lead to safe schools? *Phi Delta Kappan, 80*(5), 372–382. Accessed at www.pdkintl.org/kappan/kski9901.htm on August 10, 2008.

Sparks, D. (1994). A paradigm shift in staff development. *Journal of Staff Development, 15*(4), 26–29. Accessed at www.nsdc.org/library/publications/jsd/sparks154.cfm on August 10, 2008.

Stevens, D. W., & Kahne, J. (2006). *Professional communities and instructional improvement practices: A study of small high schools in Chicago.* Chicago: University of Chicago, Consortium on Chicago School Research.

Strong, R. W., Silver, H. F., & Robinson, A. (1995). What do students want (and what really motivates them)? *Educational Leadership, 53*(1), 8–12. Accessed at www.middleweb.com/StdntMotv.html on August 10, 2008.

Swearingen, R. (2002). *A primer: Diagnostic, formative and summative assessment.* Toppenish, WA: Heritage University. Accessed at http://slackernet.org/assessment.htm on August 21, 2008.

Tableman, B. (Ed.). (2004). *Changing school climate and school culture* (No. 31). East Lansing: Michigan State University.

Task Force on the Principalship. (2000). *Leadership for student learning: Reinventing the principalship.* Washington, DC: Institute for Educational Leadership.

Thaman, K. H. (2006, May). *Nurturing relationships: A pacific perspective of teacher education for peace and sustainable development.* Paper presented at the UNESCO Expert Meeting on ESD, Samutsongkram, Thailand.

Thorpe, P. K. (2003). *School context, school connectedness and mathematics classroom performance*. Washington, DC: Education Resources Information Center. (ERIC Document Reproduction Service No. ED480670)

Thurlow, M., Christenson, S., Sinclair, M., Evelo, D., & Thornton, H. (1995). *Staying in school: Strategies for middle school students with learning and emotional disabilities*. Minneapolis, MN: Institute on Community Integration.

Thurlow, M. L., Sinclair, M. F., & Johnson, D. R. (2002). *Students with disabilities who drop out of school: Implications for policy and practice*. Minneapolis: University of Minnesota, National Center on Secondary Education and Transition.

Timperley, H. S., Phillips, G., & Wiseman, J. (2003). *The sustainability of professional development in literacy*. Wellington: New Zealand Ministry of Education; University of Auckland, Child Literacy Foundation.

Tissington, L. D. (2007). *History: Our hope for the future*. Dallas, TX: redOrbit. Accessed at www.redorbit .com/news/education/789657/history_our_hope_for_the_future/index.html on August 10, 2008.

Togneri, W. (2003). *Beyond islands of excellence: What districts can do to improve instruction and achievement in all schools—A leadership brief*. Washington, DC: Learning First Alliance.

Togneri, W., & Anderson, S. E. (2003). *Beyond islands of excellence: What districts can do to improve instruction and achievement in all schools—A leadership brief* [Full brief]. Washington, DC: Learning First Alliance.

Tomlinson, C. A. (n.d). *Differentiation of instruction in the elementary grades: ERIC Digest*. Accessed at www .ericdigests.org/2001–2/elementary.html on August 10, 2008.

Tomlinson, C. A., Brighton, C., Hertberg, H., Callahan, C. M., Moon, T. R., Brimijoin, K., et al. (2003). Differentiating instruction in response to student readiness, interest, and learning profile in academically diverse classrooms: A review of literature. *Journal for the Education of the Gifted, 27*(2/3), 119–145.

Torgeson, J. M., Granger Meadows, J., & Howard, P. (n.d.). *Using student outcome data to help guide professional development and teacher support: Issues for Reading First and K–12 reading plans*. Tallahassee: Florida Center for Reading Research.

United States Census Bureau. (2008a). *Geographical mobility: 2006 to 2007*. Accessed at www.census.gov/ population/www/socdemo/migrate/cps2007.html on February 19, 2009.

United States Census Bureau. (2008b). *Facts for features: June 16, 2008*. Accessed at www.census.gov/ PressRelease/www/releases/archives/facts_for_features_special_editions/12084.html on August 15, 2008.

United States Department of Education. (2000). *Teacher preparation and professional development: 2000*. Washington, DC: National Center for Education Statistics. Accessed at http://nces.ed.gov/ quicktables/displaytableimage.asp?ID=QTFImage418 on August 11, 2008.

University of Minnesota. (2003, June). *The wingspread declaration on student connections to school*. Presented at The Johnson Foundation, Wingspread Conference Center, Racine, WI.

Usdan, M. (Host), & Hale, B. (Moderator). (April 2001). *Leadership for student learning: Redefining the teacher as leader.* Presented at a live panel of the National Press Club and Institute for Educational Leadership, Washington, DC.

Vaughn, S., Hughes, M. T., Moody, S. W., & Elbaum, B. (2001). Instructional grouping for reading for students with LD: Implications for practice. *LD Online.* Accessed at www.ldonline.org/article/6308 on August 11, 2008.

Waters, T., & Grubb, S. (2004). *The leadership we need: Using research to strengthen the use of standards for administrator preparation and licensure programs.* Aurora, CO: Mid-continent Research for Education and Learning.

Waters, T., & Marzano, R. (2006). *School district leadership that works: The effect of superintendent leadership on student achievement.* Aurora, CO: Mid-continent Research for Education and Learning.

Weiss, I. R., & Miller, B. (2006, October). *Deepening teacher content knowledge for teaching: A review of the evidence.* Paper presented at the Math and Science Partnership Evaluation Summit II, Minneapolis, MN. Accessed at http://hub.mspnet.org/media/data/WeissMiller.pdf?media_000000002247.pdf on August 11, 2008.

Wiggins, G., & McTighe, J. (2007). *Schooling by design.* Alexandria, VA: Association for Supervision and Curriculum Development.

Williams, T., Kirst, M., Haertel, E., et al. (2005). *Similar students, different results: Why do some schools do better? A large-scale survey of California elementary schools serving low-income students.* Mountain View, CA: EdSource.

Wilson, D. (2004). The interface of school climate and school connectedness and relationships with aggression and victimization. *Journal of School Health, 74*(7), 293–299.

Wimberly, G. L. (2002). *School relationships foster success for African American students: ACT policy report.* Iowa City, IA: ACT.

Witt, H. (2007, September 25). School discipline tougher on African Americans. *Chicago Tribune Web Edition.* Accessed at www.chicagotribune.com on August 11, 2008.

Wong, K., & Nicotera, A. (2003). *Enhancing teacher quality: Peer coaching as a professional development strategy.* Philadelphia: Mid-Atlantic Regional Educational Laboratory, the Laboratory for Student Success.

Yu, J. J., Tepper, K. H., & Russell, S. T. (n.d.). *Peer relationships and friendship.* Tucson, AZ: Building Partnerships for Youth. Accessed at http://cals-calsnet.arizona.edu/fcs/bpy/content.cfm?content=peer_rel on August 10, 2008.

INDEX

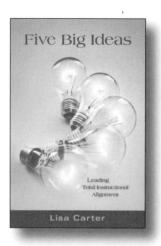

Five Big Ideas: Leading Total Instructional Alignment

Lisa Carter

In this sequel to *Total Instructional Alignment,* Lisa Carter reveals the five big ideas at the core of successful schools. Focus on these ideas to simplify decision-making, eliminate distractions, and intensify efforts to promote effective teaching and learning. **BKF263**

Total Instructional Alignment: From Standards to Student Success

Lisa Carter

Effective education in the new millennium calls for changing an antiquated system. Learn how you can create a flexible, proactive system by focusing on systemic alignment as well as alignment among standards, curriculum, classroom instruction, and assessment. **BKF222**

The Power of SMART Goals: Using Goals to Improve Student Learning

Jan O'Neill and Anne Conzemius with Carol Commodore and Carol Pulsfus

This easy-to-read guide will help your staff set effective goals that lead to real results. Four success stories illustrate how to transform challenges into opportunities for learning using an approach that is Strategic and Specific, Measurable, Attainable, Results-based and Time-bound. That's SMART! **BKF207**

Getting By or Getting Better

Wayne Hulley and Linda Dier

Learn how 14 schools became exemplary using excellent planning processes and action steps for total school improvement. Building on their work in *Harbors of Hope* (2005), the authors reveal seven lessons for success based on the Correlates of Effective Schools. **BKF262**

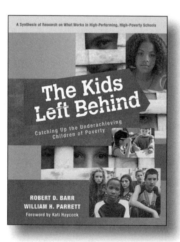

The Kids Left Behind: Catching Up the Underachieving Children of Poverty

Robert D. Barr and William H. Parrett

Successfully reach and teach the underachieving children of poverty with the help of this comprehensive resource. The authors' compiled research reveals practical, usable, best-practice strategies you can implement at district, school, and classroom levels. **BKF216**

Revisiting Professional Learning Communities At Work™: New Insights For Improving Schools

Richard DuFour, Rebecca DuFour, and Robert Eaker

This 10th-anniversary sequel to the pivotal book *Professional Learning Communities at Work™* offers advanced insights on deep implementation, the commitment/consensus issue, and the human side of PLC. Gain greater knowledge of common mistakes to avoid and new discoveries for success. **BKF252**

Solution Tree | Press

a division of
Solution Tree

Visit solution-tree.com or call 800.733.6786 to order.